With each graphic novel volume, I fix any mistakes on the pages. A common mistake is the headband mark. So complicated!

—Masashi Kishimoto, 2014

岸本斉史

D0169622

Author/artist Masashi Kishimoto was born in 1974 in rural Okayama Prefecture, Japan. After spending time in art college, he won the Hop Step Award for new manga artists with his manga **Karakuri** (Mechanism). Kishimoto decided to base his next story on traditional Japanese culture. His first version of **Naruto**, drawn in 1997, was a one-shot story about fox spirits; his final version, which debuted in **Weekly Shonen Jump** in 1999, quickly became the most popular ninja manga in Japan.

**NARUTO VOL. 70**
**SHONEN JUMP Manga Edition**

STORY AND ART BY MASASHI KISHIMOTO

Translation/Mari Morimoto
Touch-up Art & Lettering/John Hunt
Design/Sam Elzway
Editor/Alexis Kirsch

Printed in the U.S.A.

Published by VIZ Media, LLC
P.O. Box 77010
San Francisco, CA 94107

10 9 8 7 6 5 4 3 2 1
First printing, June 2015

viz
media
www.viz.com

THE WORLD'S MOST POPULAR MANGA
SHONEN JUMP
www.shonenjump.com

## Number 669: The Eight Inner Gates Formation!!

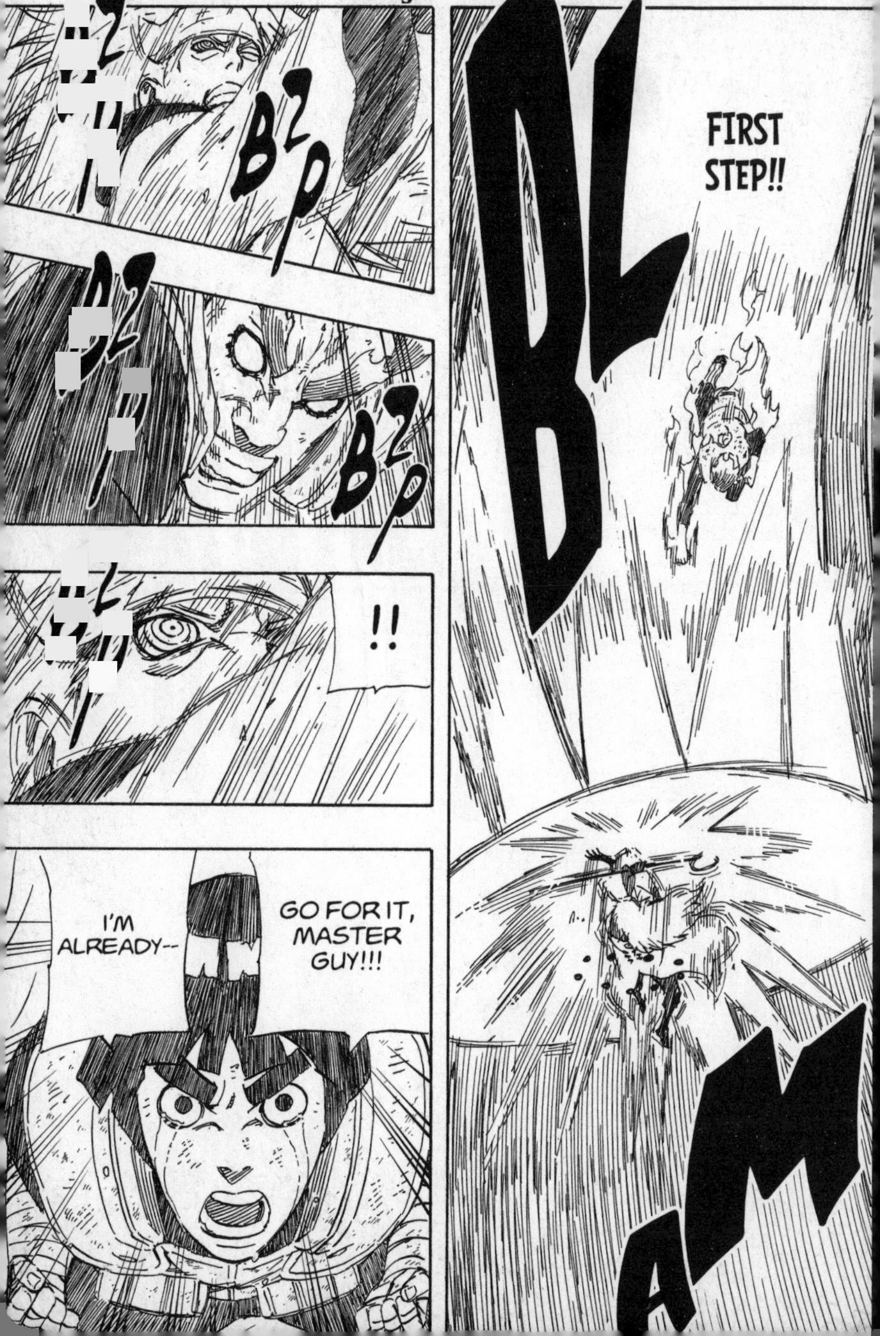
BL
FIRST STEP!!
AM
!!
GO FOR IT, MASTER GUY!!!
I'M ALREADY--

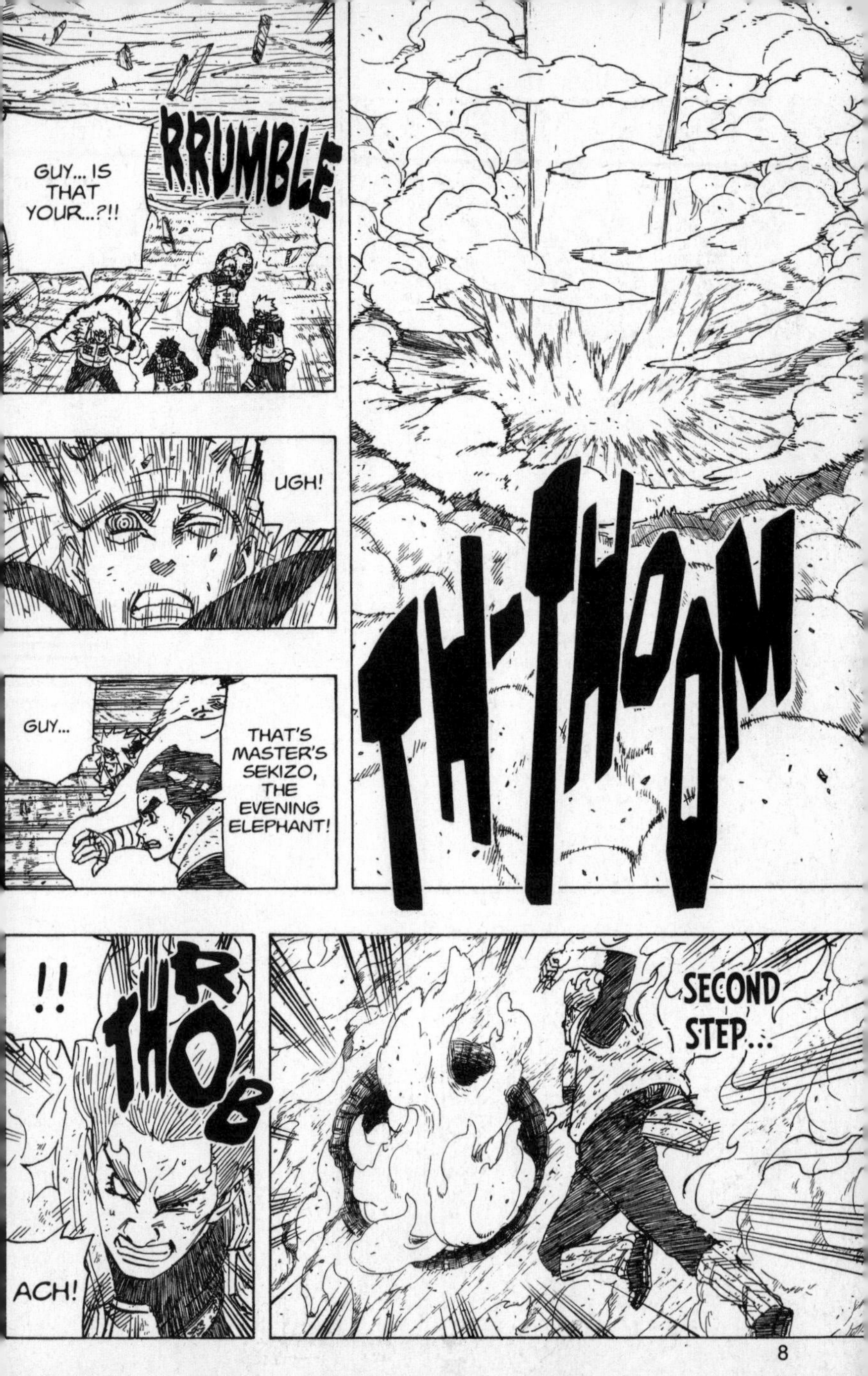
TH-THOOM
RRUMBLE
GUY... IS THAT YOUR...?!!
UGH!
THAT'S MASTER'S SEKIZO, THE EVENING ELEPHANT!
GUY...
SECOND STEP...
!!
THROB
ACH!

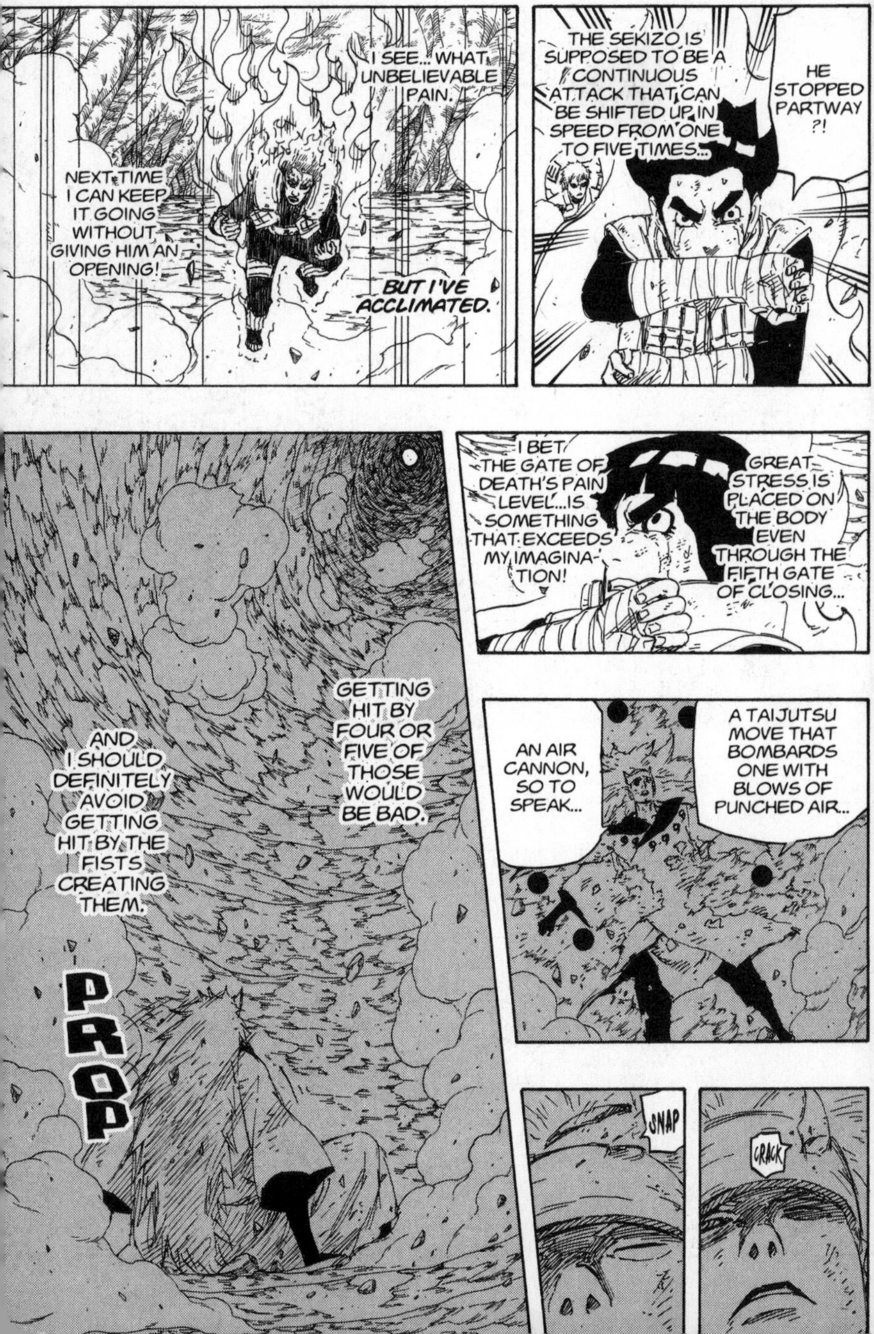
THE SEKIZO IS SUPPOSED TO BE A CONTINUOUS ATTACK THAT CAN BE SHIFTED UP IN SPEED FROM ONE TO FIVE TIMES...
HE STOPPED PARTWAY ?!
I SEE... WHAT UNBELIEVABLE PAIN.
BUT I'VE ACCLIMATED.
NEXT TIME I CAN KEEP IT GOING WITHOUT GIVING HIM AN OPENING!
GREAT STRESS IS PLACED ON THE BODY EVEN THROUGH THE FIFTH GATE OF CLOSING...
I BET THE GATE OF DEATH'S PAIN LEVEL...IS SOMETHING THAT EXCEEDS MY IMAGINA-TION!
A TAIJUTSU MOVE THAT BOMBARDS ONE WITH BLOWS OF PUNCHED AIR...
AN AIR CANNON, SO TO SPEAK...
GETTING HIT BY FOUR OR FIVE OF THOSE WOULD BE BAD.
AND I SHOULD DEFINITELY AVOID GETTING HIT BY THE FISTS CREATING THEM.
PROP
CRACK
SNAP

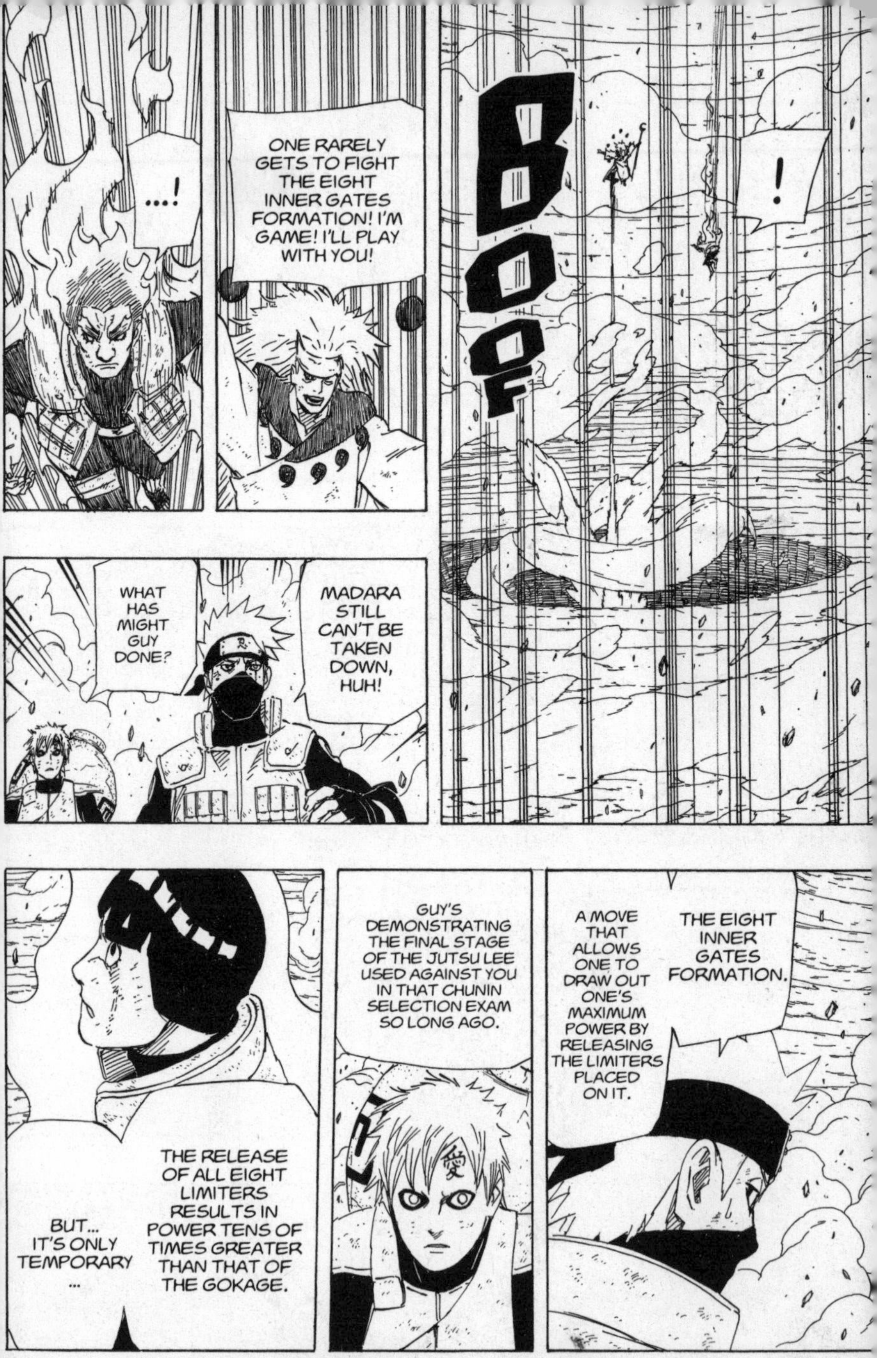
BOOF
!
ONE RARELY GETS TO FIGHT THE EIGHT INNER GATES FORMATION! I'M GAME! I'LL PLAY WITH YOU!
...!
MADARA STILL CAN'T BE TAKEN DOWN, HUH!
WHAT HAS MIGHT GUY DONE?
THE EIGHT INNER GATES FORMATION.
A MOVE THAT ALLOWS ONE TO DRAW OUT ONE'S MAXIMUM POWER BY RELEASING THE LIMITERS PLACED ON IT.
GUY'S DEMONSTRATING THE FINAL STAGE OF THE JUTSU LEE USED AGAINST YOU IN THAT CHUNIN SELECTION EXAM SO LONG AGO.
THE RELEASE OF ALL EIGHT LIMITERS RESULTS IN POWER TENS OF TIMES GREATER THAN THAT OF THE GOKAGE.
BUT... IT'S ONLY TEMPORARY...

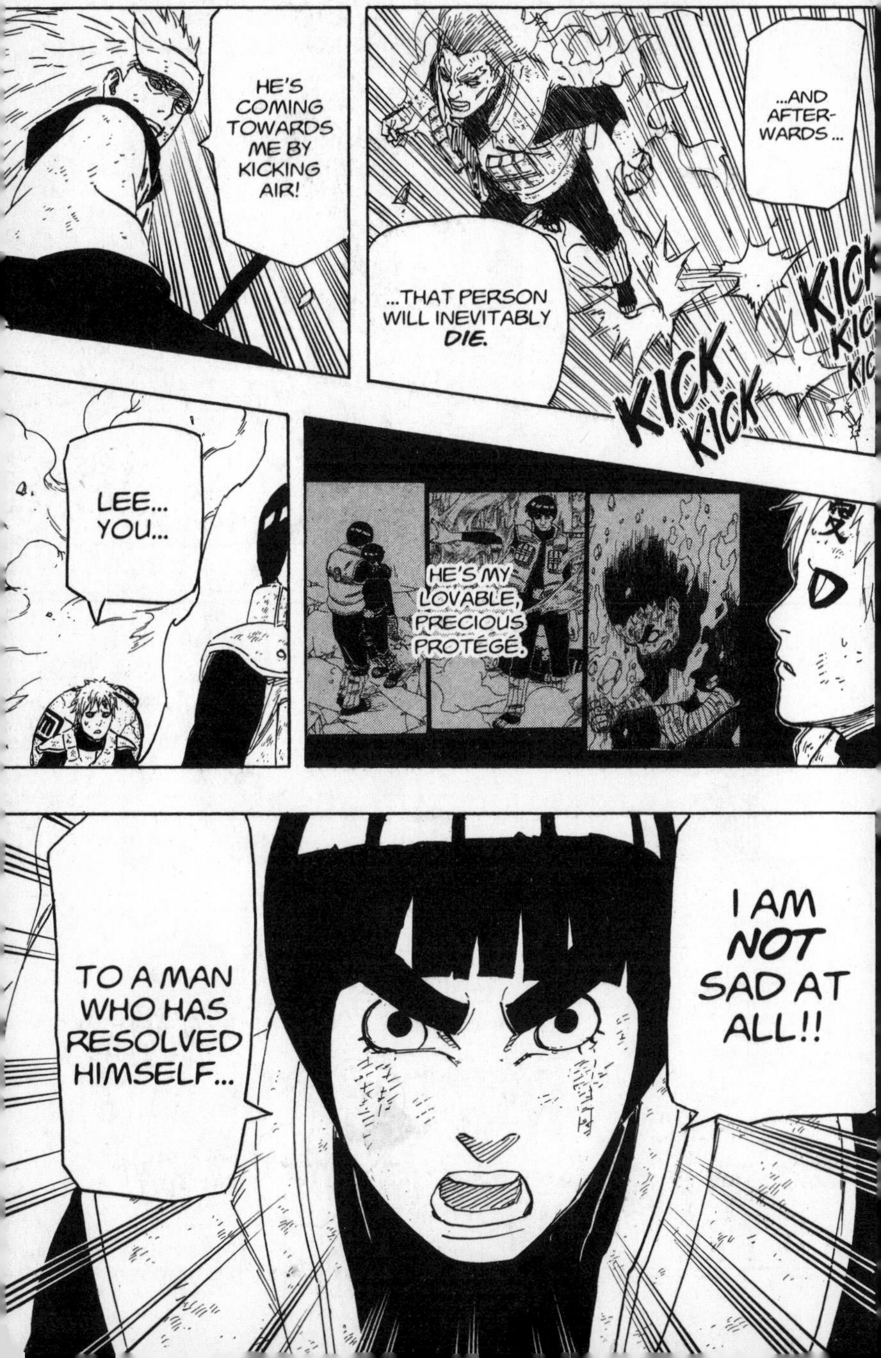

...AND AFTERWARDS...
...THAT PERSON WILL INEVITABLY *DIE.*
KICK
KICK
KICK
KICK
HE'S COMING TOWARDS ME BY KICKING AIR!
HE'S MY LOVABLE, PRECIOUS PROTÉGÉ.
LEE... YOU...
I AM *NOT* SAD AT ALL!!
TO A MAN WHO HAS RESOLVED HIMSELF...

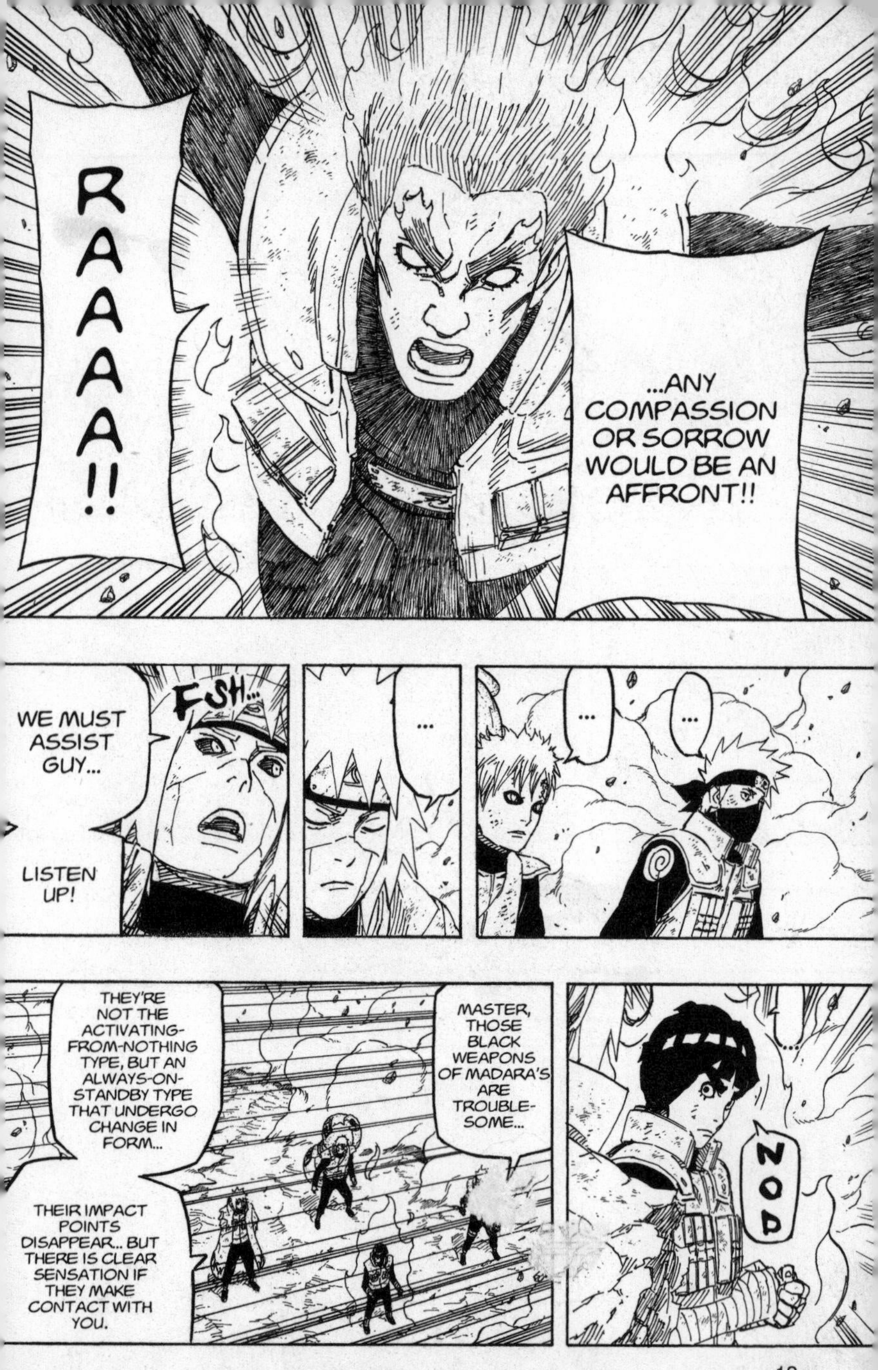
...ANY COMPASSION OR SORROW WOULD BE AN AFFRONT!!
RAAAA!!
...
...
...
FSH...
WE MUST ASSIST GUY...
LISTEN UP!
...
NOD
MASTER, THOSE BLACK WEAPONS OF MADARA'S ARE TROUBLE-SOME...
THEY'RE NOT THE ACTIVATING-FROM-NOTHING TYPE, BUT AN ALWAYS-ON-STANDBY TYPE THAT UNDERGO CHANGE IN FORM...
THEIR IMPACT POINTS DISAPPEAR... BUT THERE IS CLEAR SENSATION IF THEY MAKE CONTACT WITH YOU.

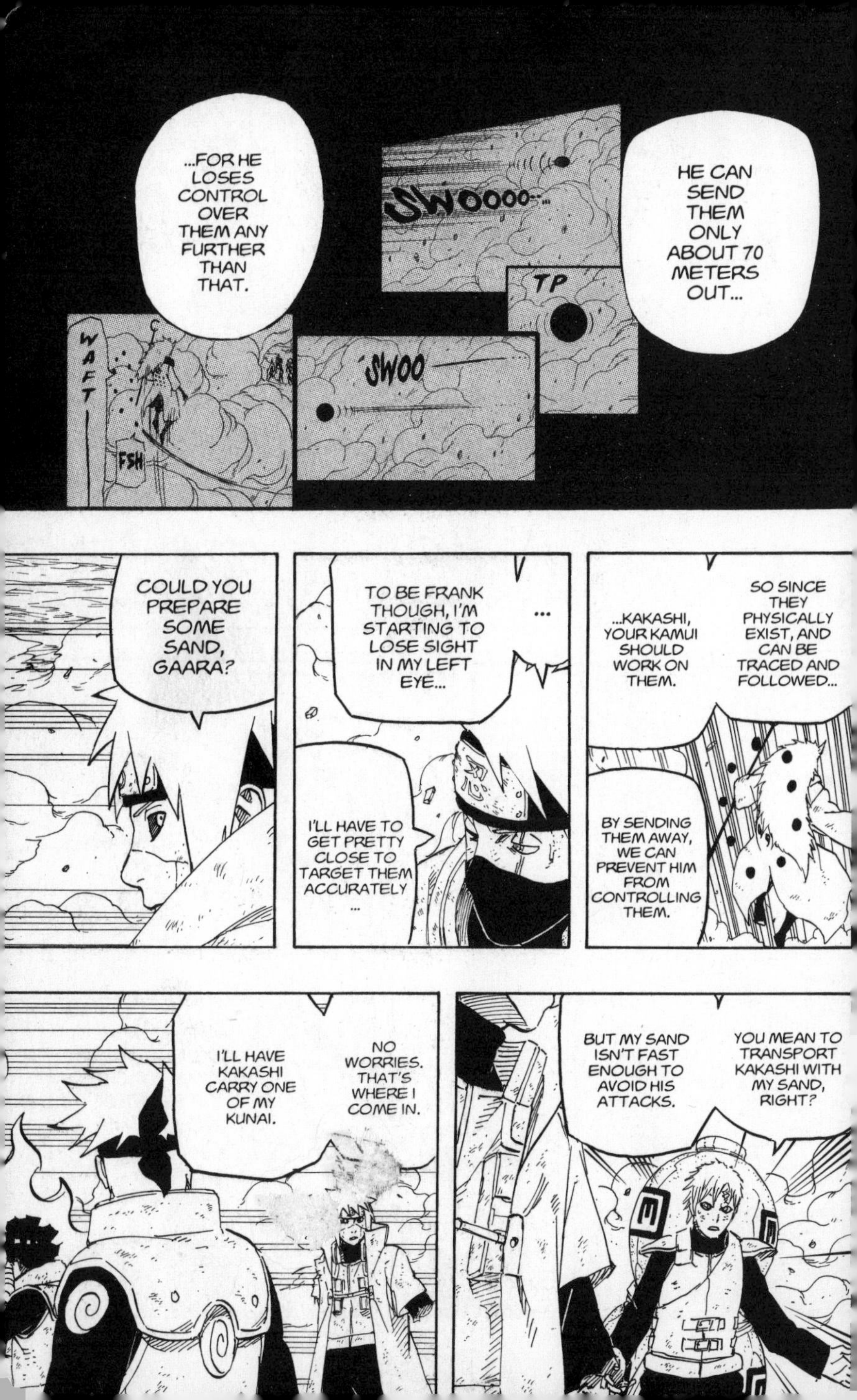
HE CAN SEND THEM ONLY ABOUT 70 METERS OUT...
SWOOOO...
TP
...FOR HE LOSES CONTROL OVER THEM ANY FURTHER THAN THAT.
SWOO
WAFT
FSH
SO SINCE THEY PHYSICALLY EXIST, AND CAN BE TRACED AND FOLLOWED...
...KAKASHI, YOUR KAMUI SHOULD WORK ON THEM.
BY SENDING THEM AWAY, WE CAN PREVENT HIM FROM CONTROLLING THEM.
...
TO BE FRANK THOUGH, I'M STARTING TO LOSE SIGHT IN MY LEFT EYE...
I'LL HAVE TO GET PRETTY CLOSE TO TARGET THEM ACCURATELY ...
COULD YOU PREPARE SOME SAND, GAARA?
YOU MEAN TO TRANSPORT KAKASHI WITH MY SAND, RIGHT?
BUT MY SAND ISN'T FAST ENOUGH TO AVOID HIS ATTACKS.
NO WORRIES. THAT'S WHERE I COME IN.
I'LL HAVE KAKASHI CARRY ONE OF MY KUNAI.

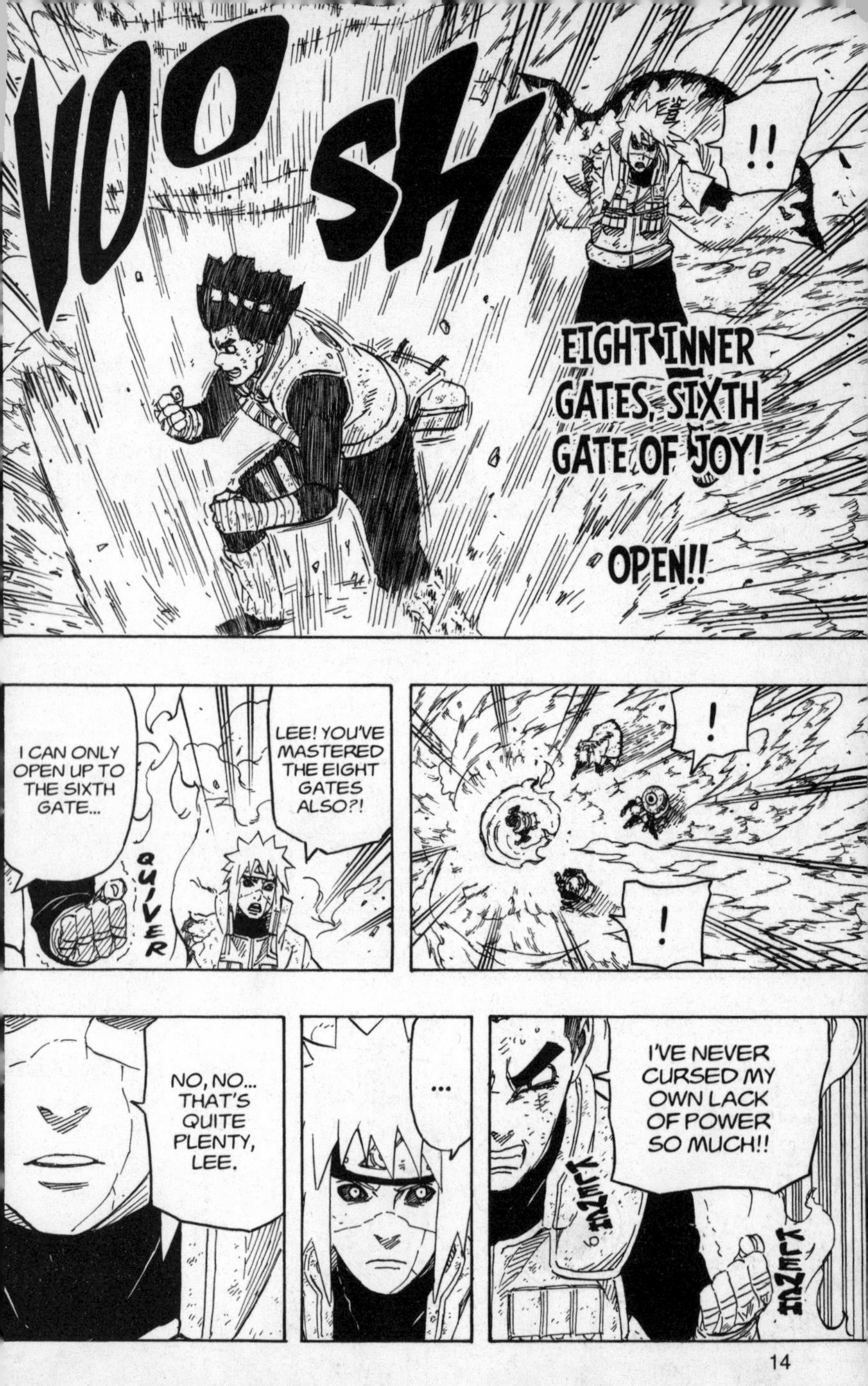
!!
VOOSH
EIGHT INNER GATES, SIXTH GATE OF JOY!
OPEN!!
!
!
LEE! YOU'VE MASTERED THE EIGHT GATES ALSO?!
I CAN ONLY OPEN UP TO THE SIXTH GATE...
QUIVER
I'VE NEVER CURSED MY OWN LACK OF POWER SO MUCH!!
KLENCH
KLENCH
...
NO, NO... THAT'S QUITE PLENTY, LEE.

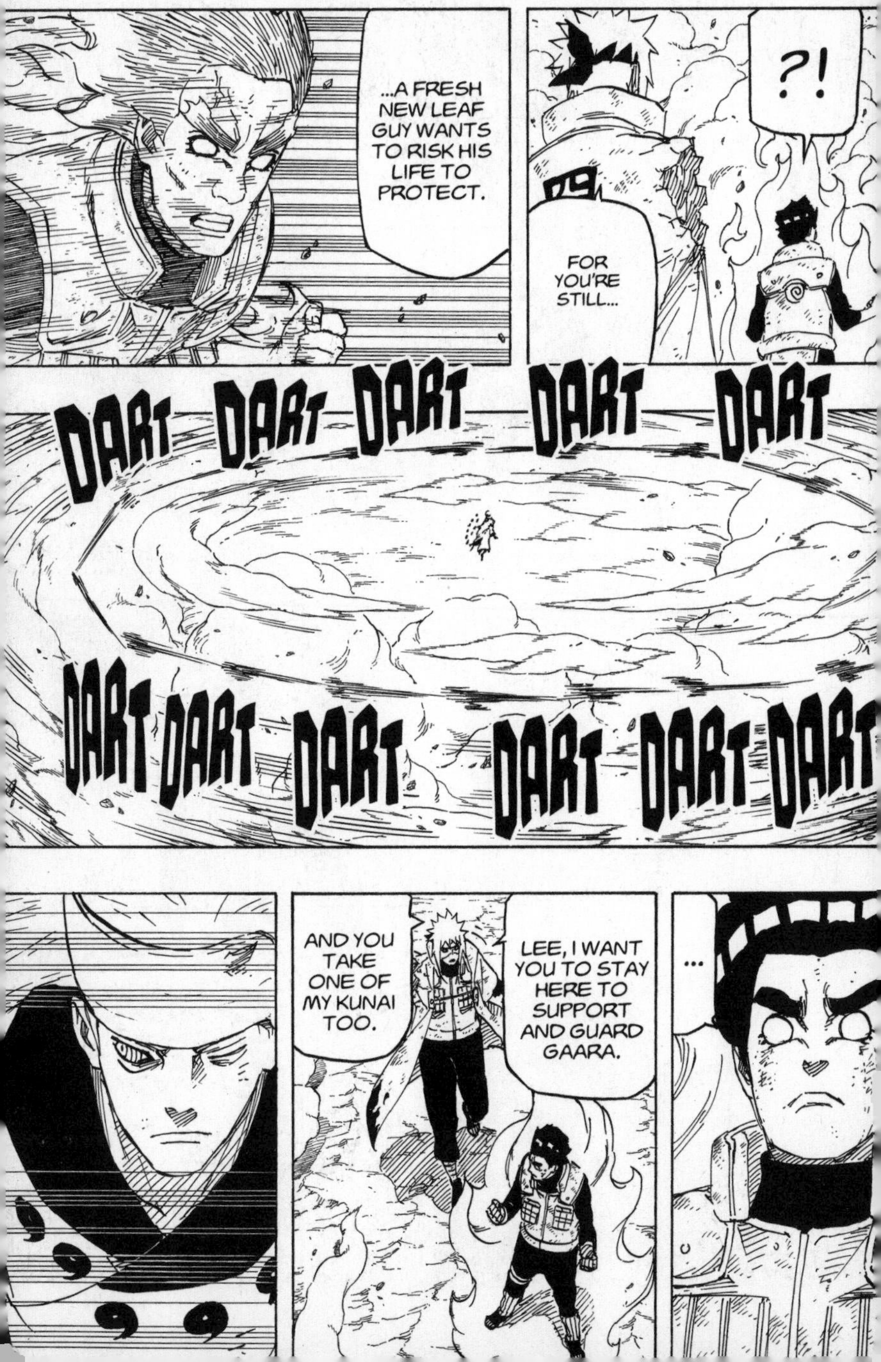
?!
FOR YOU'RE STILL...
...A FRESH NEW LEAF GUY WANTS TO RISK HIS LIFE TO PROTECT.
DART DART DART DART DART
DART DART DART DART DART DART
...
LEE, I WANT YOU TO STAY HERE TO SUPPORT AND GUARD GAARA.
AND YOU TAKE ONE OF MY KUNAI TOO.

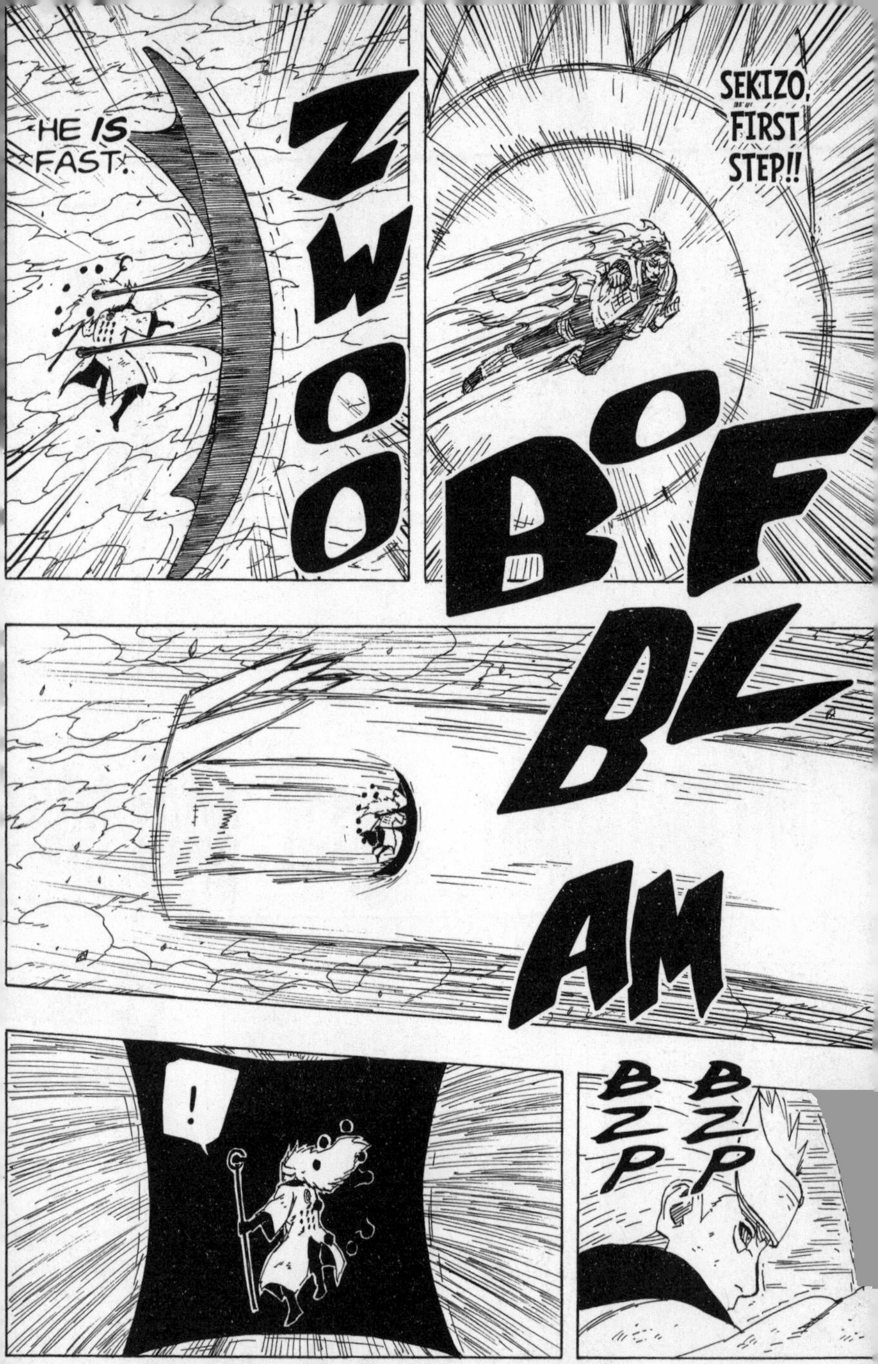
SEKIZO, FIRST STEP!!
BOF
ZWOOO
HE IS FAST.
BLAM
BZP BZP
!

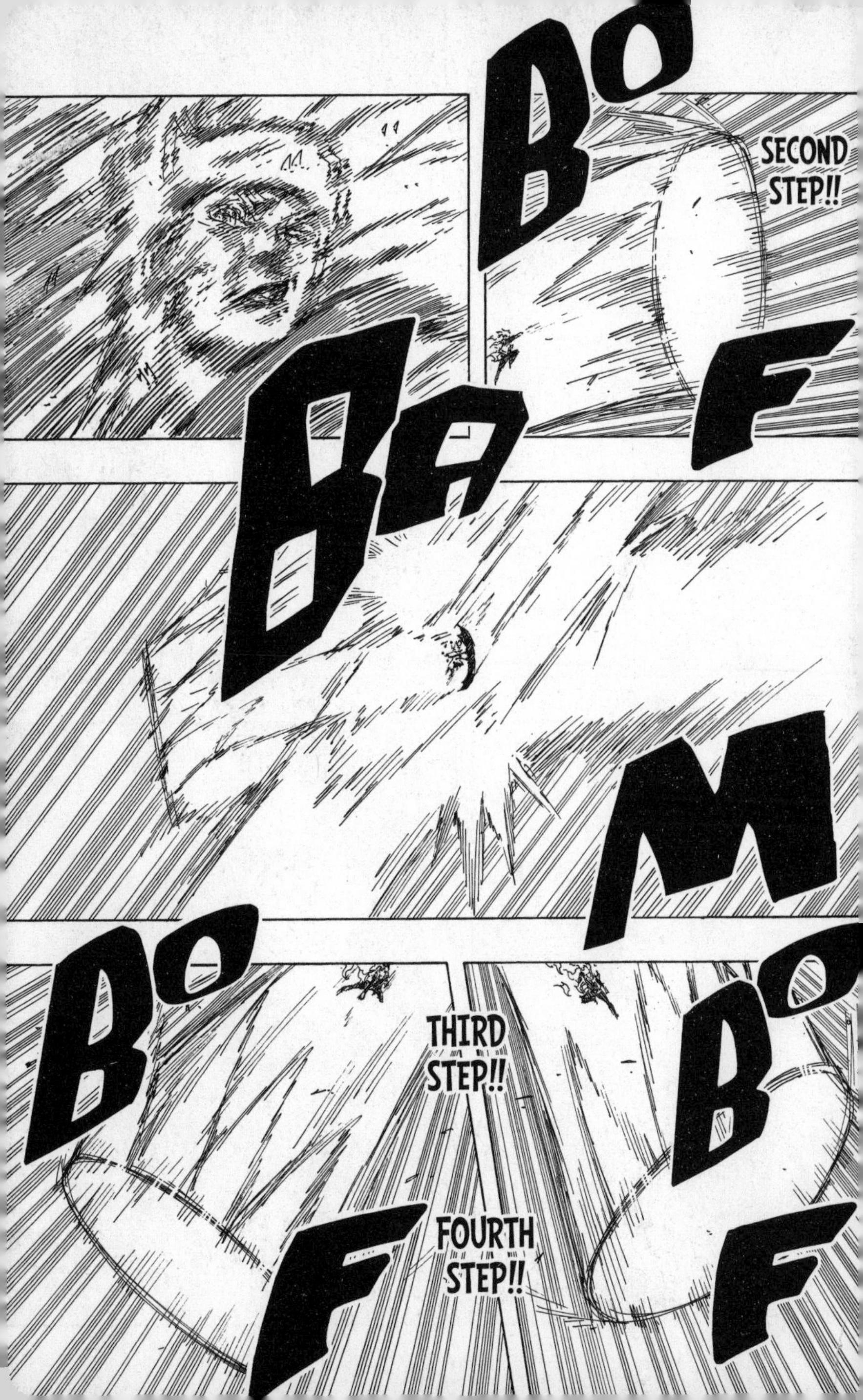
BOOF
SECOND STEP!!
BAM
BOOF
THIRD STEP!!
FOURTH STEP!!
BOOF

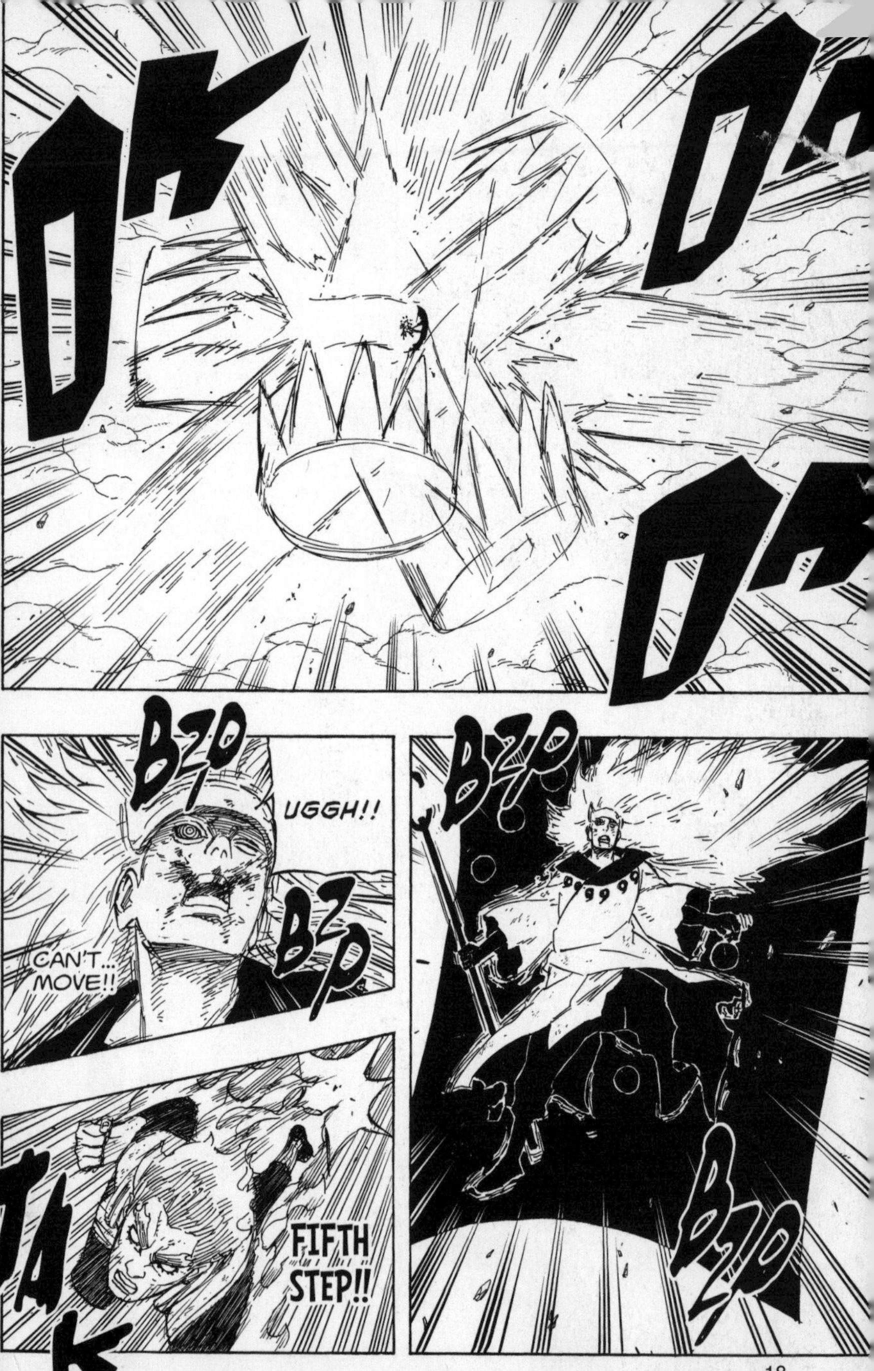
BZP
BZP
BZP
UGGH!!
BZP
CAN'T...
MOVE!!
FIFTH
STEP!!
TAK

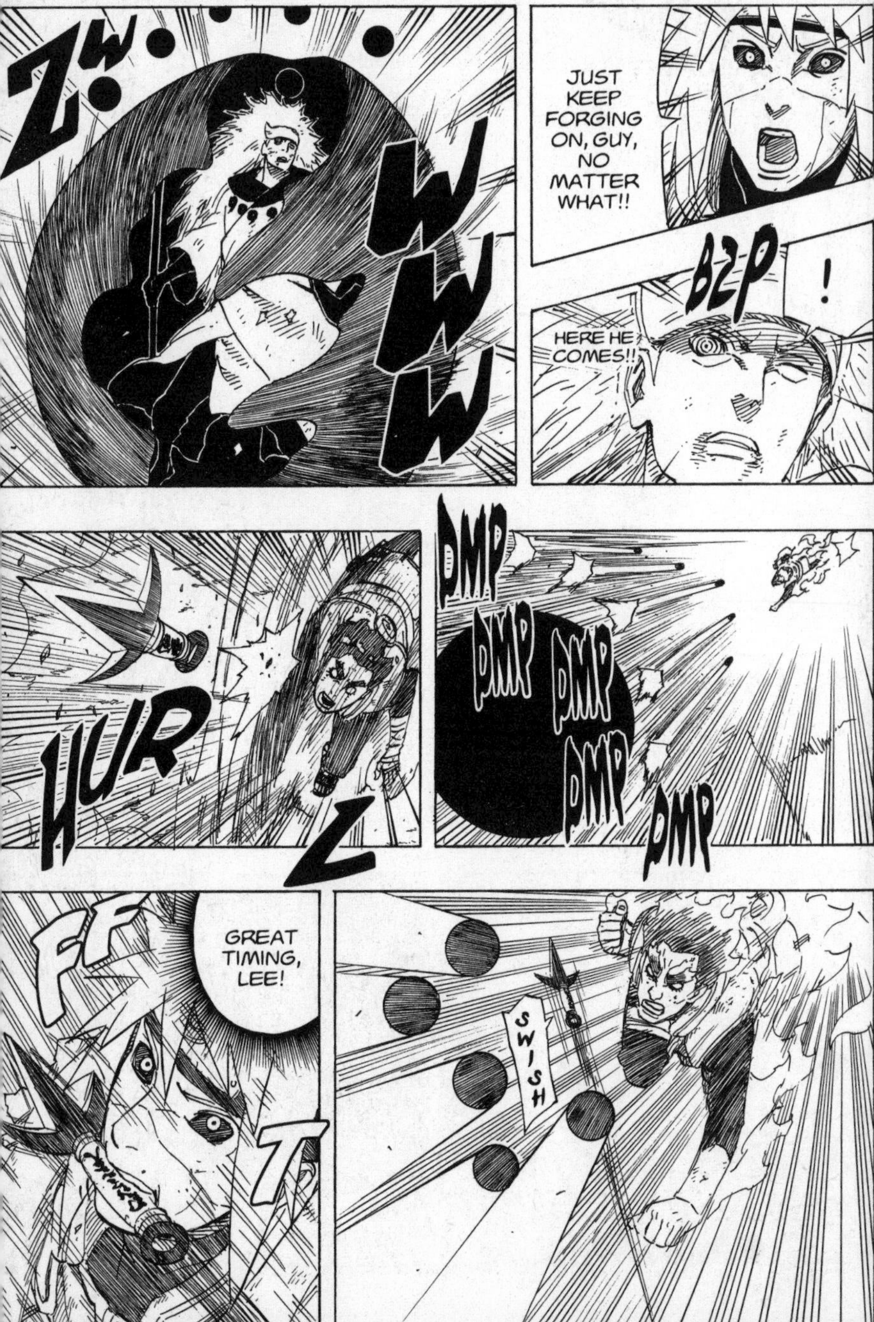
JUST KEEP FORGING ON, GUY, NO MATTER WHAT!!
BZP
!
HERE HE COMES!!
ZWWWWW
DMP DMP DMP DMP DMP DMP
HURL
SWISH
FFT
GREAT TIMING, LEE!

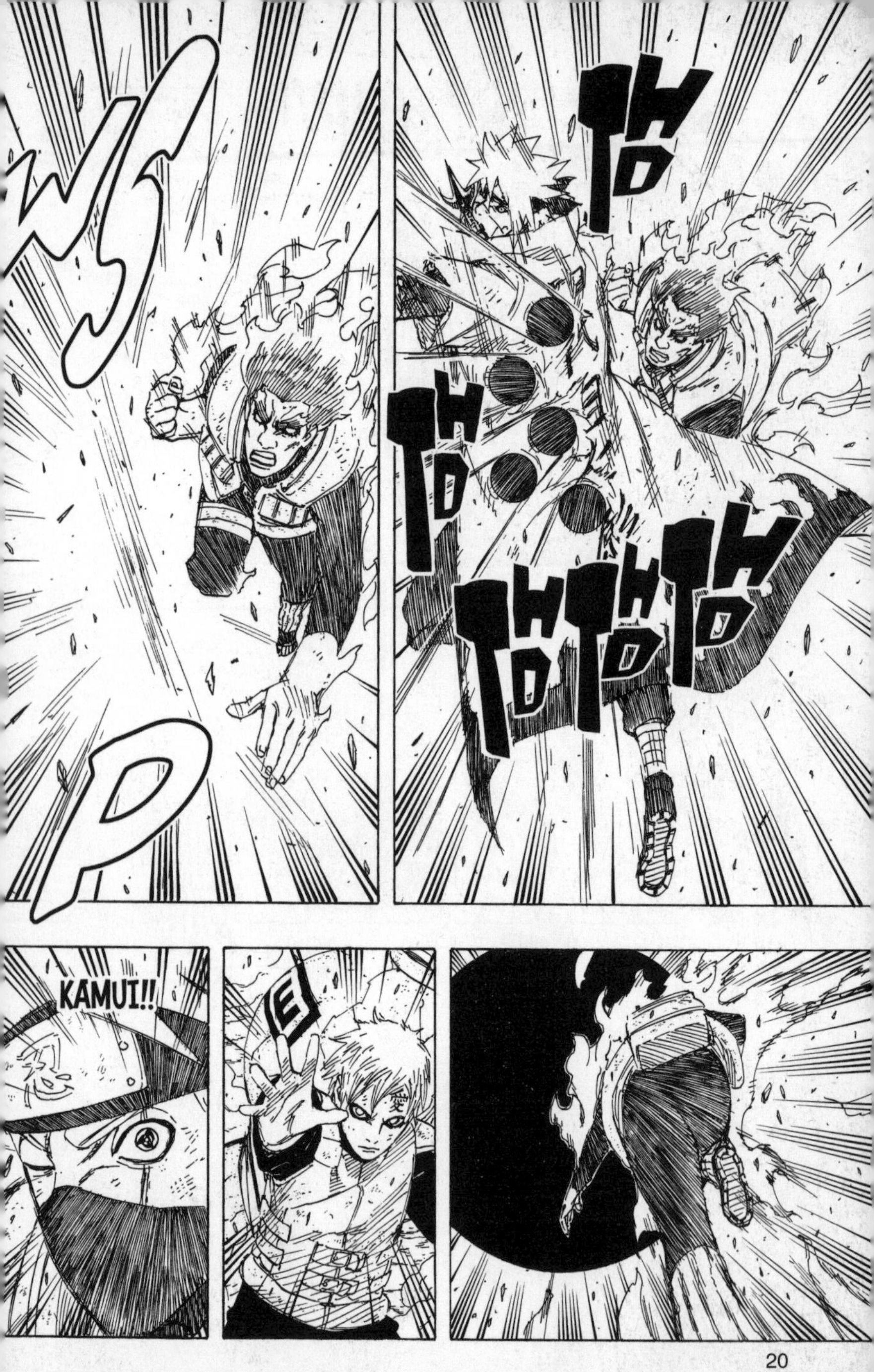
THD
THD
THD THD THD THD
KAMUI!!

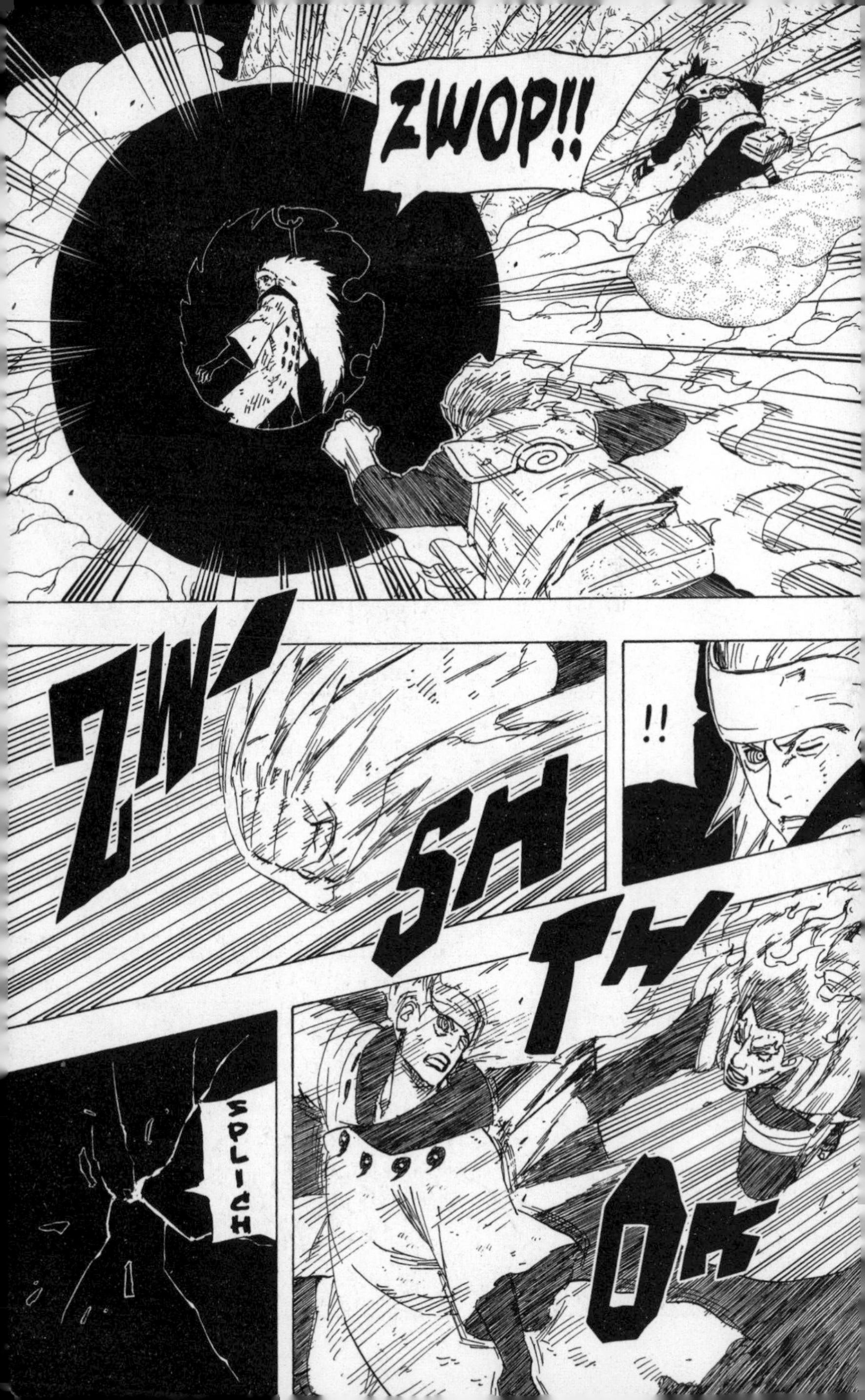
ZWOP!!
!!
ZW'
SH
TH
OK
SPLICH

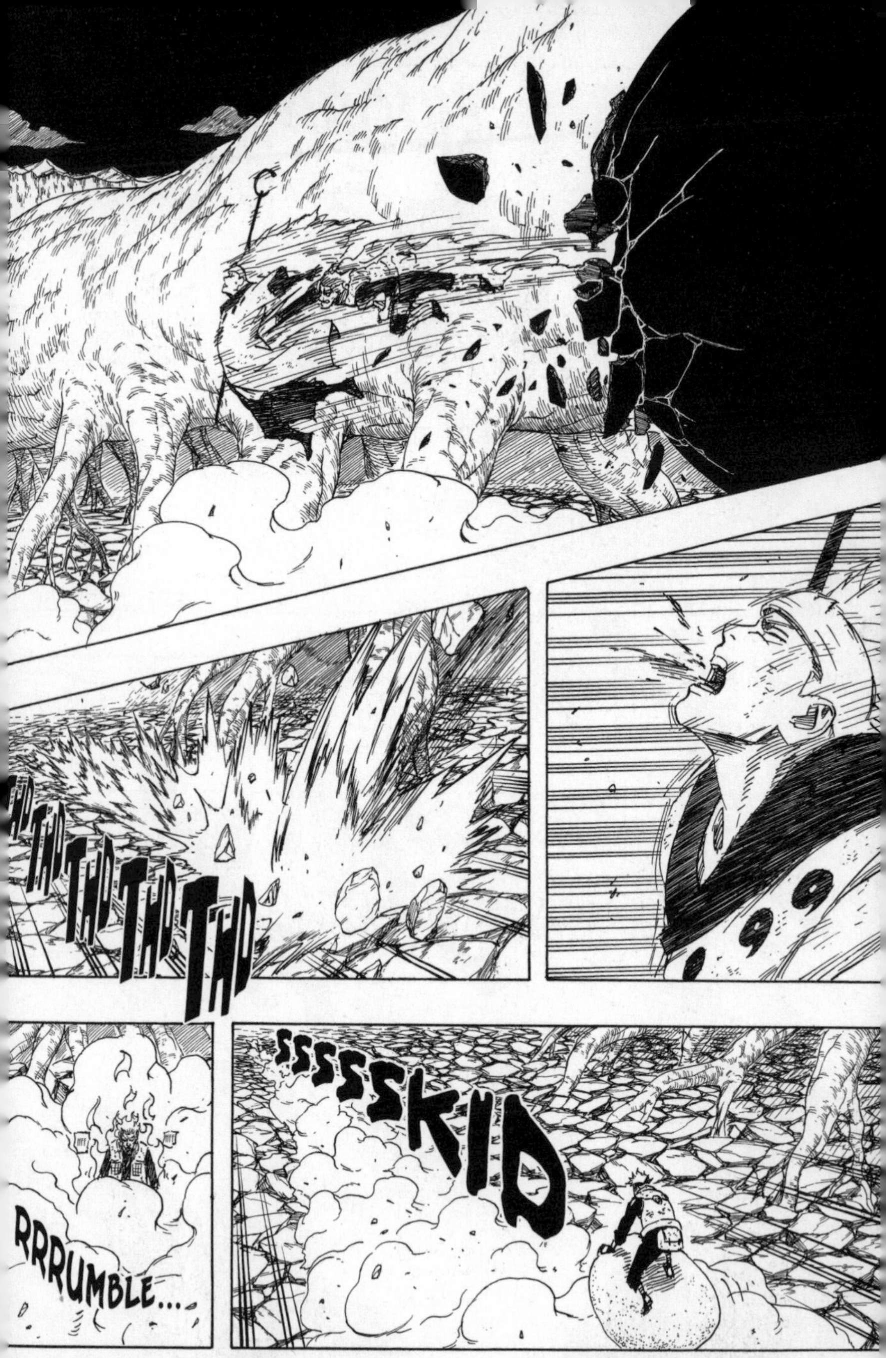
THD THD THD THD
SSSSSKID
RRRUMBLE...

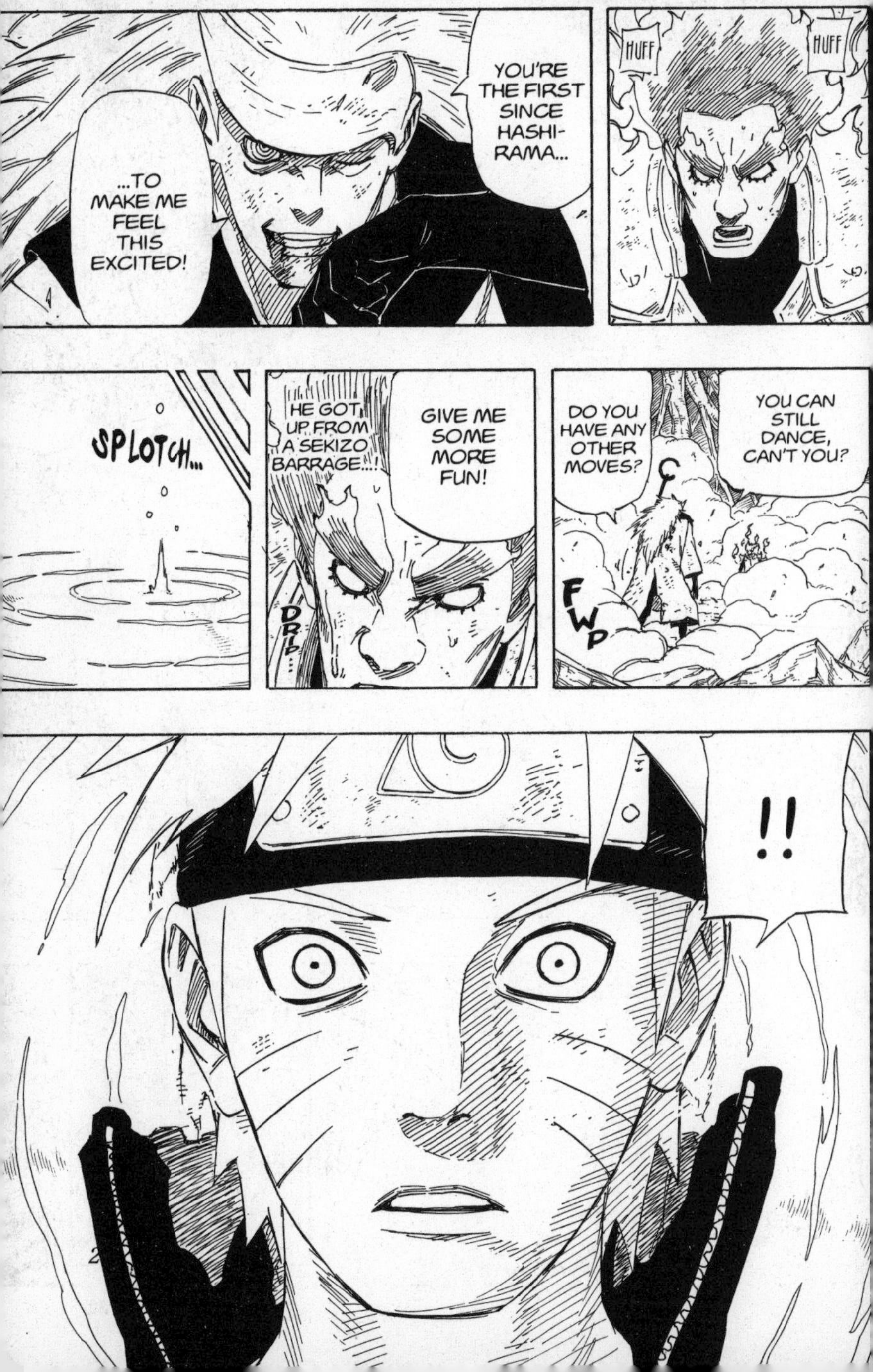
HUFF
HUFF
YOU'RE THE FIRST SINCE HASHI-RAMA...
...TO MAKE ME FEEL THIS EXCITED!
YOU CAN STILL DANCE, CAN'T YOU?
DO YOU HAVE ANY OTHER MOVES?
FWP
GIVE ME SOME MORE FUN!
HE GOT UP FROM A SEKIZO BARRAGE...!
DRIP...
SPLOTCH...
!!

Number 670: He of the Beginning...!!

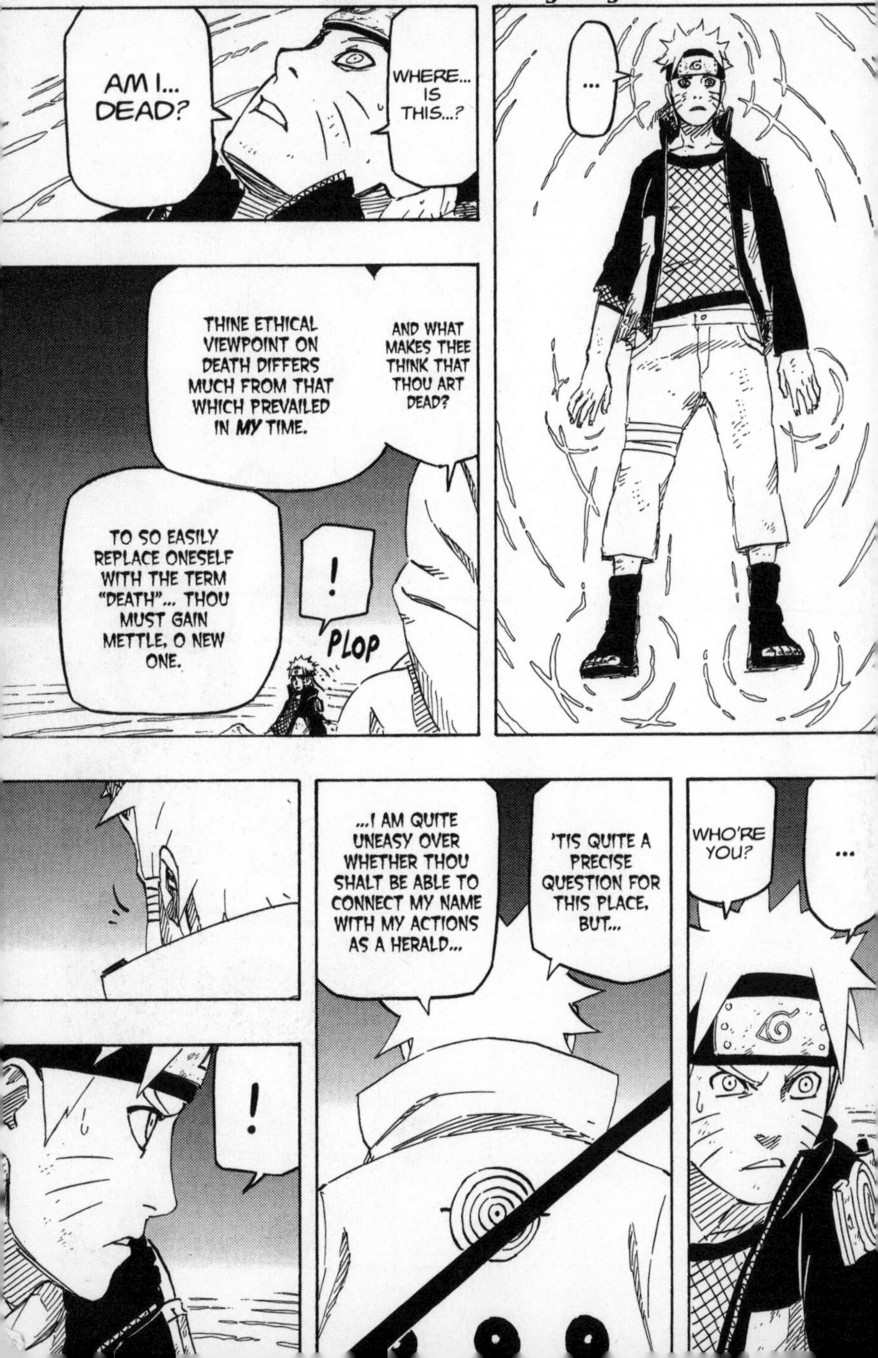
...
WHERE... IS THIS...?
AM I... DEAD?
AND WHAT MAKES THEE THINK THAT THOU ART DEAD?
THINE ETHICAL VIEWPOINT ON DEATH DIFFERS MUCH FROM THAT WHICH PREVAILED IN MY TIME.
TO SO EASILY REPLACE ONESELF WITH THE TERM "DEATH"... THOU MUST GAIN METTLE, O NEW ONE.
!
PLOP
...
WHO'RE YOU?
'TIS QUITE A PRECISE QUESTION FOR THIS PLACE, BUT...
...I AM QUITE UNEASY OVER WHETHER THOU SHALT BE ABLE TO CONNECT MY NAME WITH MY ACTIONS AS A HERALD...
!

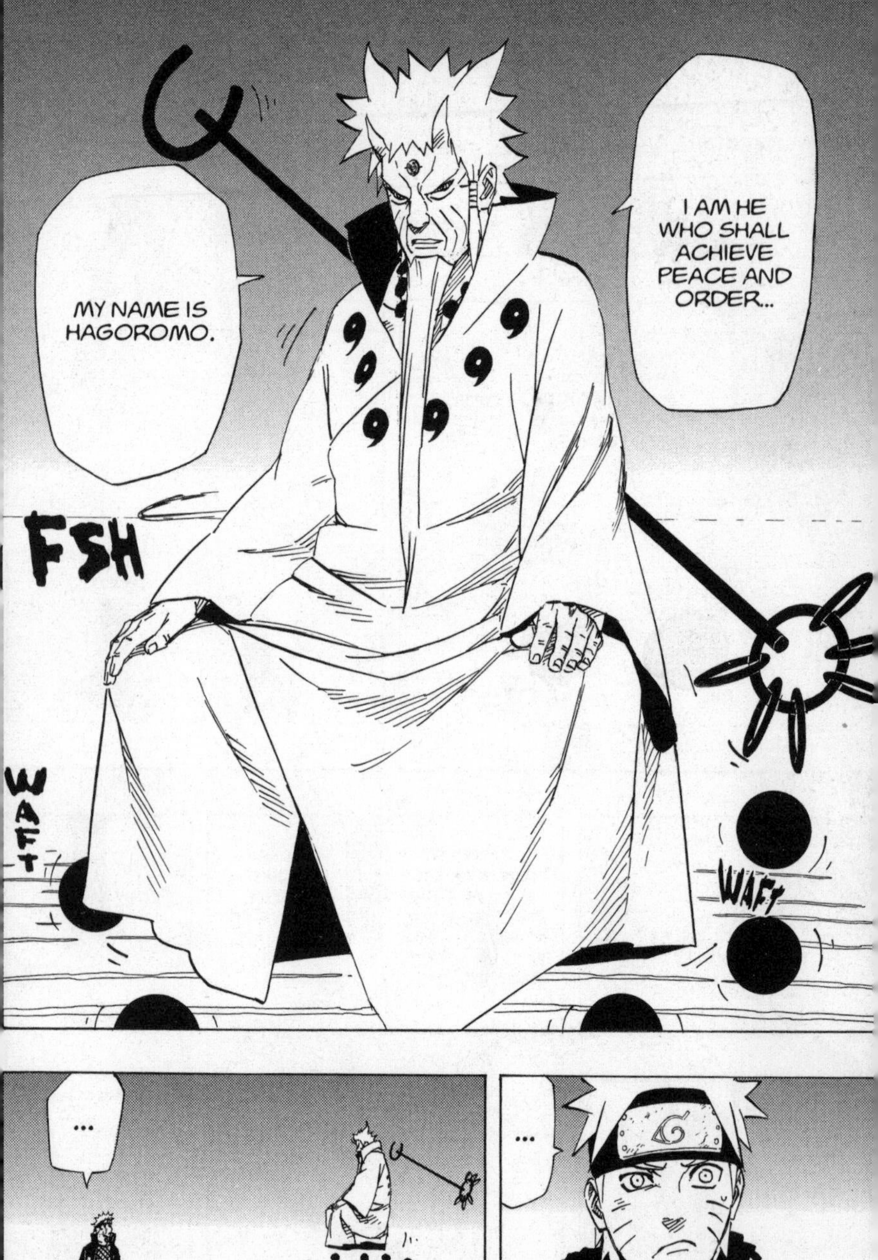
I AM HE WHO SHALL ACHIEVE PEACE AND ORDER...
MY NAME IS HAGOROMO.
FSH
WAFT
WAFT
...
...

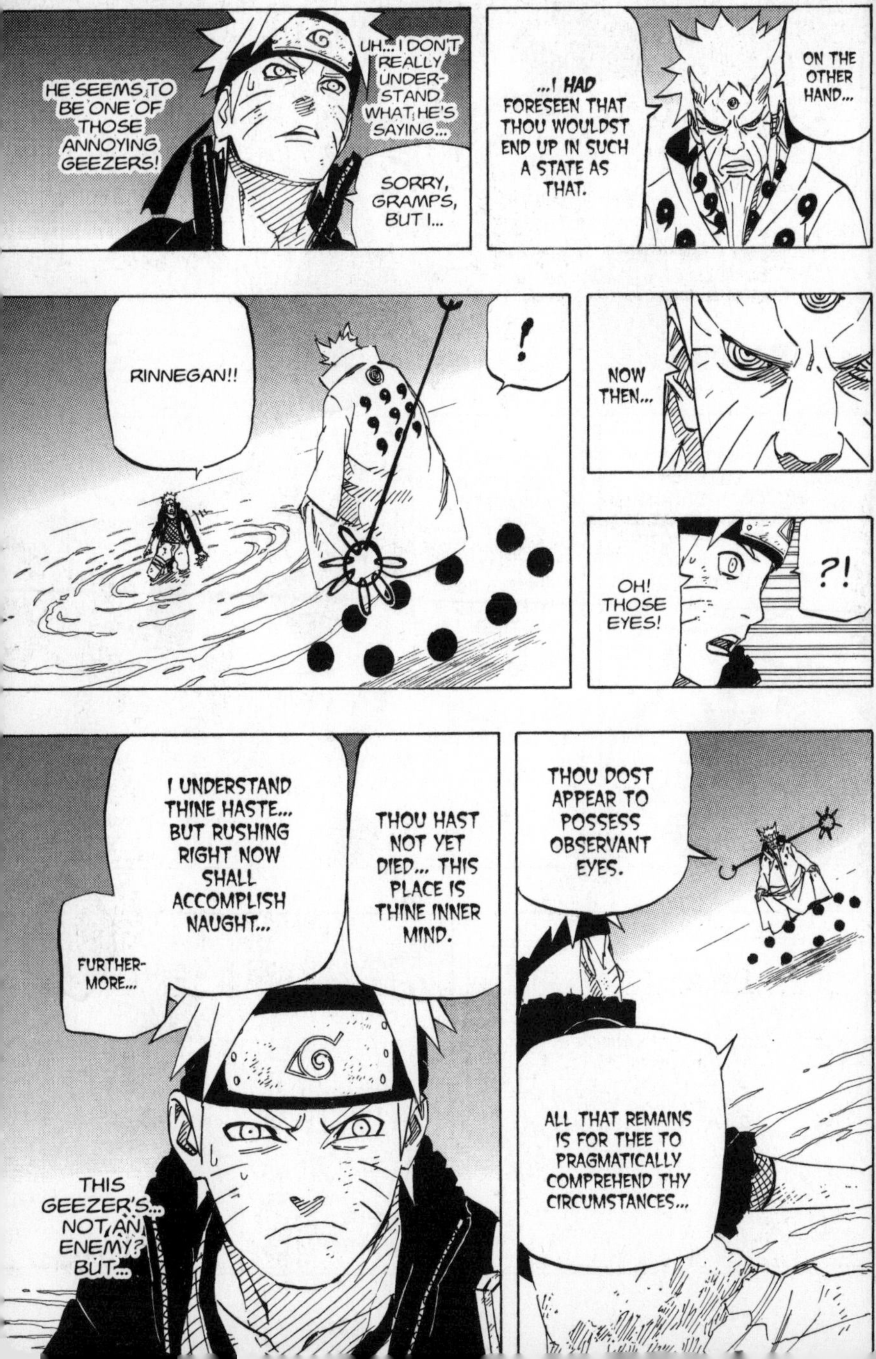
ON THE OTHER HAND...
...I HAD FORESEEN THAT THOU WOULDST END UP IN SUCH A STATE AS THAT.
UH... I DON'T REALLY UNDERSTAND WHAT HE'S SAYING...
SORRY, GRAMPS, BUT I...
HE SEEMS TO BE ONE OF THOSE ANNOYING GEEZERS!
NOW THEN...
?!
OH! THOSE EYES!
!
RINNEGAN!!
THOU DOST APPEAR TO POSSESS OBSERVANT EYES.
ALL THAT REMAINS IS FOR THEE TO PRAGMATICALLY COMPREHEND THY CIRCUMSTANCES...
THOU HAST NOT YET DIED... THIS PLACE IS THINE INNER MIND.
I UNDERSTAND THINE HASTE... BUT RUSHING RIGHT NOW SHALL ACCOMPLISH NAUGHT...
FURTHERMORE...
THIS GEEZER'S... NOT AN ENEMY? BUT...

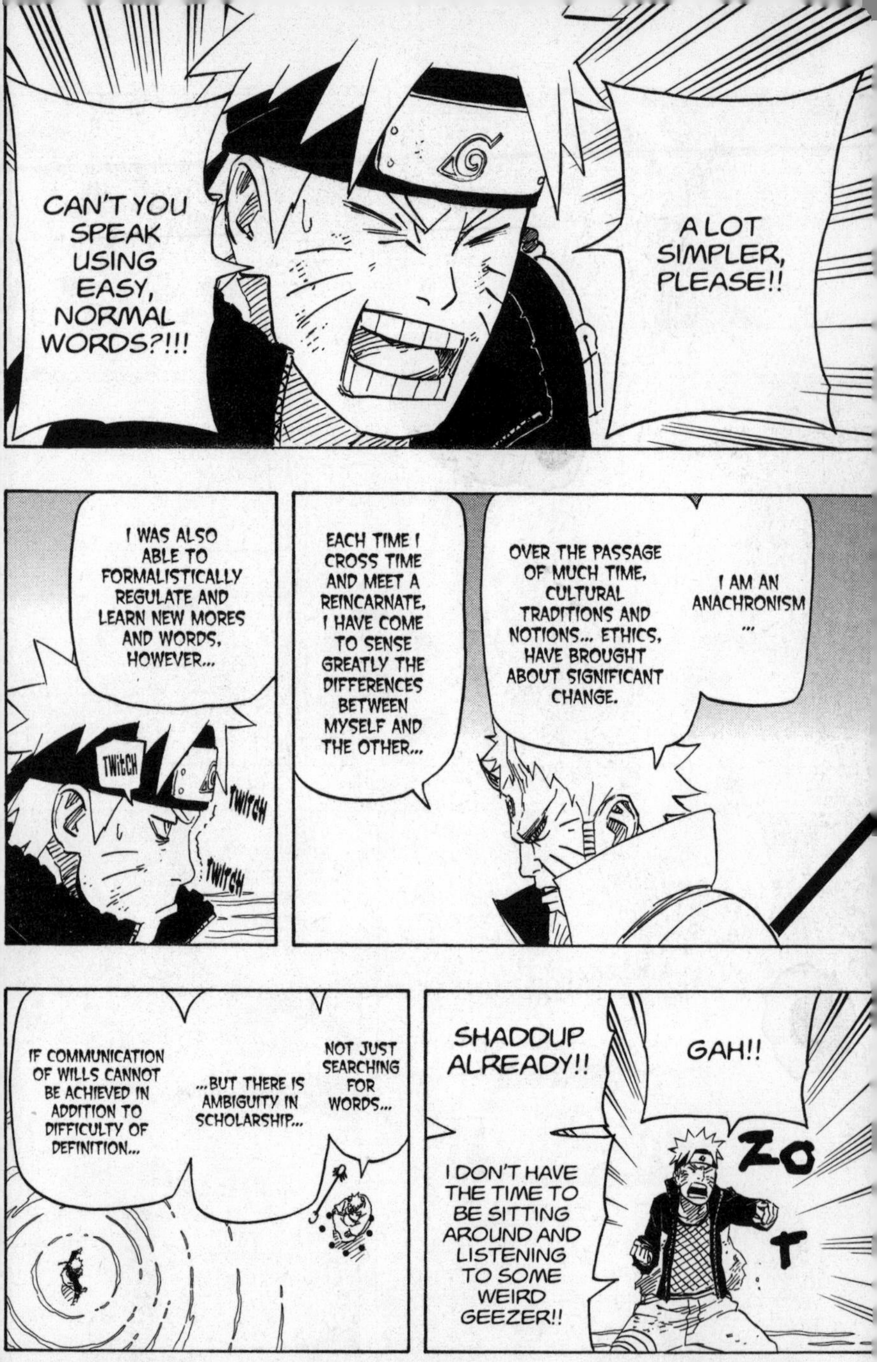
A LOT SIMPLER, PLEASE!!
CAN'T YOU SPEAK USING EASY, NORMAL WORDS?!!!
I AM AN ANACHRONISM ...
OVER THE PASSAGE OF MUCH TIME, CULTURAL TRADITIONS AND NOTIONS... ETHICS, HAVE BROUGHT ABOUT SIGNIFICANT CHANGE.
EACH TIME I CROSS TIME AND MEET A REINCARNATE, I HAVE COME TO SENSE GREATLY THE DIFFERENCES BETWEEN MYSELF AND THE OTHER...
I WAS ALSO ABLE TO FORMALISTICALLY REGULATE AND LEARN NEW MORES AND WORDS, HOWEVER...
TWITCH
TWITCH
TWITCH
GAH!!
SHADDUP ALREADY!!
ZOT
I DON'T HAVE THE TIME TO BE SITTING AROUND AND LISTENING TO SOME WEIRD GEEZER!!
NOT JUST SEARCHING FOR WORDS...
...BUT THERE IS AMBIGUITY IN SCHOLARSHIP...
IF COMMUNICATION OF WILLS CANNOT BE ACHIEVED IN ADDITION TO DIFFICULTY OF DEFINITION...

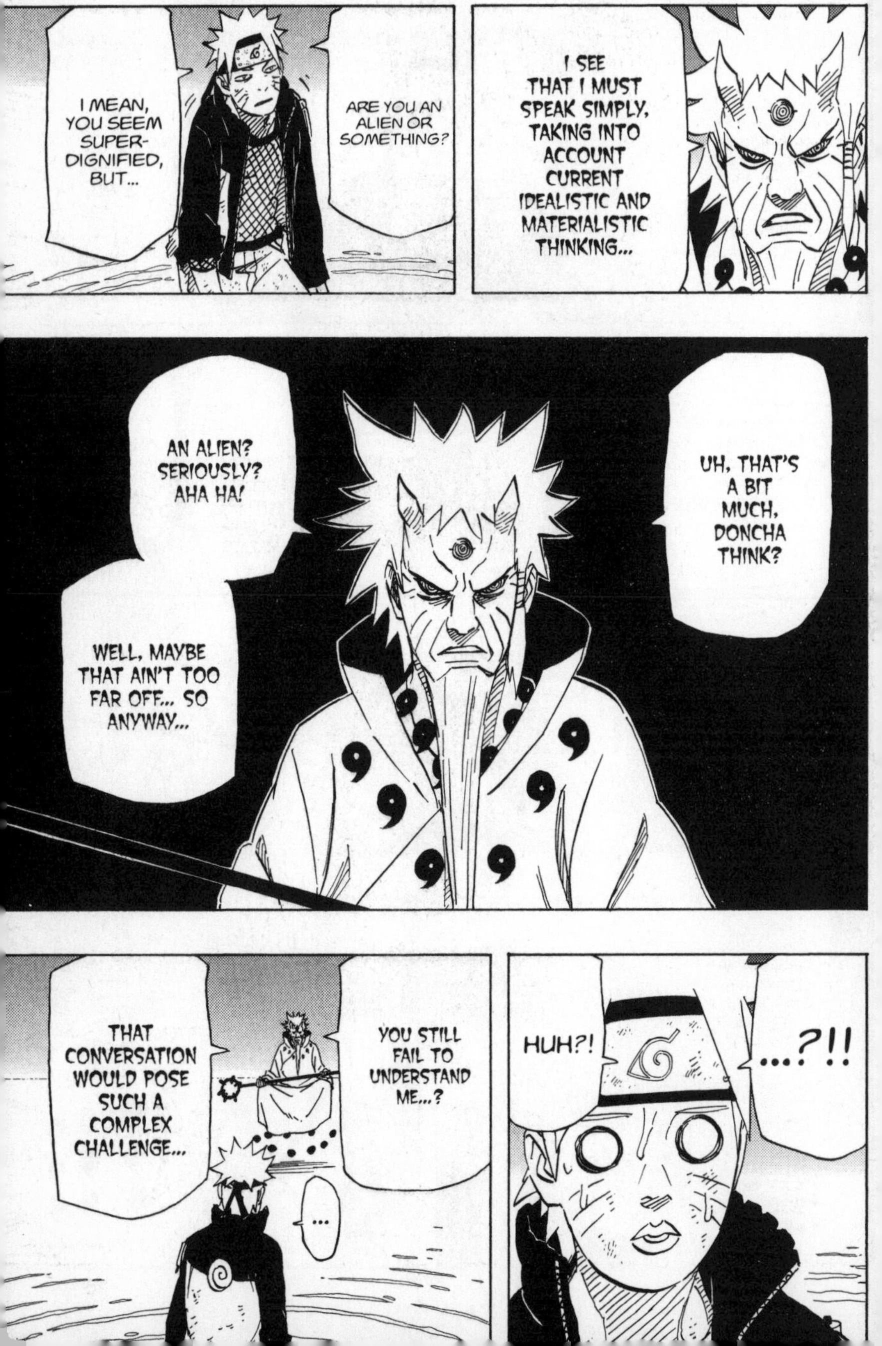
I SEE THAT I MUST SPEAK SIMPLY, TAKING INTO ACCOUNT CURRENT IDEALISTIC AND MATERIALISTIC THINKING...
ARE YOU AN ALIEN OR SOMETHING?
I MEAN, YOU SEEM SUPER-DIGNIFIED, BUT...
UH, THAT'S A BIT MUCH, DONCHA THINK?
AN ALIEN? SERIOUSLY? AHA HA!
WELL, MAYBE THAT AIN'T TOO FAR OFF... SO ANYWAY...
...?!!
HUH?!
YOU STILL FAIL TO UNDERSTAND ME...?
THAT CONVERSATION WOULD POSE SUCH A COMPLEX CHALLENGE...
...

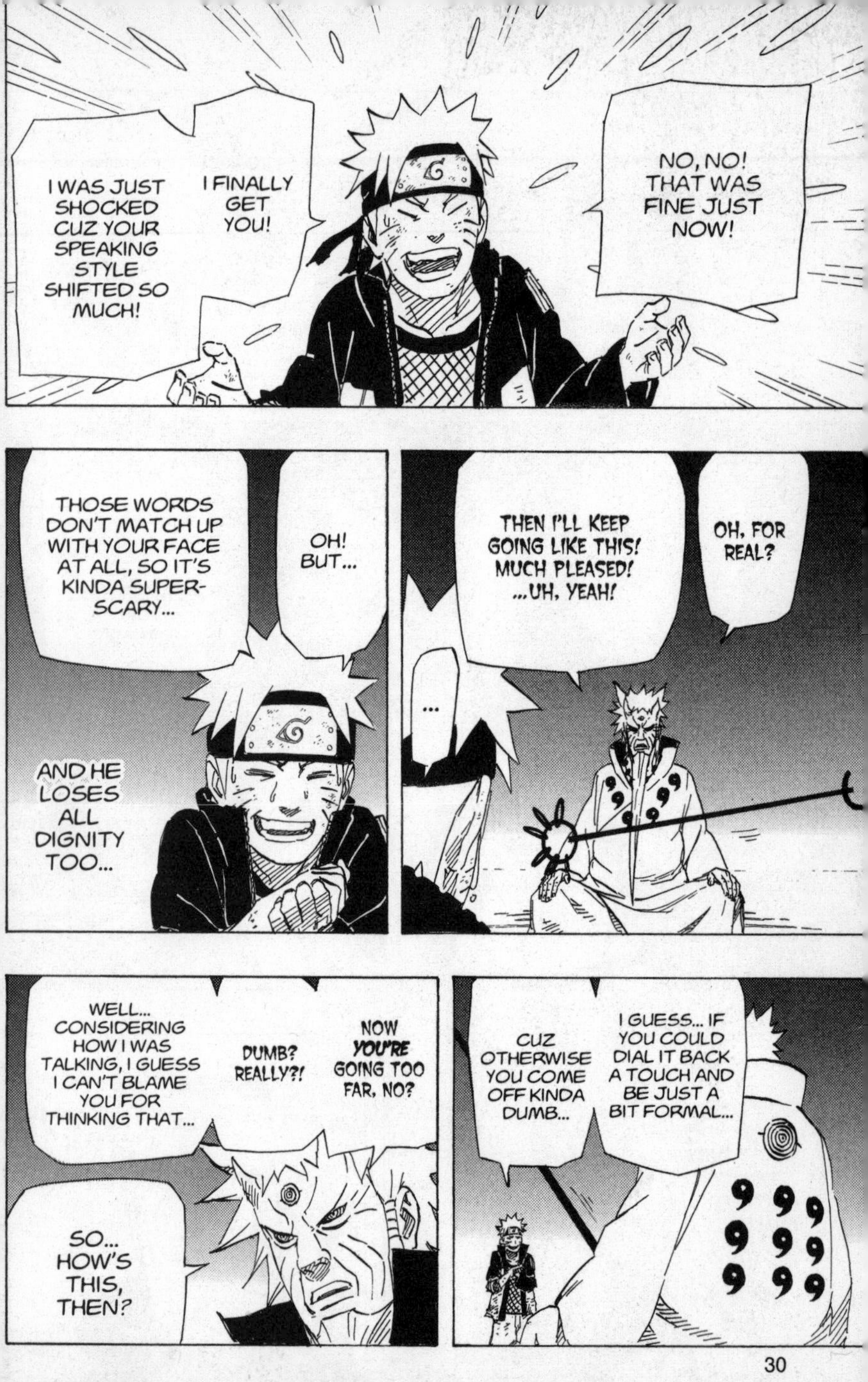
NO, NO! THAT WAS FINE JUST NOW!
I FINALLY GET YOU!
I WAS JUST SHOCKED CUZ YOUR SPEAKING STYLE SHIFTED SO MUCH!
OH, FOR REAL?
THEN I'LL KEEP GOING LIKE THIS! MUCH PLEASED! ...UH, YEAH!
...
OH! BUT...
THOSE WORDS DON'T MATCH UP WITH YOUR FACE AT ALL, SO IT'S KINDA SUPER-SCARY...
AND HE LOSES ALL DIGNITY TOO...
I GUESS... IF YOU COULD DIAL IT BACK A TOUCH AND BE JUST A BIT FORMAL...
CUZ OTHERWISE YOU COME OFF KINDA DUMB...
NOW *YOU'RE* GOING TOO FAR, NO?
DUMB? REALLY?!
WELL... CONSIDERING HOW I WAS TALKING, I GUESS I CAN'T BLAME YOU FOR THINKING THAT...
SO... HOW'S THIS, THEN?

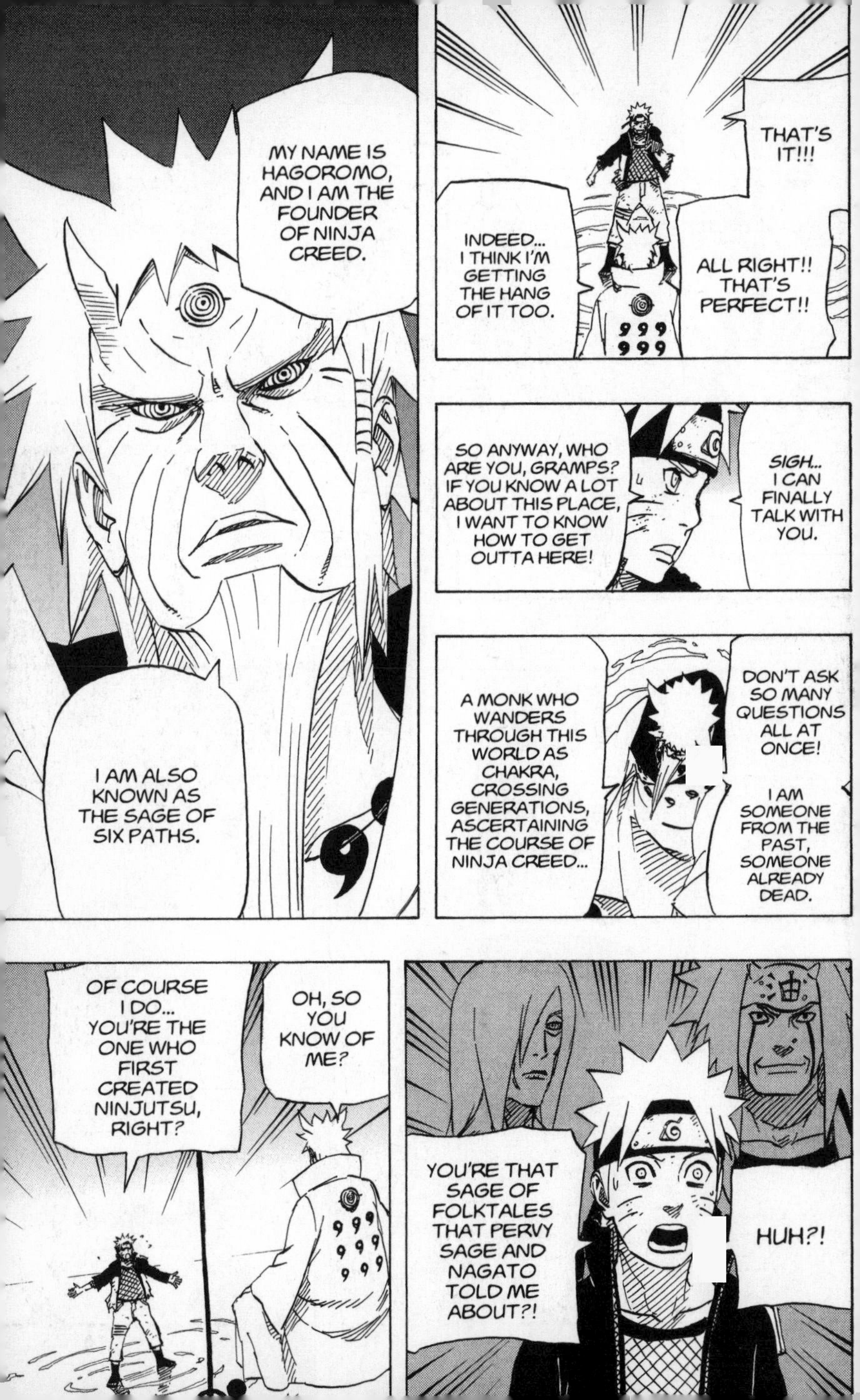
THAT'S IT!!!
ALL RIGHT!! THAT'S PERFECT!!
INDEED... I THINK I'M GETTING THE HANG OF IT TOO.
SIGH... I CAN FINALLY TALK WITH YOU.
SO ANYWAY, WHO ARE YOU, GRAMPS? IF YOU KNOW A LOT ABOUT THIS PLACE, I WANT TO KNOW HOW TO GET OUTTA HERE!
DON'T ASK SO MANY QUESTIONS ALL AT ONCE!
I AM SOMEONE FROM THE PAST, SOMEONE ALREADY DEAD.
A MONK WHO WANDERS THROUGH THIS WORLD AS CHAKRA, CROSSING GENERATIONS, ASCERTAINING THE COURSE OF NINJA CREED...
MY NAME IS HAGOROMO, AND I AM THE FOUNDER OF NINJA CREED.
I AM ALSO KNOWN AS THE SAGE OF SIX PATHS.
HUH?!
YOU'RE THAT SAGE OF FOLKTALES THAT PERVY SAGE AND NAGATO TOLD ME ABOUT?!
OH, SO YOU KNOW OF ME?
OF COURSE I DO... YOU'RE THE ONE WHO FIRST CREATED NINJUTSU, RIGHT?

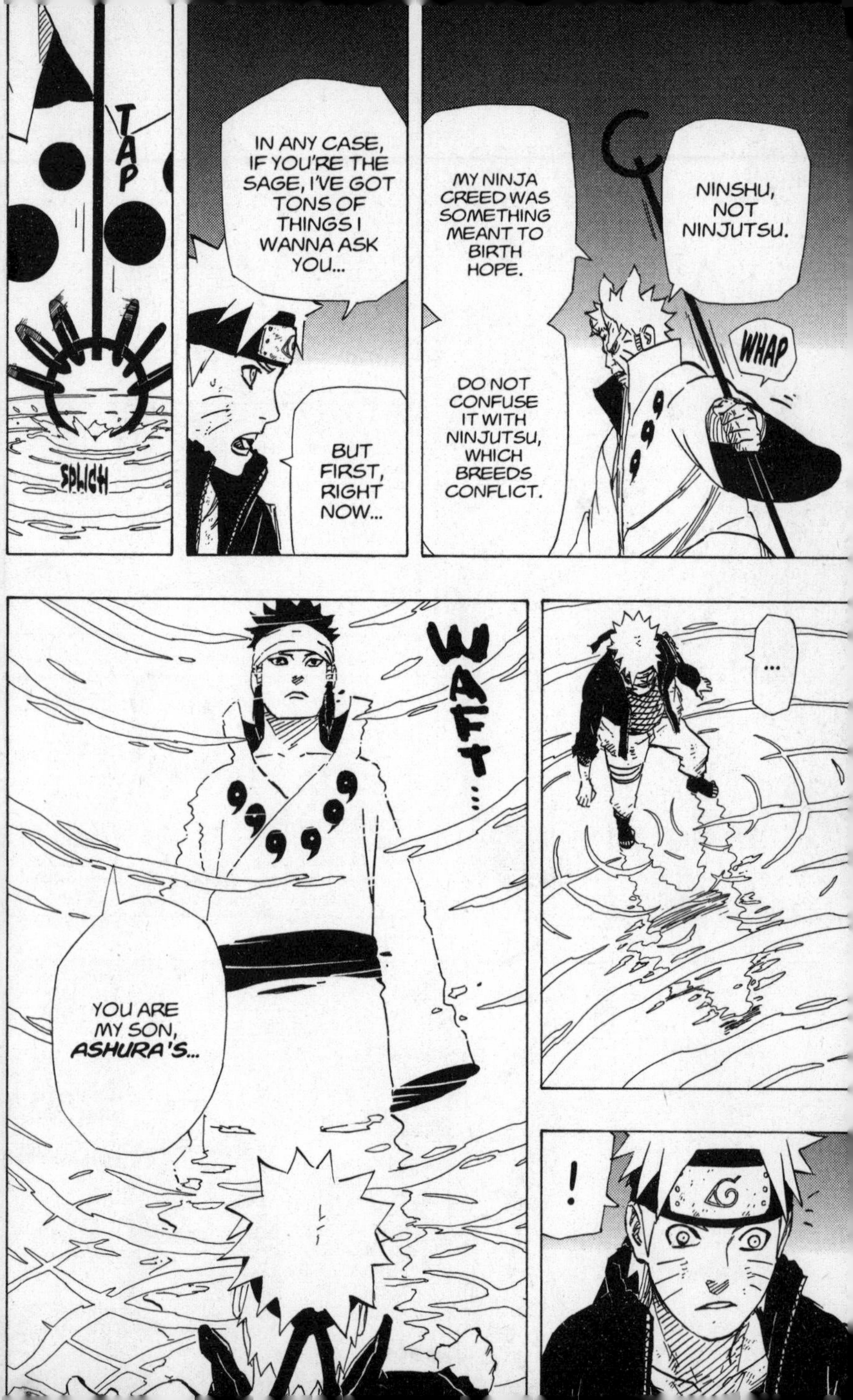
NINSHU, NOT NINJUTSU.
WHAP
MY NINJA CREED WAS SOMETHING MEANT TO BIRTH HOPE.
DO NOT CONFUSE IT WITH NINJUTSU, WHICH BREEDS CONFLICT.
IN ANY CASE, IF YOU'RE THE SAGE, I'VE GOT TONS OF THINGS I WANNA ASK YOU...
BUT FIRST, RIGHT NOW...
TAP
SPLICH
...
!
WAFT...
YOU ARE MY SON, **ASHURA'S**...

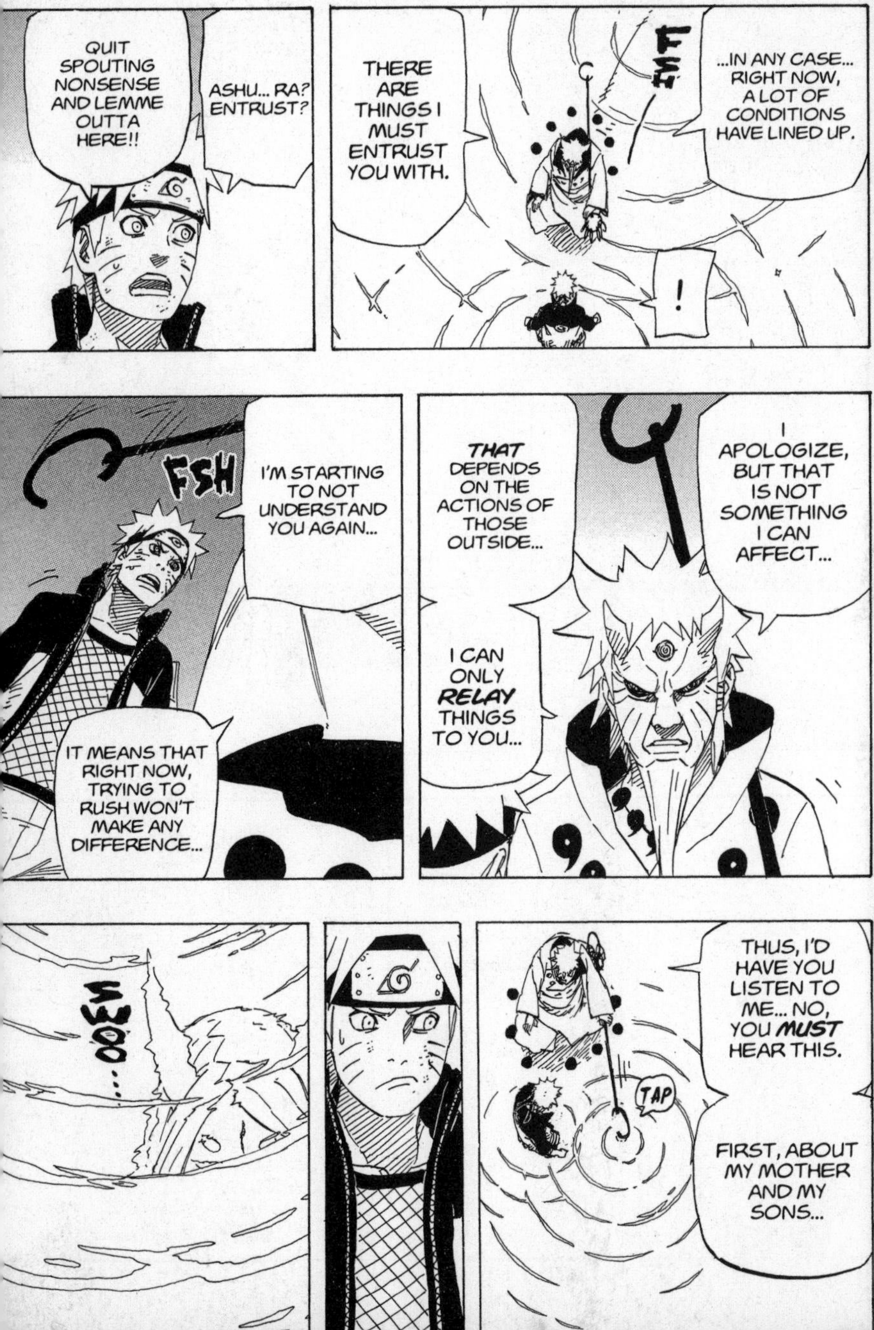

...IN ANY CASE... RIGHT NOW, A LOT OF CONDITIONS HAVE LINED UP.
FSH
THERE ARE THINGS I MUST ENTRUST YOU WITH.
!
ASHU... RA? ENTRUST?
QUIT SPOUTING NONSENSE AND LEMME OUTTA HERE!!
I APOLOGIZE, BUT THAT IS NOT SOMETHING I CAN AFFECT...
THAT DEPENDS ON THE ACTIONS OF THOSE OUTSIDE...
I CAN ONLY RELAY THINGS TO YOU...
I'M STARTING TO NOT UNDERSTAND YOU AGAIN...
FSH
IT MEANS THAT RIGHT NOW, TRYING TO RUSH WON'T MAKE ANY DIFFERENCE...
THUS, I'D HAVE YOU LISTEN TO ME... NO, YOU MUST HEAR THIS.
TAP
FIRST, ABOUT MY MOTHER AND MY SONS...
SWOO...

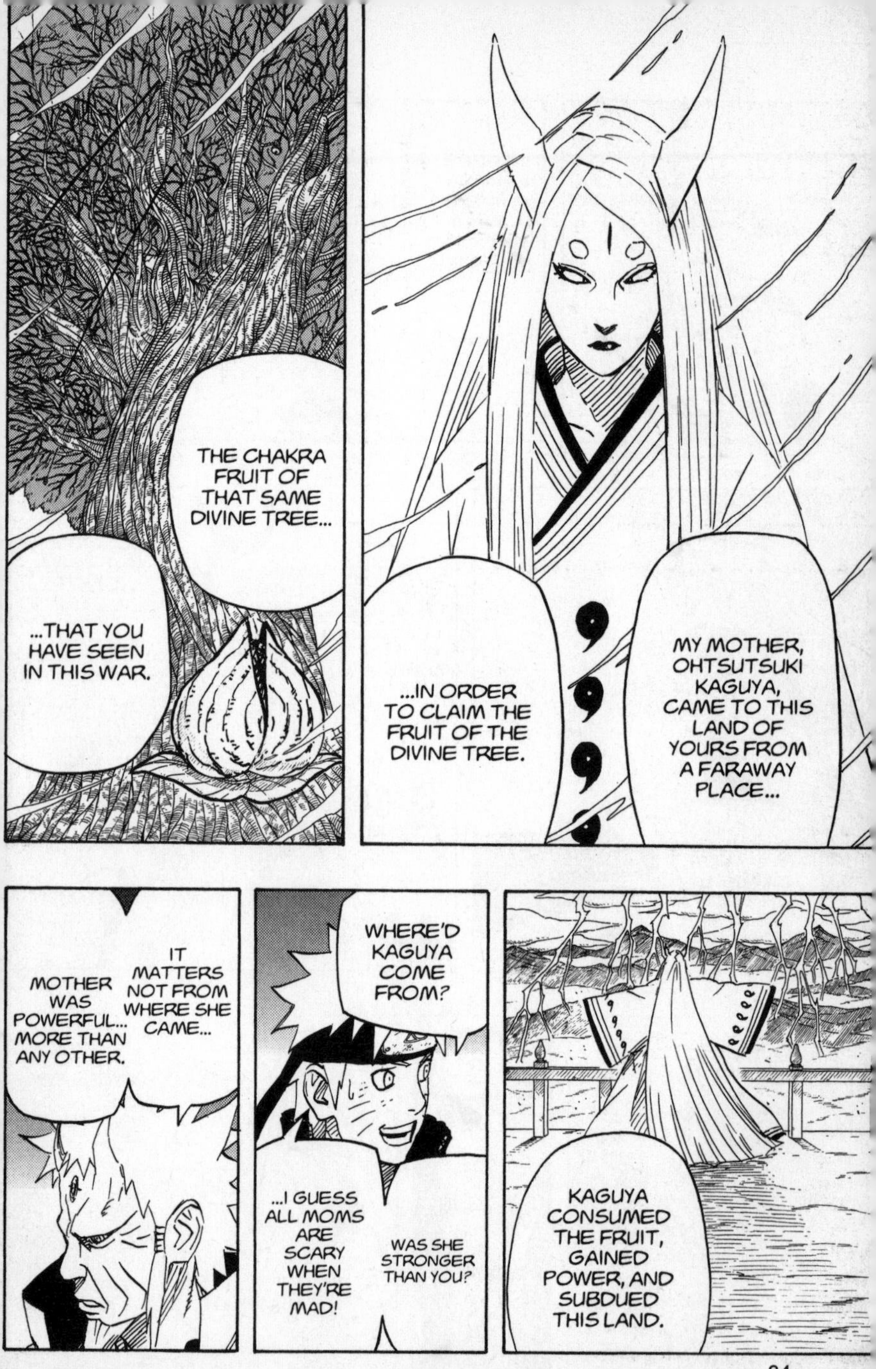
MY MOTHER, OHTSUTSUKI KAGUYA, CAME TO THIS LAND OF YOURS FROM A FARAWAY PLACE...
...IN ORDER TO CLAIM THE FRUIT OF THE DIVINE TREE.
THE CHAKRA FRUIT OF THAT SAME DIVINE TREE...
...THAT YOU HAVE SEEN IN THIS WAR.
KAGUYA CONSUMED THE FRUIT, GAINED POWER, AND SUBDUED THIS LAND.
WHERE'D KAGUYA COME FROM?
WAS SHE STRONGER THAN YOU?
...I GUESS ALL MOMS ARE SCARY WHEN THEY'RE MAD!
IT MATTERS NOT FROM WHERE SHE CAME...
MOTHER WAS POWERFUL... MORE THAN ANY OTHER.

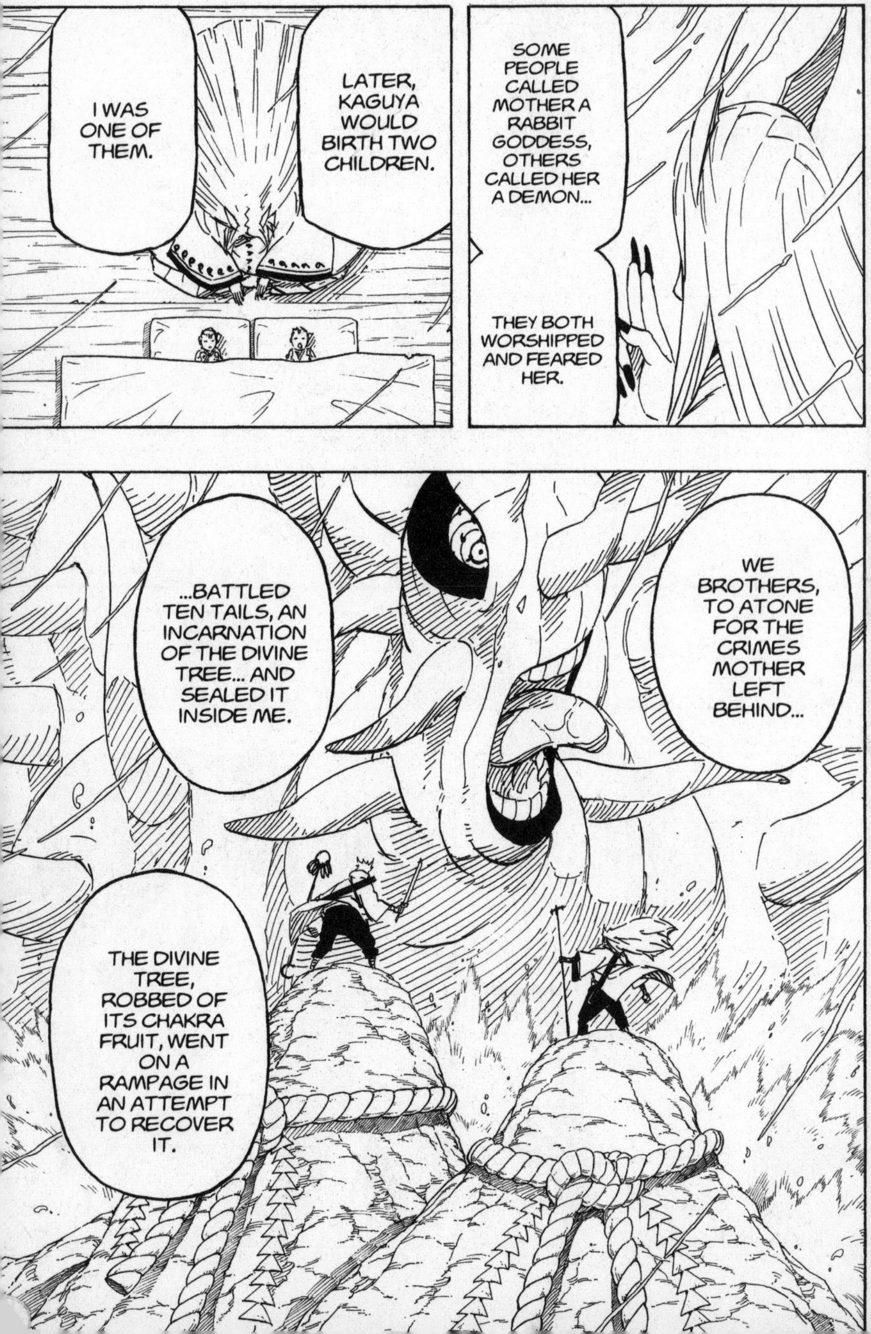
SOME PEOPLE CALLED MOTHER A RABBIT GODDESS, OTHERS CALLED HER A DEMON...
THEY BOTH WORSHIPPED AND FEARED HER.
LATER, KAGUYA WOULD BIRTH TWO CHILDREN.
I WAS ONE OF THEM.
WE BROTHERS, TO ATONE FOR THE CRIMES MOTHER LEFT BEHIND...
...BATTLED TEN TAILS, AN INCARNATION OF THE DIVINE TREE... AND SEALED IT INSIDE ME.
THE DIVINE TREE, ROBBED OF ITS CHAKRA FRUIT, WENT ON A RAMPAGE IN AN ATTEMPT TO RECOVER IT.

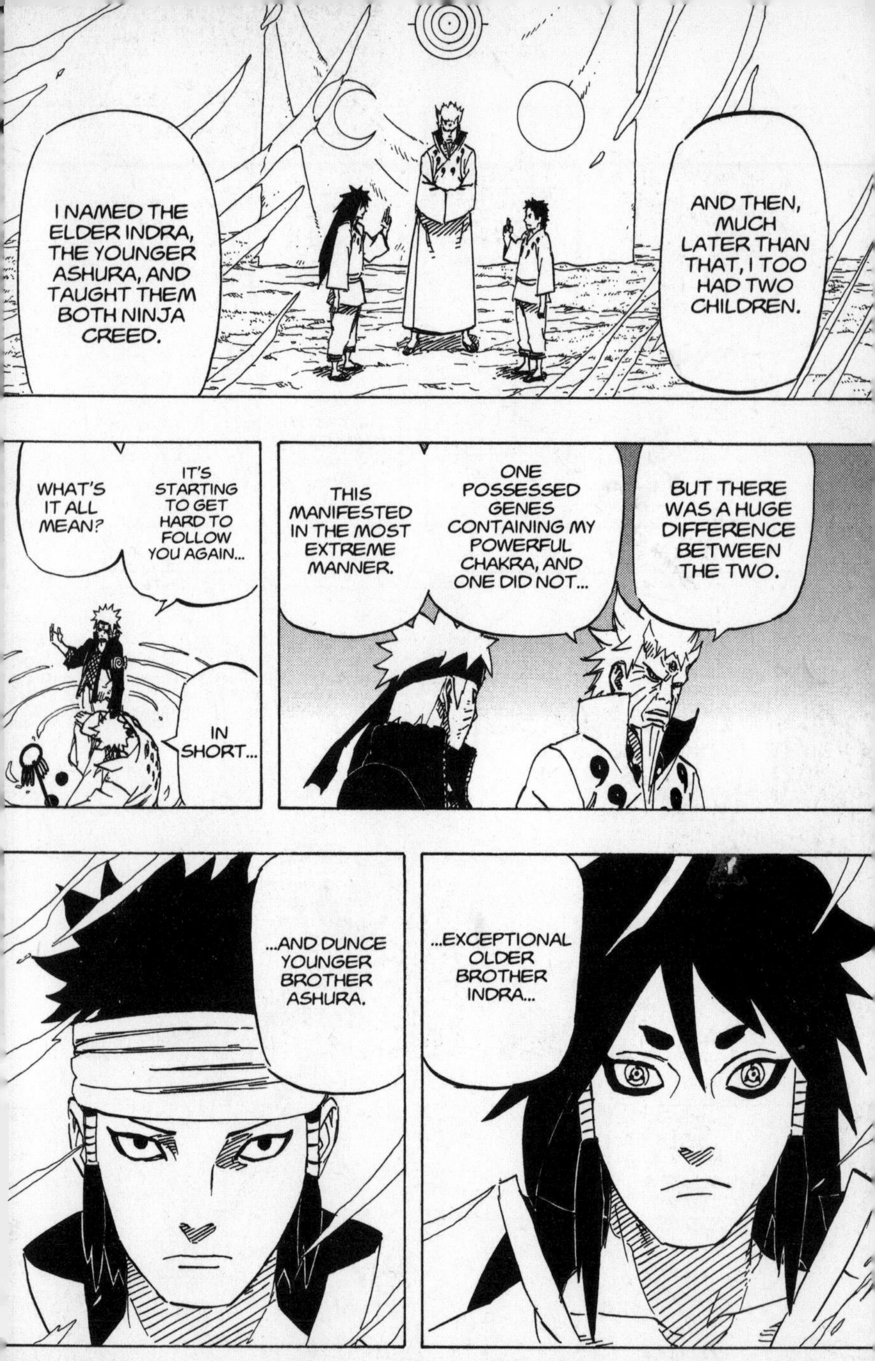
AND THEN, MUCH LATER THAN THAT, I TOO HAD TWO CHILDREN.
I NAMED THE ELDER INDRA, THE YOUNGER ASHURA, AND TAUGHT THEM BOTH NINJA CREED.
BUT THERE WAS A HUGE DIFFERENCE BETWEEN THE TWO.
ONE POSSESSED GENES CONTAINING MY POWERFUL CHAKRA, AND ONE DID NOT...
THIS MANIFESTED IN THE MOST EXTREME MANNER.
IT'S STARTING TO GET HARD TO FOLLOW YOU AGAIN...
WHAT'S IT ALL MEAN?
IN SHORT...
...EXCEPTIONAL OLDER BROTHER INDRA...
...AND DUNCE YOUNGER BROTHER ASHURA.

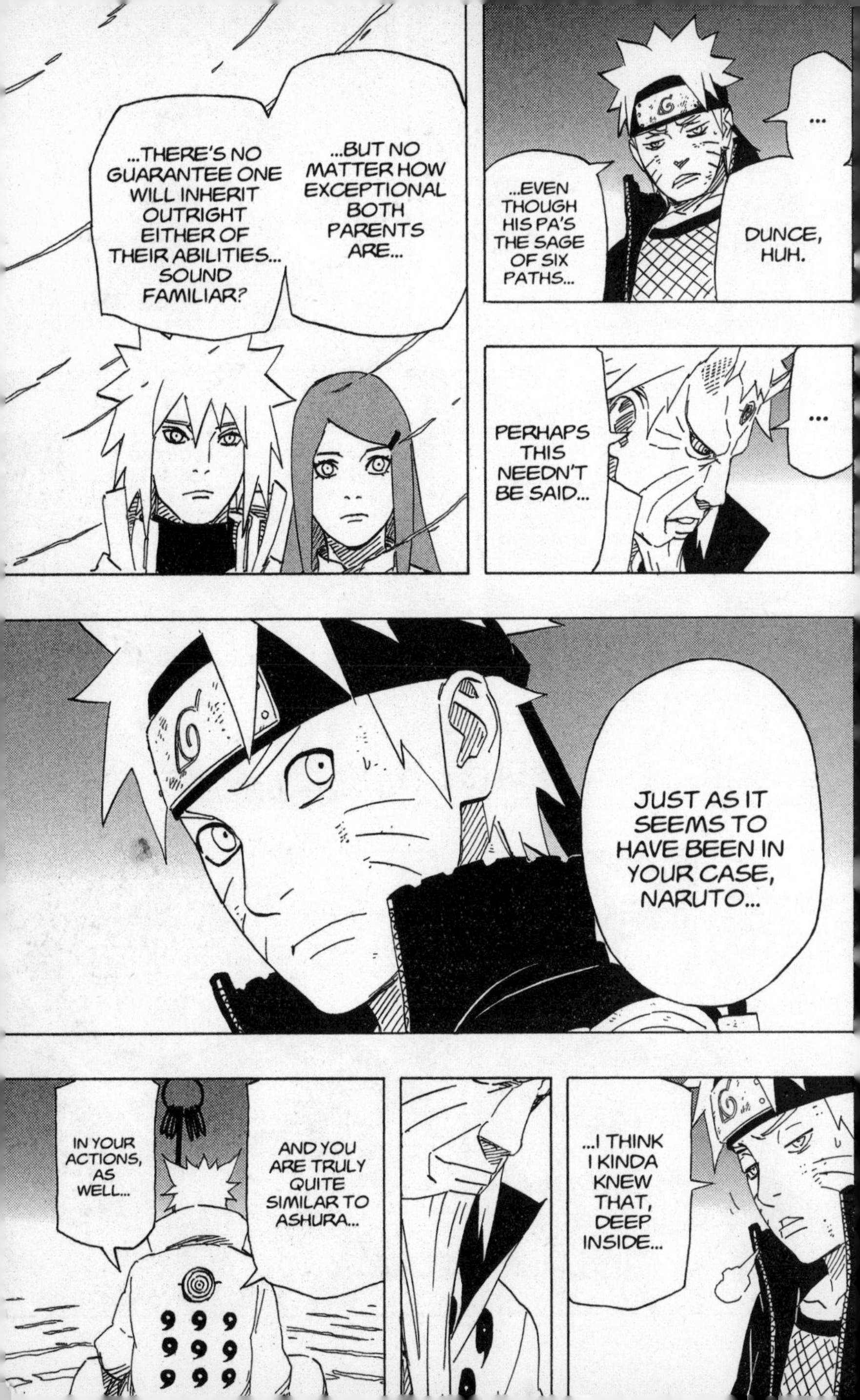
...
DUNCE, HUH.
...EVEN THOUGH HIS PA'S THE SAGE OF SIX PATHS...
...
PERHAPS THIS NEEDN'T BE SAID...
...BUT NO MATTER HOW EXCEPTIONAL BOTH PARENTS ARE...
...THERE'S NO GUARANTEE ONE WILL INHERIT OUTRIGHT EITHER OF THEIR ABILITIES... SOUND FAMILIAR?
JUST AS IT SEEMS TO HAVE BEEN IN YOUR CASE, NARUTO...
...I THINK I KINDA KNEW THAT, DEEP INSIDE...
AND YOU ARE TRULY QUITE SIMILAR TO ASHURA...
IN YOUR ACTIONS, AS WELL...

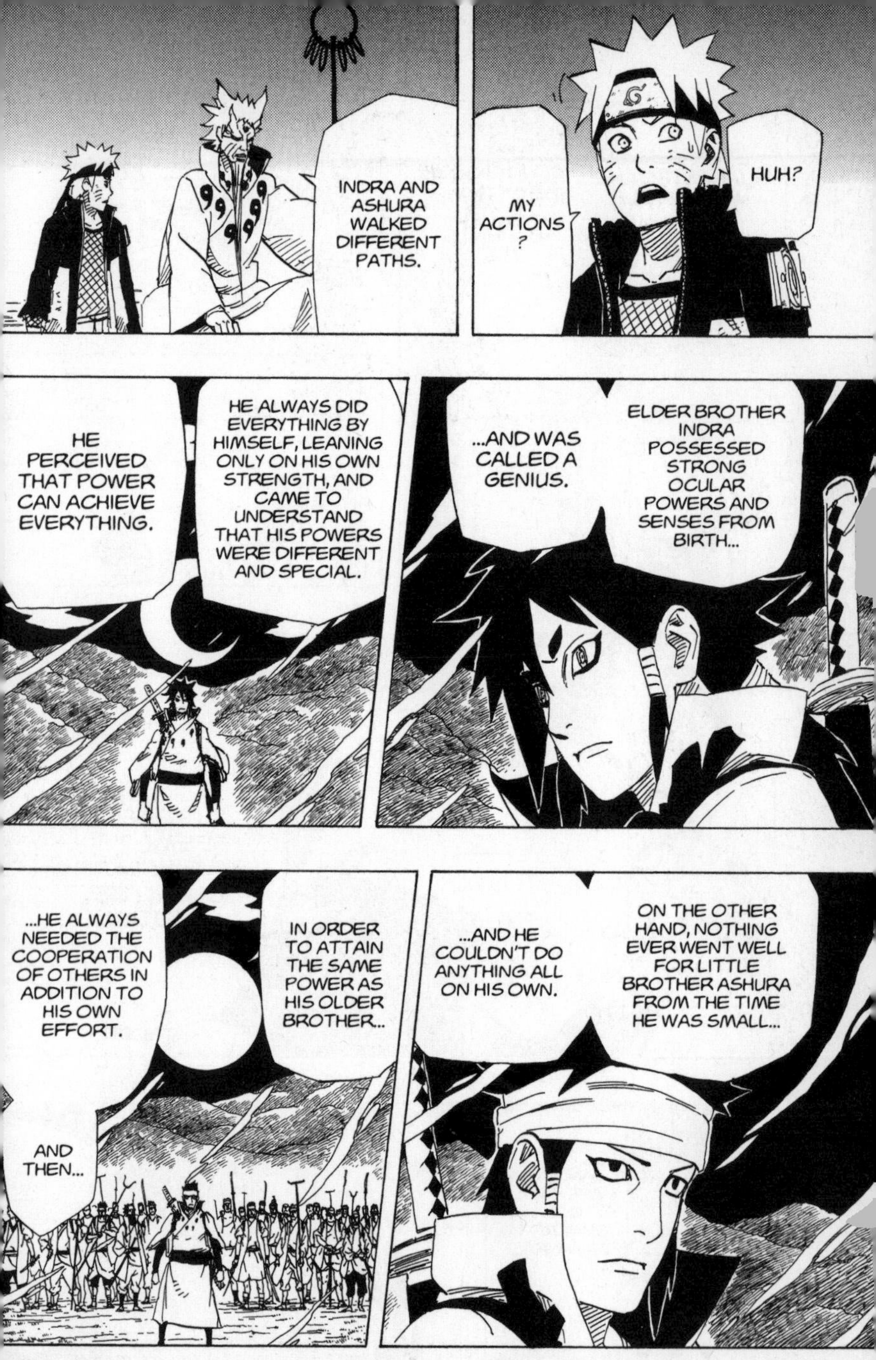
HUH?
MY ACTIONS?
INDRA AND ASHURA WALKED DIFFERENT PATHS.
ELDER BROTHER INDRA POSSESSED STRONG OCULAR POWERS AND SENSES FROM BIRTH...
...AND WAS CALLED A GENIUS.
HE ALWAYS DID EVERYTHING BY HIMSELF, LEANING ONLY ON HIS OWN STRENGTH, AND CAME TO UNDERSTAND THAT HIS POWERS WERE DIFFERENT AND SPECIAL.
HE PERCEIVED THAT POWER CAN ACHIEVE EVERYTHING.
ON THE OTHER HAND, NOTHING EVER WENT WELL FOR LITTLE BROTHER ASHURA FROM THE TIME HE WAS SMALL...
...AND HE COULDN'T DO ANYTHING ALL ON HIS OWN.
IN ORDER TO ATTAIN THE SAME POWER AS HIS OLDER BROTHER...
...HE ALWAYS NEEDED THE COOPERATION OF OTHERS IN ADDITION TO HIS OWN EFFORT.
AND THEN...

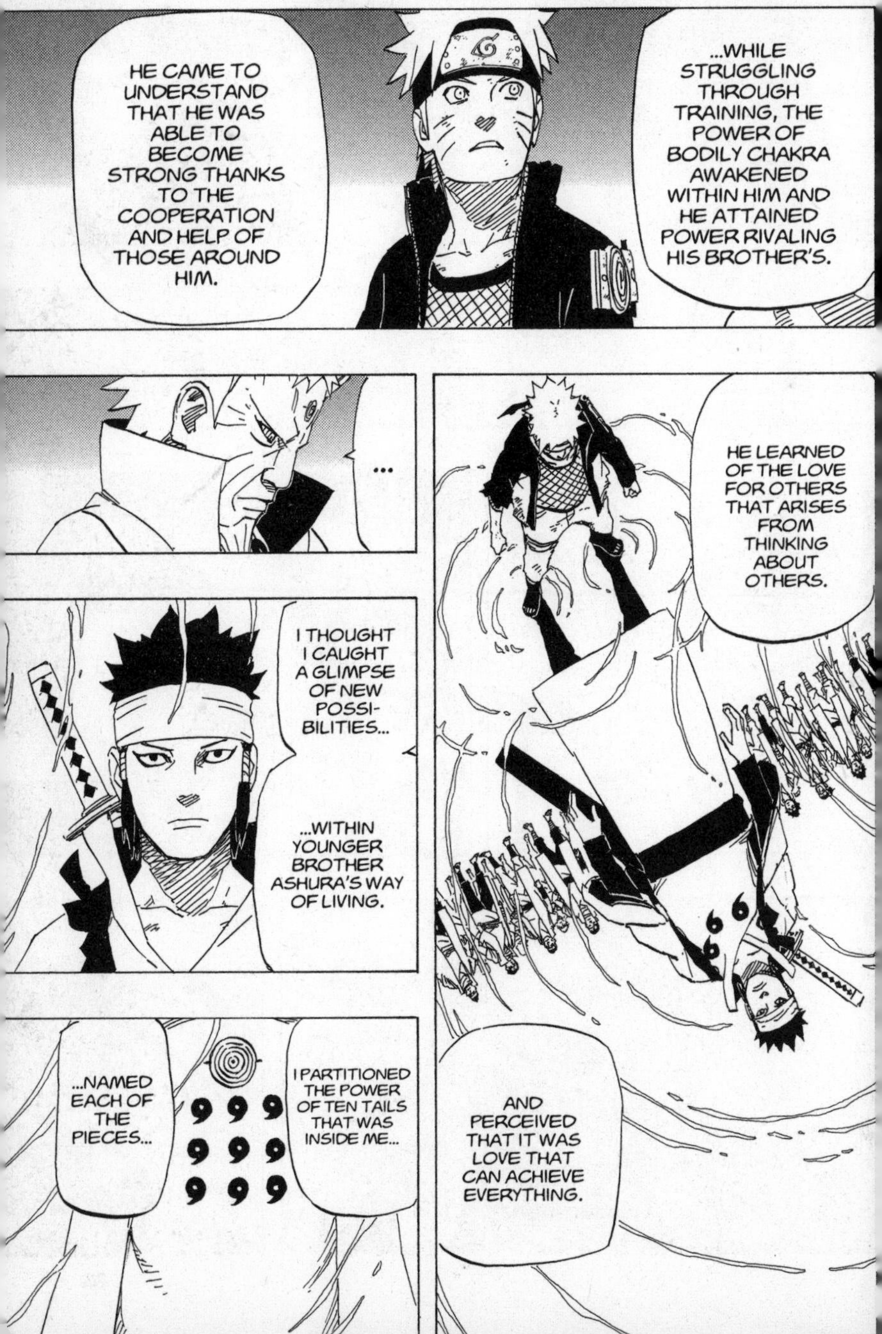
...WHILE STRUGGLING THROUGH TRAINING, THE POWER OF BODILY CHAKRA AWAKENED WITHIN HIM AND HE ATTAINED POWER RIVALING HIS BROTHER'S.
HE CAME TO UNDERSTAND THAT HE WAS ABLE TO BECOME STRONG THANKS TO THE COOPERATION AND HELP OF THOSE AROUND HIM.
HE LEARNED OF THE LOVE FOR OTHERS THAT ARISES FROM THINKING ABOUT OTHERS.
AND PERCEIVED THAT IT WAS LOVE THAT CAN ACHIEVE EVERYTHING.
...
I THOUGHT I CAUGHT A GLIMPSE OF NEW POSSI-BILITIES...
...WITHIN YOUNGER BROTHER ASHURA'S WAY OF LIVING.
I PARTITIONED THE POWER OF TEN TAILS THAT WAS INSIDE ME...
...NAMED EACH OF THE PIECES...

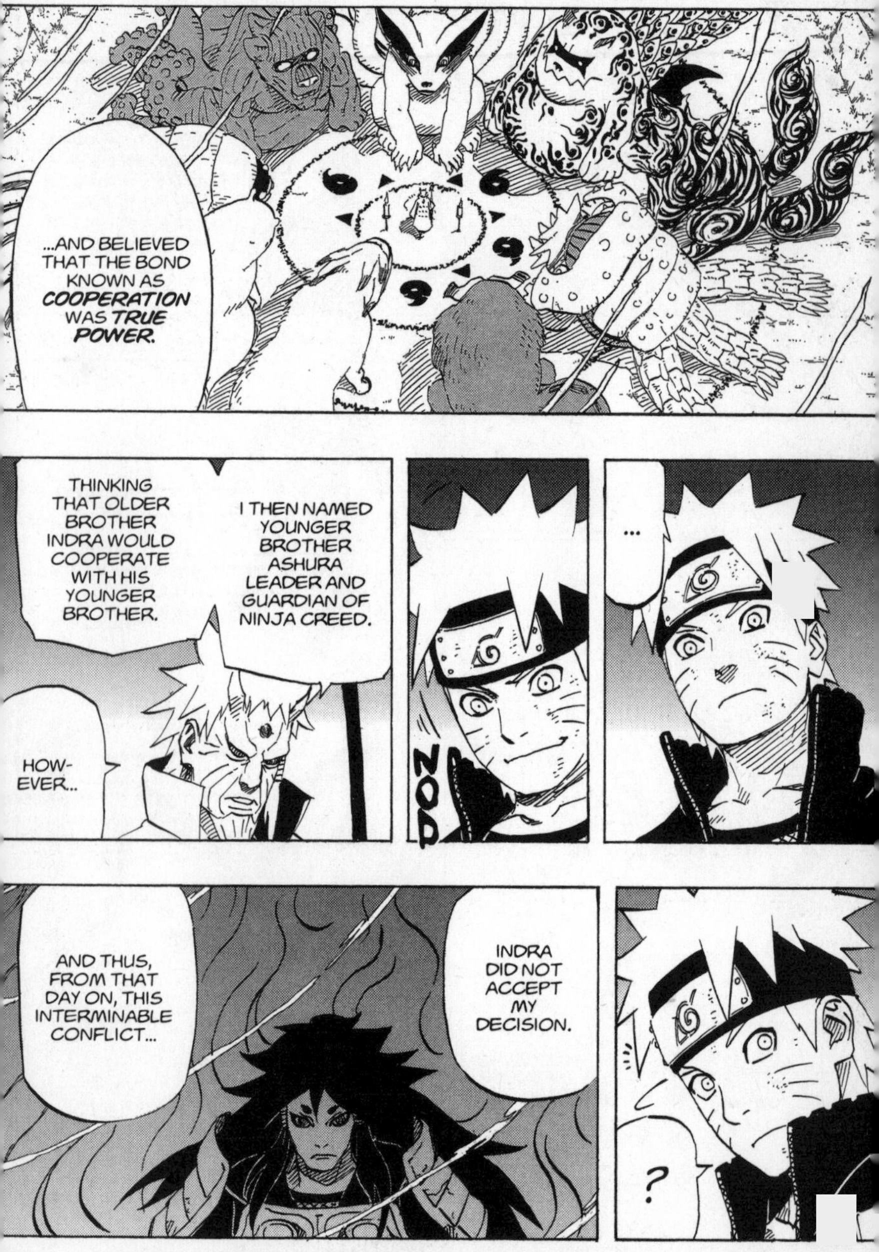

...AND BELIEVED THAT THE BOND KNOWN AS COOPERATION WAS TRUE POWER.
...
NOD
I THEN NAMED YOUNGER BROTHER ASHURA LEADER AND GUARDIAN OF NINJA CREED.
THINKING THAT OLDER BROTHER INDRA WOULD COOPERATE WITH HIS YOUNGER BROTHER.
HOW-EVER...
?
INDRA DID NOT ACCEPT MY DECISION.
AND THUS, FROM THAT DAY ON, THIS INTERMINABLE CONFLICT...

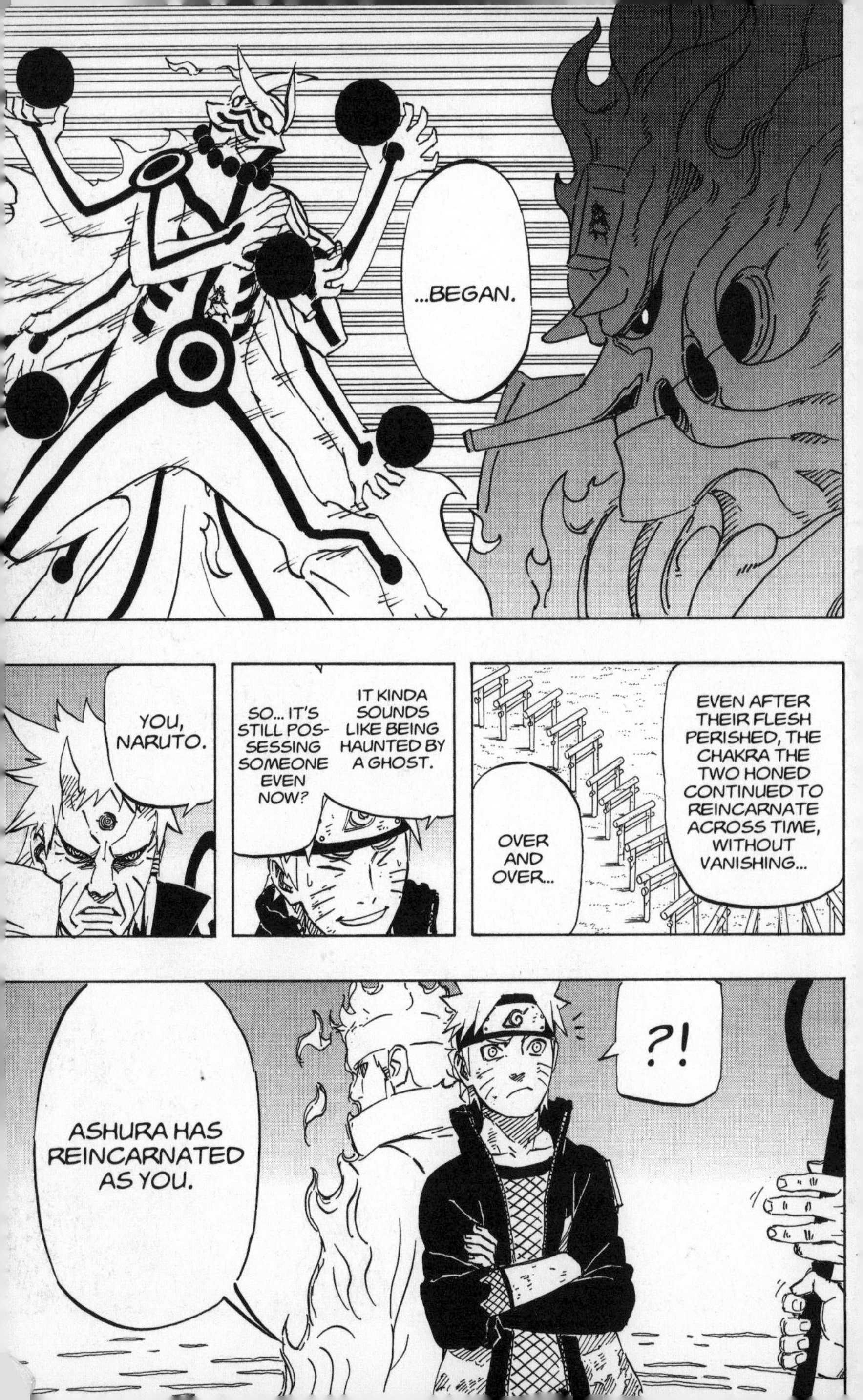
...BEGAN.
EVEN AFTER THEIR FLESH PERISHED, THE CHAKRA THE TWO HONED CONTINUED TO REINCARNATE ACROSS TIME, WITHOUT VANISHING...
OVER AND OVER...
IT KINDA SOUNDS LIKE BEING HAUNTED BY A GHOST.
SO... IT'S STILL POS-SESSING SOMEONE EVEN NOW?
YOU, NARUTO.
?!
ASHURA HAS REINCARNATED AS YOU.

# Number 671: Naruto and the Sage of Six Paths

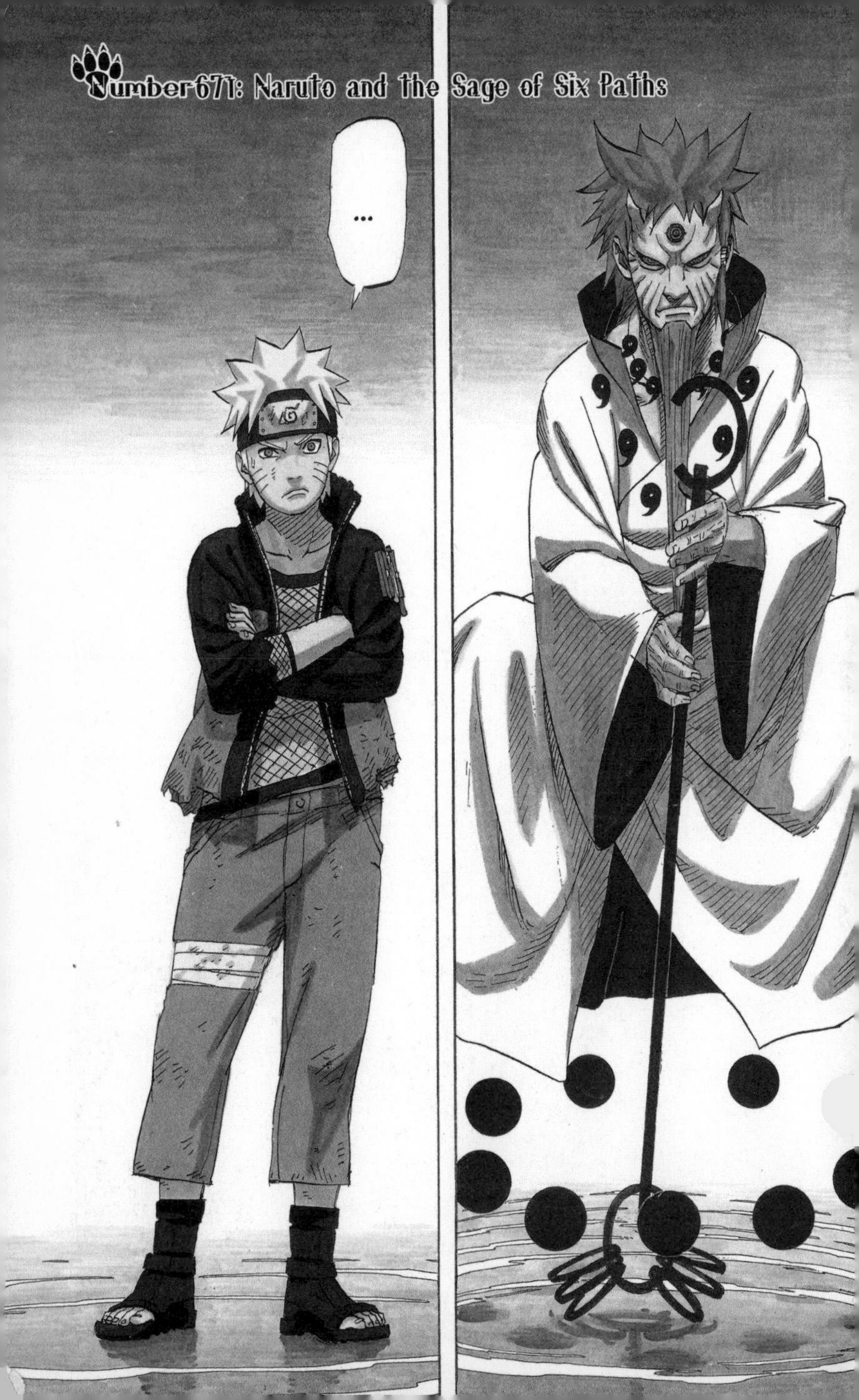

...

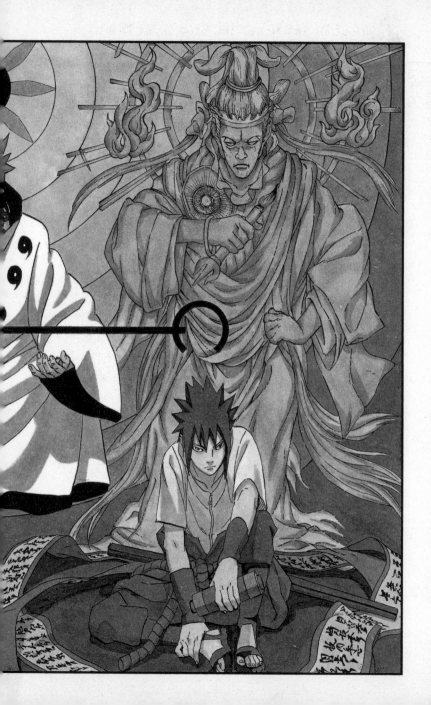

# Number 671: Naruto and the Sage of Six Paths

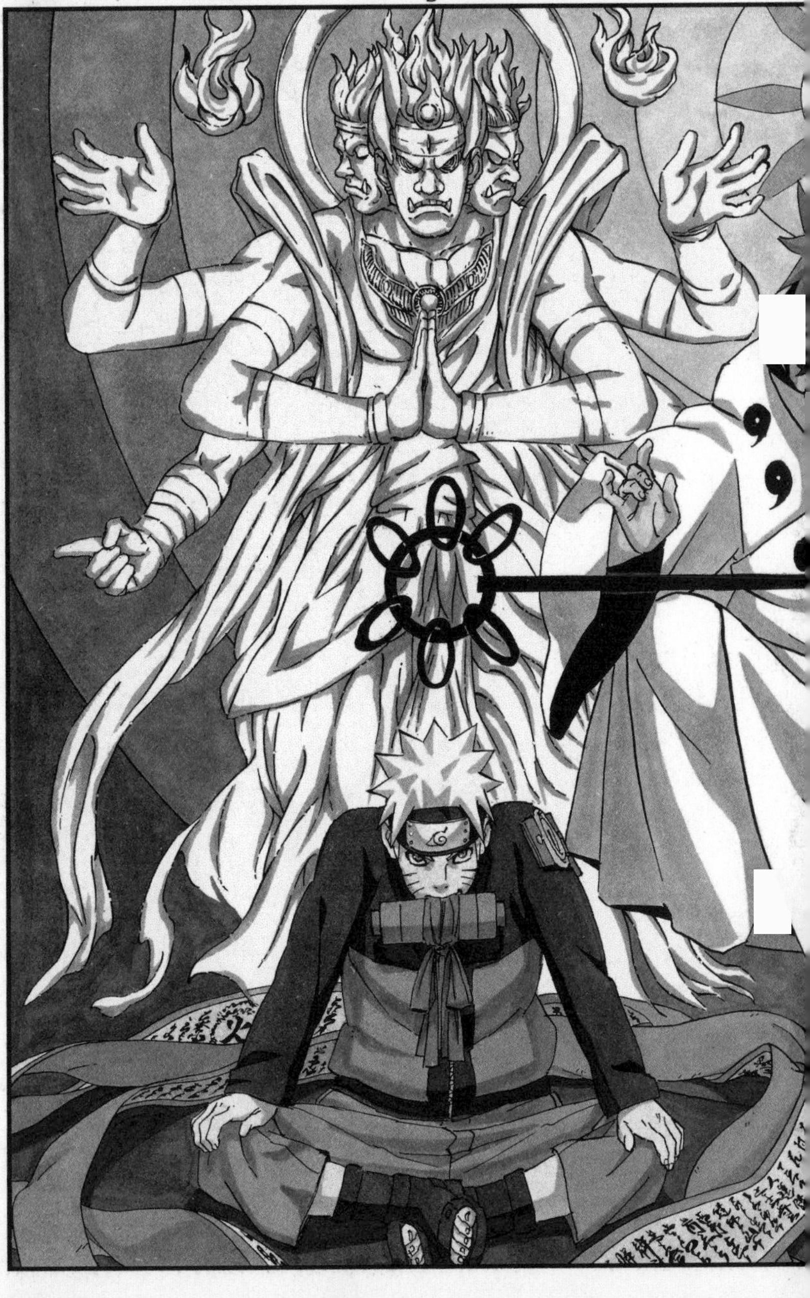

NARUTO

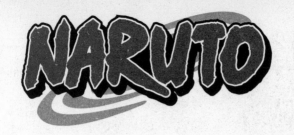

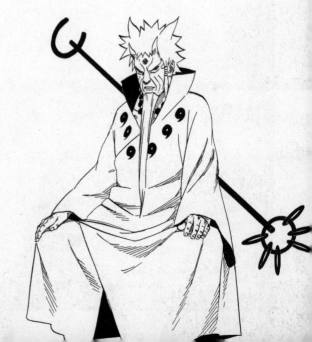

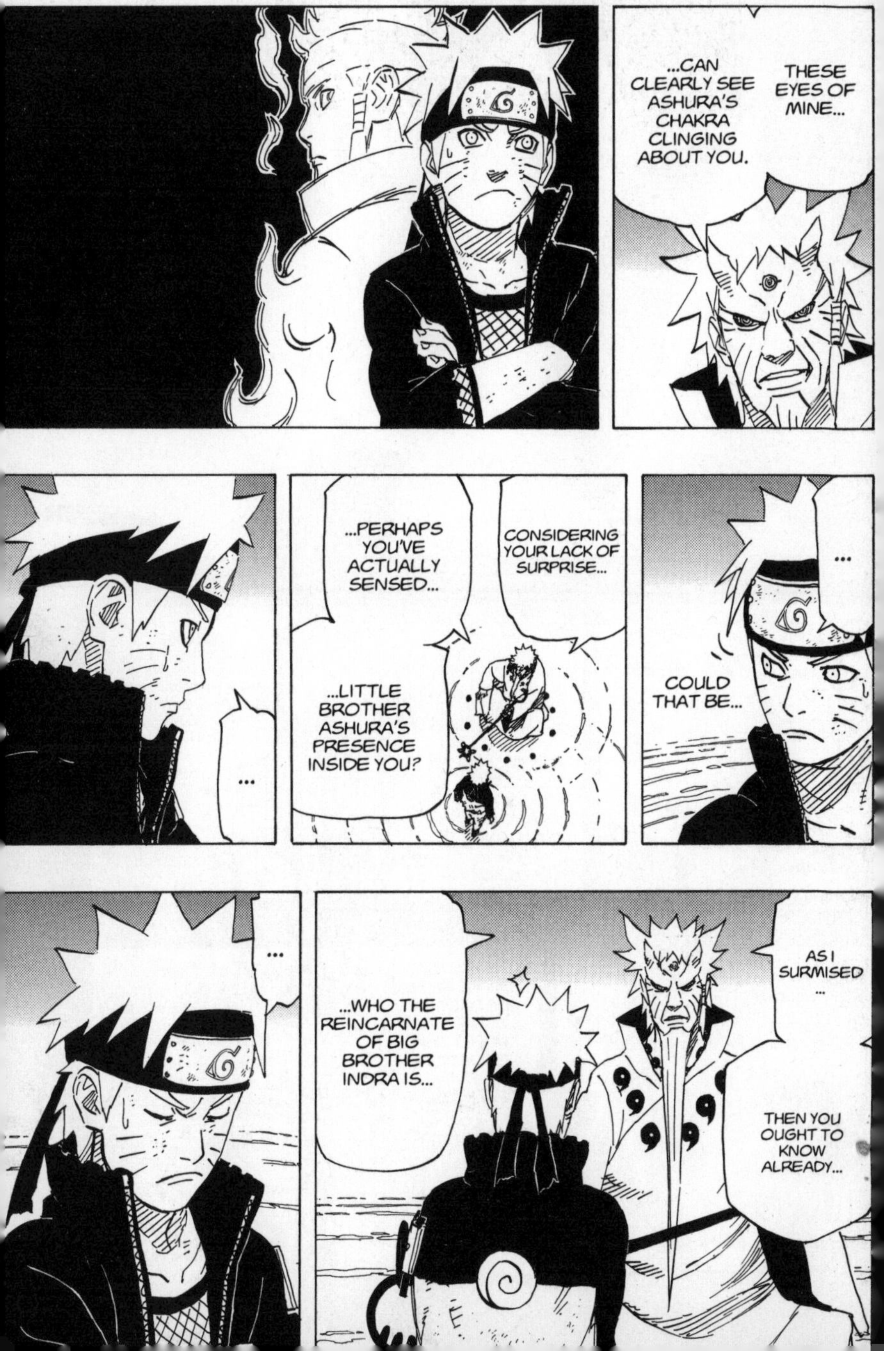
THESE EYES OF MINE...
...CAN CLEARLY SEE ASHURA'S CHAKRA CLINGING ABOUT YOU.
...
COULD THAT BE...
CONSIDERING YOUR LACK OF SURPRISE...
...PERHAPS YOU'VE ACTUALLY SENSED...
...LITTLE BROTHER ASHURA'S PRESENCE INSIDE YOU?
...
AS I SURMISED ...
THEN YOU OUGHT TO KNOW ALREADY...
...WHO THE REINCARNATE OF BIG BROTHER INDRA IS...
...

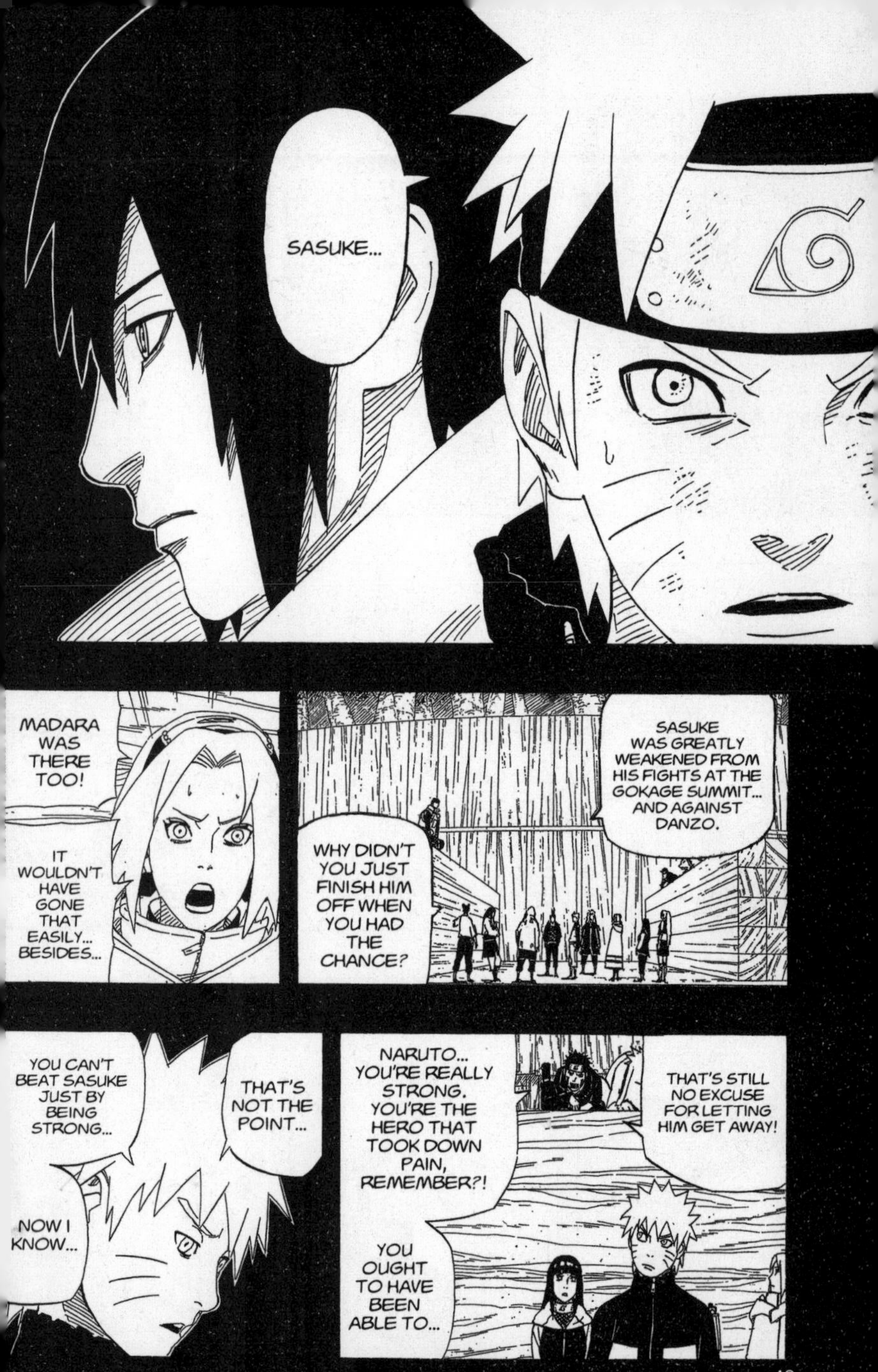

SASUKE...
SASUKE WAS GREATLY WEAKENED FROM HIS FIGHTS AT THE GOKAGE SUMMIT... AND AGAINST DANZO.
WHY DIDN'T YOU JUST FINISH HIM OFF WHEN YOU HAD THE CHANCE?
MADARA WAS THERE TOO!
IT WOULDN'T HAVE GONE THAT EASILY... BESIDES...
THAT'S STILL NO EXCUSE FOR LETTING HIM GET AWAY!
NARUTO... YOU'RE REALLY STRONG. YOU'RE THE HERO THAT TOOK DOWN PAIN, REMEMBER?!
YOU OUGHT TO HAVE BEEN ABLE TO...
THAT'S NOT THE POINT...
YOU CAN'T BEAT SASUKE JUST BY BEING STRONG...
NOW I KNOW...

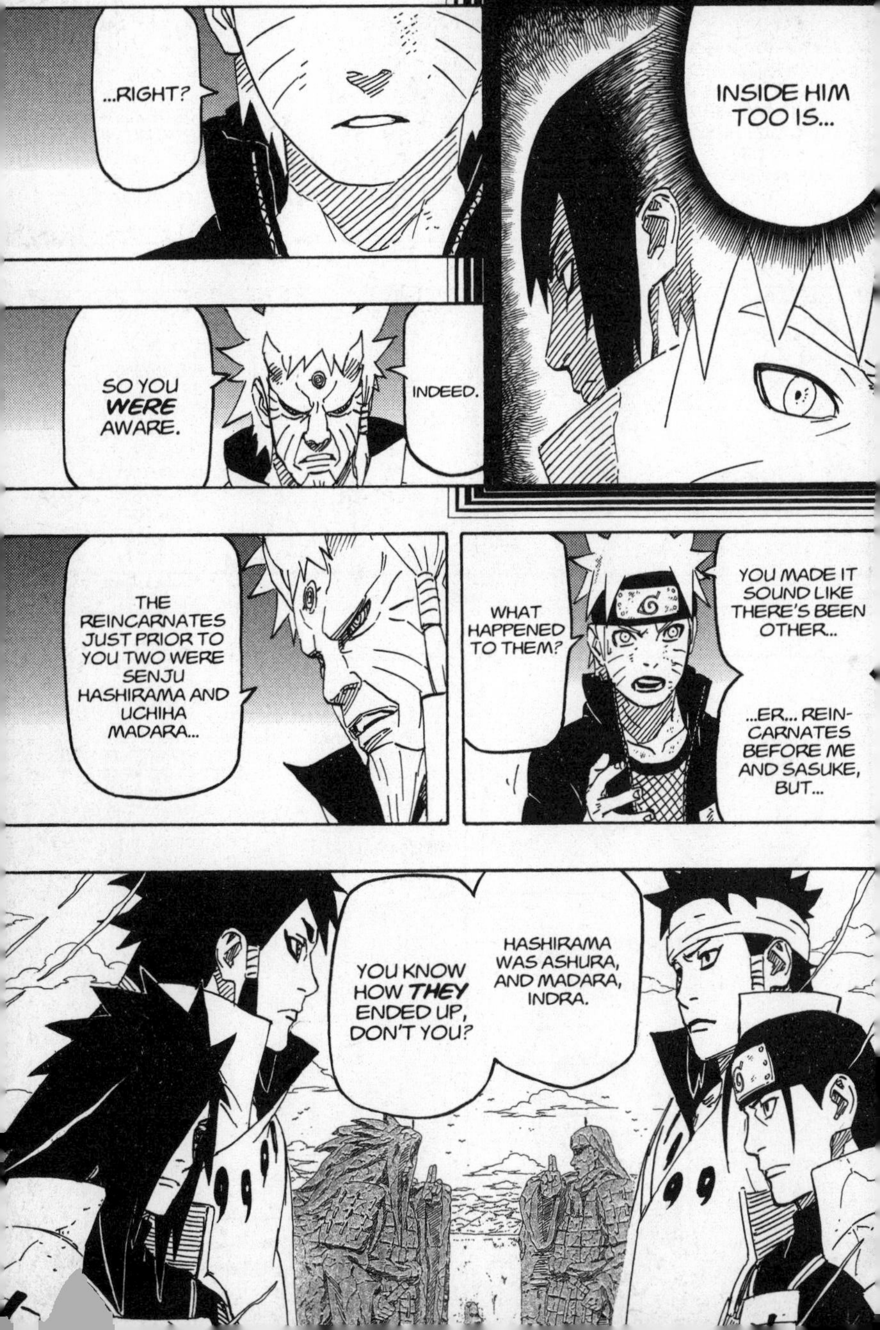
INSIDE HIM TOO IS...
...RIGHT?
INDEED.
SO YOU *WERE* AWARE.
YOU MADE IT SOUND LIKE THERE'S BEEN OTHER...
...ER... REIN-CARNATES BEFORE ME AND SASUKE, BUT...
WHAT HAPPENED TO THEM?
THE REINCARNATES JUST PRIOR TO YOU TWO WERE SENJU HASHIRAMA AND UCHIHA MADARA...
HASHIRAMA WAS ASHURA, AND MADARA, INDRA.
YOU KNOW HOW *THEY* ENDED UP, DON'T YOU?

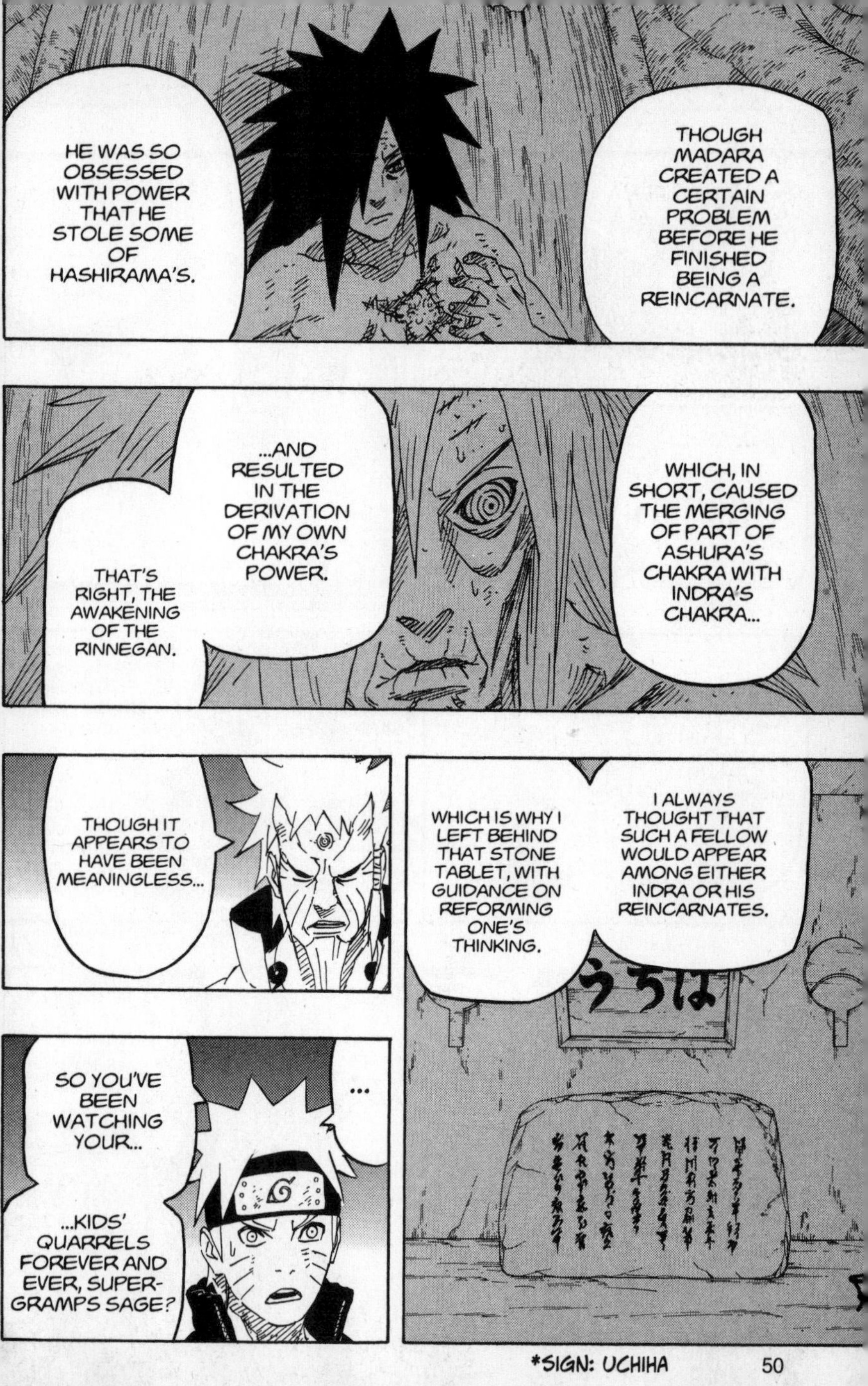
THOUGH MADARA CREATED A CERTAIN PROBLEM BEFORE HE FINISHED BEING A REINCARNATE.
HE WAS SO OBSESSED WITH POWER THAT HE STOLE SOME OF HASHIRAMA'S.
WHICH, IN SHORT, CAUSED THE MERGING OF PART OF ASHURA'S CHAKRA WITH INDRA'S CHAKRA...
...AND RESULTED IN THE DERIVATION OF MY OWN CHAKRA'S POWER.
THAT'S RIGHT, THE AWAKENING OF THE RINNEGAN.
I ALWAYS THOUGHT THAT SUCH A FELLOW WOULD APPEAR AMONG EITHER INDRA OR HIS REINCARNATES.
WHICH IS WHY I LEFT BEHIND THAT STONE TABLET, WITH GUIDANCE ON REFORMING ONE'S THINKING.
うちは
THOUGH IT APPEARS TO HAVE BEEN MEANINGLESS...
...
SO YOU'VE BEEN WATCHING YOUR...
...KIDS' QUARRELS FOREVER AND EVER, SUPER-GRAMPS SAGE?

*SIGN: UCHIHA

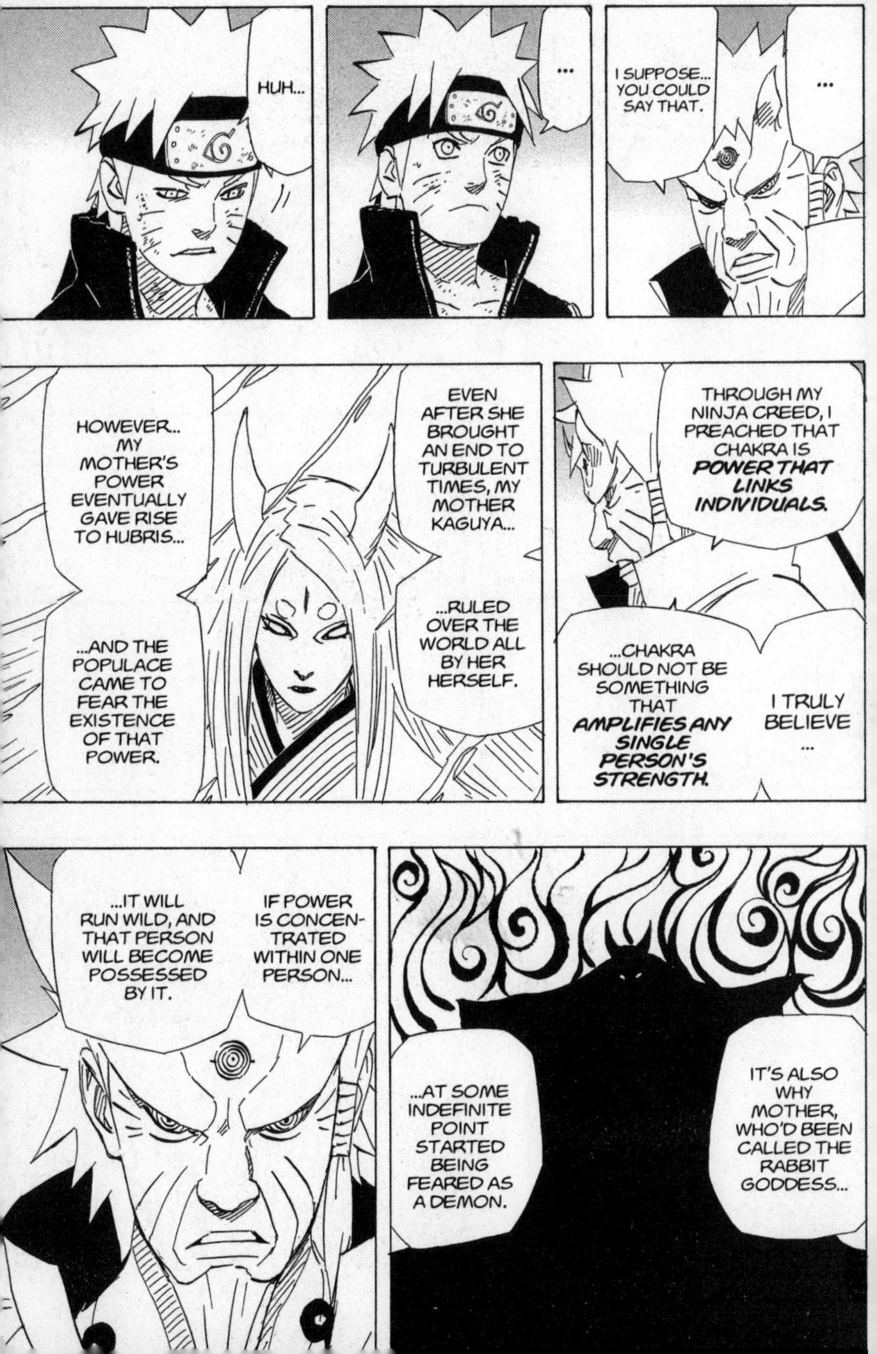
...
I SUPPOSE... YOU COULD SAY THAT.
...
HUH...
THROUGH MY NINJA CREED, I PREACHED THAT CHAKRA IS **POWER THAT LINKS INDIVIDUALS.**
I TRULY BELIEVE ...
...CHAKRA SHOULD NOT BE SOMETHING THAT **AMPLIFIES ANY SINGLE PERSON'S STRENGTH.**
EVEN AFTER SHE BROUGHT AN END TO TURBULENT TIMES, MY MOTHER KAGUYA...
...RULED OVER THE WORLD ALL BY HER HERSELF.
HOWEVER... MY MOTHER'S POWER EVENTUALLY GAVE RISE TO HUBRIS...
...AND THE POPULACE CAME TO FEAR THE EXISTENCE OF THAT POWER.
IT'S ALSO WHY MOTHER, WHO'D BEEN CALLED THE RABBIT GODDESS...
...AT SOME INDEFINITE POINT STARTED BEING FEARED AS A DEMON.
IF POWER IS CONCEN-TRATED WITHIN ONE PERSON...
...IT WILL RUN WILD, AND THAT PERSON WILL BECOME POSSESSED BY IT.

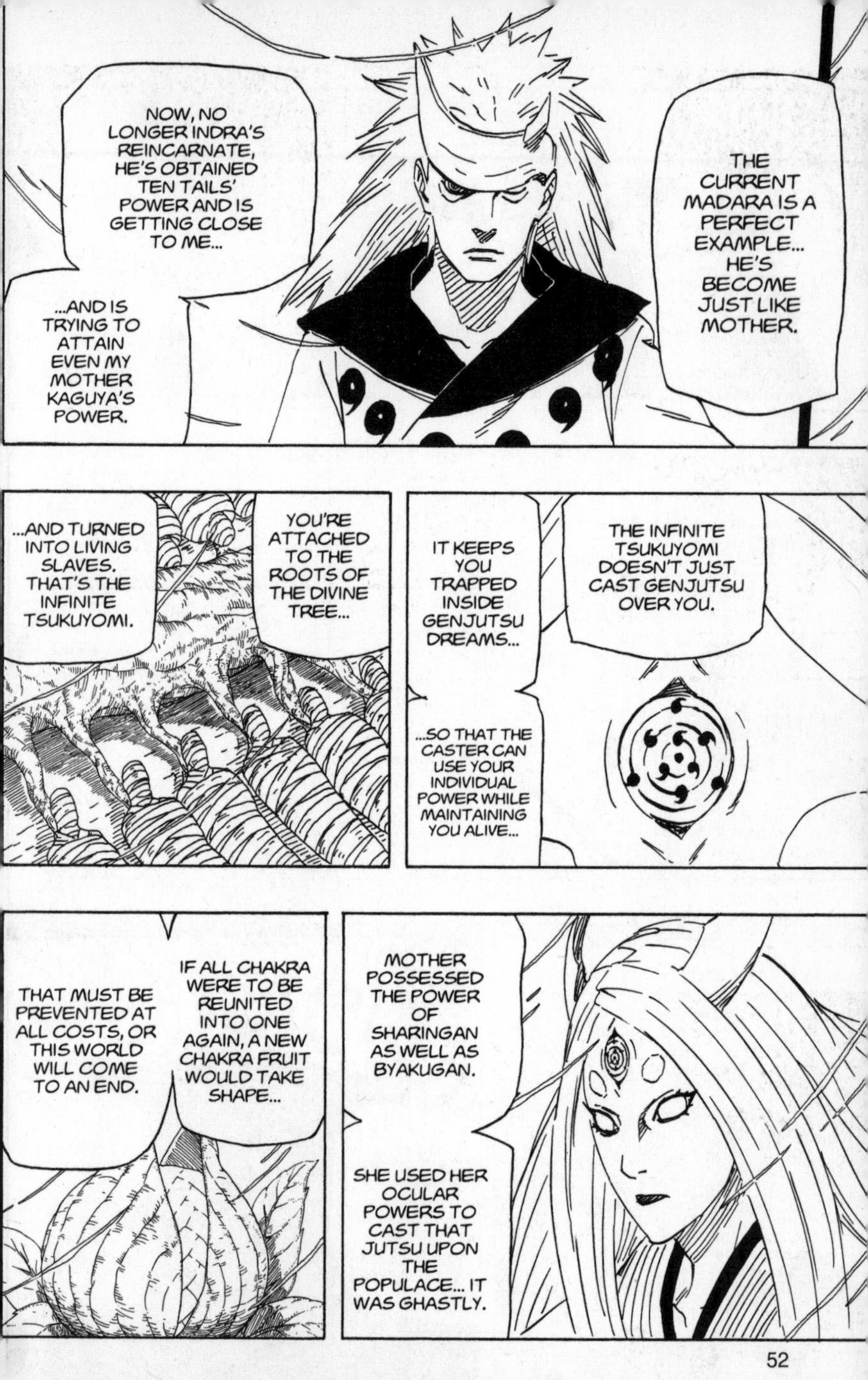
THE CURRENT MADARA IS A PERFECT EXAMPLE... HE'S BECOME JUST LIKE MOTHER.
NOW, NO LONGER INDRA'S REINCARNATE, HE'S OBTAINED TEN TAILS' POWER AND IS GETTING CLOSE TO ME...
...AND IS TRYING TO ATTAIN EVEN MY MOTHER KAGUYA'S POWER.
THE INFINITE TSUKUYOMI DOESN'T JUST CAST GENJUTSU OVER YOU.
IT KEEPS YOU TRAPPED INSIDE GENJUTSU DREAMS...
...SO THAT THE CASTER CAN USE YOUR INDIVIDUAL POWER WHILE MAINTAINING YOU ALIVE...
YOU'RE ATTACHED TO THE ROOTS OF THE DIVINE TREE...
...AND TURNED INTO LIVING SLAVES. THAT'S THE INFINITE TSUKUYOMI.
MOTHER POSSESSED THE POWER OF SHARINGAN AS WELL AS BYAKUGAN.
SHE USED HER OCULAR POWERS TO CAST THAT JUTSU UPON THE POPULACE... IT WAS GHASTLY.
IF ALL CHAKRA WERE TO BE REUNITED INTO ONE AGAIN, A NEW CHAKRA FRUIT WOULD TAKE SHAPE...
THAT MUST BE PREVENTED AT ALL COSTS, OR THIS WORLD WILL COME TO AN END.

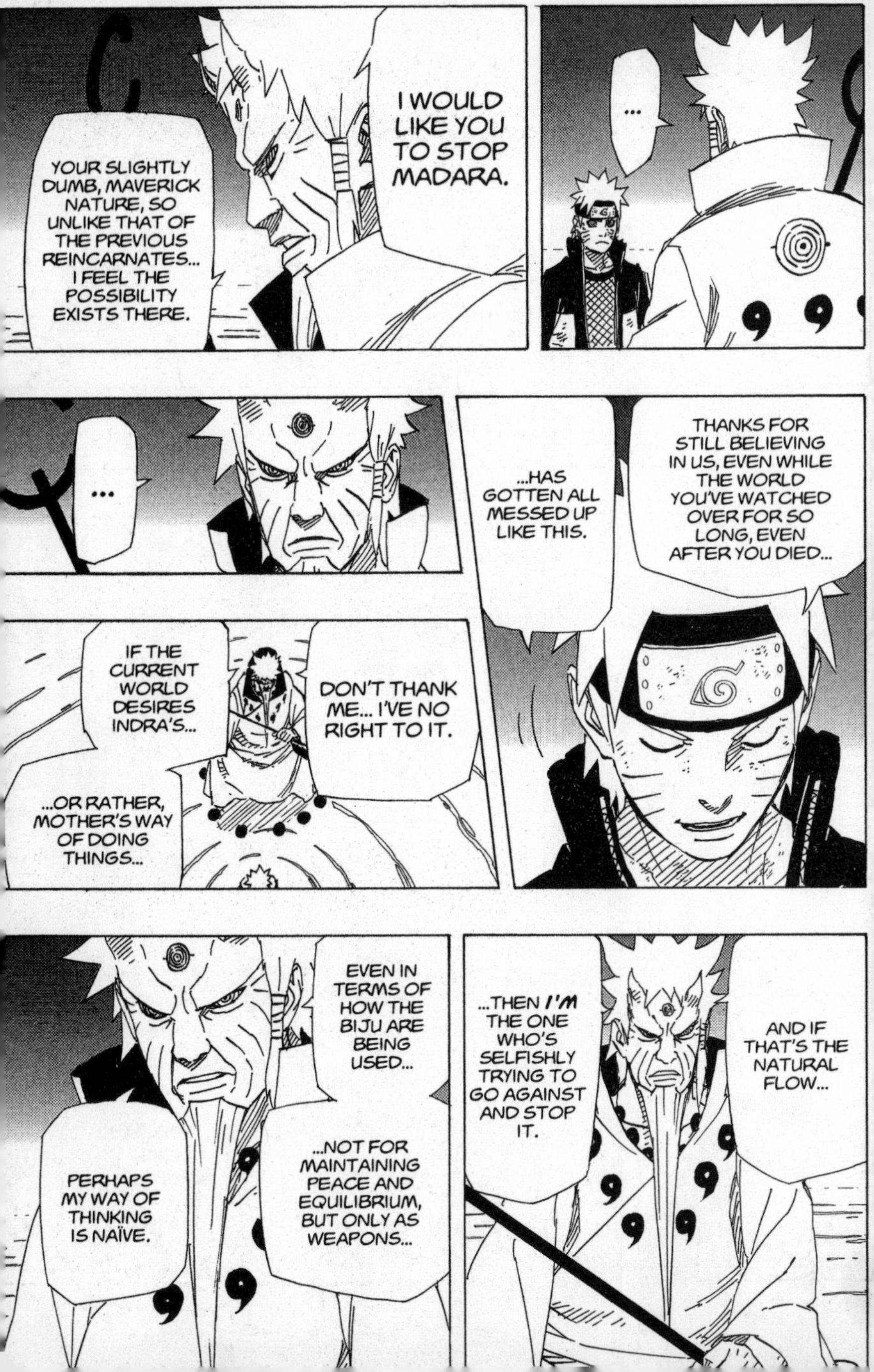
...
I WOULD LIKE YOU TO STOP MADARA.
YOUR SLIGHTLY DUMB, MAVERICK NATURE, SO UNLIKE THAT OF THE PREVIOUS REINCARNATES... I FEEL THE POSSIBILITY EXISTS THERE.
THANKS FOR STILL BELIEVING IN US, EVEN WHILE THE WORLD YOU'VE WATCHED OVER FOR SO LONG, EVEN AFTER YOU DIED...
...HAS GOTTEN ALL MESSED UP LIKE THIS.
...
DON'T THANK ME... I'VE NO RIGHT TO IT.
IF THE CURRENT WORLD DESIRES INDRA'S...
...OR RATHER, MOTHER'S WAY OF DOING THINGS...
AND IF THAT'S THE NATURAL FLOW...
...THEN *I'M* THE ONE WHO'S SELFISHLY TRYING TO GO AGAINST AND STOP IT.
EVEN IN TERMS OF HOW THE BIJU ARE BEING USED...
...NOT FOR MAINTAINING PEACE AND EQUILIBRIUM, BUT ONLY AS WEAPONS...
PERHAPS MY WAY OF THINKING IS NAÏVE.

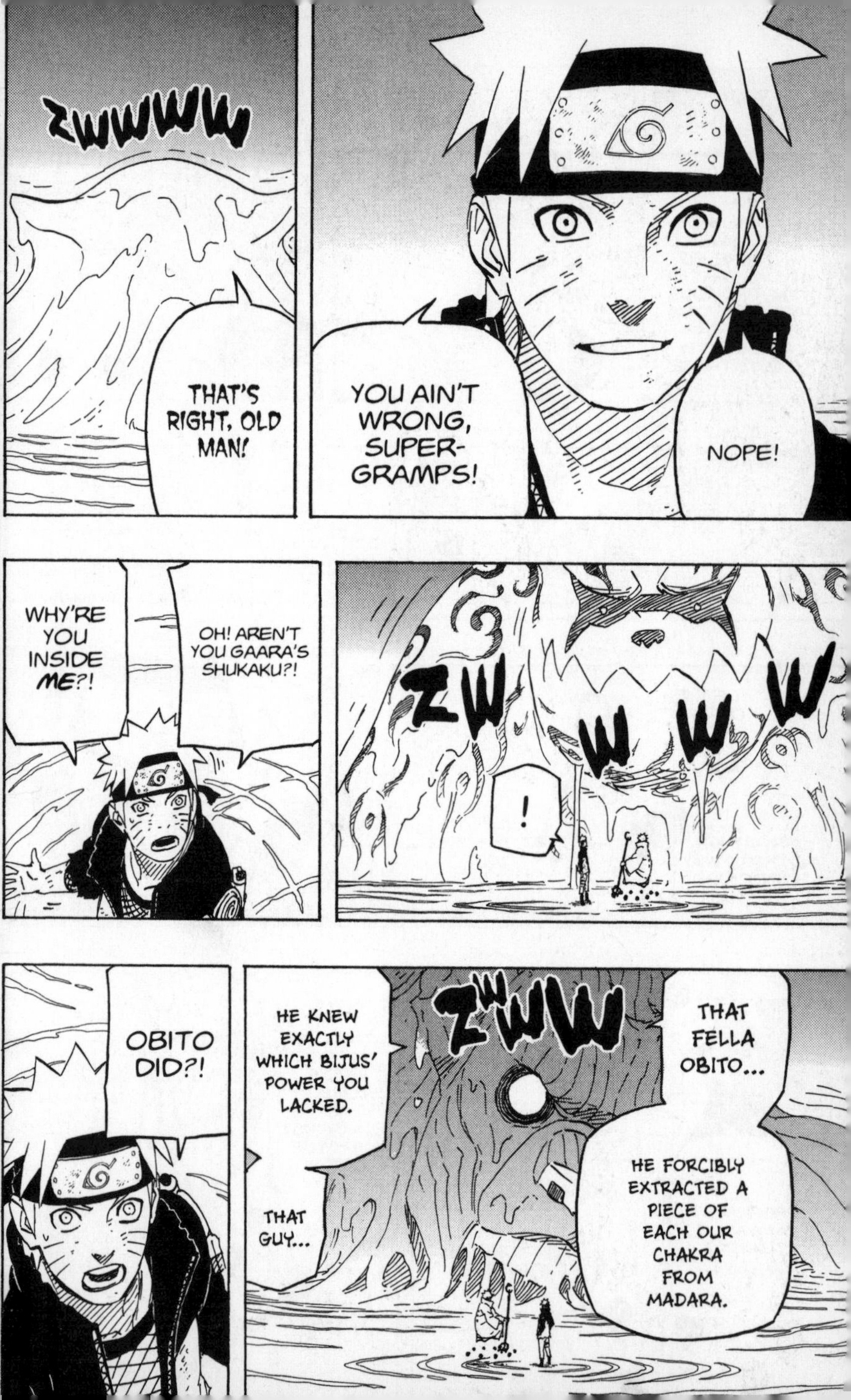
NOPE!
YOU AIN'T WRONG, SUPER-GRAMPS!
ZWWWW
THAT'S RIGHT, OLD MAN!
ZWWWW
!
OH! AREN'T YOU GAARA'S SHUKAKU?!
WHY'RE YOU INSIDE *ME*?!
THAT FELLA OBITO...
ZWWW
HE FORCIBLY EXTRACTED A PIECE OF EACH OUR CHAKRA FROM MADARA.
HE KNEW EXACTLY WHICH BIJUS' POWER YOU LACKED.
THAT GUY...
OBITO DID?!

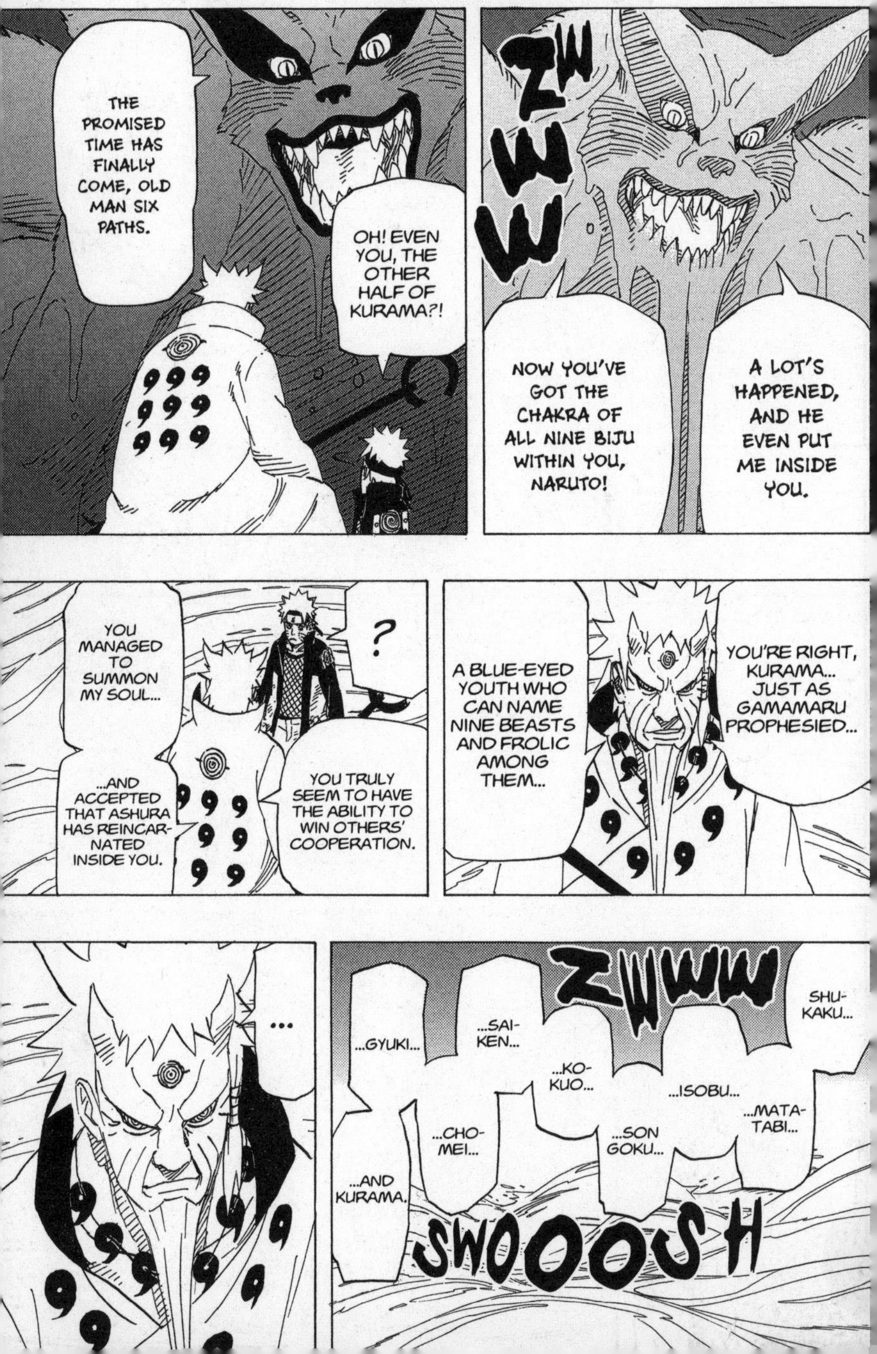
ZWWW
A LOT'S HAPPENED, AND HE EVEN PUT ME INSIDE YOU.
NOW YOU'VE GOT THE CHAKRA OF ALL NINE BIJU WITHIN YOU, NARUTO!
THE PROMISED TIME HAS FINALLY COME, OLD MAN SIX PATHS.
OH! EVEN YOU, THE OTHER HALF OF KURAMA?!
YOU'RE RIGHT, KURAMA... JUST AS GAMAMARU PROPHESIED...
A BLUE-EYED YOUTH WHO CAN NAME NINE BEASTS AND FROLIC AMONG THEM...
?
YOU MANAGED TO SUMMON MY SOUL...
...AND ACCEPTED THAT ASHURA HAS REINCARNATED INSIDE YOU.
YOU TRULY SEEM TO HAVE THE ABILITY TO WIN OTHERS' COOPERATION.
ZWWW
SHUKAKU...
...MATATABI...
...ISOBU...
...SON GOKU...
...KOKUO...
...SAIKEN...
...CHOMEI...
...GYUKI...
...AND KURAMA.
SWOOOSH
...

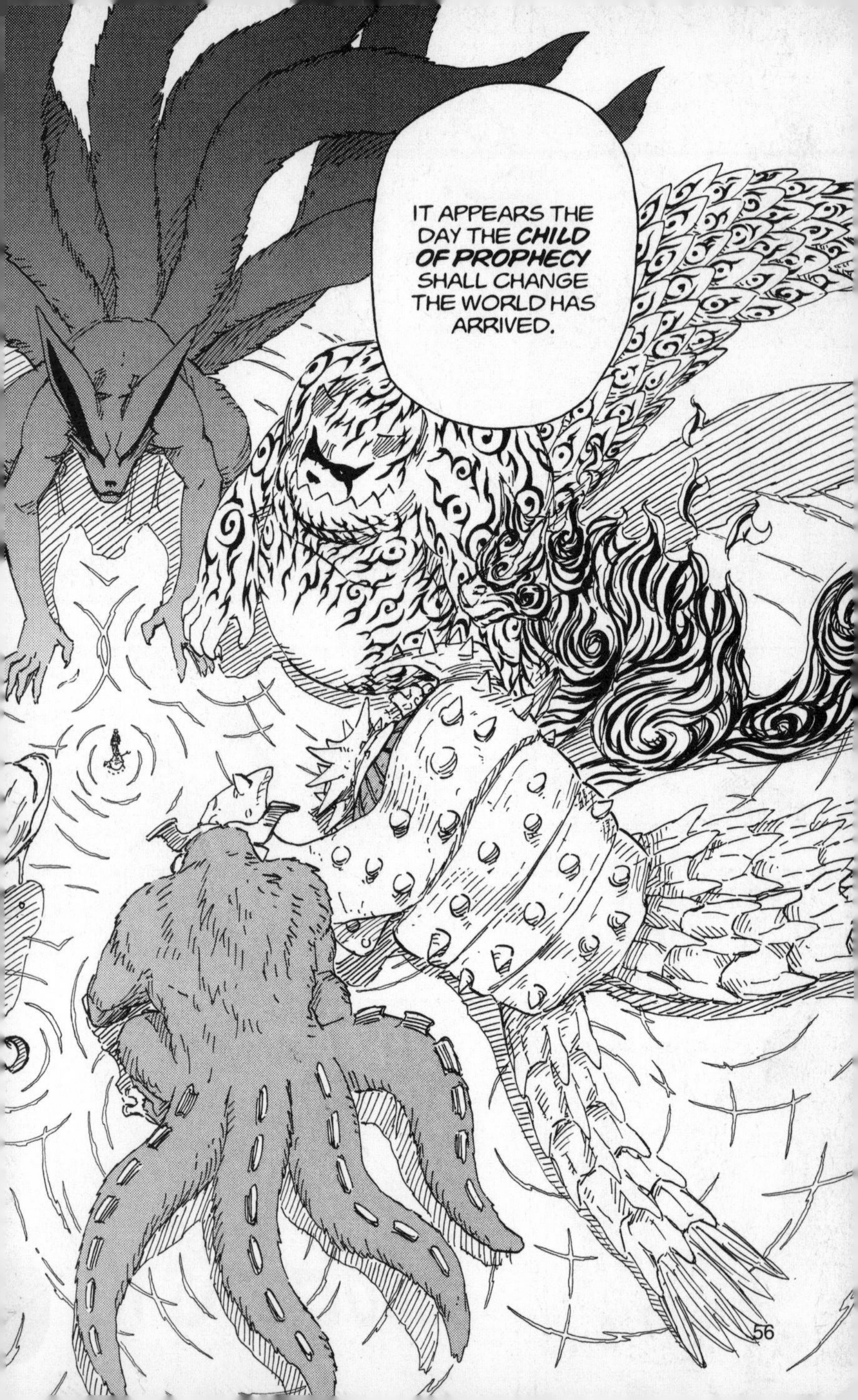
IT APPEARS THE DAY THE **CHILD OF PROPHECY** SHALL CHANGE THE WORLD HAS ARRIVED.

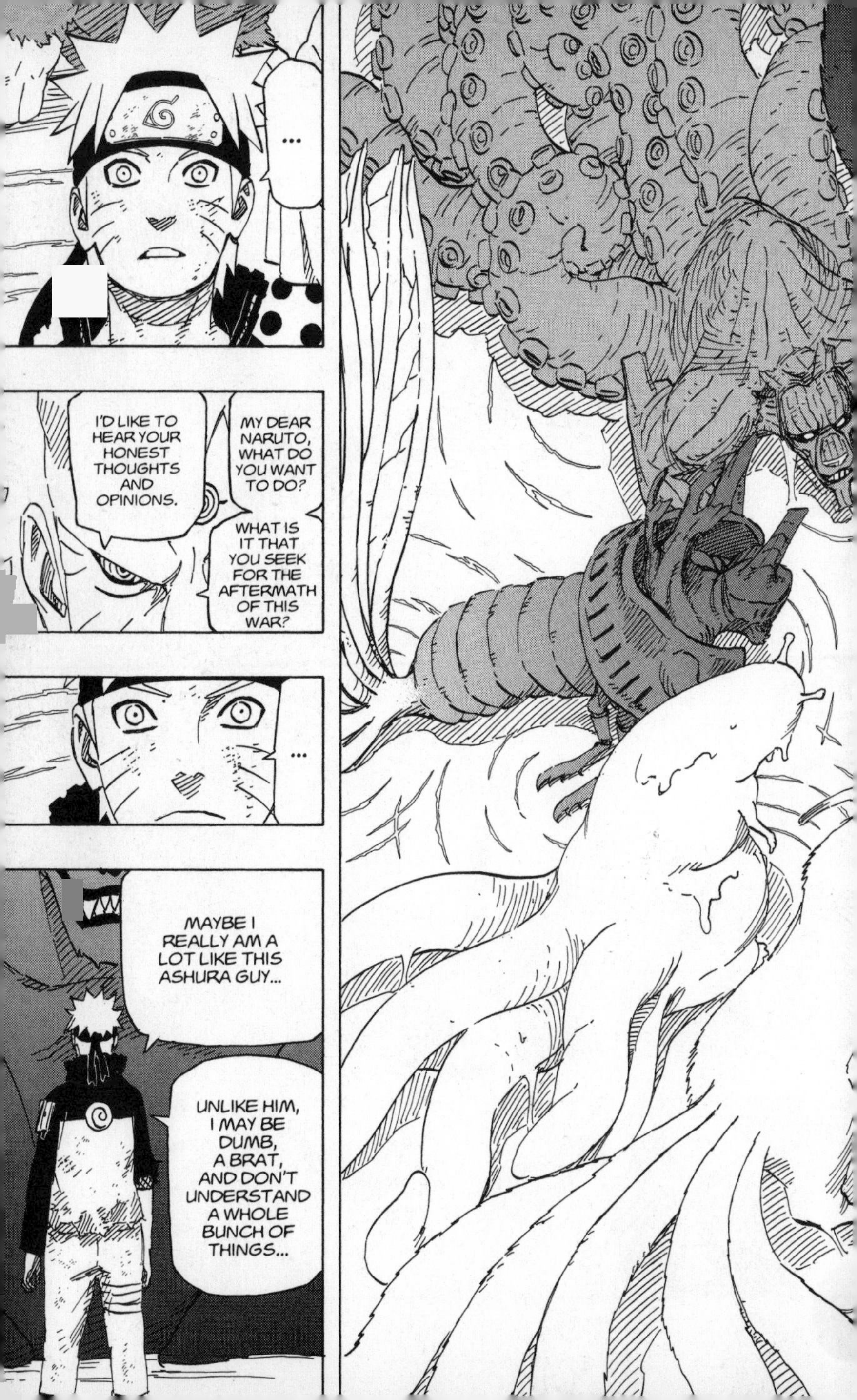
...
MY DEAR NARUTO, WHAT DO YOU WANT TO DO?
WHAT IS IT THAT YOU SEEK FOR THE AFTERMATH OF THIS WAR?
I'D LIKE TO HEAR YOUR HONEST THOUGHTS AND OPINIONS.
...
MAYBE I REALLY AM A LOT LIKE THIS ASHURA GUY...
UNLIKE HIM, I MAY BE DUMB, A BRAT, AND DON'T UNDERSTAND A WHOLE BUNCH OF THINGS...

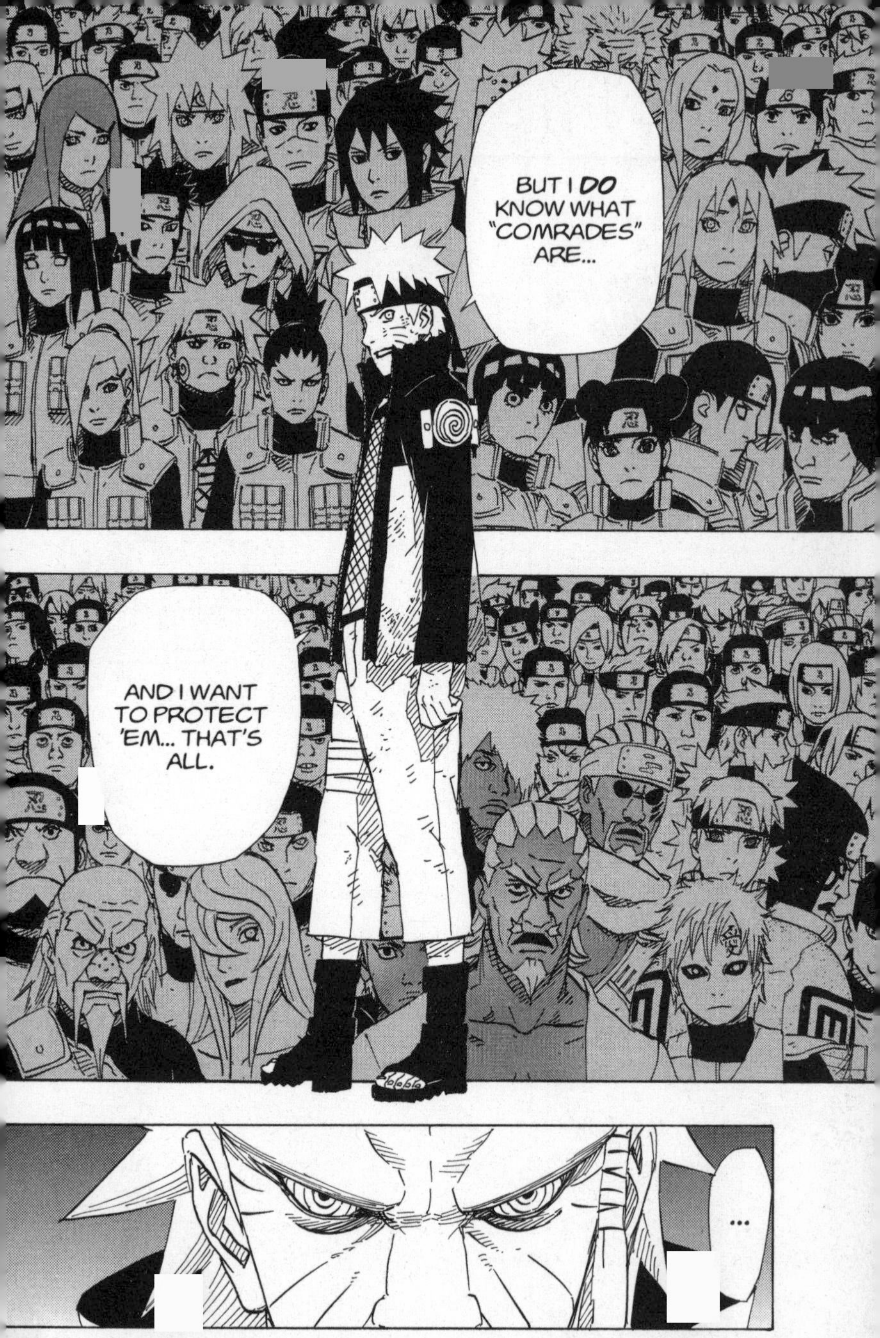
BUT I DO KNOW WHAT "COMRADES" ARE...
AND I WANT TO PROTECT 'EM... THAT'S ALL.
...

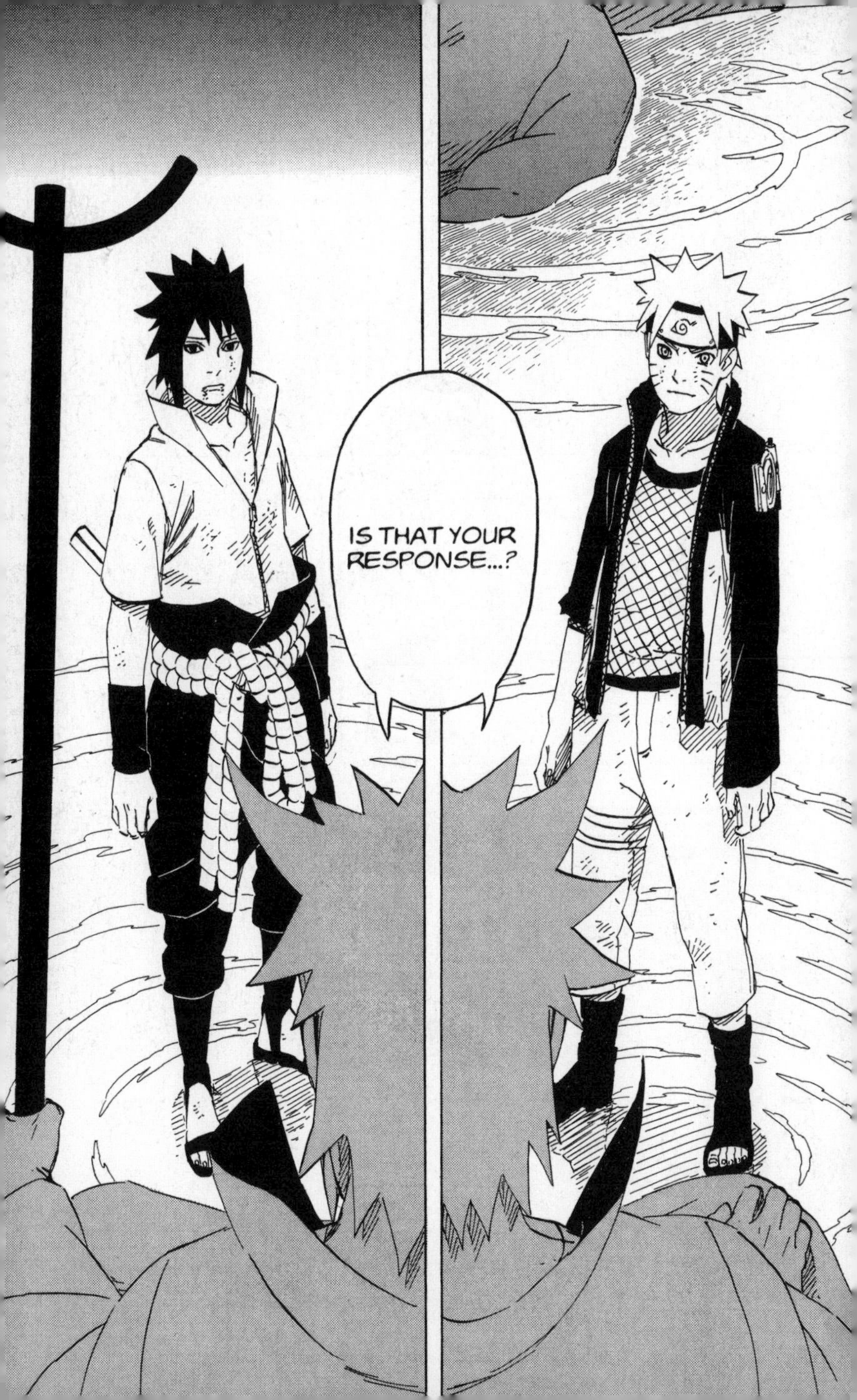
IS THAT YOUR RESPONSE...?

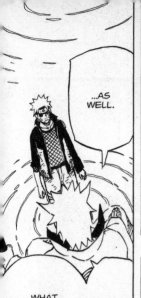

YEAH...
...AS WELL.
LONG AGO, I ENTRUSTED EVERYTHING TO LITTLE BROTHER ASHURA AND DIDN'T PAY ANY ATTENTION TO ELDER BROTHER INDRA.
THAT PROVED TO BE THE SOURCE OF CALAMITY.
THIS TIME, I SHALL SHARE MY POWER WITH YOU, INDRA'S REINCARNATE...
PROFFER ME YOUR DOMINANT ARM.
AND FROM THIS POINT ON, NARUTO AND SASUKE...
...WHAT YOU BOTH SHALL DO, AND WHAT SHALL TRANSPIRE, WILL BE UP TO THE TWO OF YOU.

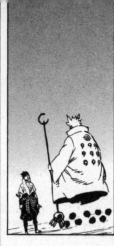

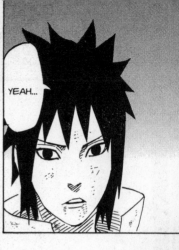

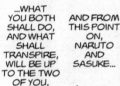

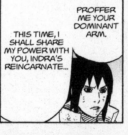

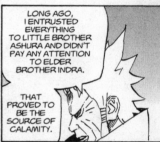

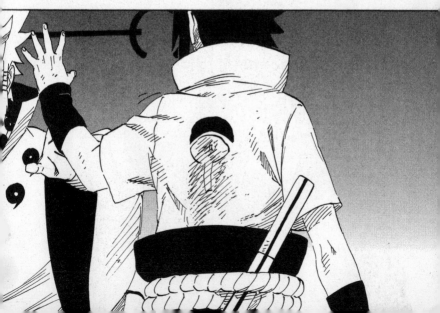

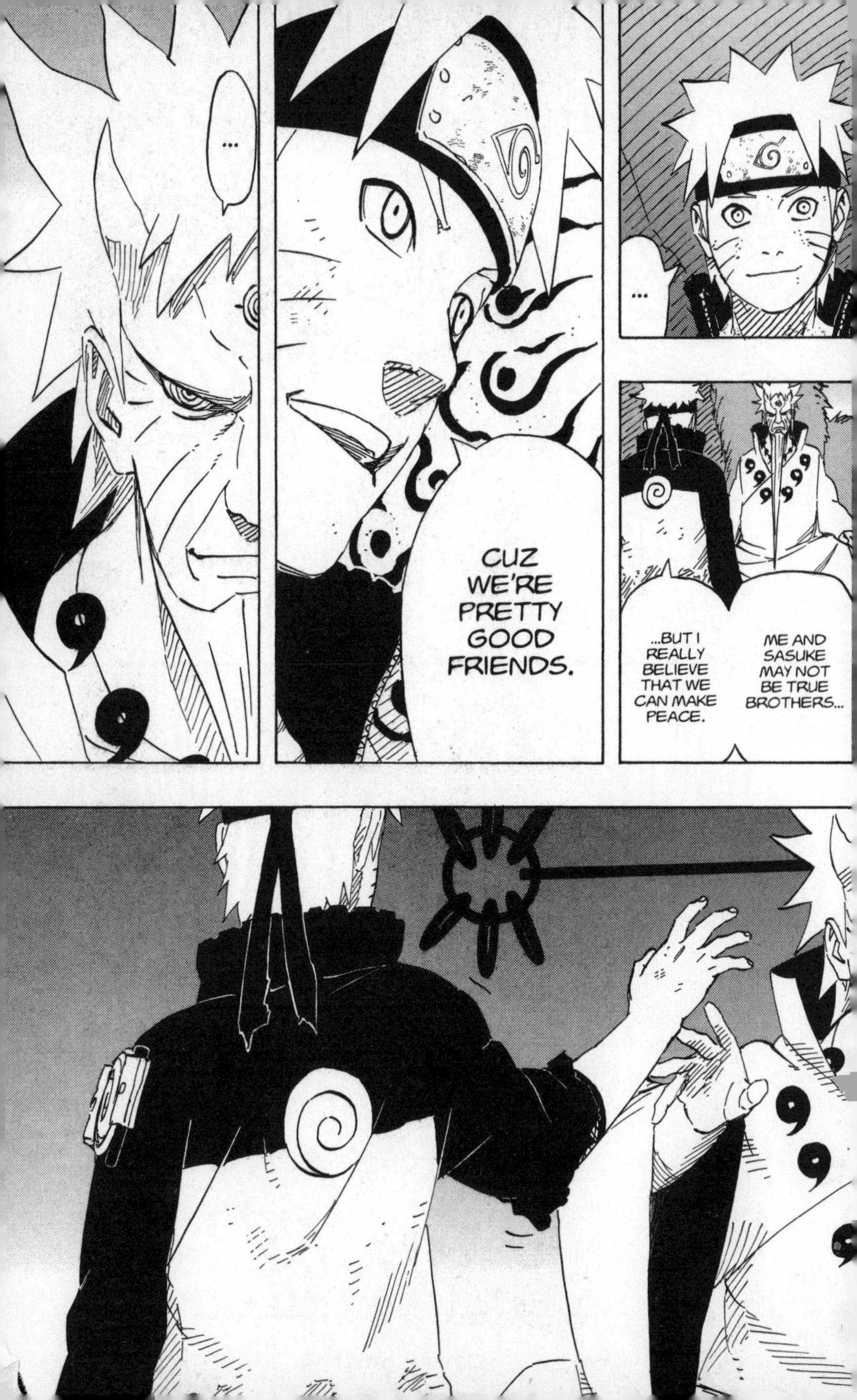
...
ME AND SASUKE MAY NOT BE TRUE BROTHERS...
...BUT I REALLY BELIEVE THAT WE CAN MAKE PEACE.
CUZ WE'RE PRETTY GOOD FRIENDS.
...

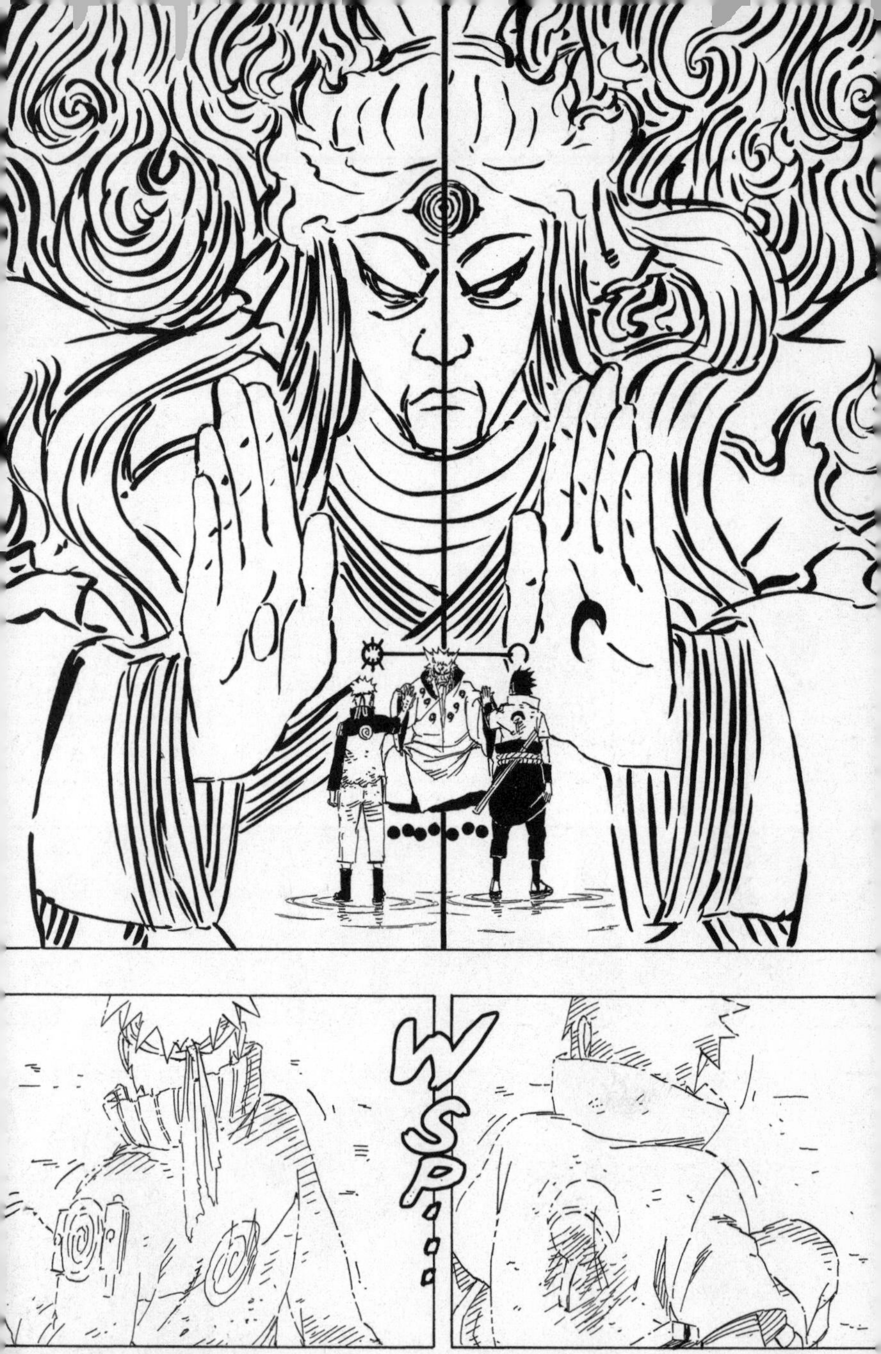
WSPooo

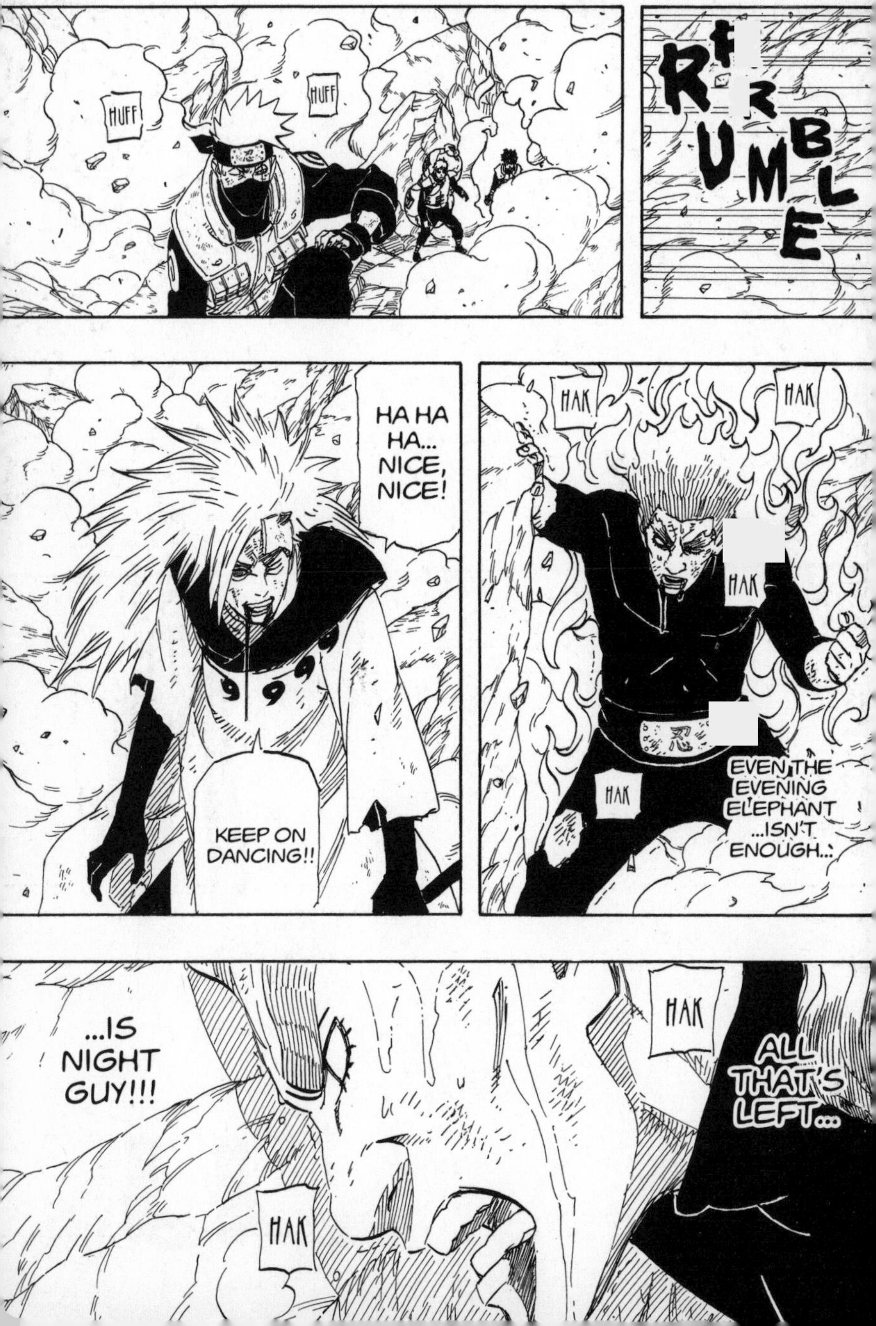
RRRUMBLE
HUFF
HUFF
HAK
HAK
HAK
EVEN THE EVENING ELEPHANT ...ISN'T ENOUGH...
HAK
HA HA HA... NICE, NICE!
KEEP ON DANCING!!
HAK
ALL THAT'S LEFT...
...IS NIGHT GUY!!!
HAK

HUFF

HAK

FSH

HAK

**Number 672: Night Guy!!**

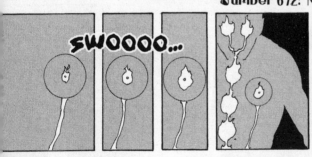

SWOOOO...

...

HUFF

HAK

CHARGE!!!

RMM

GIVEN THE STATE OF YOUR HEART NODE...

...IT SEEMS THE NEXT ATTACK WILL BE YOUR LAST...

RMM

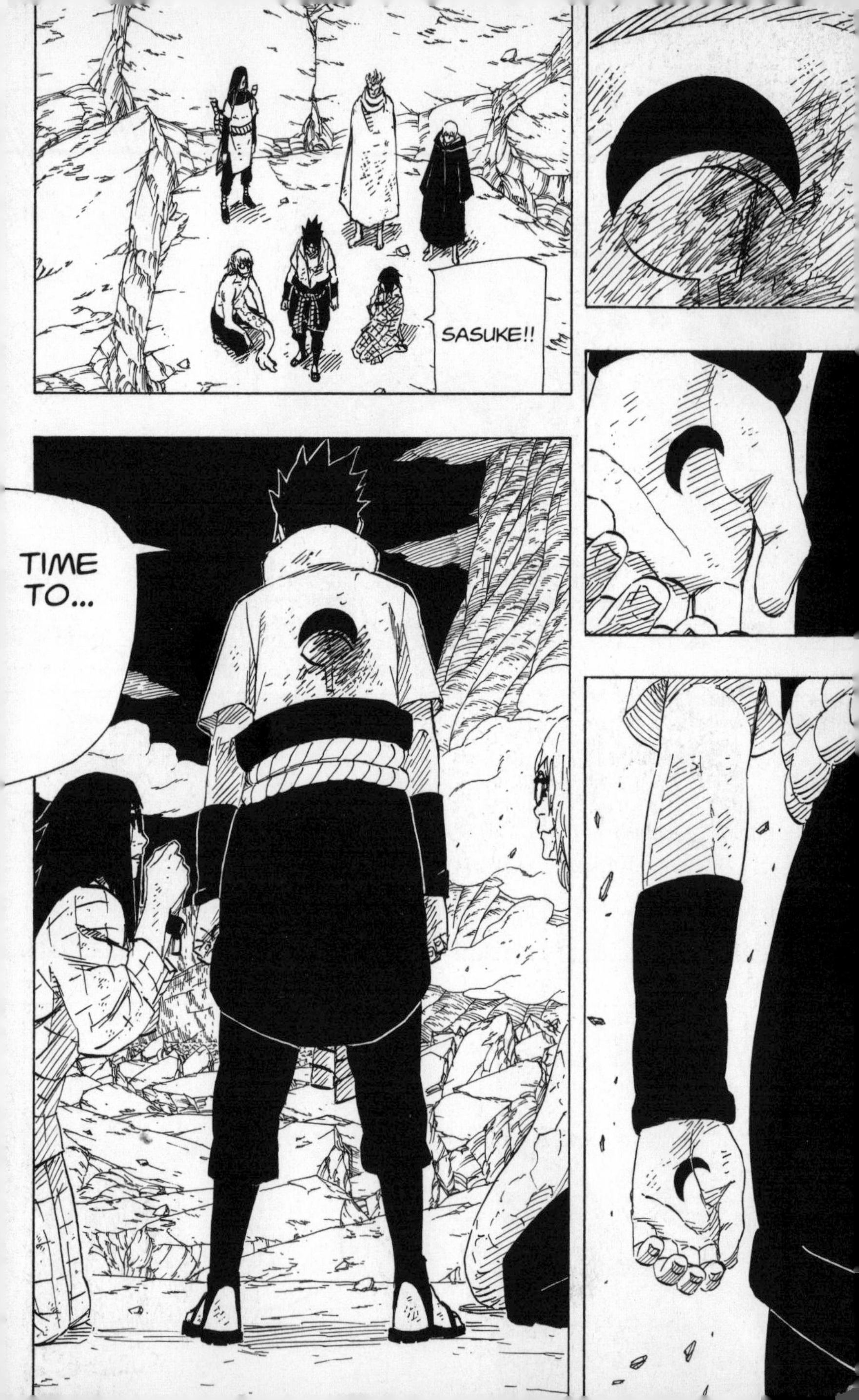
SASUKE!!
TIME TO...

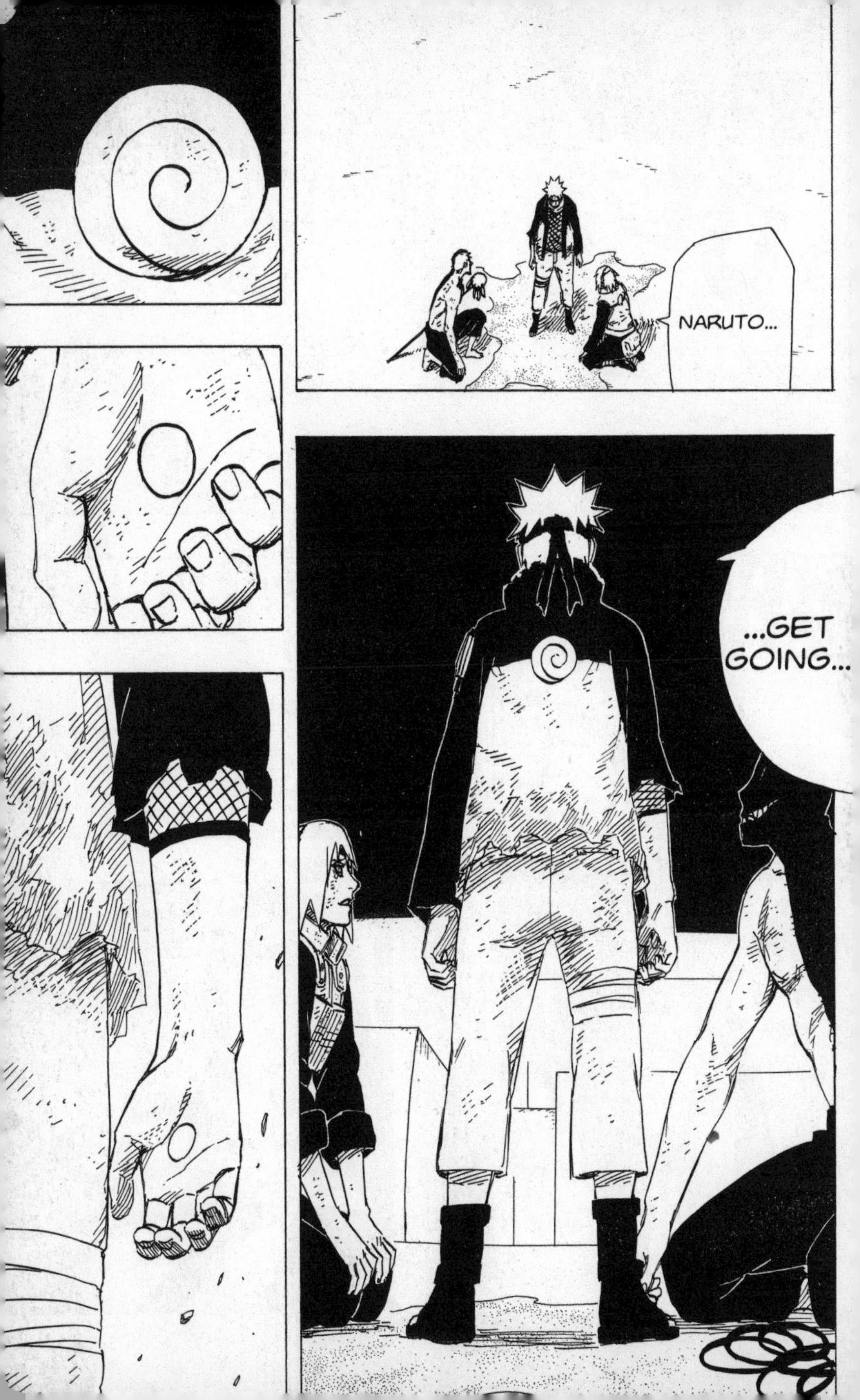
NARUTO...
...GET GOING...

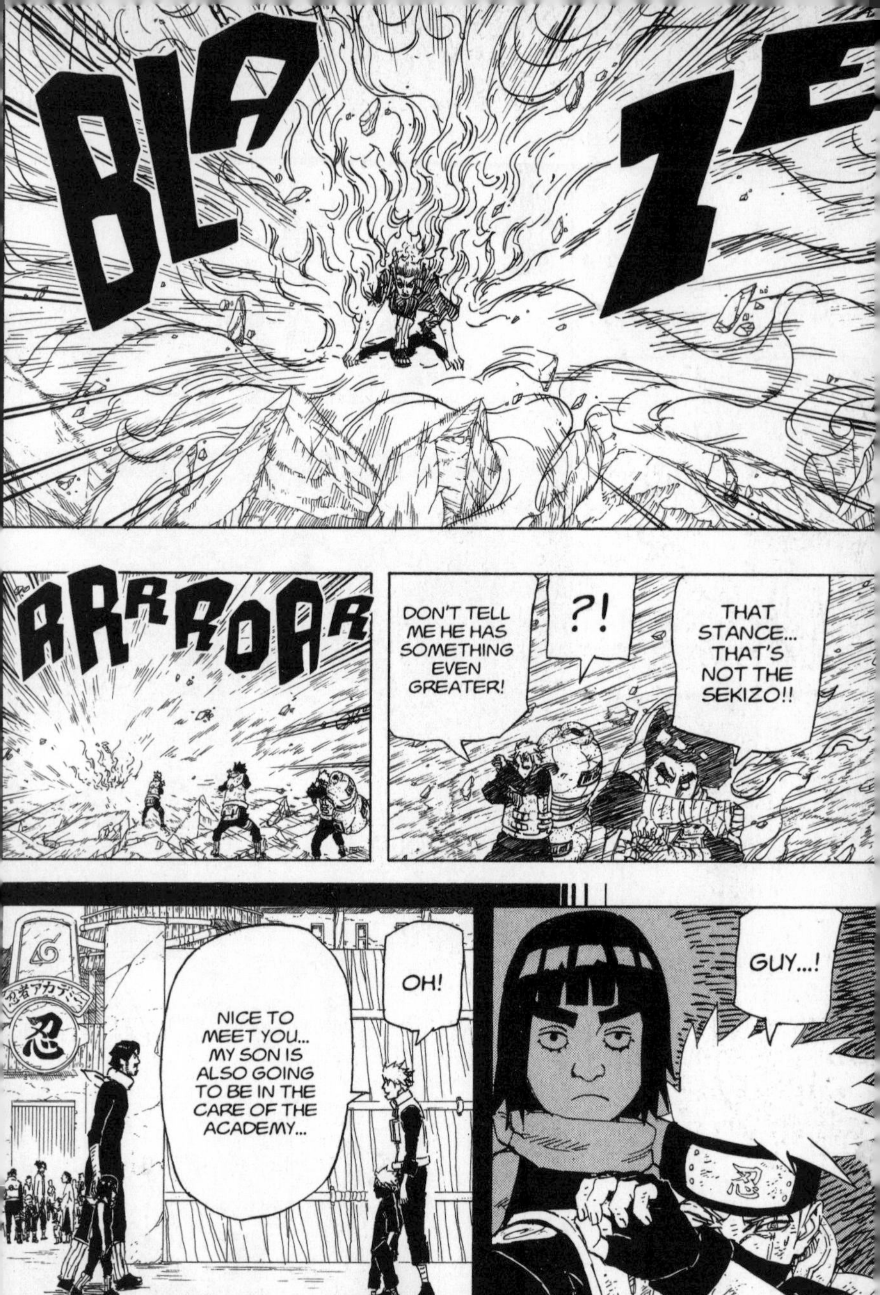
BLAZE
THAT STANCE... THAT'S NOT THE SEKIZO!!
?!
DON'T TELL ME HE HAS SOMETHING EVEN GREATER!
RRRROAR
GUY...!
OH!
NICE TO MEET YOU... MY SON IS ALSO GOING TO BE IN THE CARE OF THE ACADEMY...

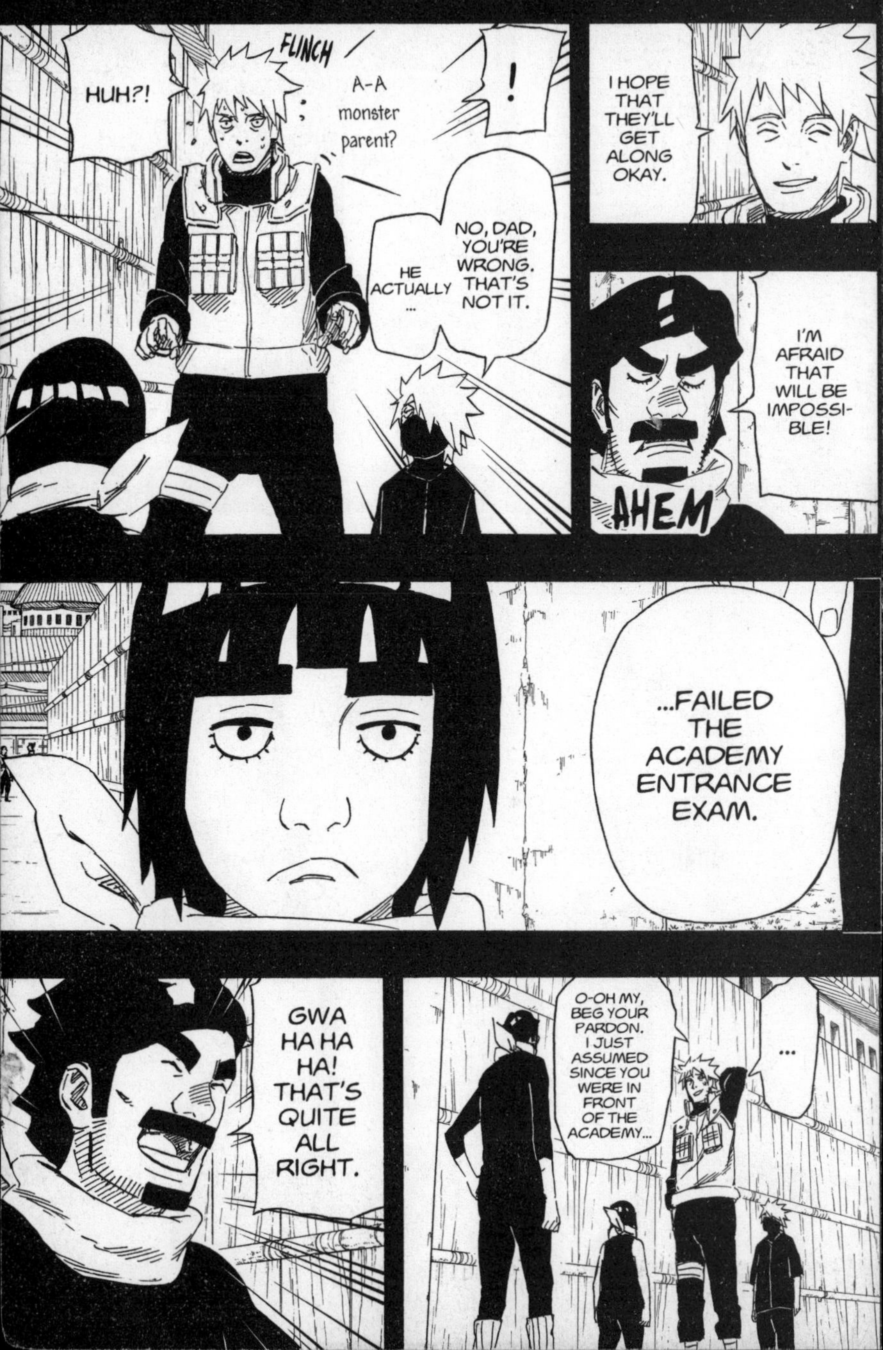

I HOPE THAT THEY'LL GET ALONG OKAY.
I'M AFRAID THAT WILL BE IMPOSSIBLE!
AHEM
!
NO, DAD, YOU'RE WRONG. THAT'S NOT IT.
HE ACTUALLY ...
FLINCH
A-A monster parent?
HUH?!
...FAILED THE ACADEMY ENTRANCE EXAM.
...
O-OH MY, BEG YOUR PARDON. I JUST ASSUMED SINCE YOU WERE IN FRONT OF THE ACADEMY...
GWA HA HA HA! THAT'S QUITE ALL RIGHT.

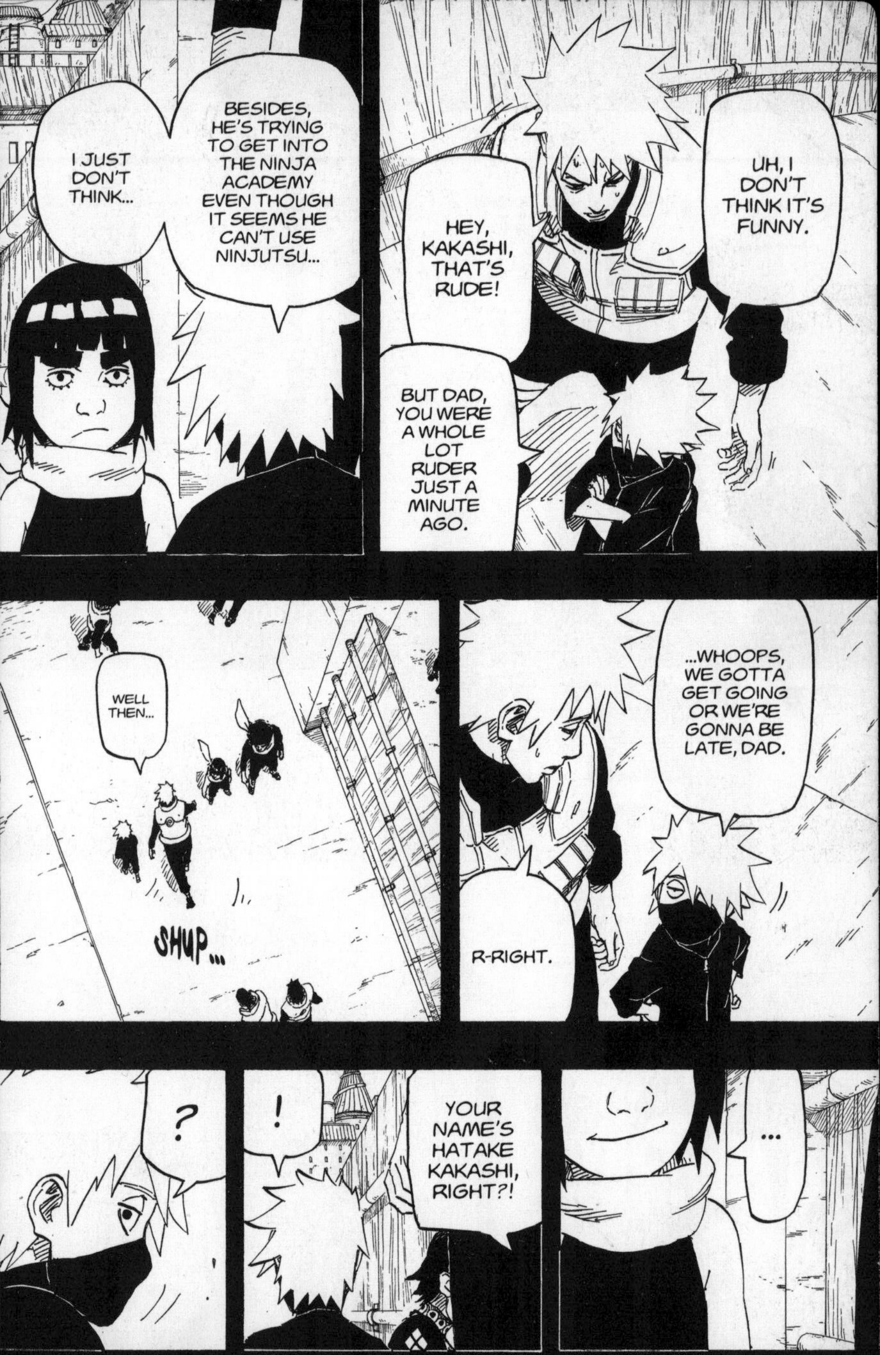
UH, I DON'T THINK IT'S FUNNY.
HEY, KAKASHI, THAT'S RUDE!
BUT DAD, YOU WERE A WHOLE LOT RUDER JUST A MINUTE AGO.
BESIDES, HE'S TRYING TO GET INTO THE NINJA ACADEMY EVEN THOUGH IT SEEMS HE CAN'T USE NINJUTSU...
I JUST DON'T THINK...
...WHOOPS, WE GOTTA GET GOING OR WE'RE GONNA BE LATE, DAD.
R-RIGHT.
WELL THEN...
SHUP...
...
YOUR NAME'S HATAKE KAKASHI, RIGHT?!
!
?

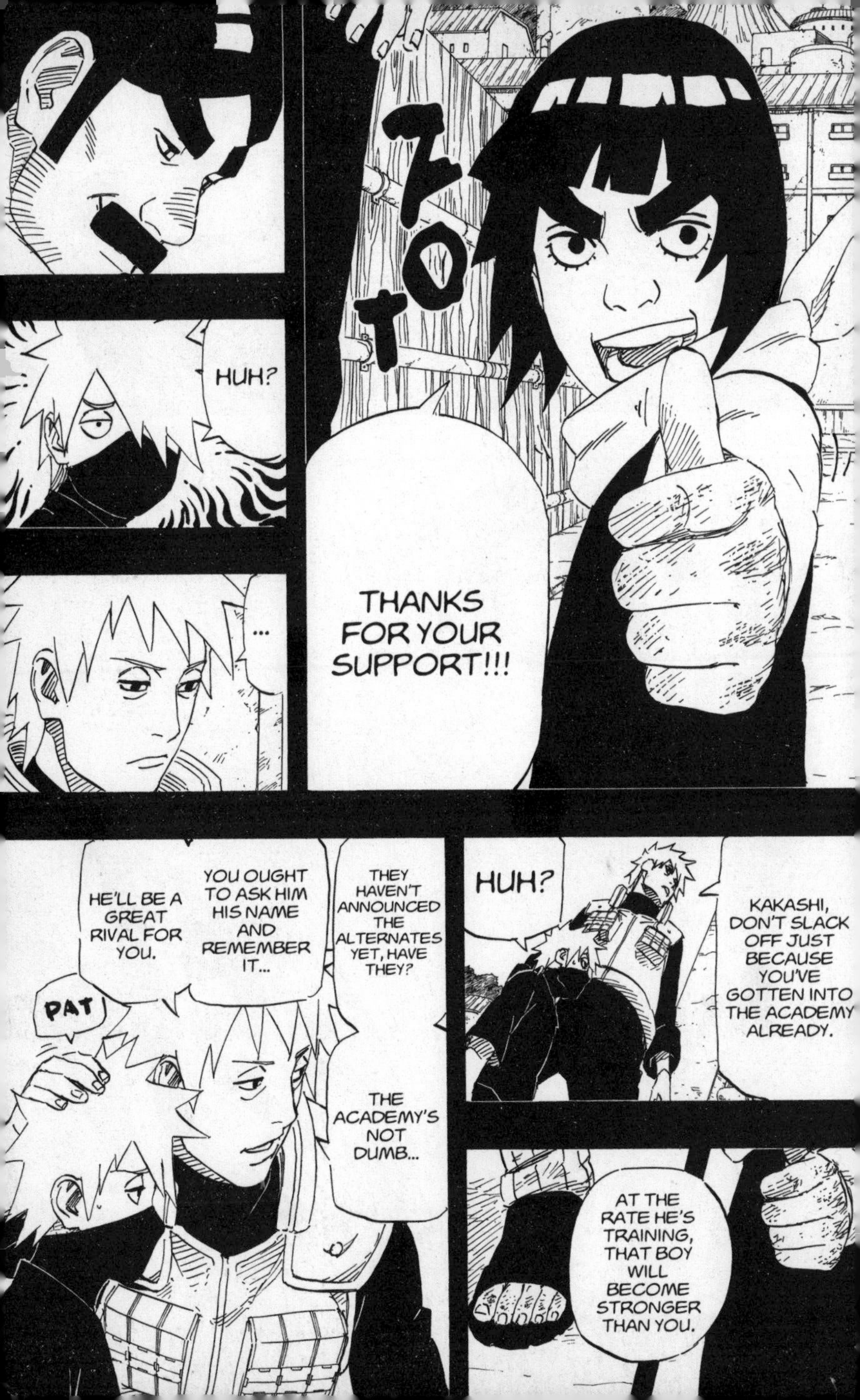

ZOT
THANKS FOR YOUR SUPPORT!!!
HUH?
...
KAKASHI, DON'T SLACK OFF JUST BECAUSE YOU'VE GOTTEN INTO THE ACADEMY ALREADY.
HUH?
AT THE RATE HE'S TRAINING, THAT BOY WILL BECOME STRONGER THAN YOU.
THEY HAVEN'T ANNOUNCED THE ALTERNATES YET, HAVE THEY?
THE ACADEMY'S NOT DUMB...
YOU OUGHT TO ASK HIM HIS NAME AND REMEMBER IT...
HE'LL BE A GREAT RIVAL FOR YOU.
PAT

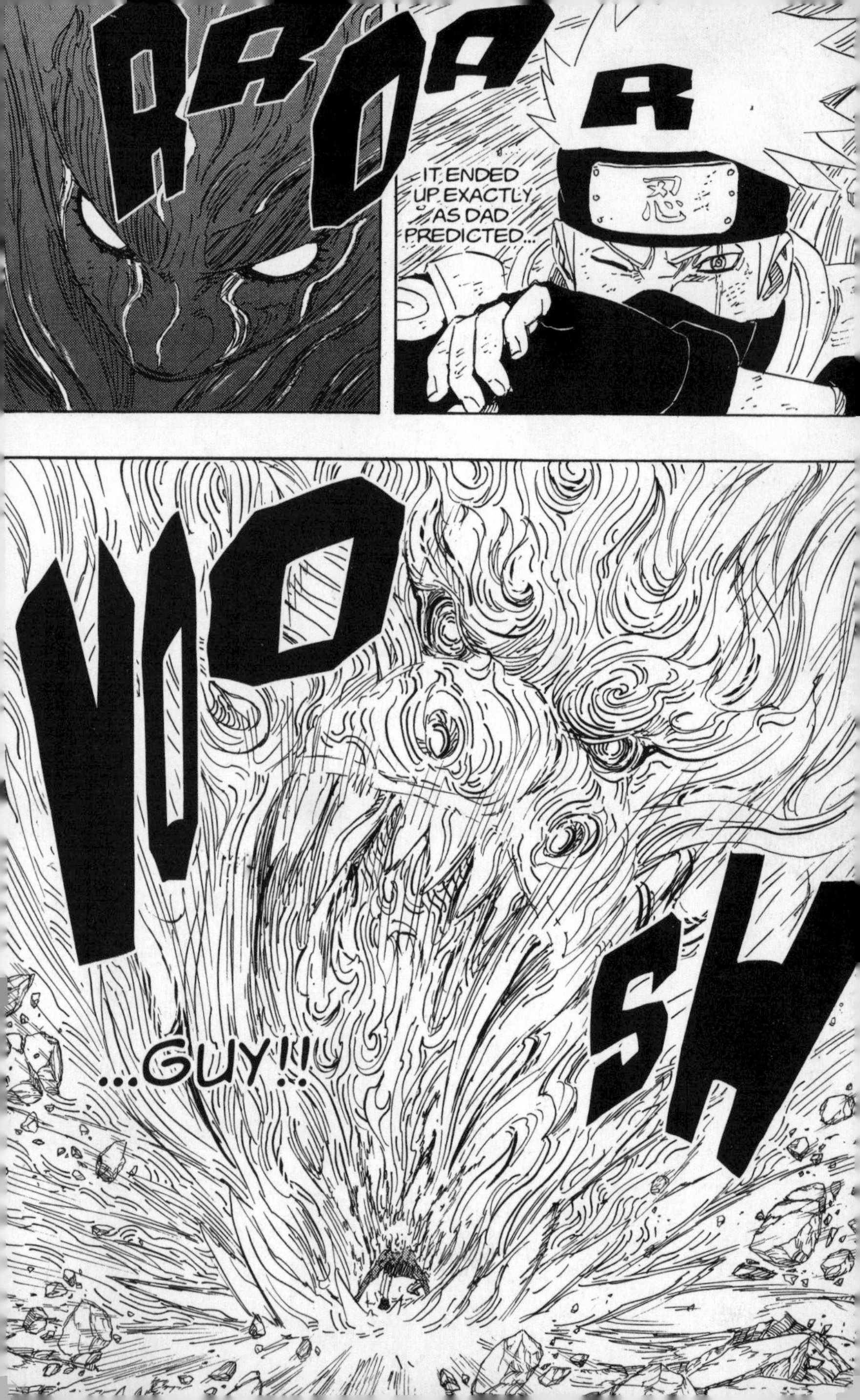
RROAR
IT ENDED UP EXACTLY AS DAD PREDICTED...
VOOSH
...GUY!!

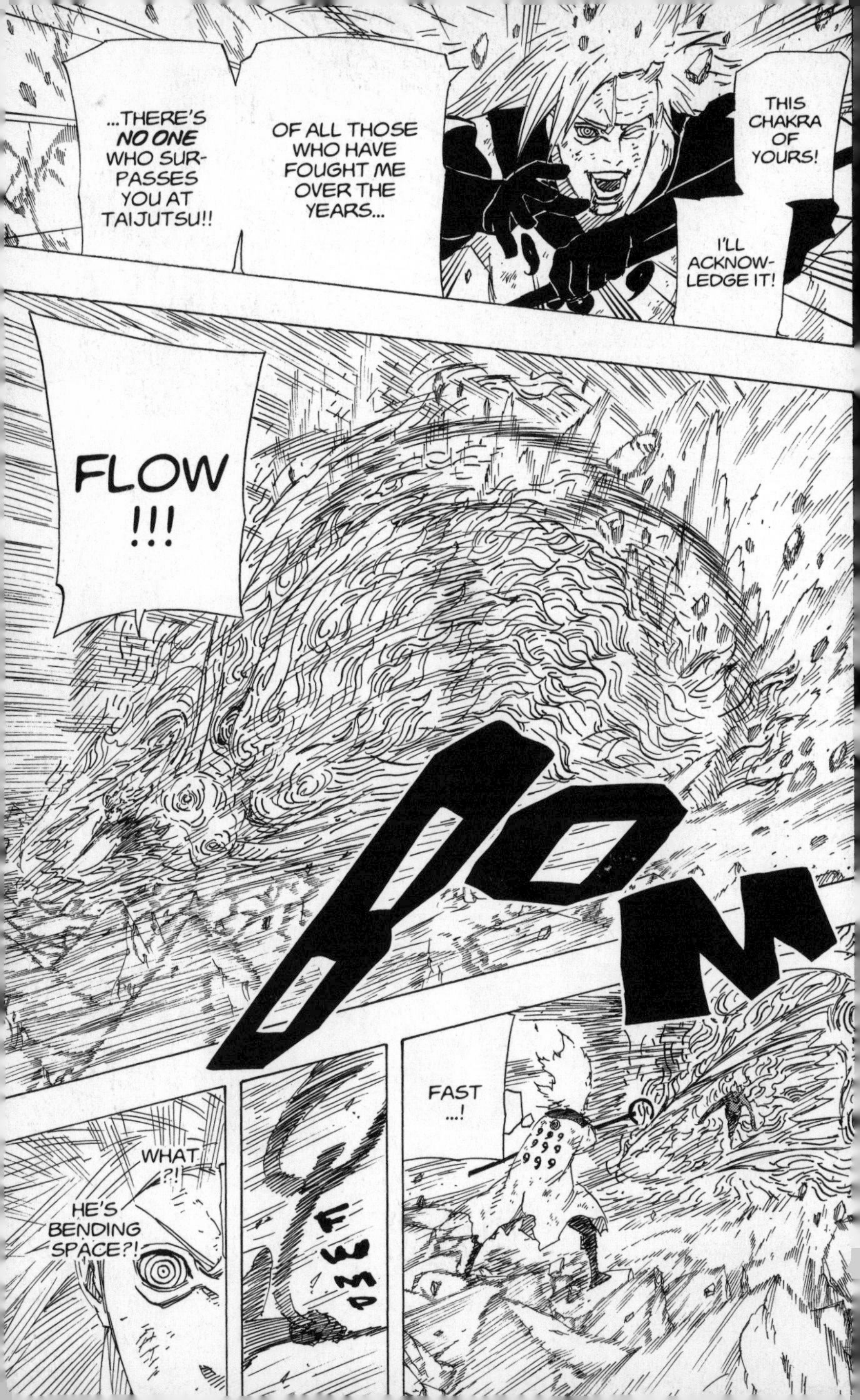
THIS CHAKRA OF YOURS!
I'LL ACKNOWLEDGE IT!
OF ALL THOSE WHO HAVE FOUGHT ME OVER THE YEARS...
...THERE'S NO ONE WHO SURPASSES YOU AT TAIJUTSU!!
FLOW !!!
BOM
FAST ...!
FWMP
WHAT ?!
HE'S BENDING SPACE?!

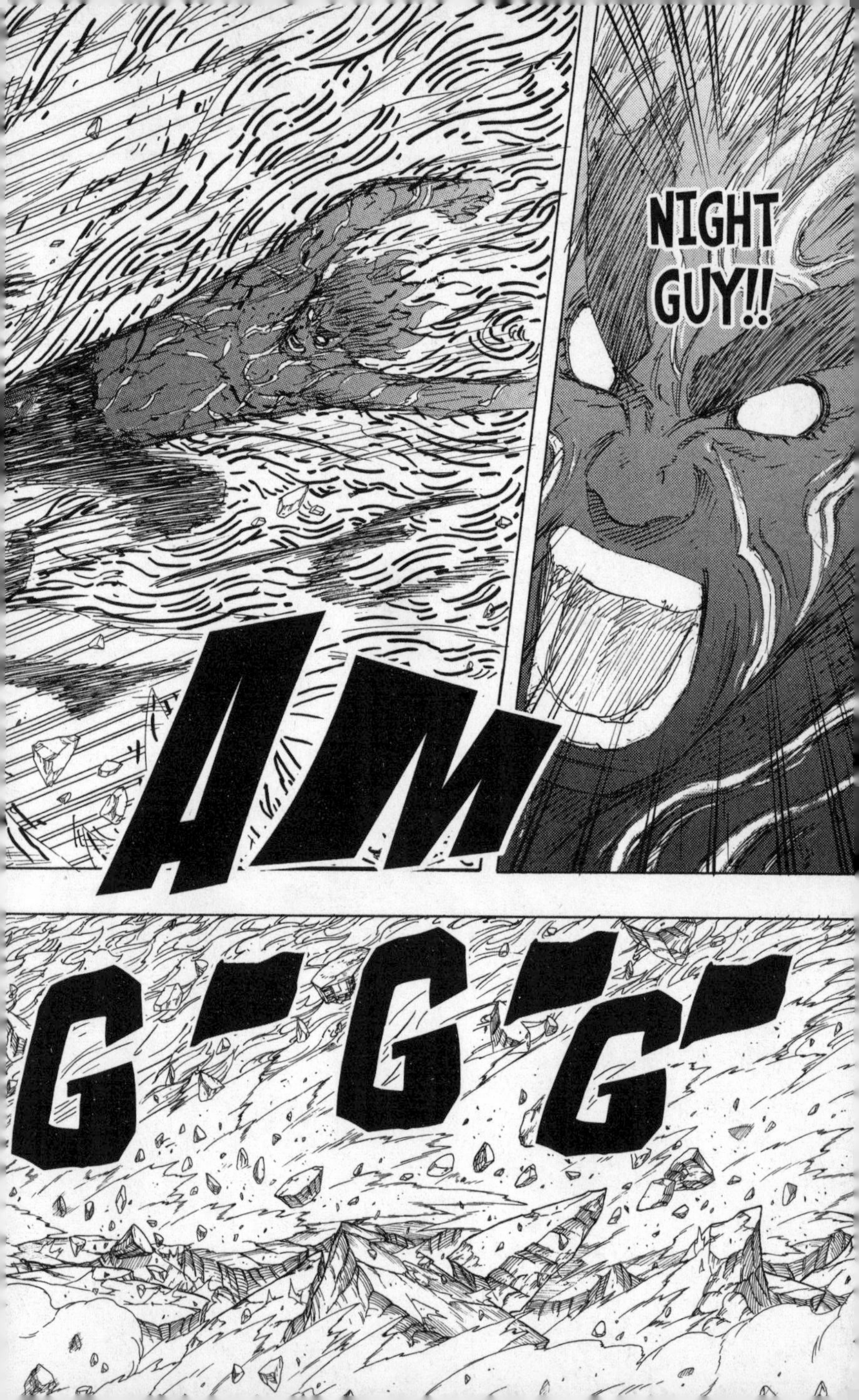
NIGHT GUY!!
G-G-G

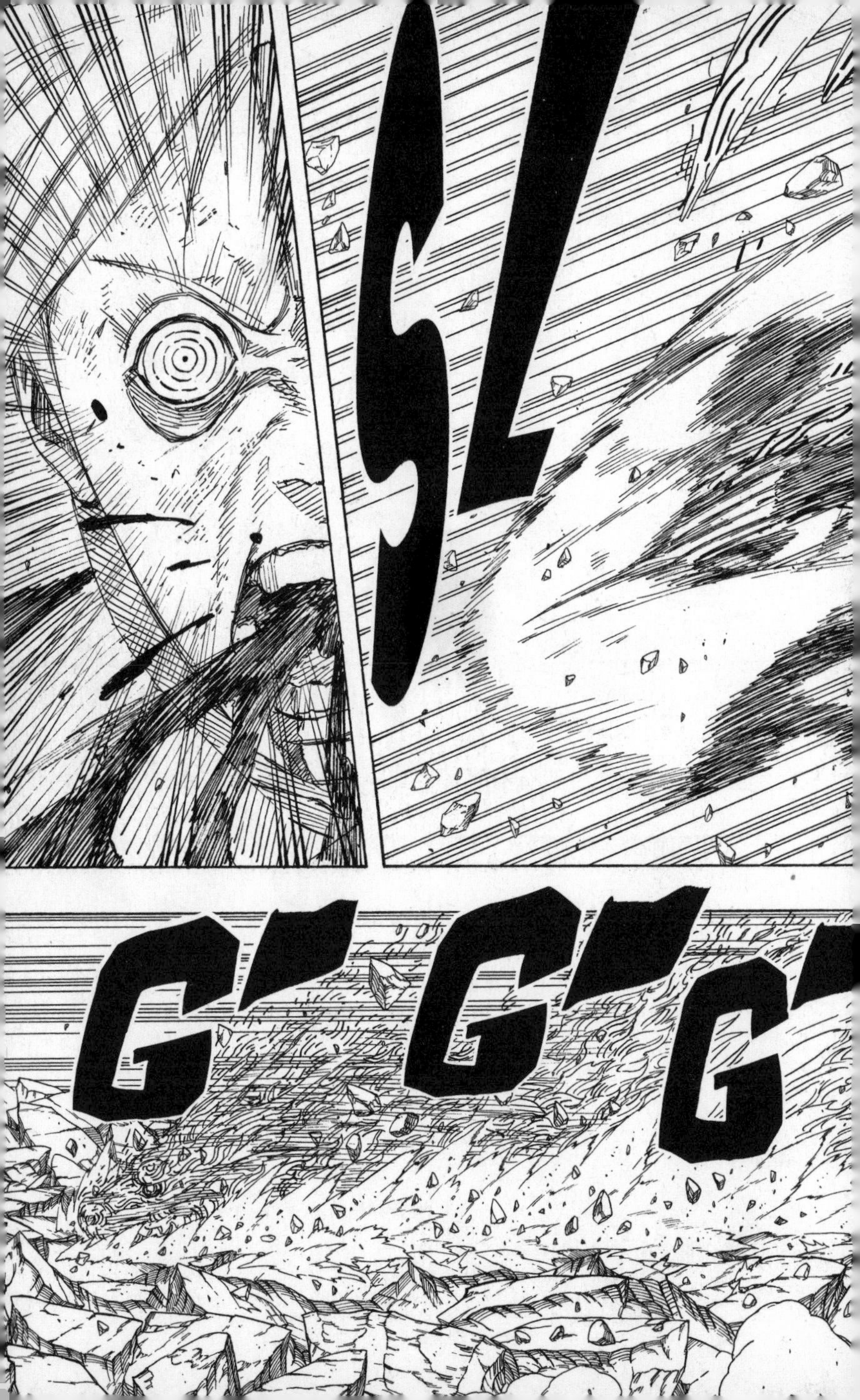
SL
G'G'G

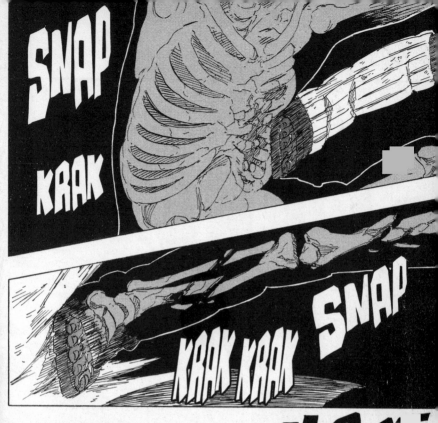

SNAP

KRAK

KRAK KRAK SNAP

THO THO THO
THO THO THO THO

BLA...!

ARGH!

WAH!

GAH!

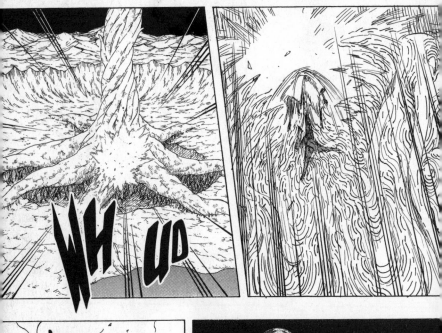

WH UD

RRRUMBLE

R RUMBLE

UGH...

THAT WAS GUY'S FINAL MOVE!

WHAT HAPPENED ?!

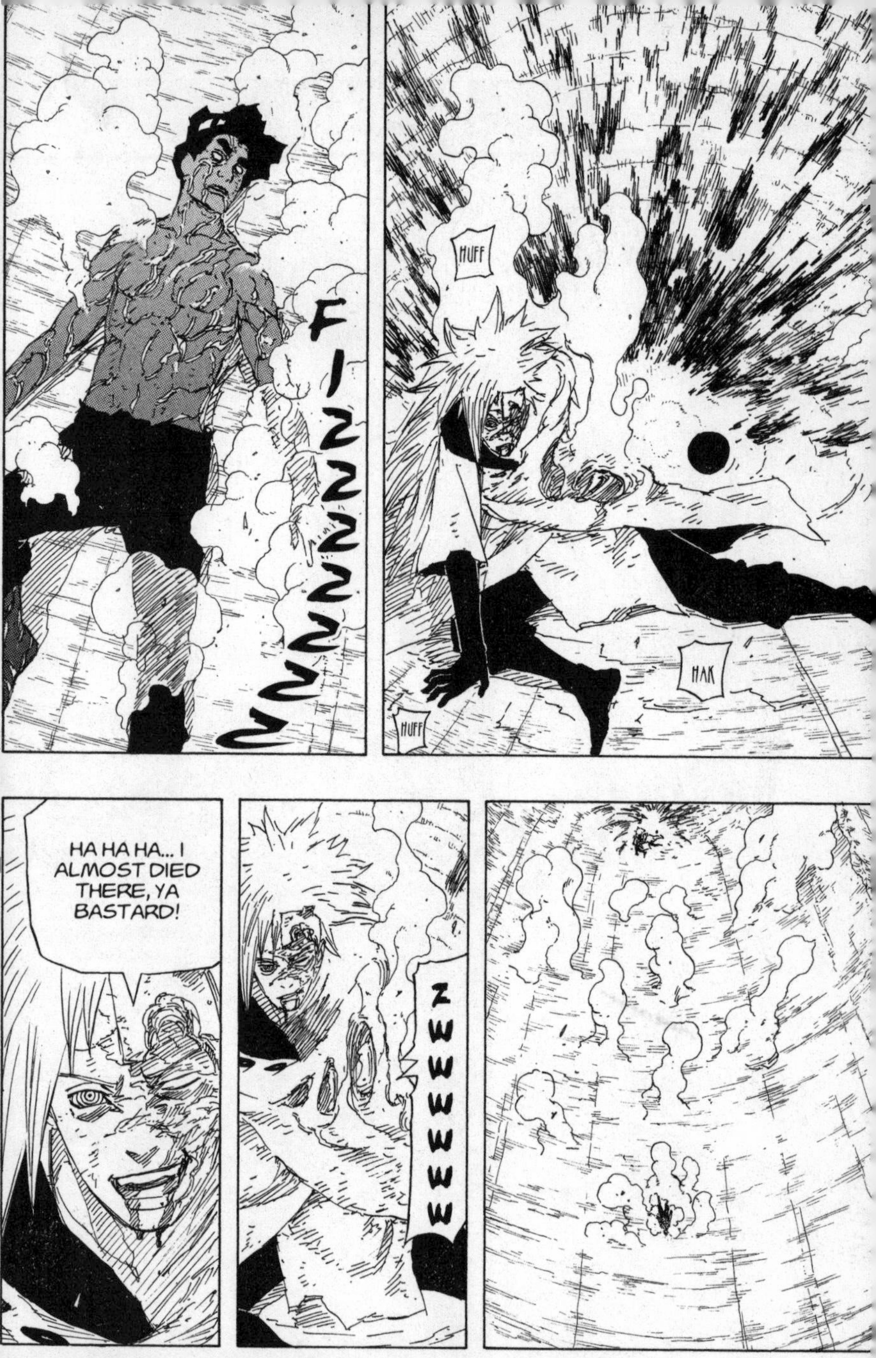
HUFF
HAK
HUFF
FIZZZZZZZZ
ZWWWWWWW
HA HA HA... I ALMOST DIED THERE, YA BASTARD!

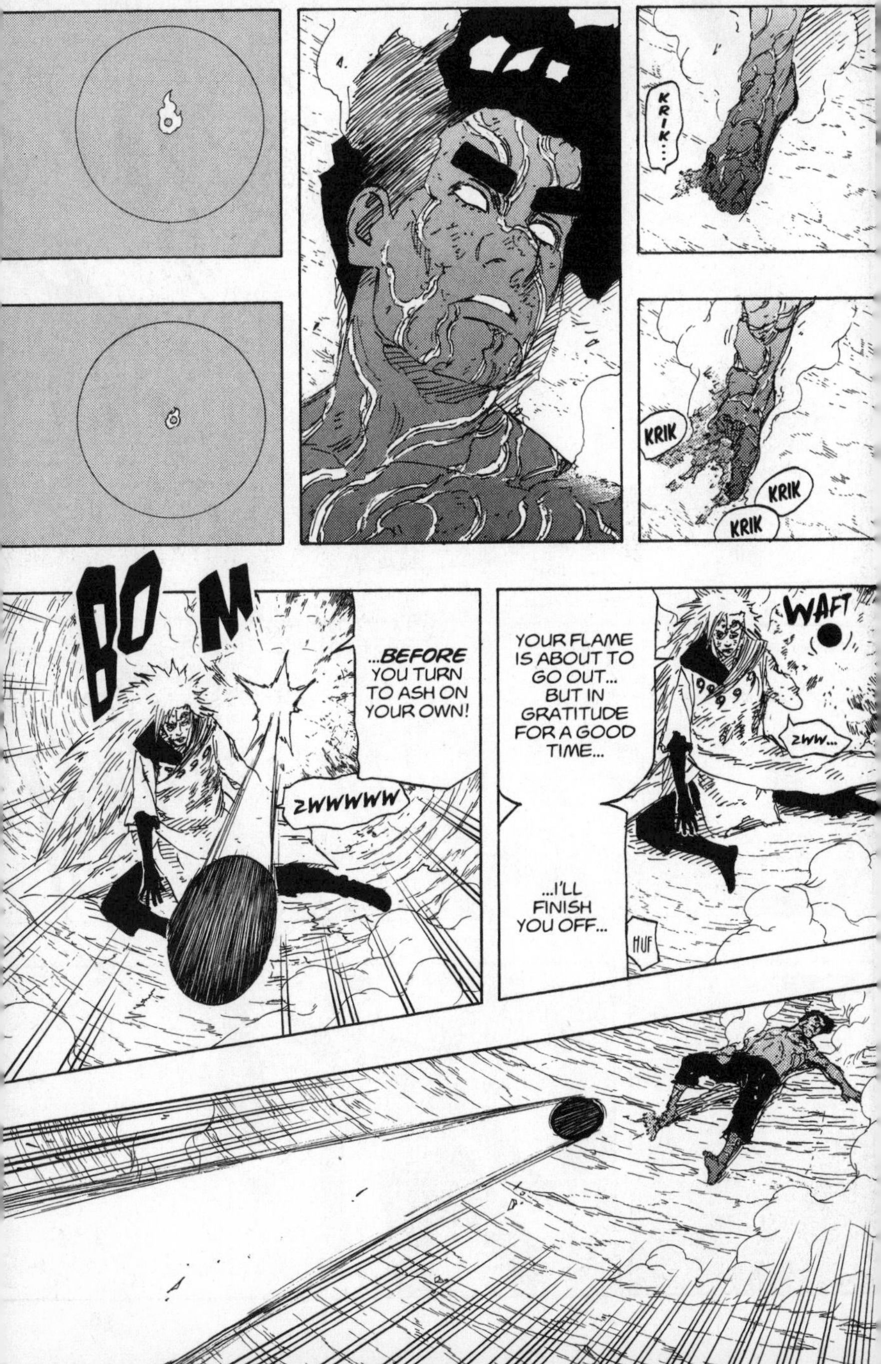
KRIK...
KRIK
KRIK
KRIK
WAFT
ZWW...
YOUR FLAME IS ABOUT TO GO OUT... BUT IN GRATITUDE FOR A GOOD TIME...
...I'LL FINISH YOU OFF...
HUF
BOOM
...BEFORE YOU TURN TO ASH ON YOUR OWN!
ZWWWWW

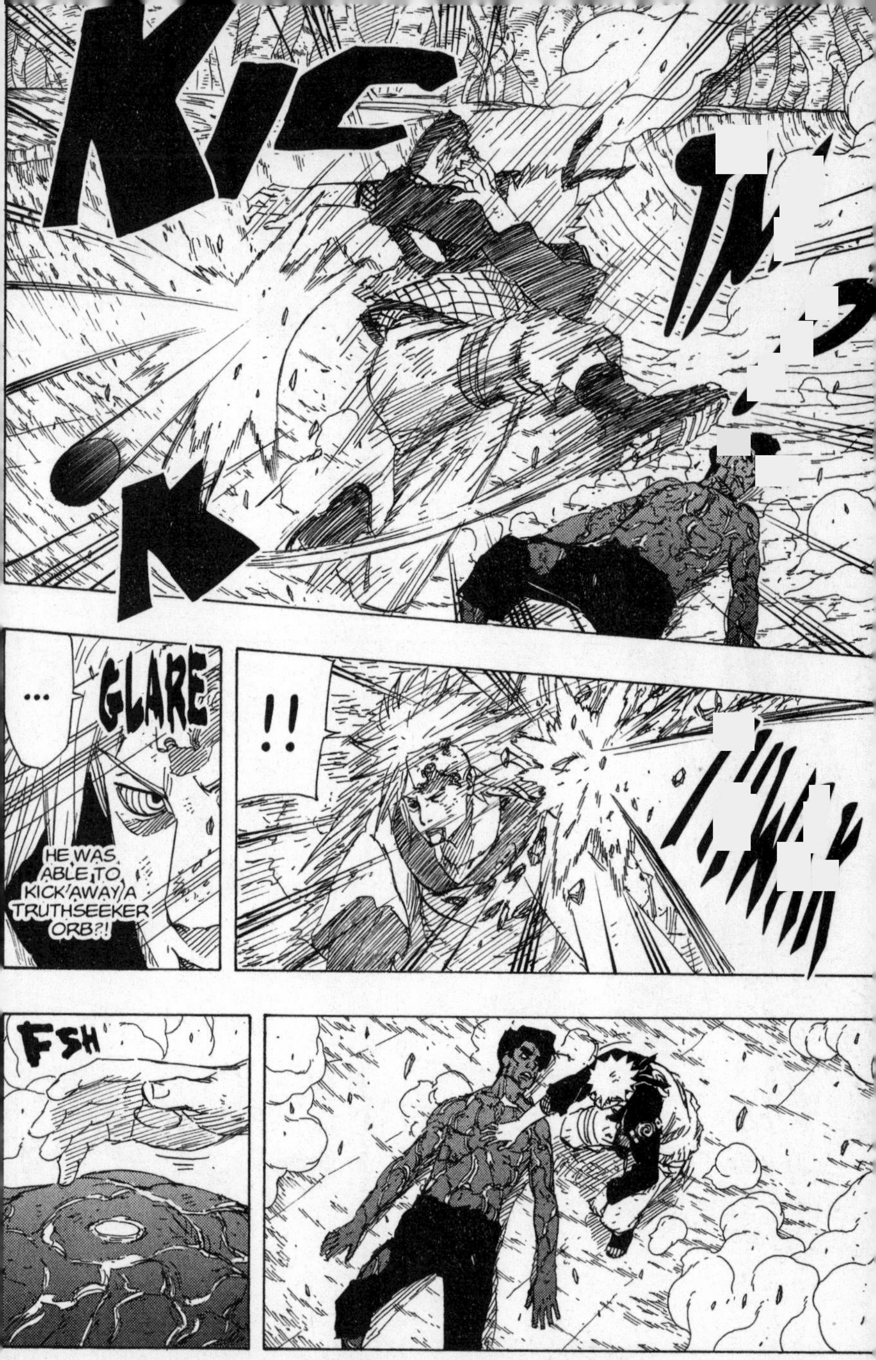
KICK
!!
GLARE
...
HE WAS ABLE TO KICK AWAY A TRUTHSEEKER ORB?!
FSH

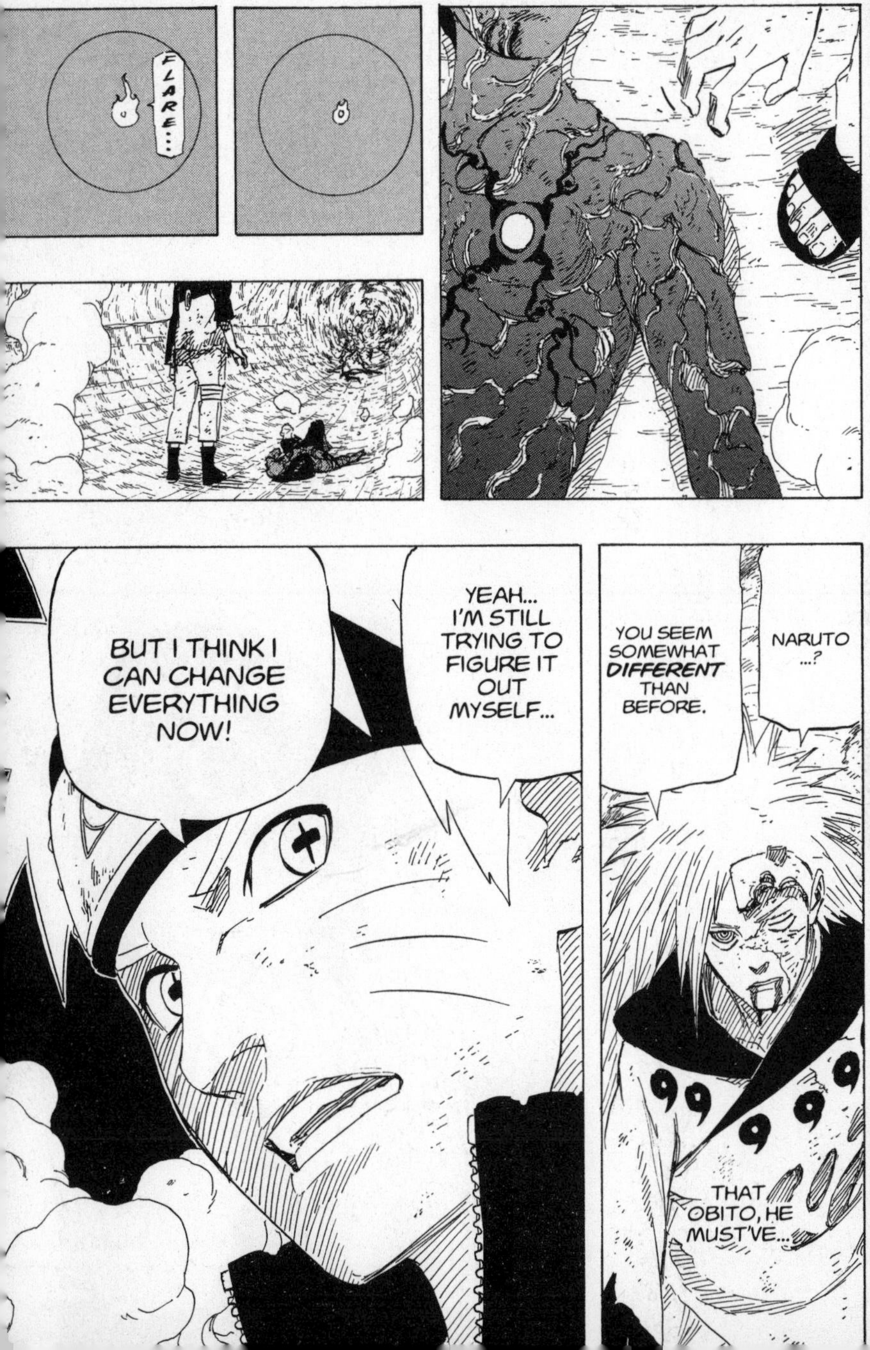
FLARE...
NARUTO ...?
YOU SEEM SOMEWHAT **DIFFERENT** THAN BEFORE.
THAT OBITO, HE MUST'VE...
YEAH... I'M STILL TRYING TO FIGURE IT OUT MYSELF...
BUT I THINK I CAN CHANGE EVERYTHING NOW!

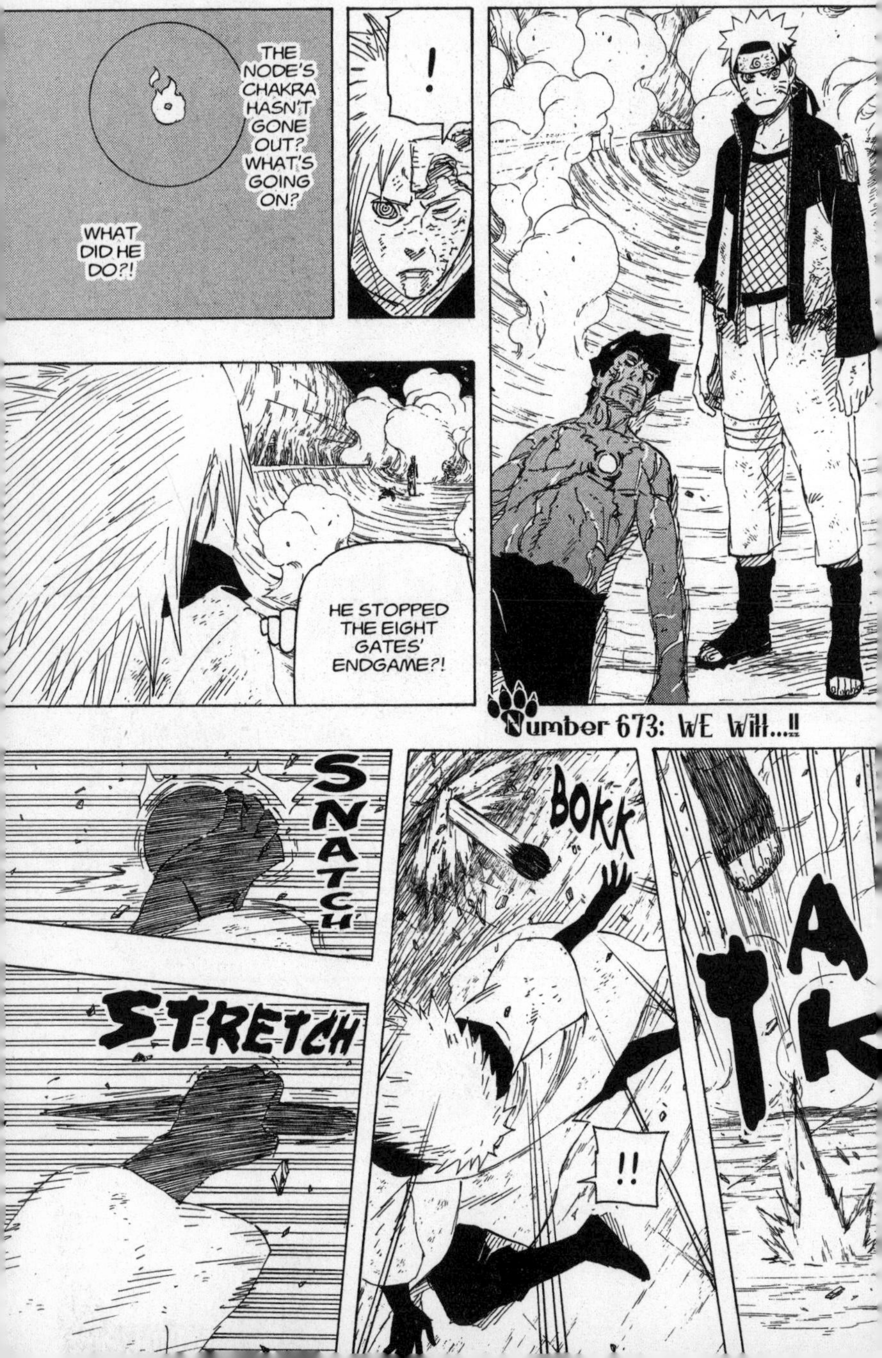
Number 673: We Will...!!
!
THE NODE'S CHAKRA HASN'T GONE OUT? WHAT'S GOING ON?
WHAT DID HE DO?!
HE STOPPED THE EIGHT GATES' ENDGAME?!
TAK
BOKK
!!
SNATCH
STRETCH

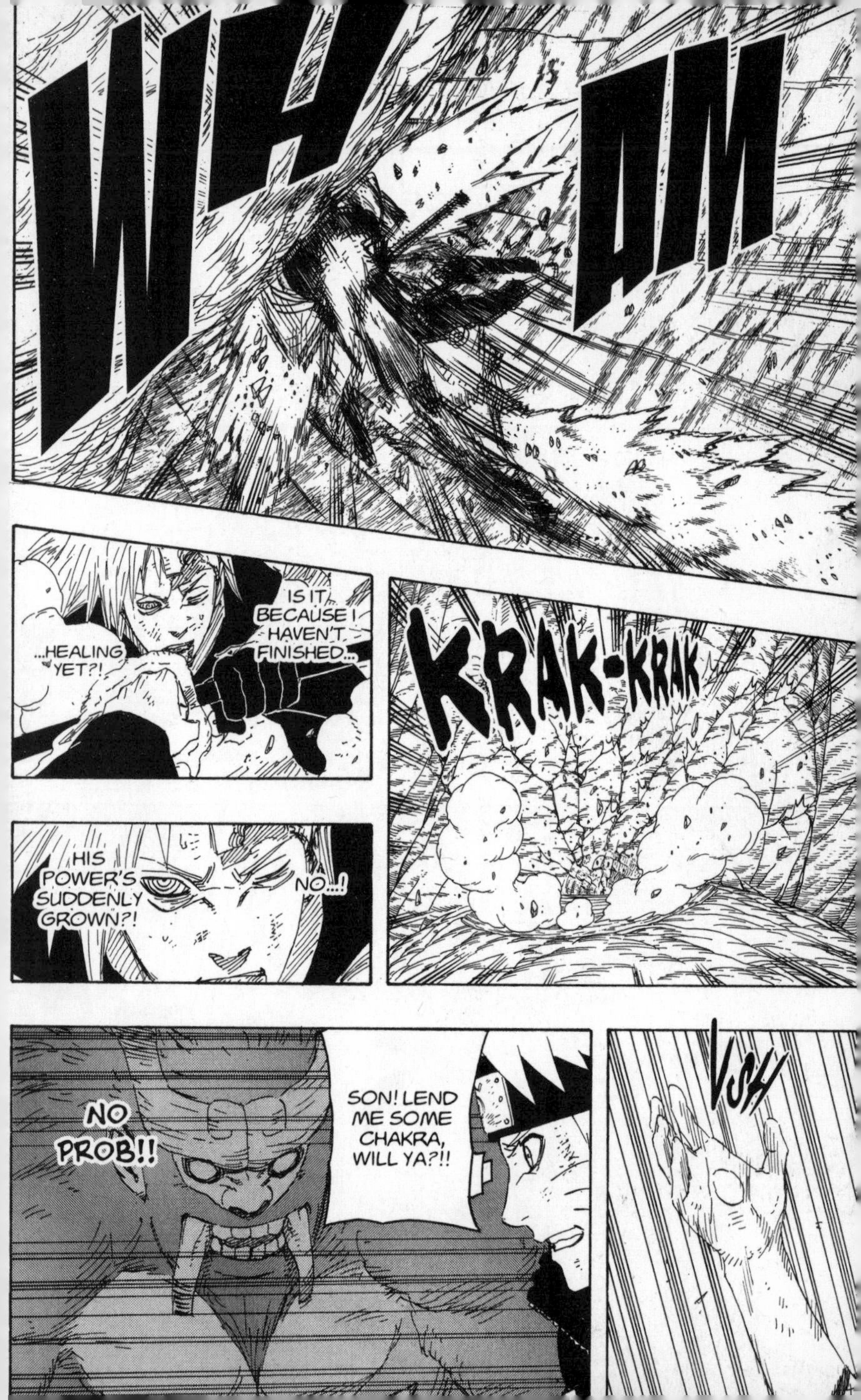
WHAM
KRAK-KRAK
IS IT BECAUSE I HAVEN'T FINISHED...
...HEALING YET?!
NO...!
HIS POWER'S SUDDENLY GROWN?!
VSH
SON! LEND ME SOME CHAKRA, WILL YA?!!
NO PROB!!

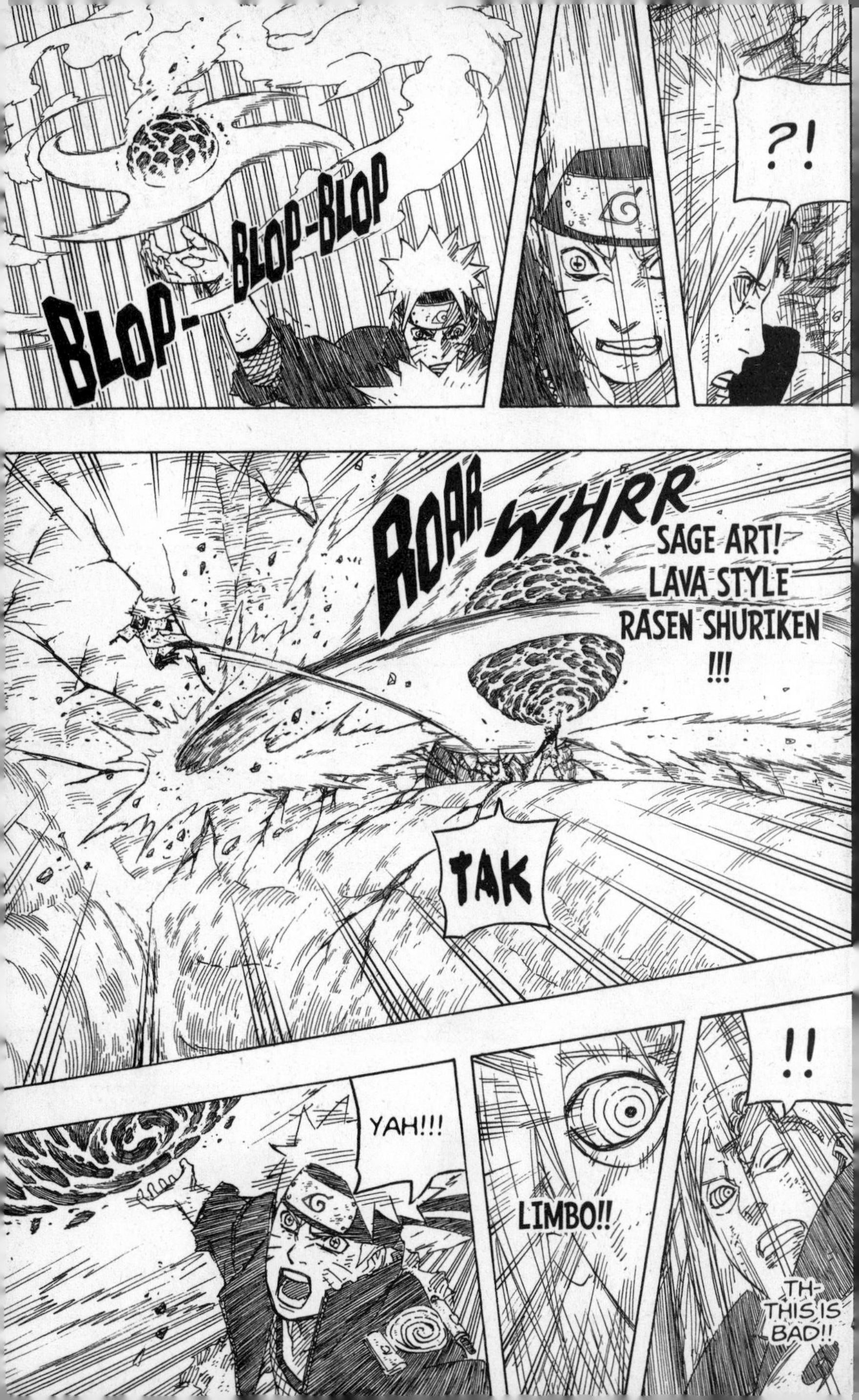
?!
BLOP-BLOP-BLOP
ROAR
WHRR
SAGE ART! LAVA STYLE RASEN SHURIKEN !!!
TAK
!!
TH-THIS IS BAD!!
LIMBO!!
YAH!!!

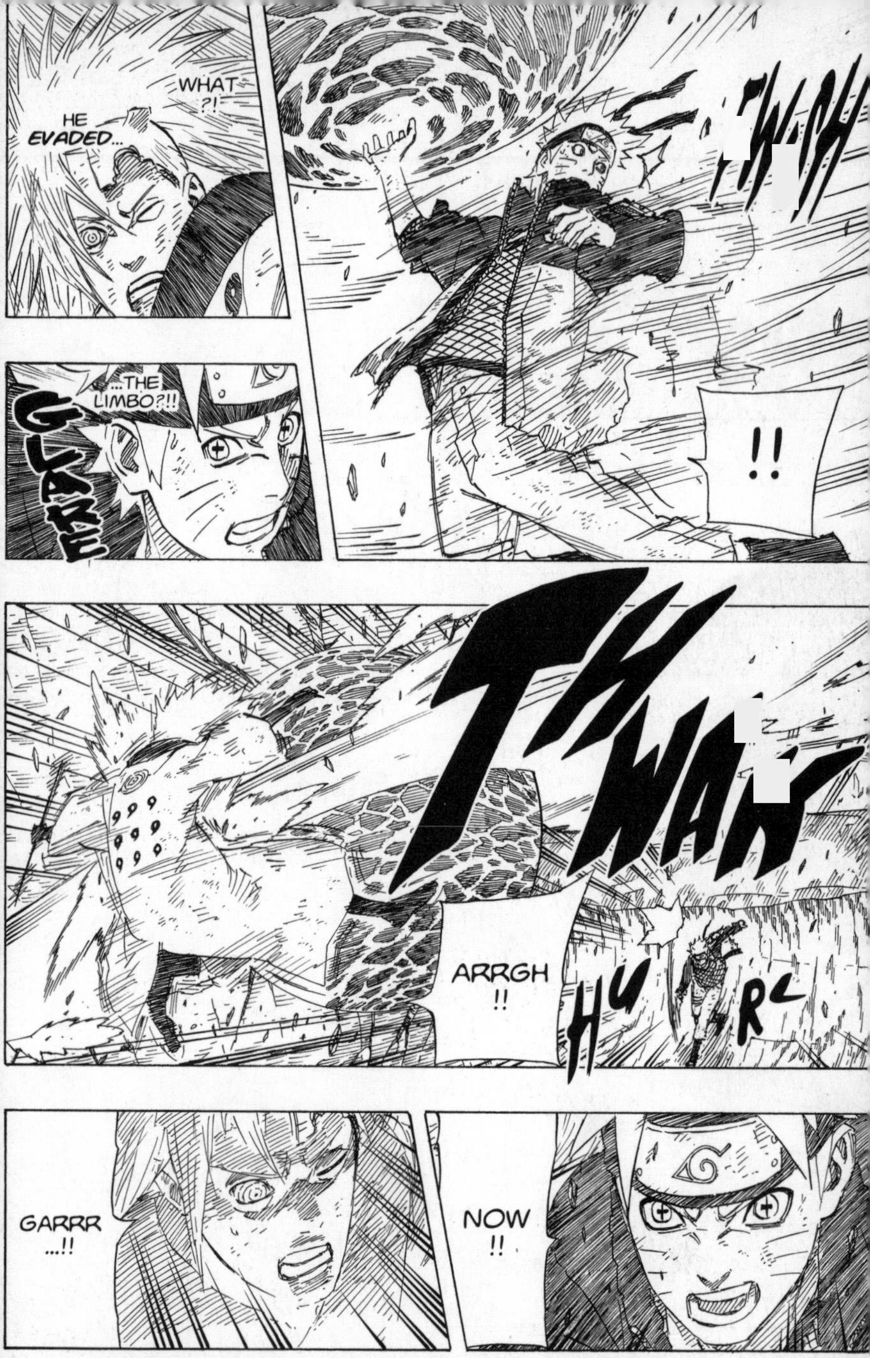
!!
WHAT ?!
HE EVADED...
...THE LIMBO?!!
GLARE
ARRGH !!
NOW !!
GARRR ...!!

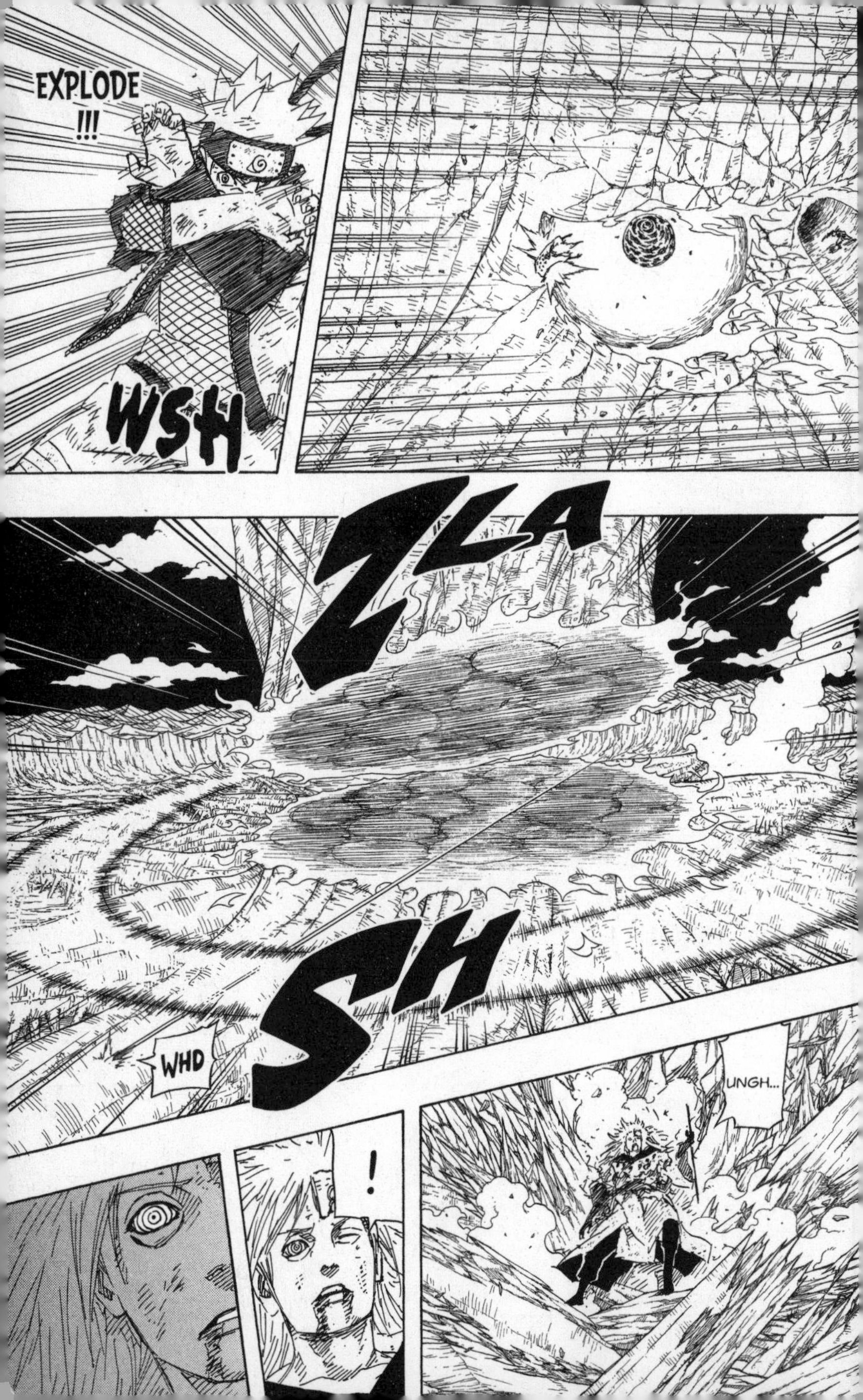
EXPLODE !!!
WSH
ZLA
SH
WHD
UNGH...
!

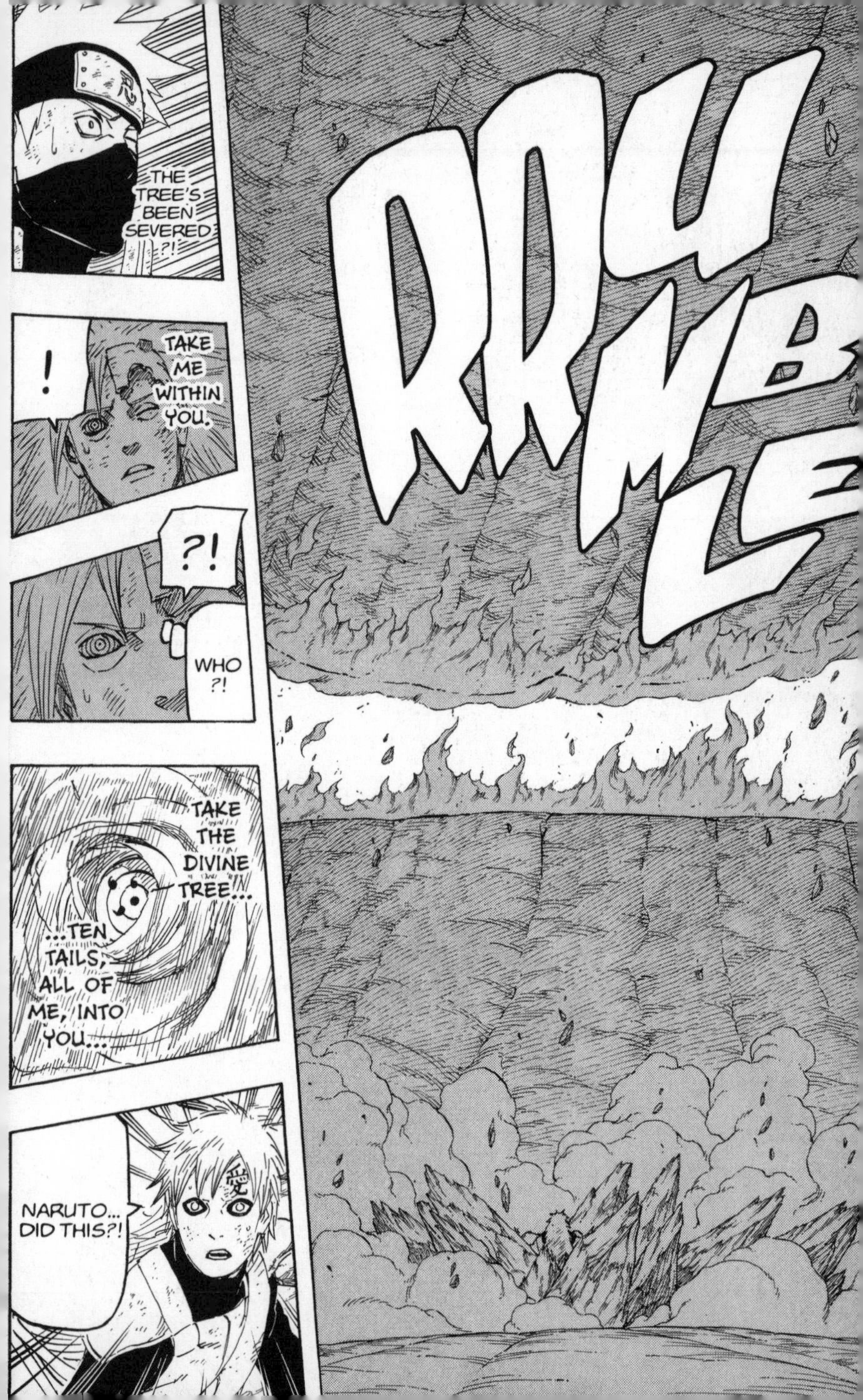
RRUMBLE
THE TREE'S BEEN SEVERED?!
TAKE ME WITHIN YOU.
!
?!
WHO?!
TAKE THE DIVINE TREE...
...TEN TAILS, ALL OF ME, INTO YOU...
NARUTO... DID THIS?!

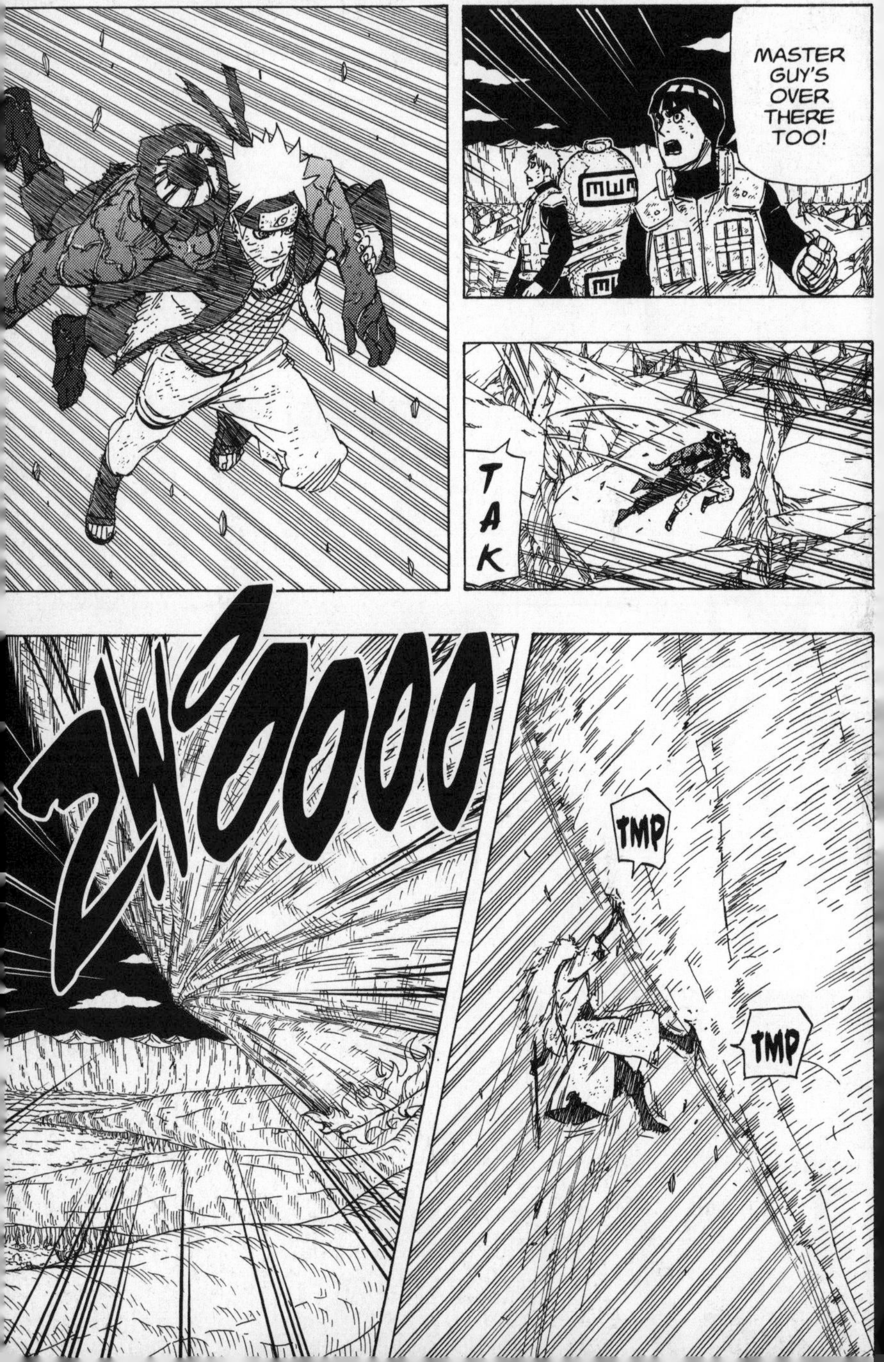
MASTER GUY'S OVER THERE TOO!
TAK
TMP
TMP
ZWOOOO

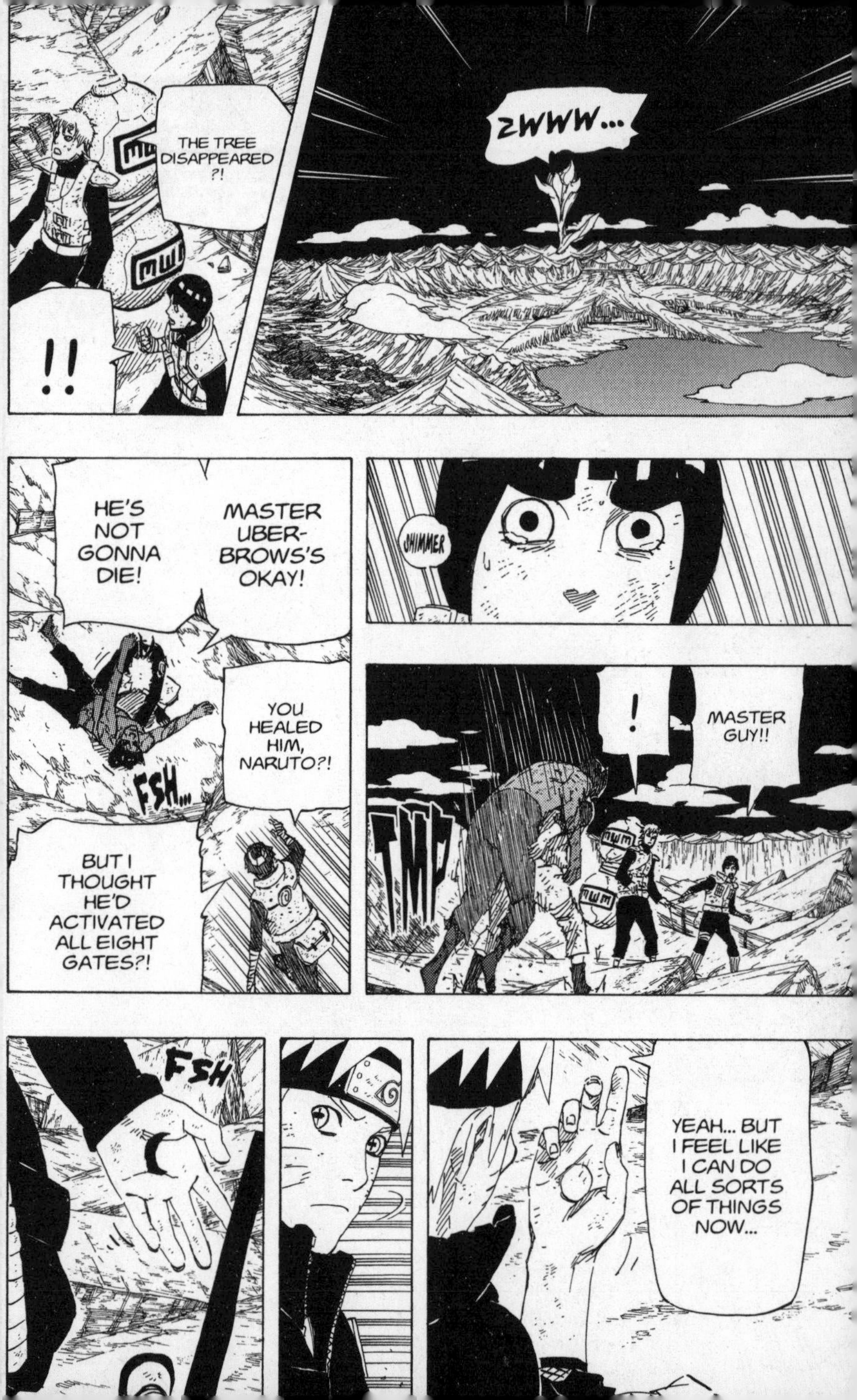
ZWWW...
THE TREE DISAPPEARED?!
!!
SHIMMER
MASTER GUY!!
!
TMP
MASTER UBER-BROWS'S OKAY!
HE'S NOT GONNA DIE!
YOU HEALED HIM, NARUTO?!
FSH...
BUT I THOUGHT HE'D ACTIVATED ALL EIGHT GATES?!
YEAH... BUT I FEEL LIKE I CAN DO ALL SORTS OF THINGS NOW...
FSH

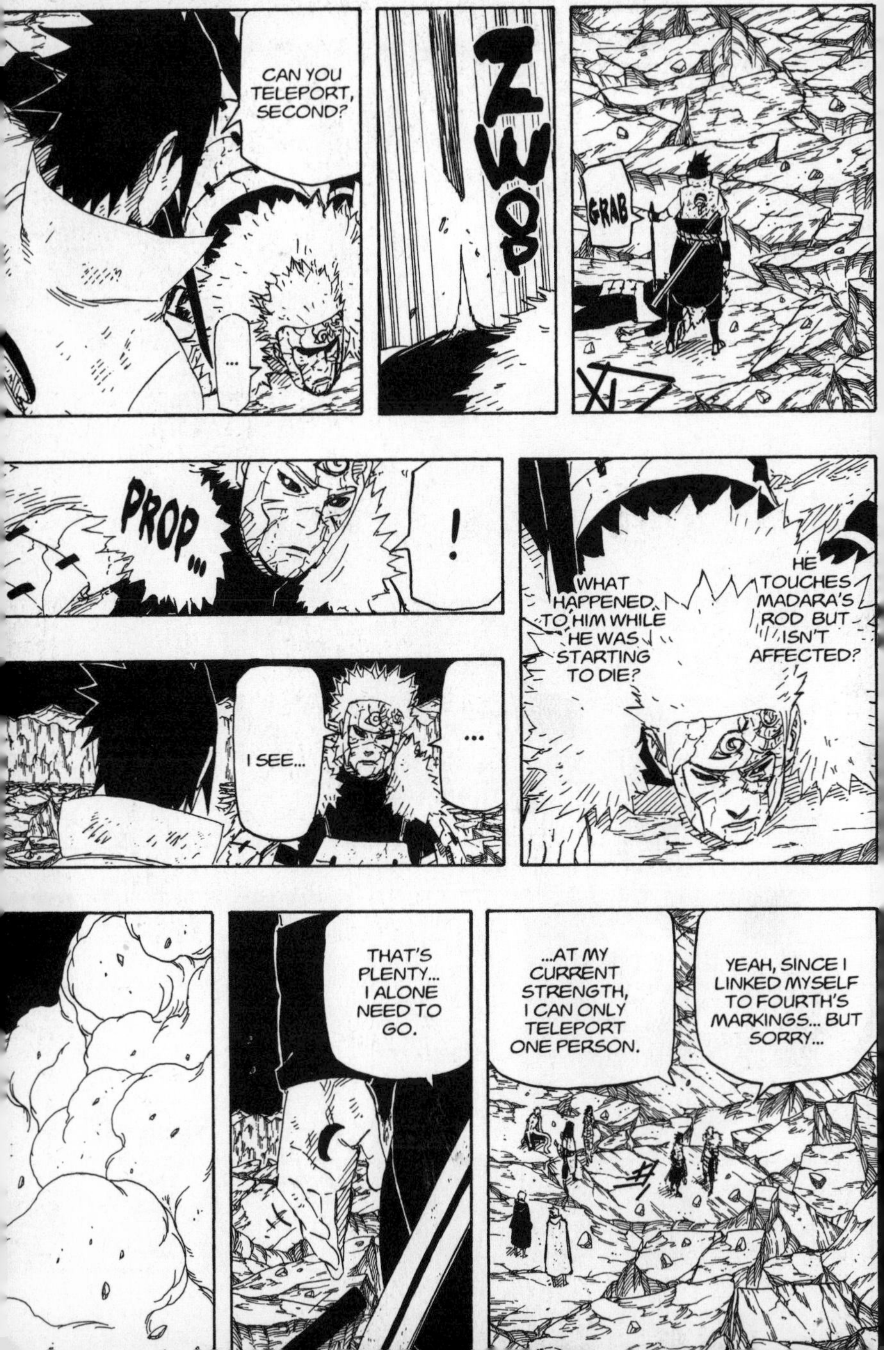
GRAB
ZWOP
CAN YOU TELEPORT, SECOND?
...
HE TOUCHES MADARA'S ROD BUT ISN'T AFFECTED?
WHAT HAPPENED TO HIM WHILE HE WAS STARTING TO DIE?
!
PROP...
...
I SEE...
YEAH, SINCE I LINKED MYSELF TO FOURTH'S MARKINGS... BUT SORRY...
...AT MY CURRENT STRENGTH, I CAN ONLY TELEPORT ONE PERSON.
THAT'S PLENTY... I ALONE NEED TO GO.

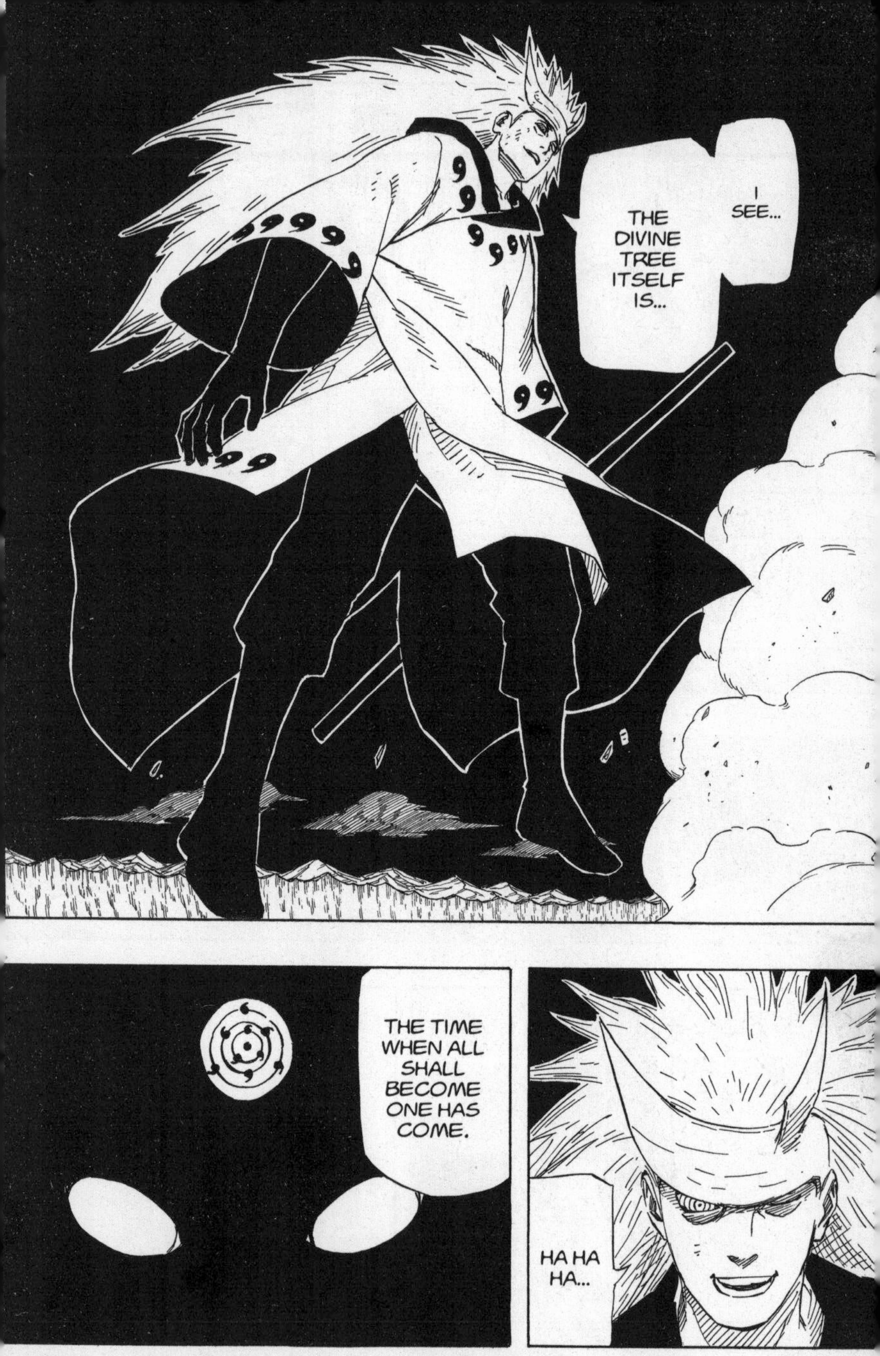
I SEE...
THE DIVINE TREE ITSELF IS...
HA HA HA...
THE TIME WHEN ALL SHALL BECOME ONE HAS COME.

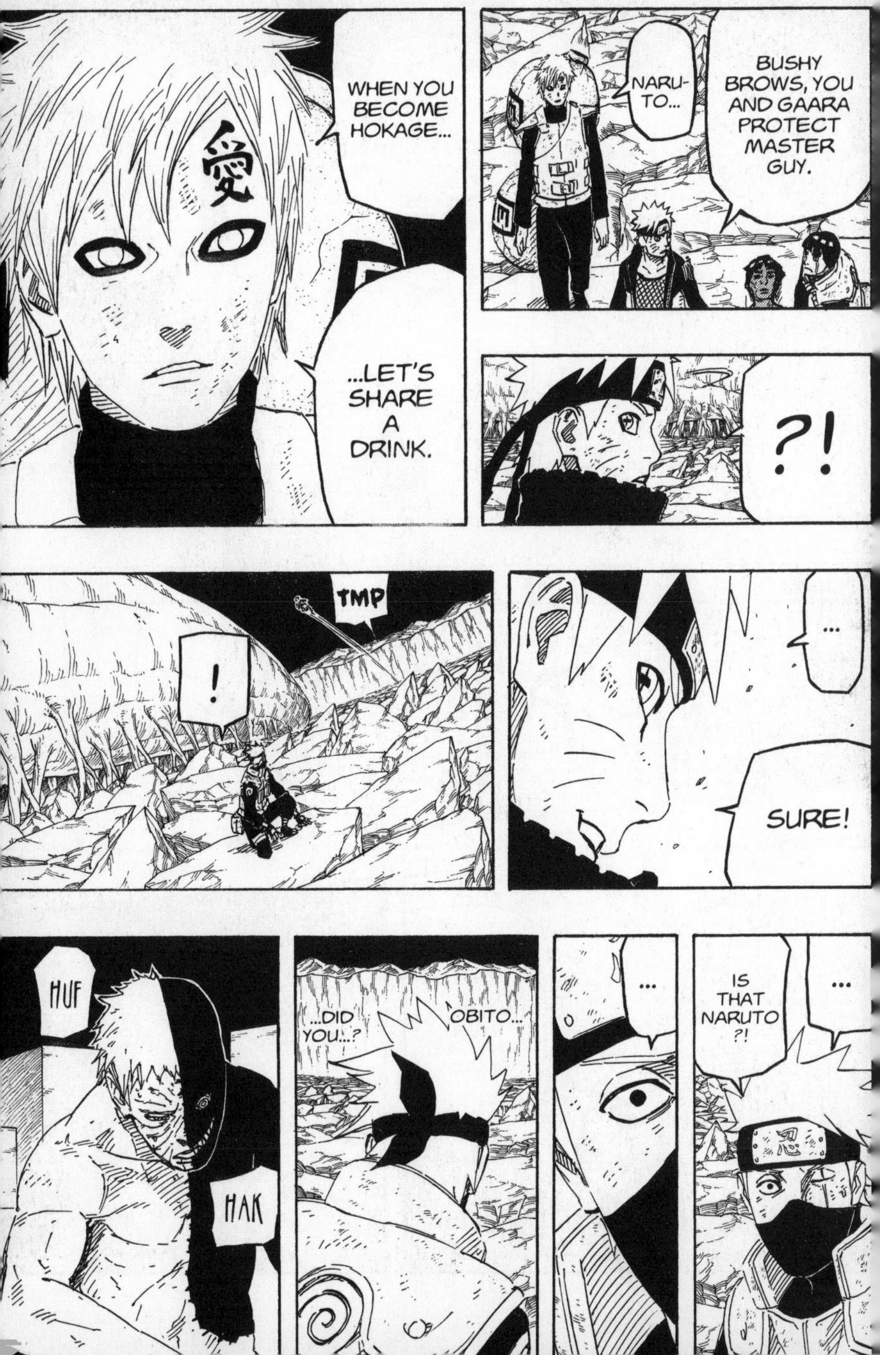
BUSHY BROWS, YOU AND GAARA PROTECT MASTER GUY.
NARU-TO...
?!
WHEN YOU BECOME HOKAGE...
...LET'S SHARE A DRINK.
...
SURE!
TMP
!
...
IS THAT NARUTO ?!
...
OBITO...
...DID YOU...?
HUF
HAK

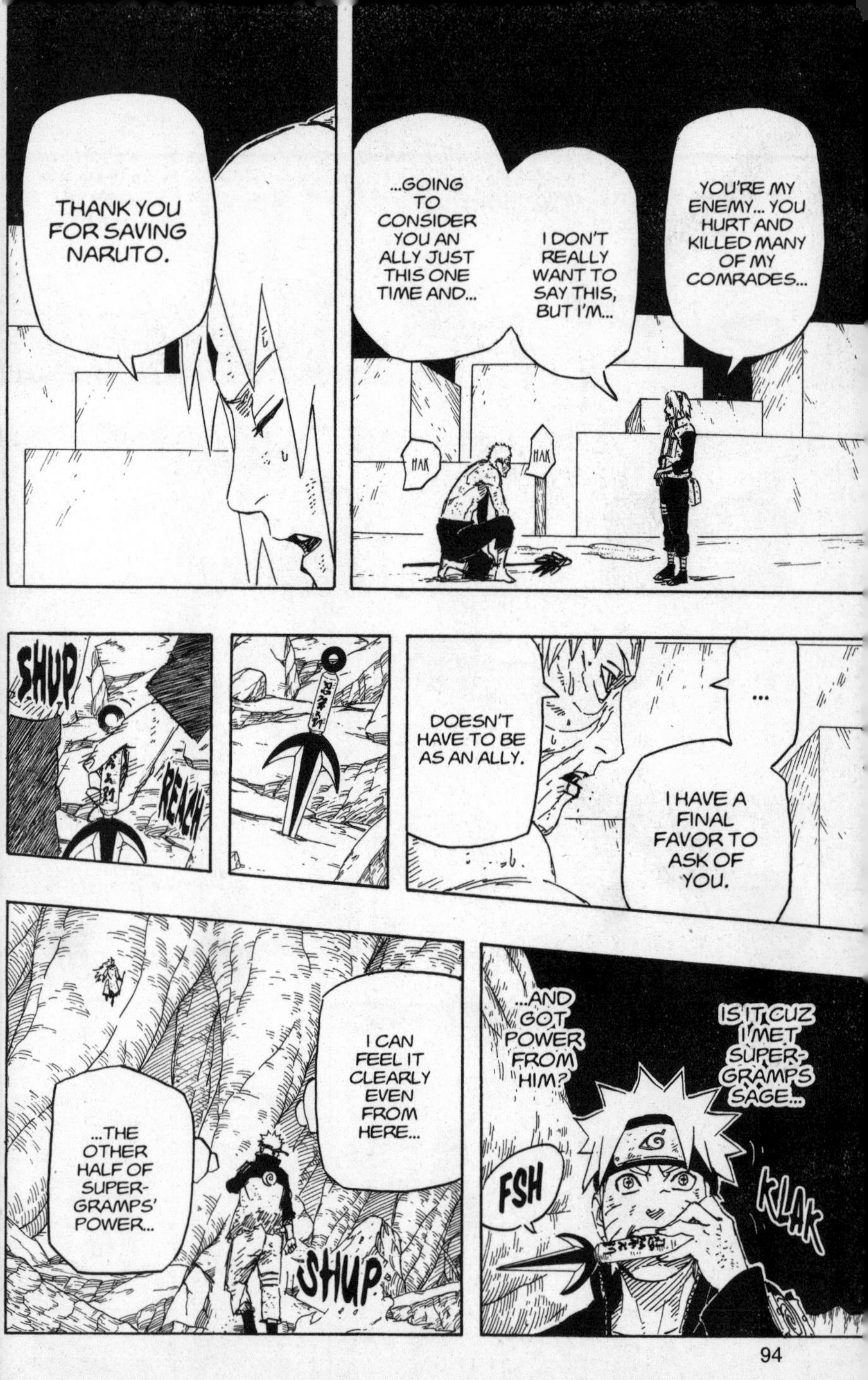
YOU'RE MY ENEMY... YOU HURT AND KILLED MANY OF MY COMRADES...
I DON'T REALLY WANT TO SAY THIS, BUT I'M...
...GOING TO CONSIDER YOU AN ALLY JUST THIS ONE TIME AND...
HAK
HAK
THANK YOU FOR SAVING NARUTO.
...
I HAVE A FINAL FAVOR TO ASK OF YOU.
DOESN'T HAVE TO BE AS AN ALLY.
SHUP
REACH
IS IT CUZ I MET SUPER-GRAMPS SAGE...
...AND GOT POWER FROM HIM?
KLAK
FSH
I CAN FEEL IT CLEARLY EVEN FROM HERE...
...THE OTHER HALF OF SUPER-GRAMPS' POWER...
SHUP

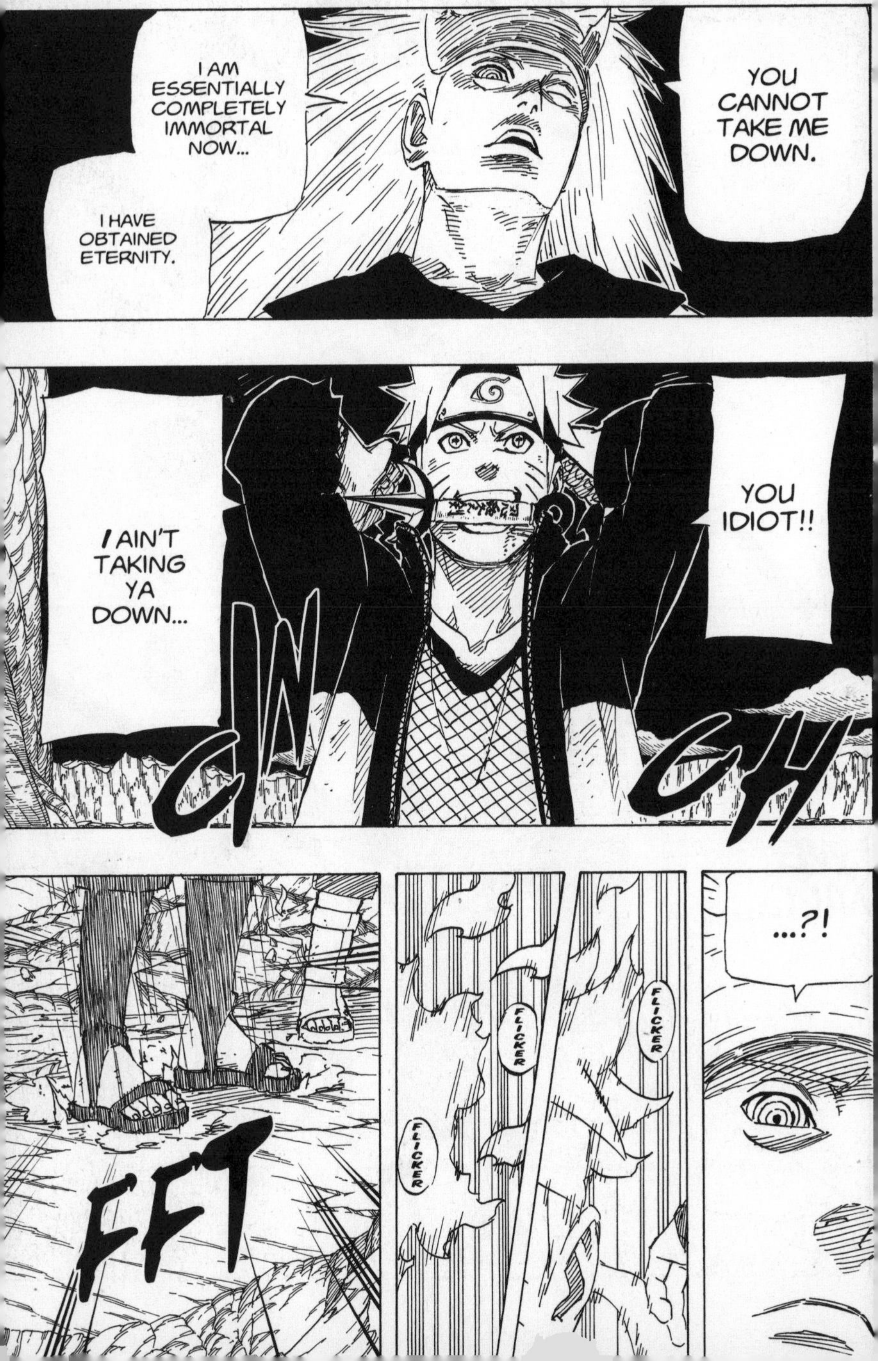
YOU CANNOT TAKE ME DOWN.
I AM ESSENTIALLY COMPLETELY IMMORTAL NOW...
I HAVE OBTAINED ETERNITY.
YOU IDIOT!!
I AIN'T TAKING YA DOWN...
...?!
FLICKER
FLICKER
FLICKER
FFT

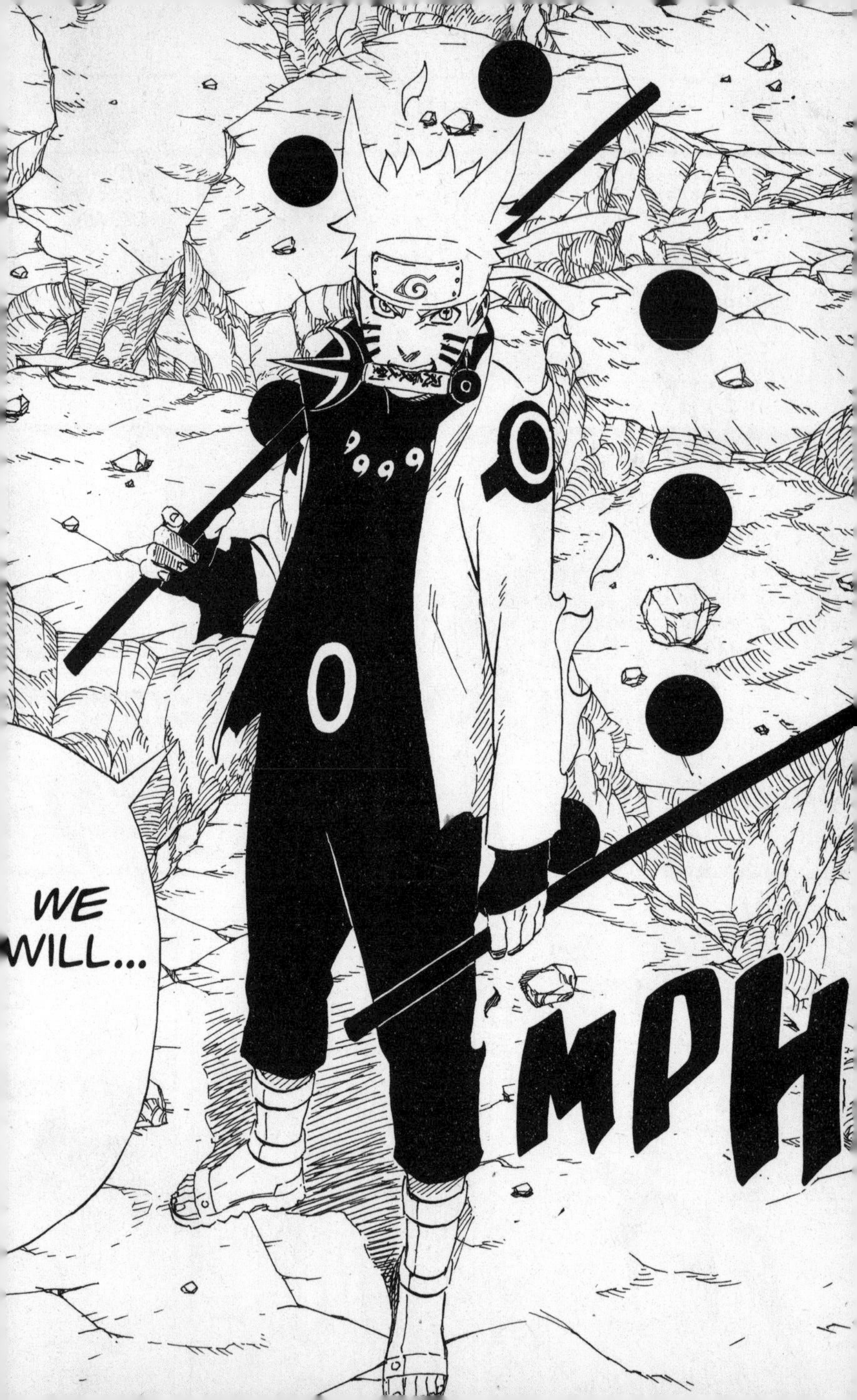
WE WILL...
MPH

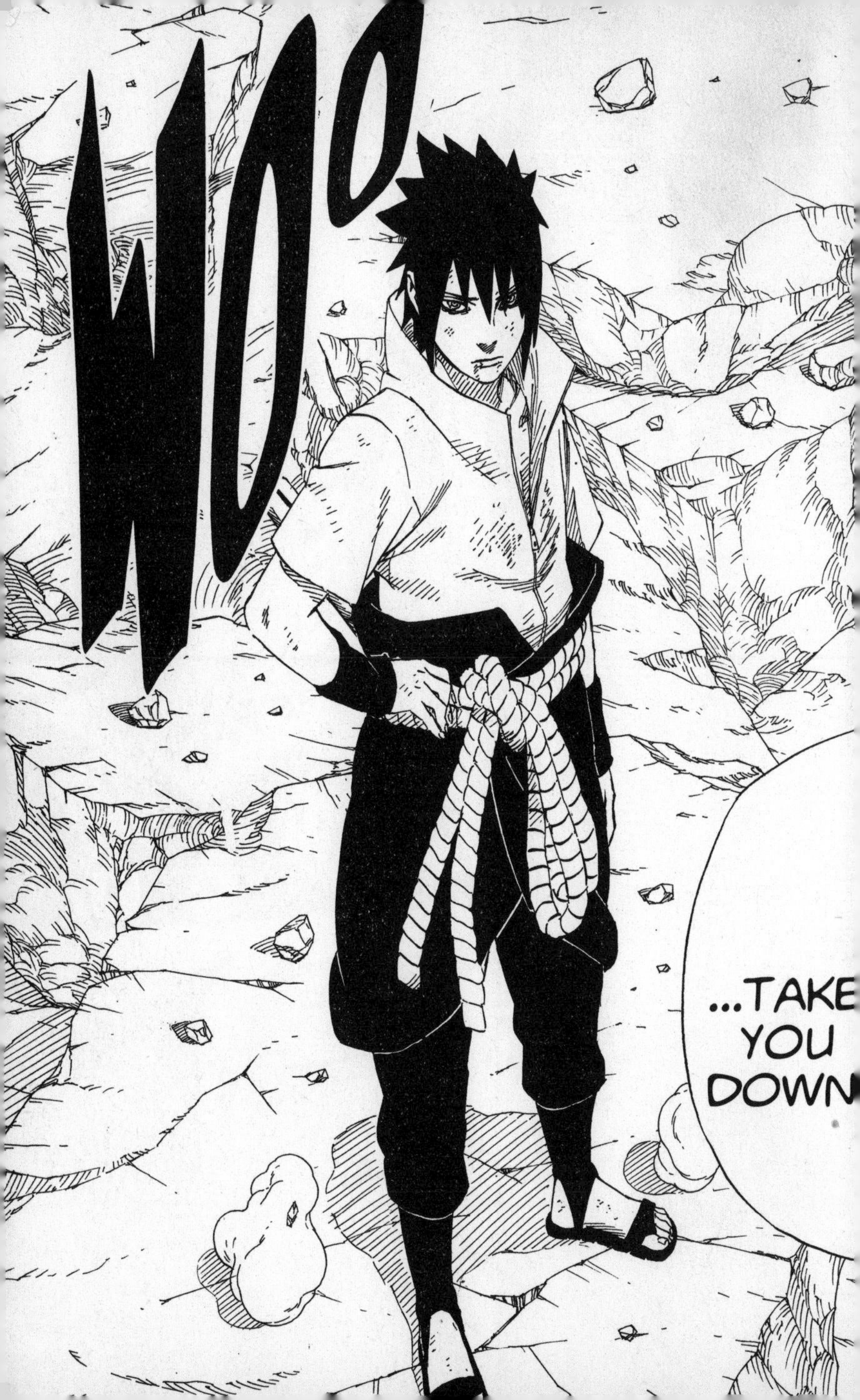
WOO
...TAKE YOU DOWN

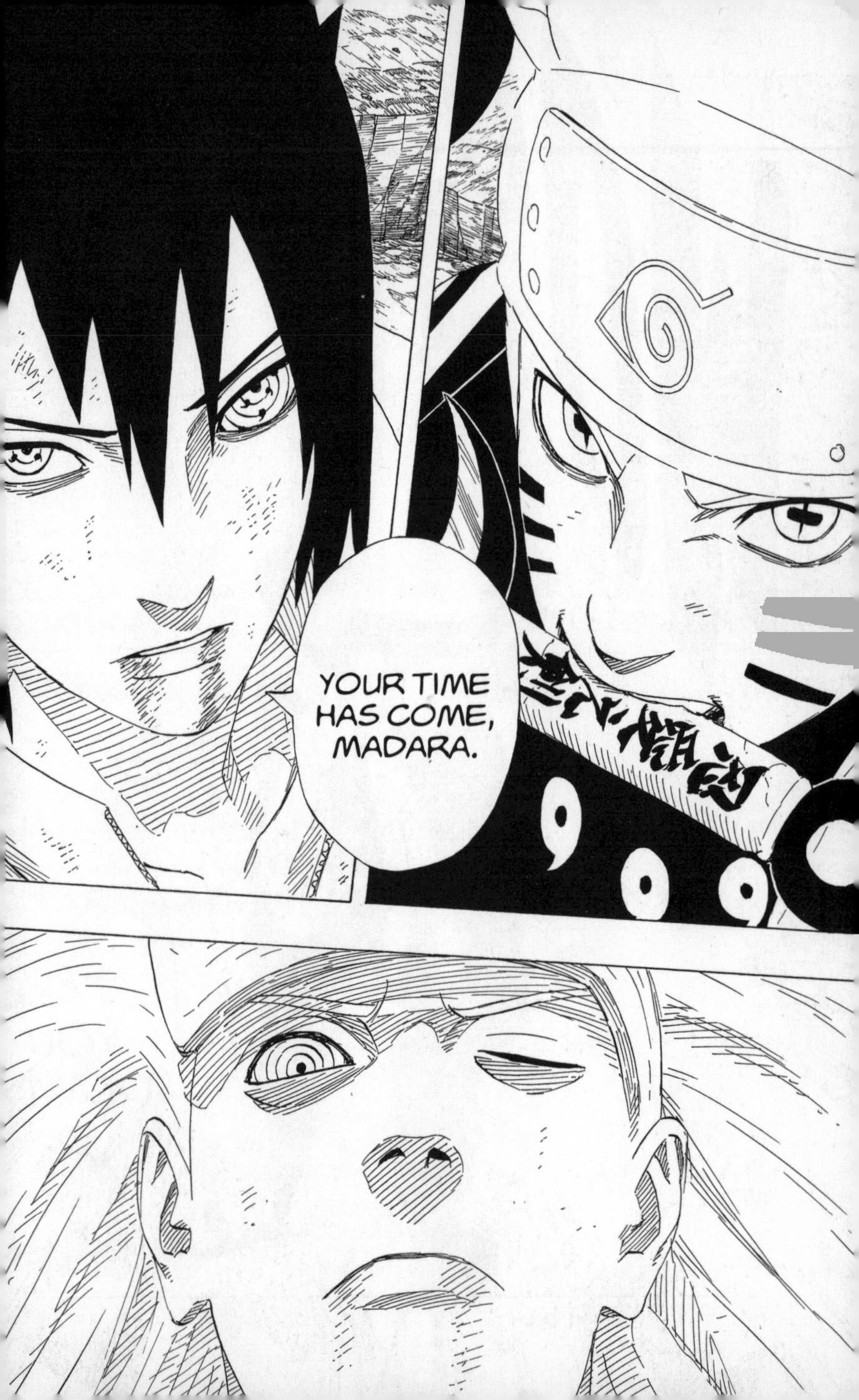
YOUR TIME HAS COME, MADARA.

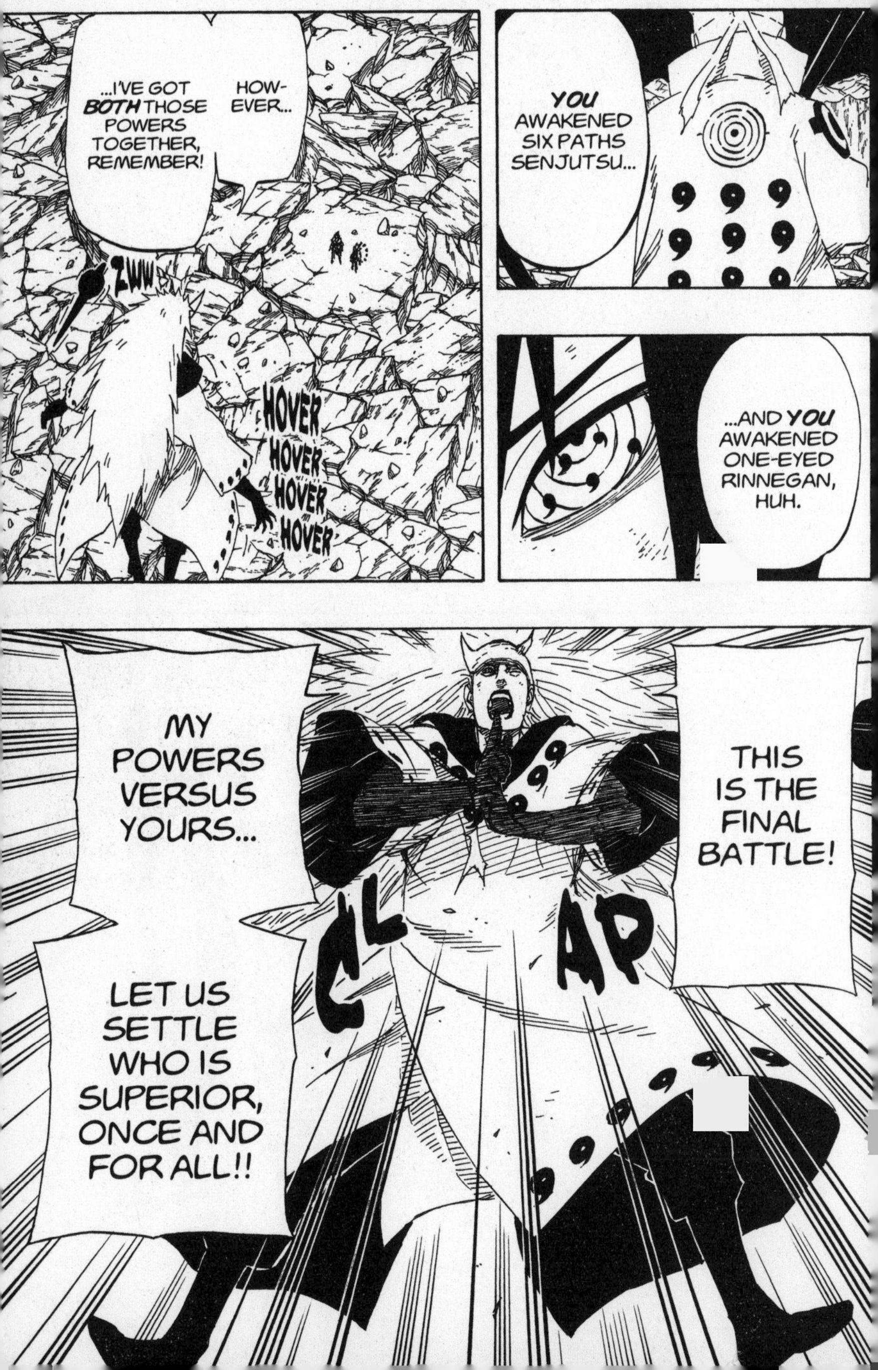
YOU AWAKENED SIX PATHS SENJUTSU...
...AND YOU AWAKENED ONE-EYED RINNEGAN, HUH.
HOW-EVER...
...I'VE GOT BOTH THOSE POWERS TOGETHER, REMEMBER!
ZWW
HOVER HOVER HOVER HOVER
THIS IS THE FINAL BATTLE!
MY POWERS VERSUS YOURS...
LET US SETTLE WHO IS SUPERIOR, ONCE AND FOR ALL!!
CLAP

# Number 674: Sasuke's Rinnegan

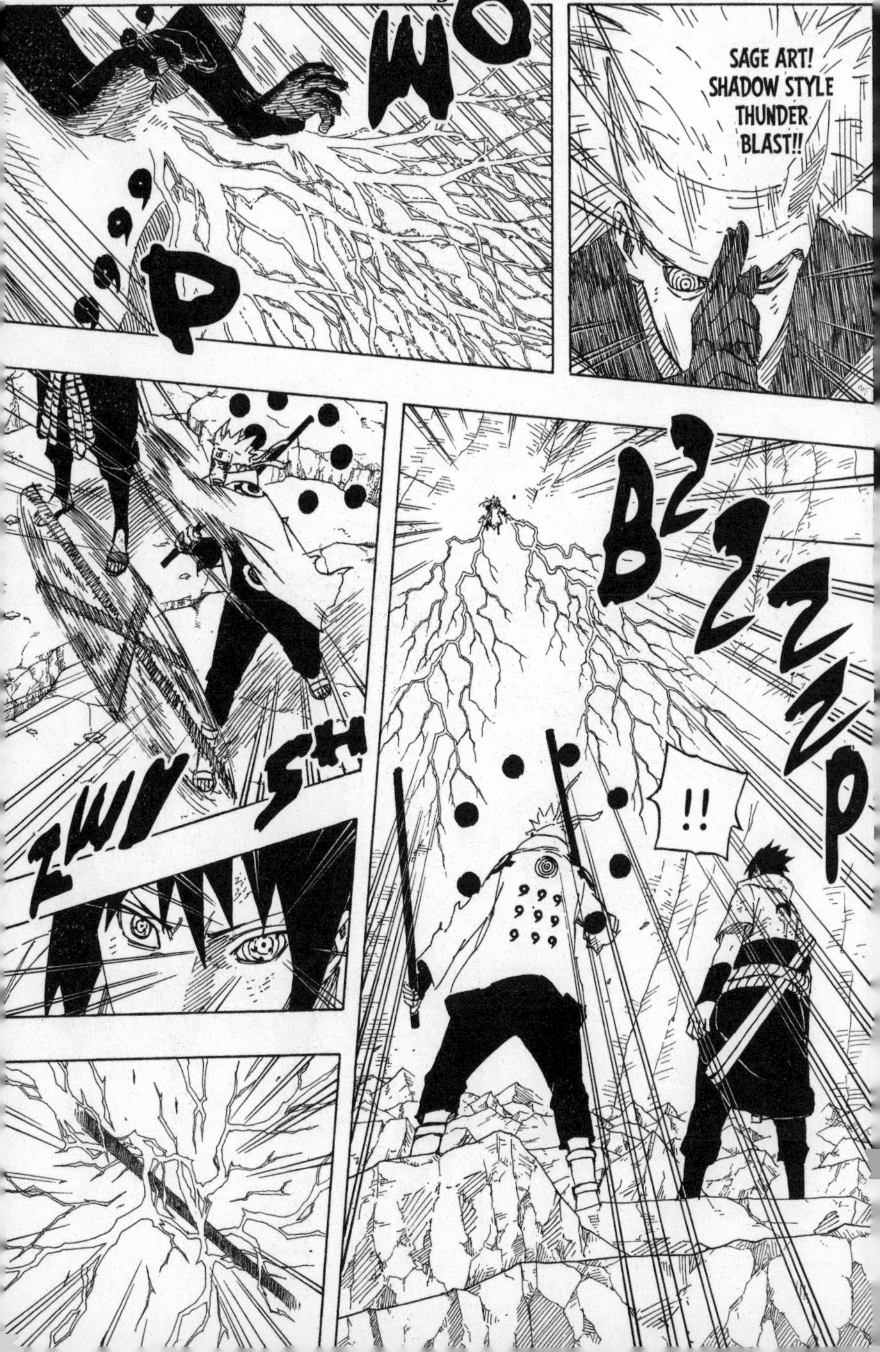
SAGE ART! SHADOW STYLE THUNDER BLAST!!
WOP
BZZZZP
!!
ZWISH

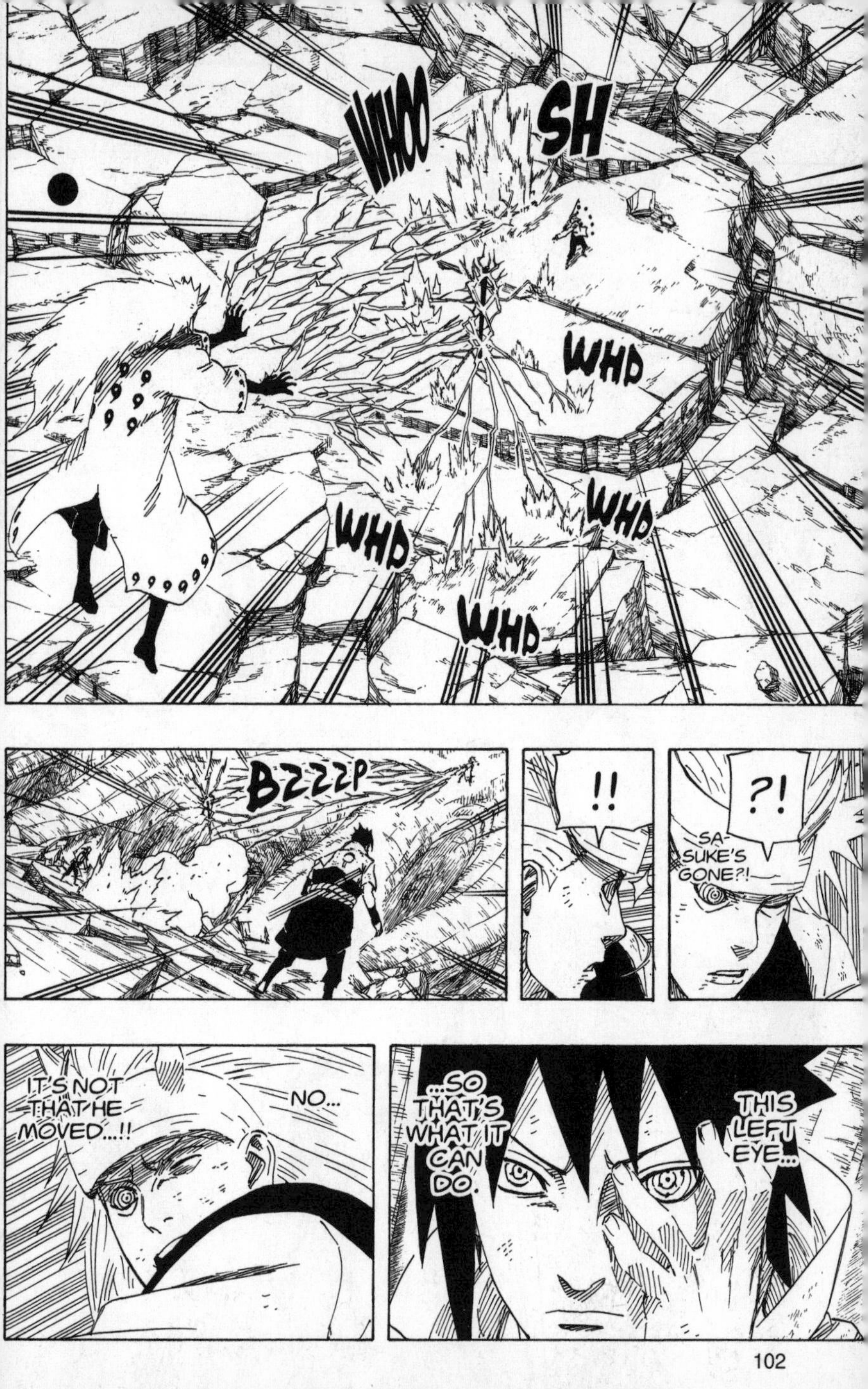
WHOOSH
WHD
WHD
WHD
WHD
?!
SA-SUKE'S GONE?!
!!
BZZZP
THIS LEFT EYE...
...SO THAT'S WHAT IT CAN DO.
NO...
IT'S NOT THAT HE MOVED...!!

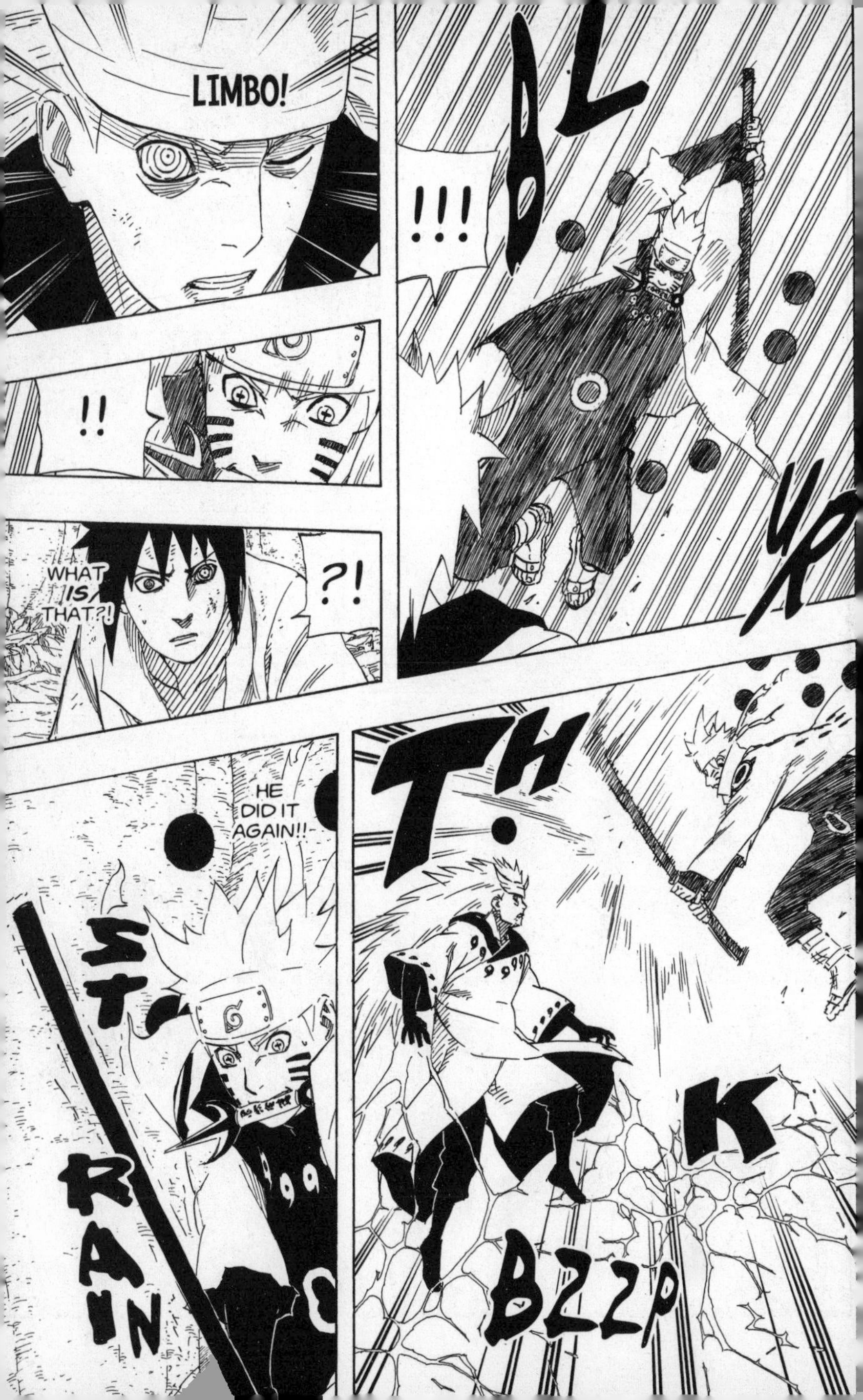
!!!
LIMBO!
!!
?!
WHAT IS THAT?!
HE DID IT AGAIN!!

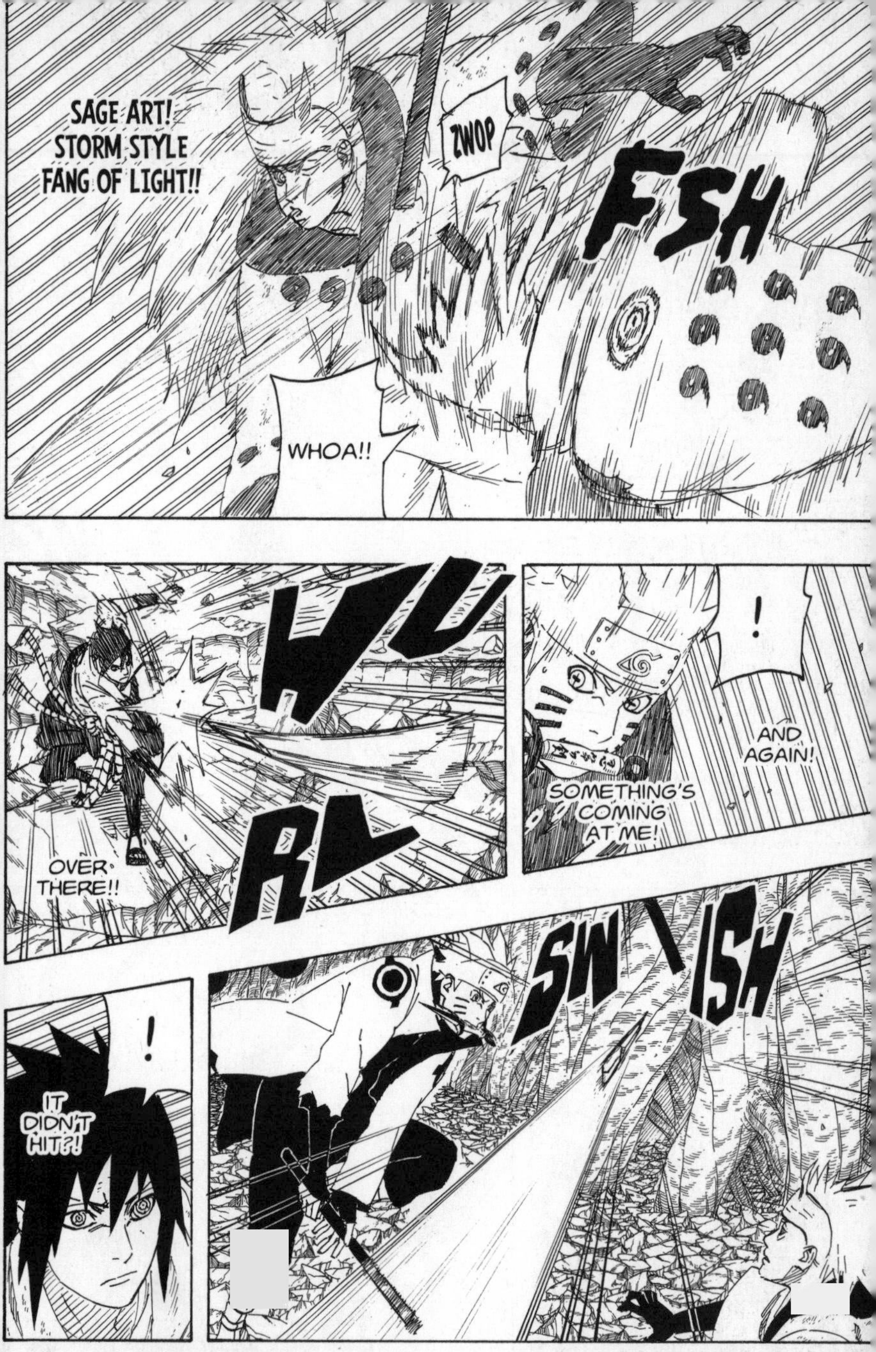
FSH
ZWOP
SAGE ART! STORM STYLE FANG OF LIGHT!!
WHOA!!
!
AND AGAIN!
SOMETHING'S COMING AT ME!
WHURL
OVER THERE!!
SWISH
!
IT DIDN'T HIT?!

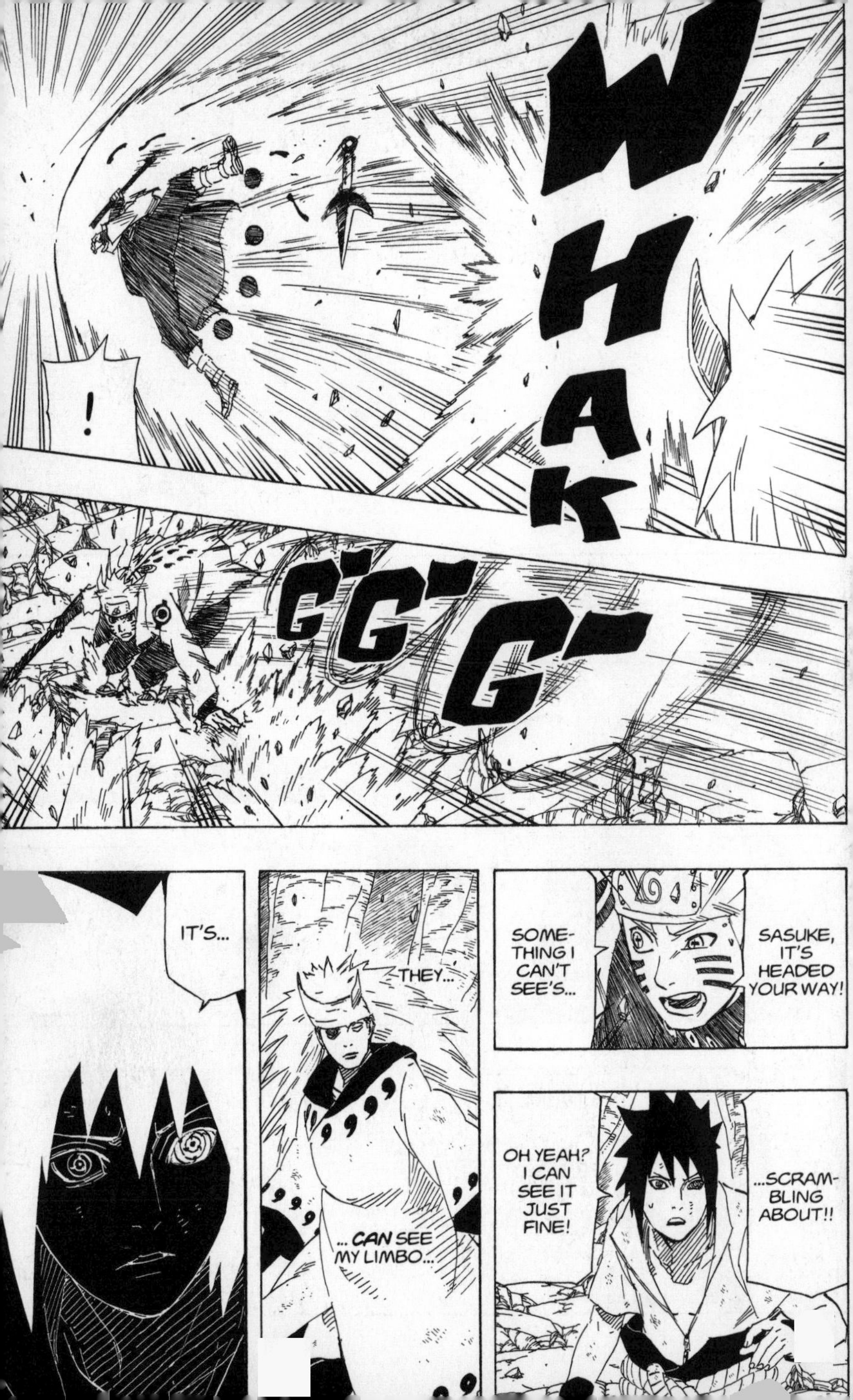
WHAK
!
GGG
SASUKE, IT'S HEADED YOUR WAY!
SOME-THING I CAN'T SEE'S...
...SCRAM-BLING ABOUT!!
OH YEAH? I CAN SEE IT JUST FINE!
THEY...
...CAN SEE MY LIMBO...
IT'S...

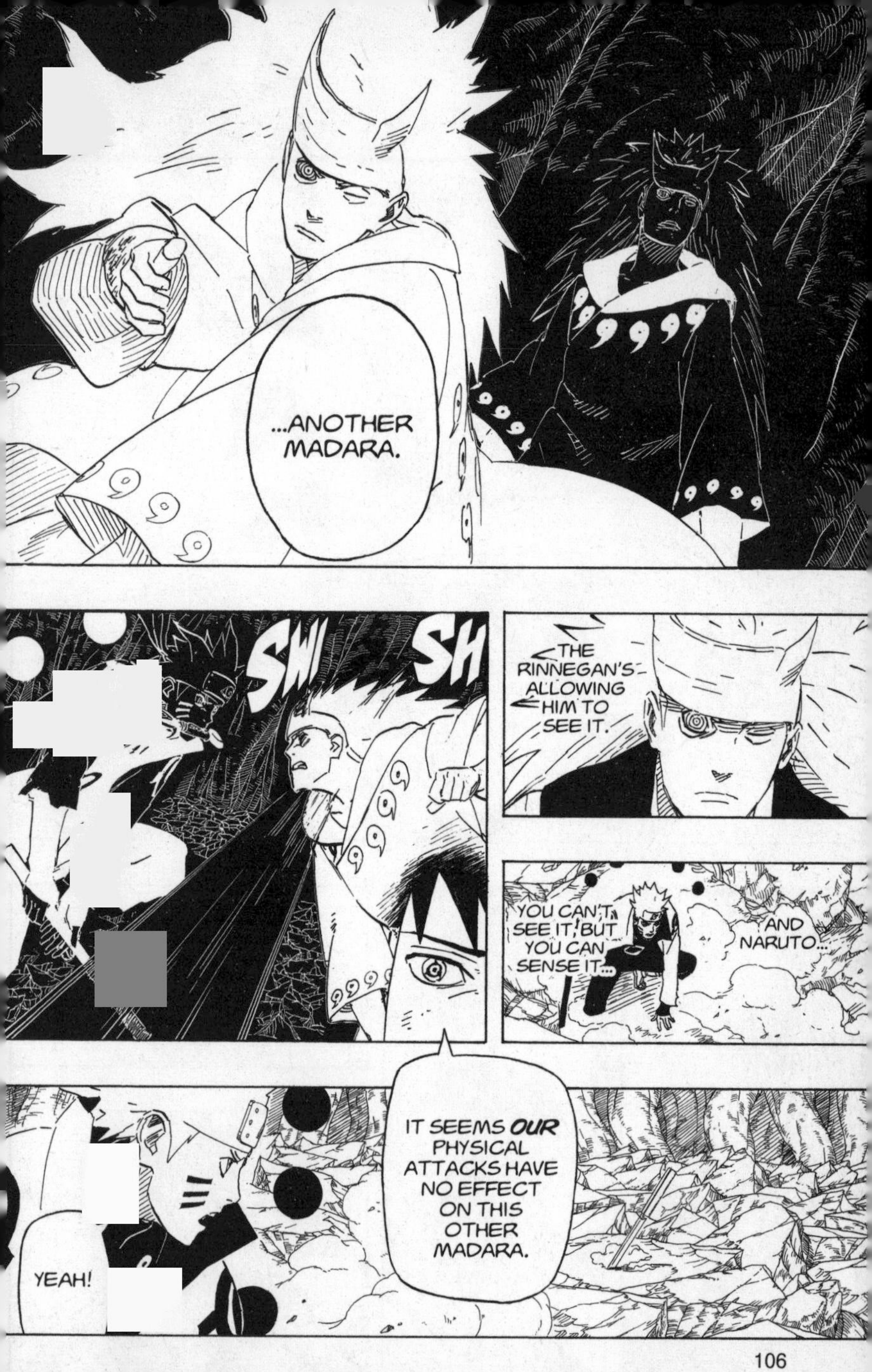

...ANOTHER MADARA.
THE RINNEGAN'S ALLOWING HIM TO SEE IT.
AND NARUTO...
YOU CAN'T SEE IT, BUT YOU CAN SENSE IT...
SH
SHI
IT SEEMS **OUR** PHYSICAL ATTACKS HAVE NO EFFECT ON THIS OTHER MADARA.
YEAH!

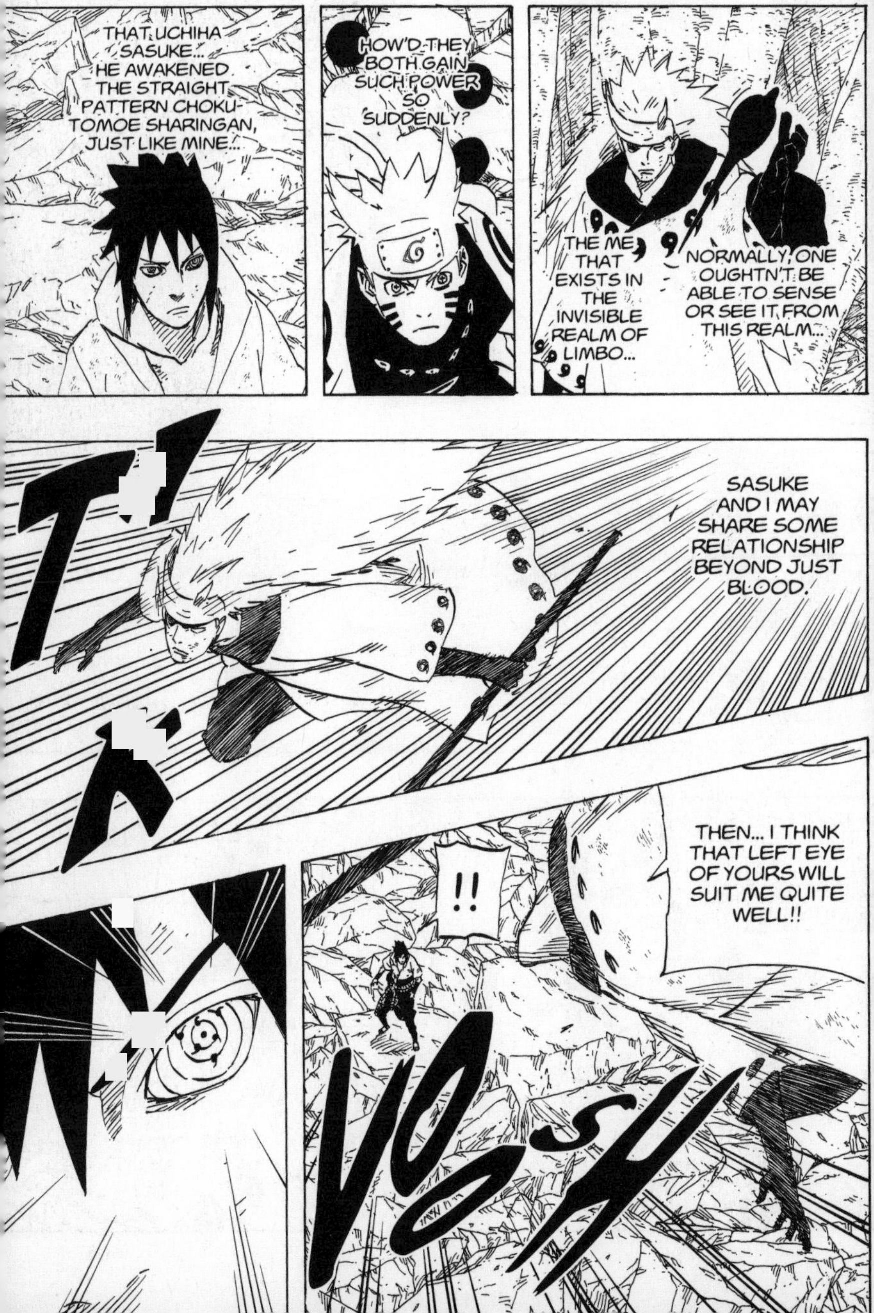
THE ME THAT EXISTS IN THE INVISIBLE REALM OF LIMBO...
NORMALLY, ONE OUGHTN'T BE ABLE TO SENSE OR SEE IT FROM THIS REALM...
HOW'D THEY BOTH GAIN SUCH POWER SO SUDDENLY?
THAT UCHIHA SASUKE... HE AWAKENED THE STRAIGHT PATTERN CHOKU-TOMOE SHARINGAN, JUST LIKE MINE...
SASUKE AND I MAY SHARE SOME RELATIONSHIP BEYOND JUST BLOOD.
THEN... I THINK THAT LEFT EYE OF YOURS WILL SUIT ME QUITE WELL!!
!!
VOSH

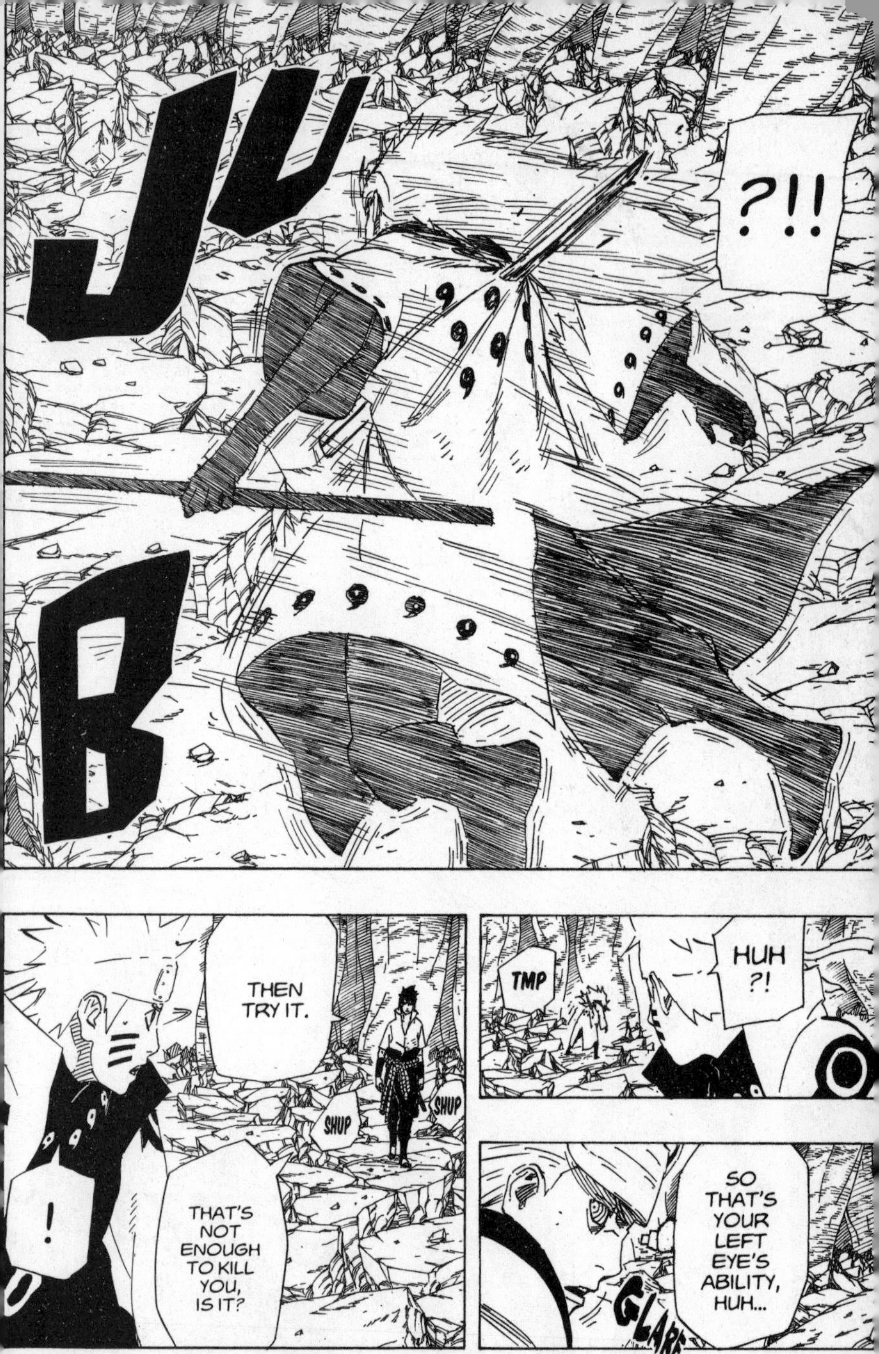
?!!
JU
B
HUH ?!
TMP
SO THAT'S YOUR LEFT EYE'S ABILITY, HUH...
GLARE
THEN TRY IT.
SHUP
SHUP
!
THAT'S NOT ENOUGH TO KILL YOU, IS IT?

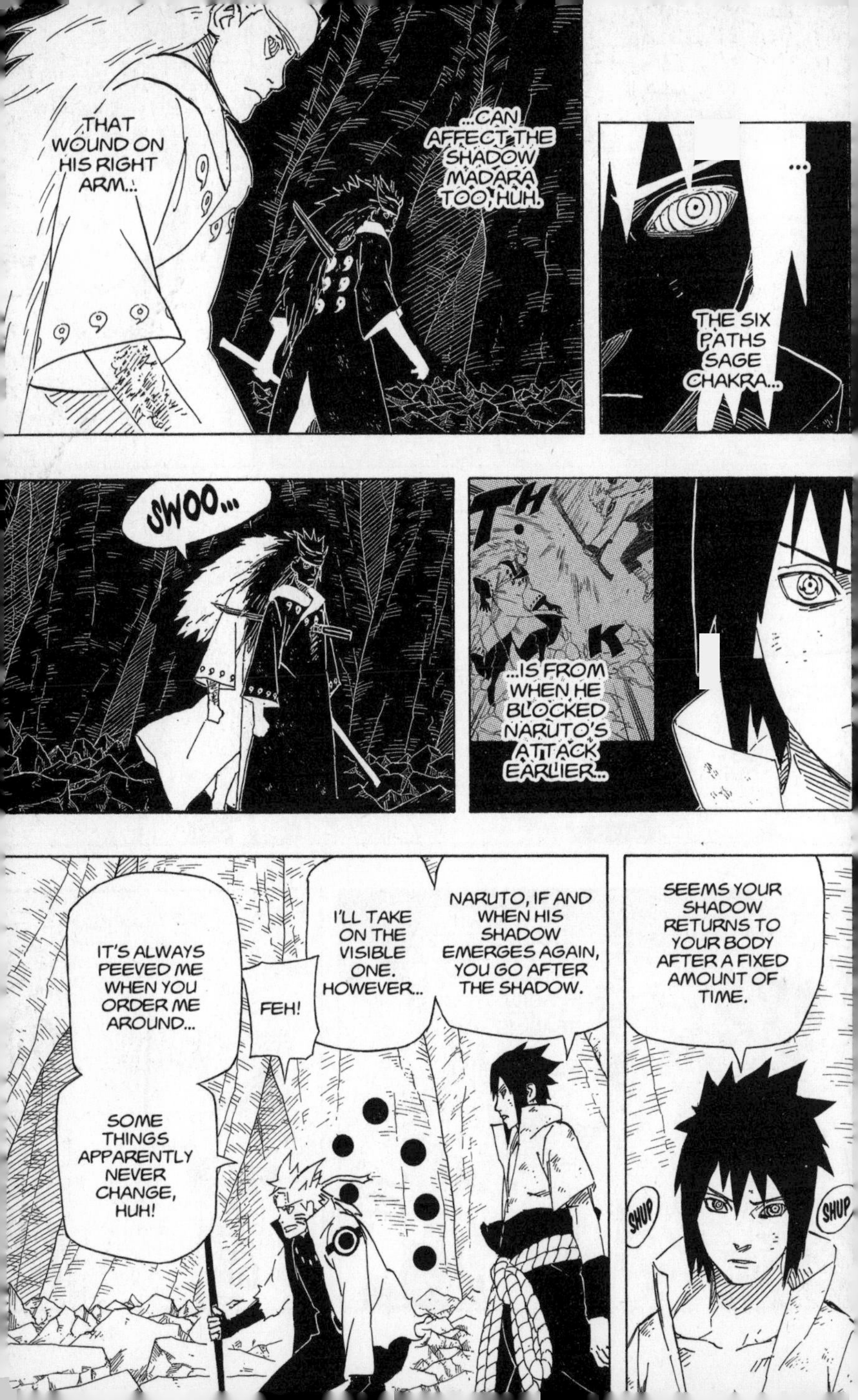
...
THE SIX PATHS SAGE CHAKRA...
...CAN AFFECT THE SHADOW MADARA TOO, HUH.
THAT WOUND ON HIS RIGHT ARM...
...IS FROM WHEN HE BLOCKED NARUTO'S ATTACK EARLIER...
TH
K
SWOO...
SEEMS YOUR SHADOW RETURNS TO YOUR BODY AFTER A FIXED AMOUNT OF TIME.
SHUP
SHUP
NARUTO, IF AND WHEN HIS SHADOW EMERGES AGAIN, YOU GO AFTER THE SHADOW.
I'LL TAKE ON THE VISIBLE ONE. HOWEVER...
FEH!
IT'S ALWAYS PEEVED ME WHEN YOU ORDER ME AROUND...
SOME THINGS APPARENTLY NEVER CHANGE, HUH!

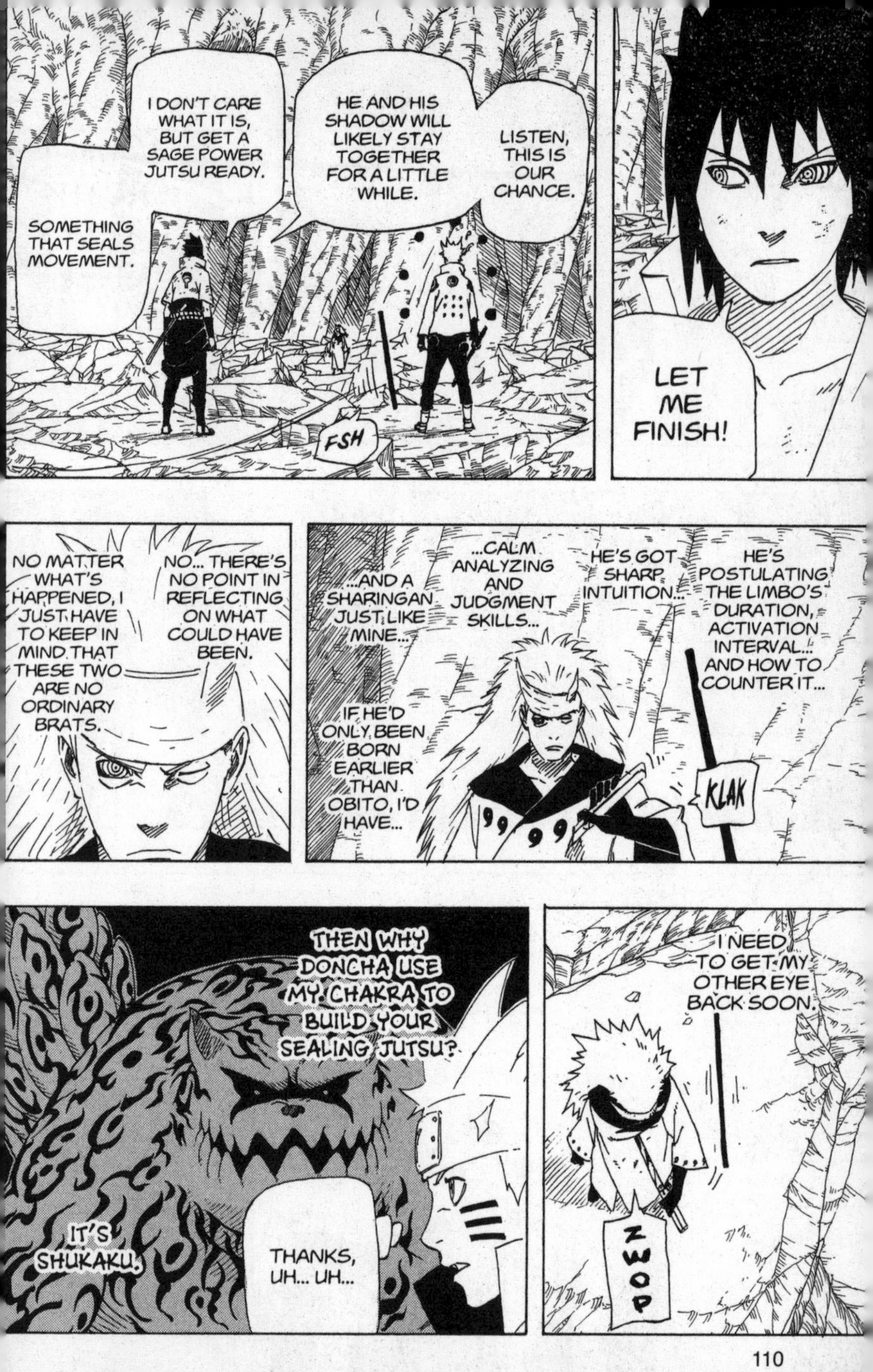
LET ME FINISH!
LISTEN, THIS IS OUR CHANCE.
HE AND HIS SHADOW WILL LIKELY STAY TOGETHER FOR A LITTLE WHILE.
I DON'T CARE WHAT IT IS, BUT GET A SAGE POWER JUTSU READY.
SOMETHING THAT SEALS MOVEMENT.
FSH
HE'S POSTULATING THE LIMBO'S DURATION, ACTIVATION INTERVAL... AND HOW TO COUNTER IT...
HE'S GOT SHARP INTUITION...
...CALM ANALYZING AND JUDGMENT SKILLS...
...AND A SHARINGAN JUST LIKE MINE...
KLAK
IF HE'D ONLY BEEN BORN EARLIER THAN OBITO, I'D HAVE...
NO... THERE'S NO POINT IN REFLECTING ON WHAT COULD HAVE BEEN.
NO MATTER WHAT'S HAPPENED, I JUST HAVE TO KEEP IN MIND THAT THESE TWO ARE NO ORDINARY BRATS.
I NEED TO GET MY OTHER EYE BACK SOON.
ZWOP
THEN WHY DONCHA USE MY CHAKRA TO BUILD YOUR SEALING JUTSU?
THANKS, UH... UH...
IT'S SHUKAKU.

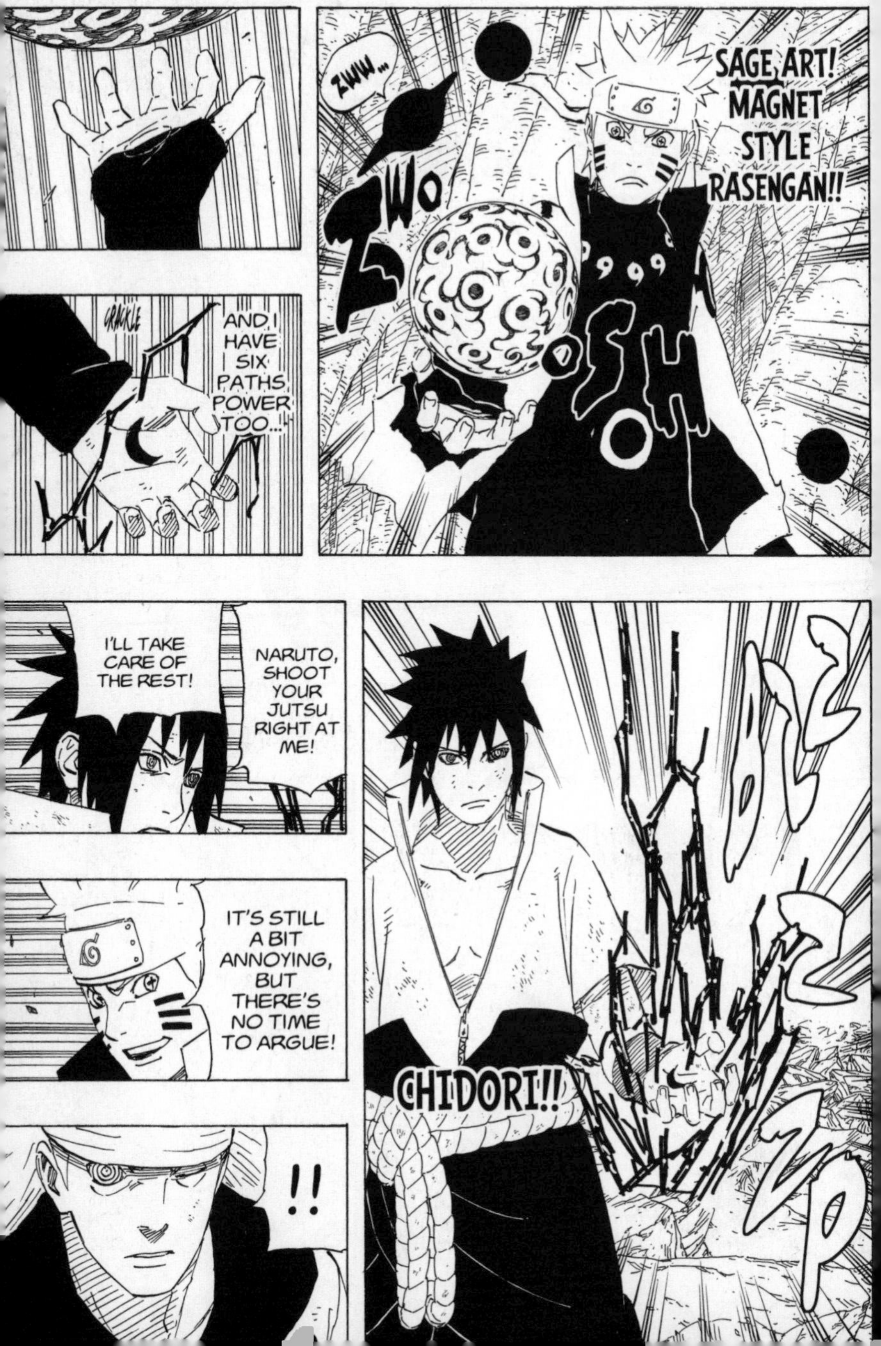
ZWW...
ZWOOSH
SAGE ART! MAGNET STYLE RASENGAN!!
CRACKLE
AND I HAVE SIX PATHS POWER TOO...
CHIDORI!!
NARUTO, SHOOT YOUR JUTSU RIGHT AT ME!
I'LL TAKE CARE OF THE REST!
IT'S STILL A BIT ANNOYING, BUT THERE'S NO TIME TO ARGUE!
!!

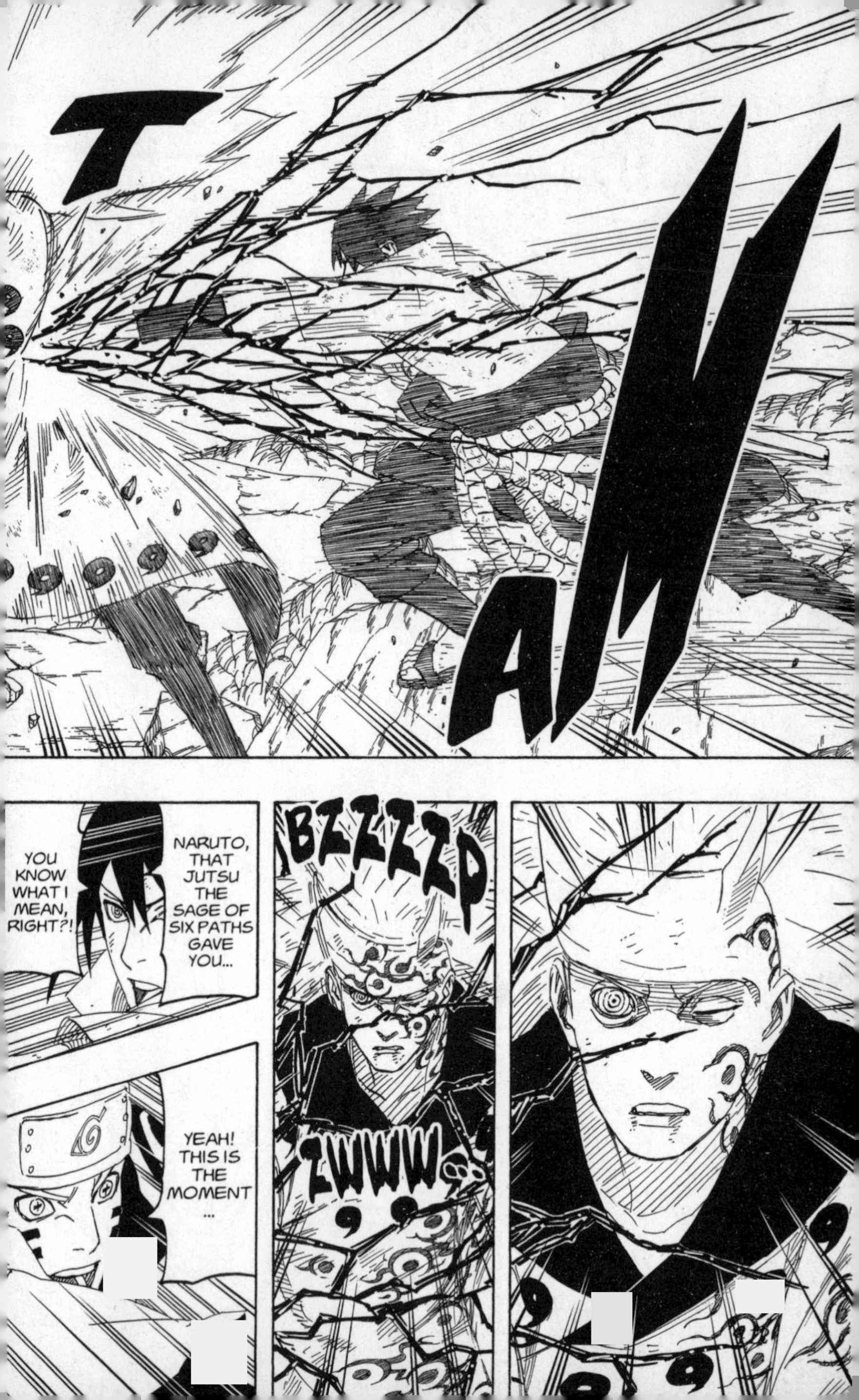
TAM
BZZZZP
ZWWW...
NARUTO, THAT JUTSU THE SAGE OF SIX PATHS GAVE YOU...
YOU KNOW WHAT I MEAN, RIGHT?!
YEAH! THIS IS THE MOMENT ...

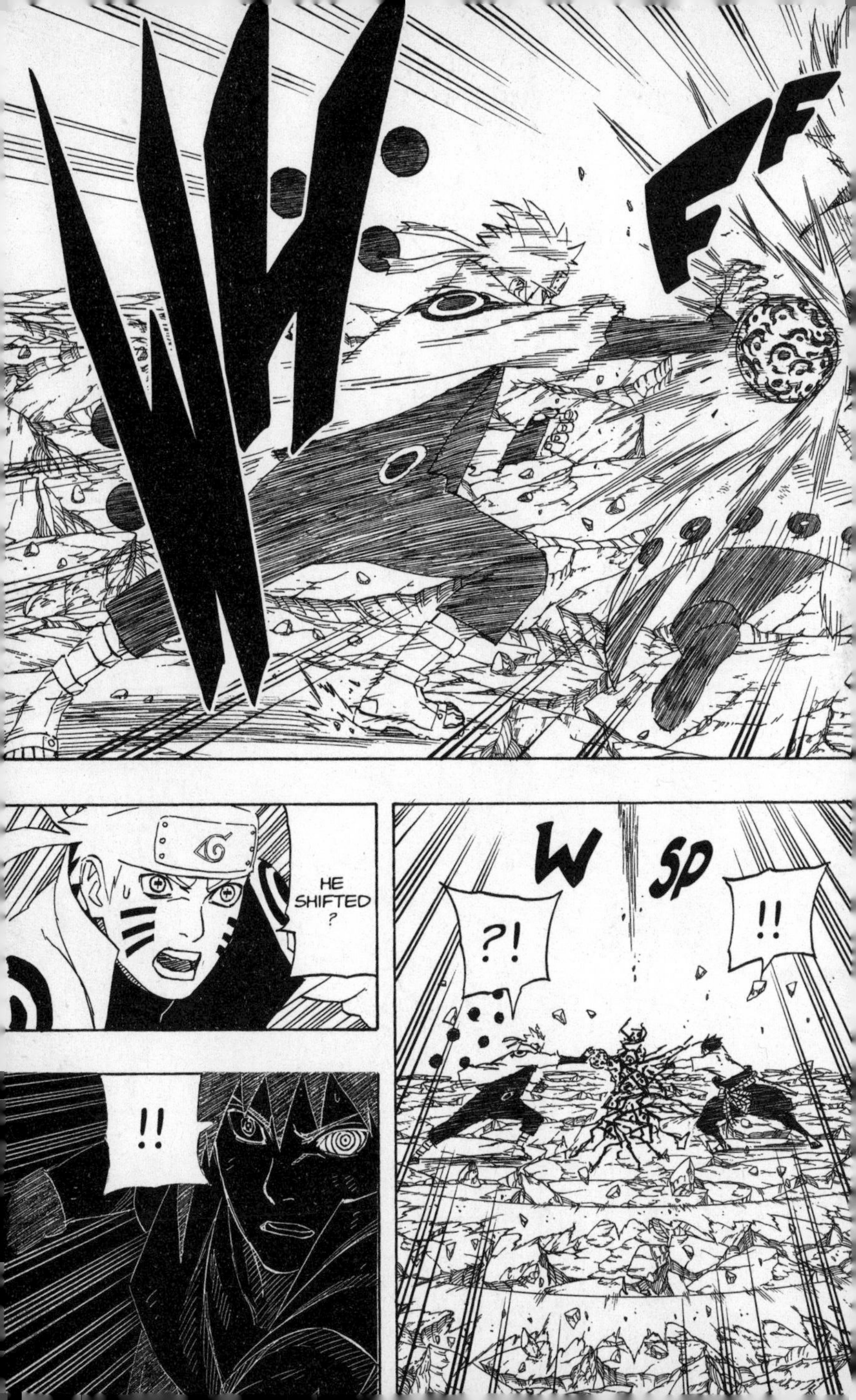
WHFF
W SP
!!
?!
HE SHIFTED?
!!

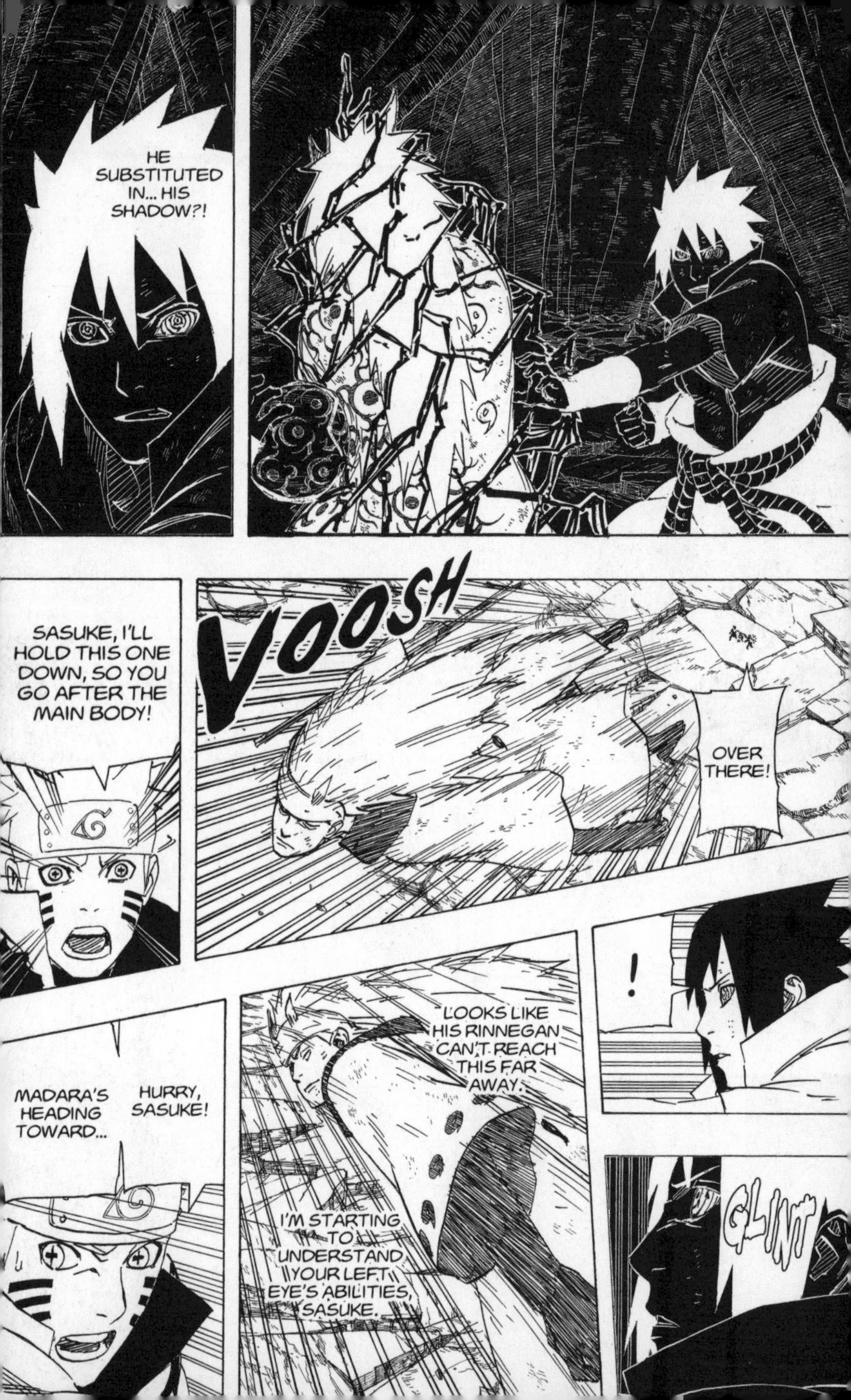
HE SUBSTITUTED IN... HIS SHADOW?!
VOOSH
OVER THERE!
SASUKE, I'LL HOLD THIS ONE DOWN, SO YOU GO AFTER THE MAIN BODY!
!
GLINT
LOOKS LIKE HIS RINNEGAN CAN'T REACH THIS FAR AWAY.
I'M STARTING TO UNDERSTAND YOUR LEFT EYE'S ABILITIES, SASUKE.
HURRY, SASUKE!
MADARA'S HEADING TOWARD...

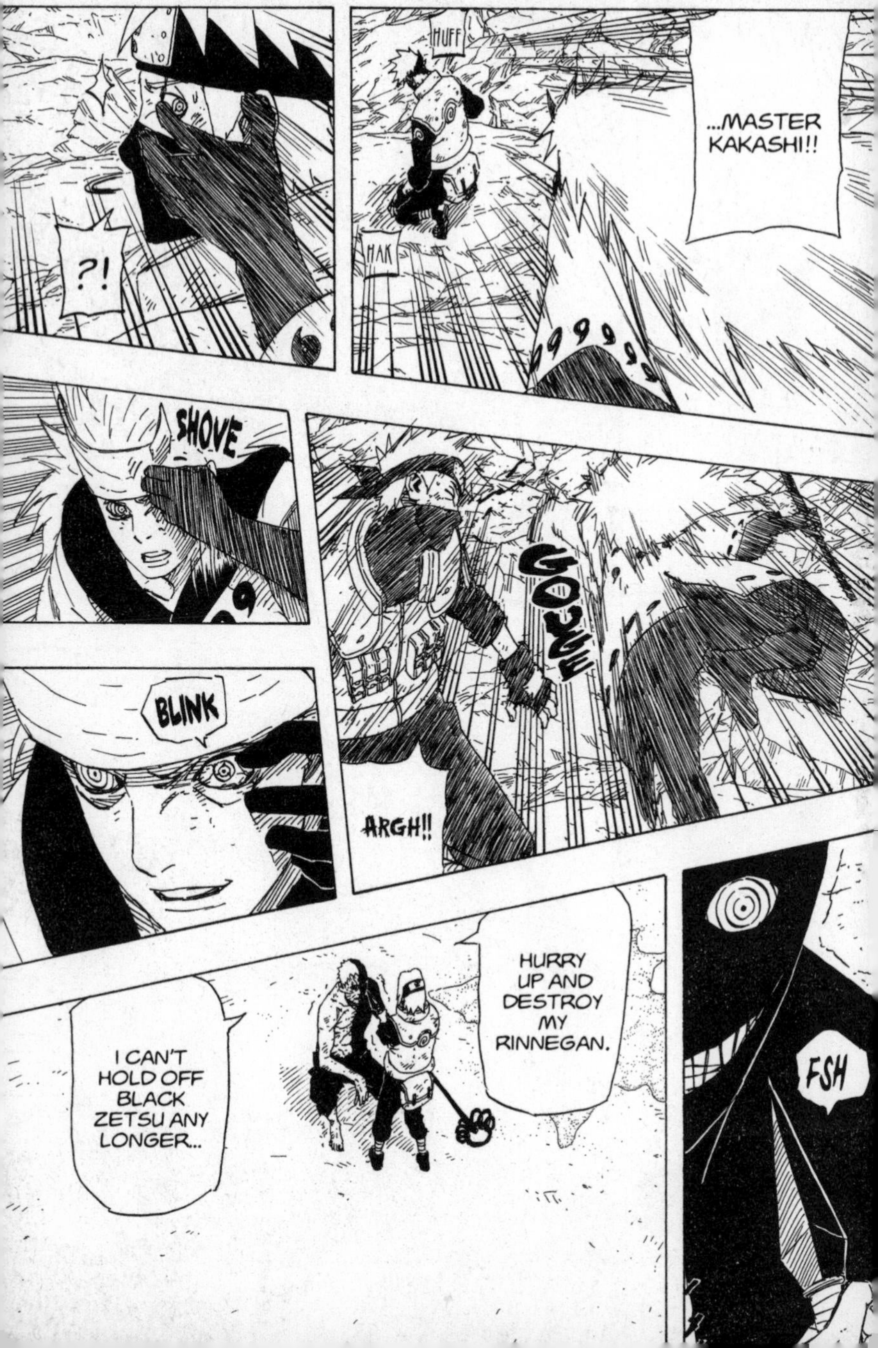
...MASTER KAKASHI!!
HUFF
HAK
?!
GOUGE
ARGH!!
SHOVE
BLINK
FSH
HURRY UP AND DESTROY MY RINNEGAN.
I CAN'T HOLD OFF BLACK ZETSU ANY LONGER...

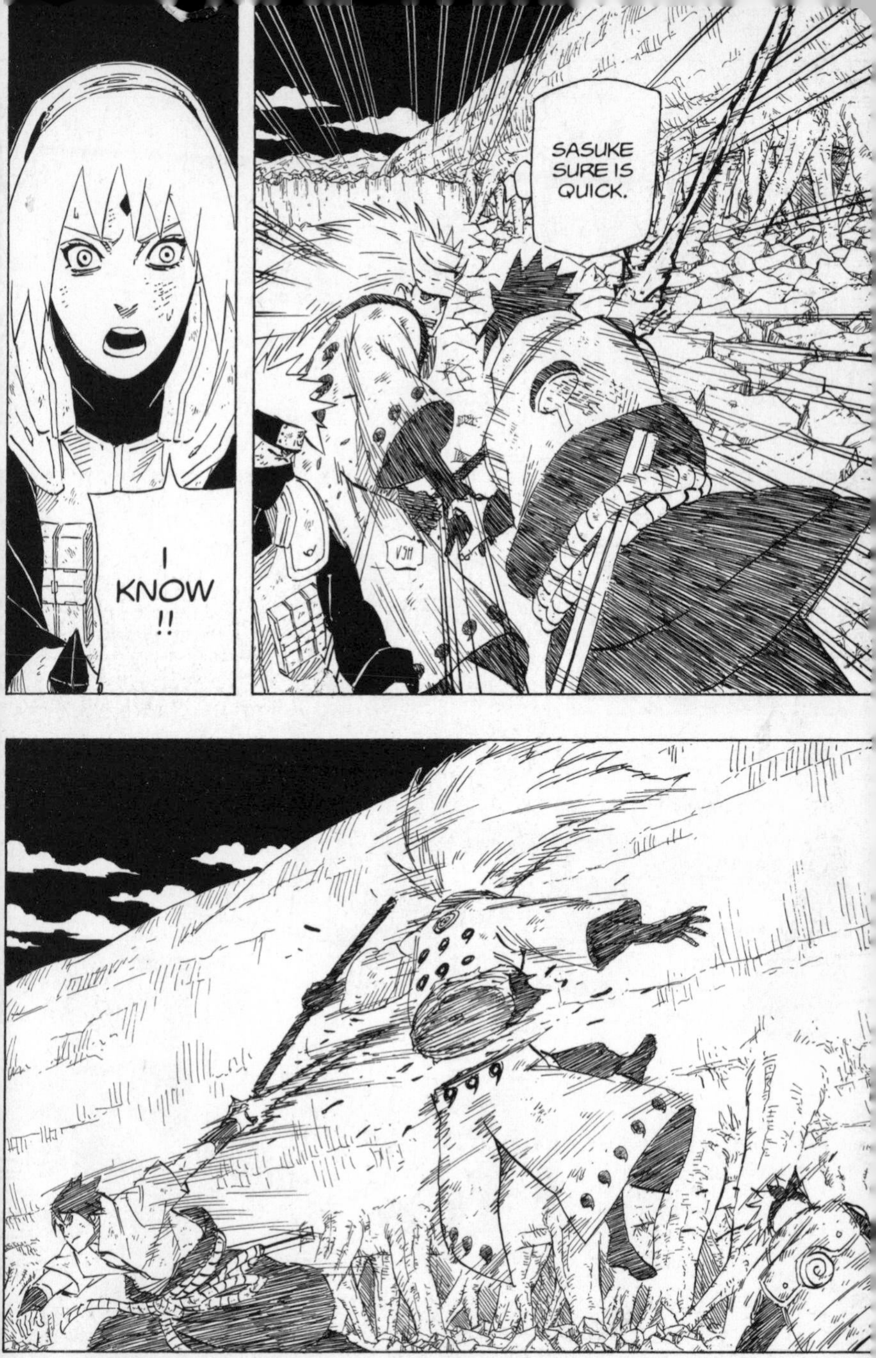
SASUKE SURE IS QUICK.
I KNOW!!

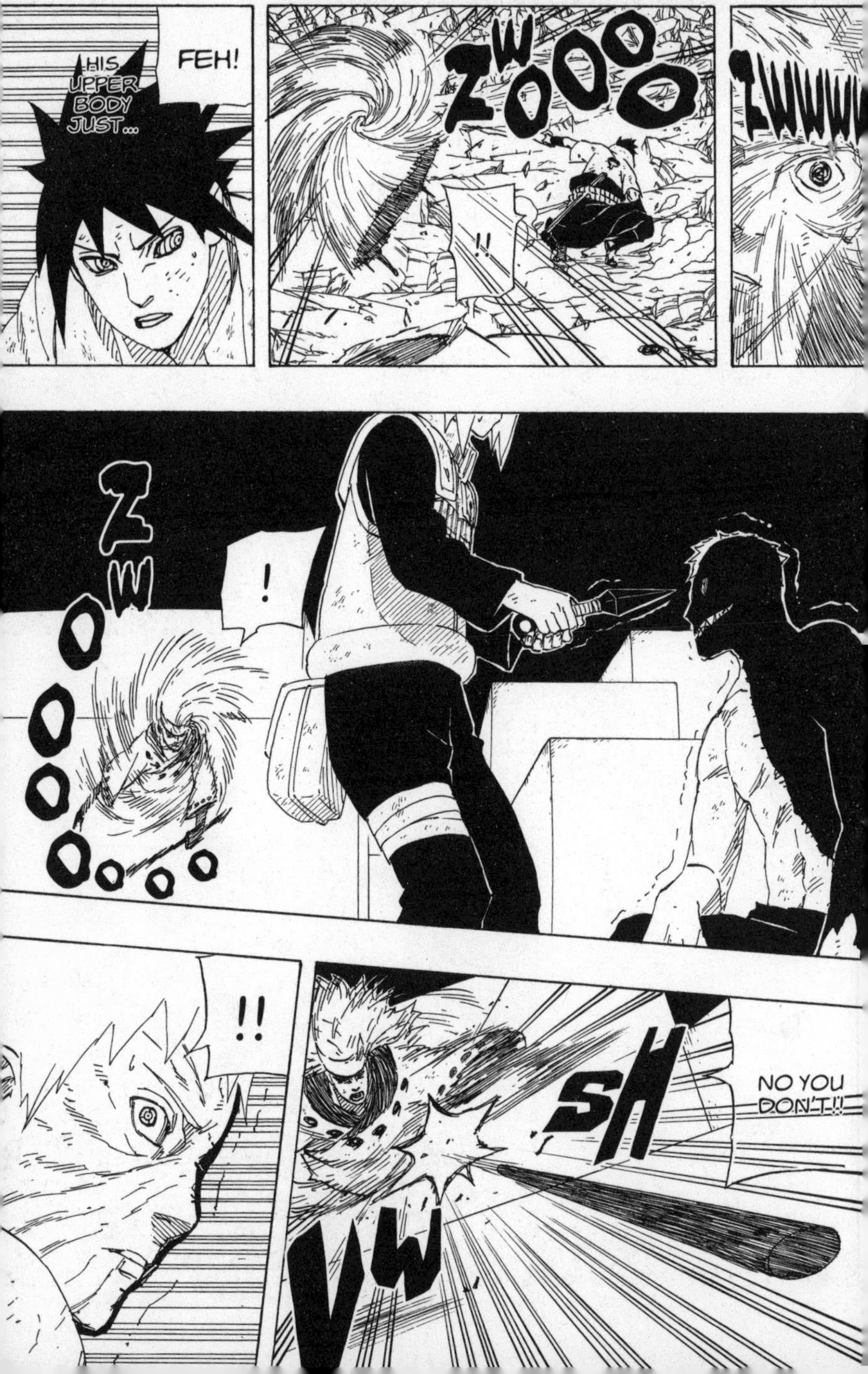
ZWWWW
ZWOOOO
!!
FEH!
HIS UPPER BODY JUST...
!
ZWOOOOOOOOO
NO YOU DON'T!!
SH
VW
!!

ZWW...
ZWOOSH

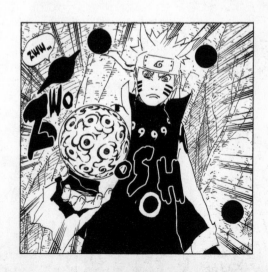

# Number 675: Your Current Dream

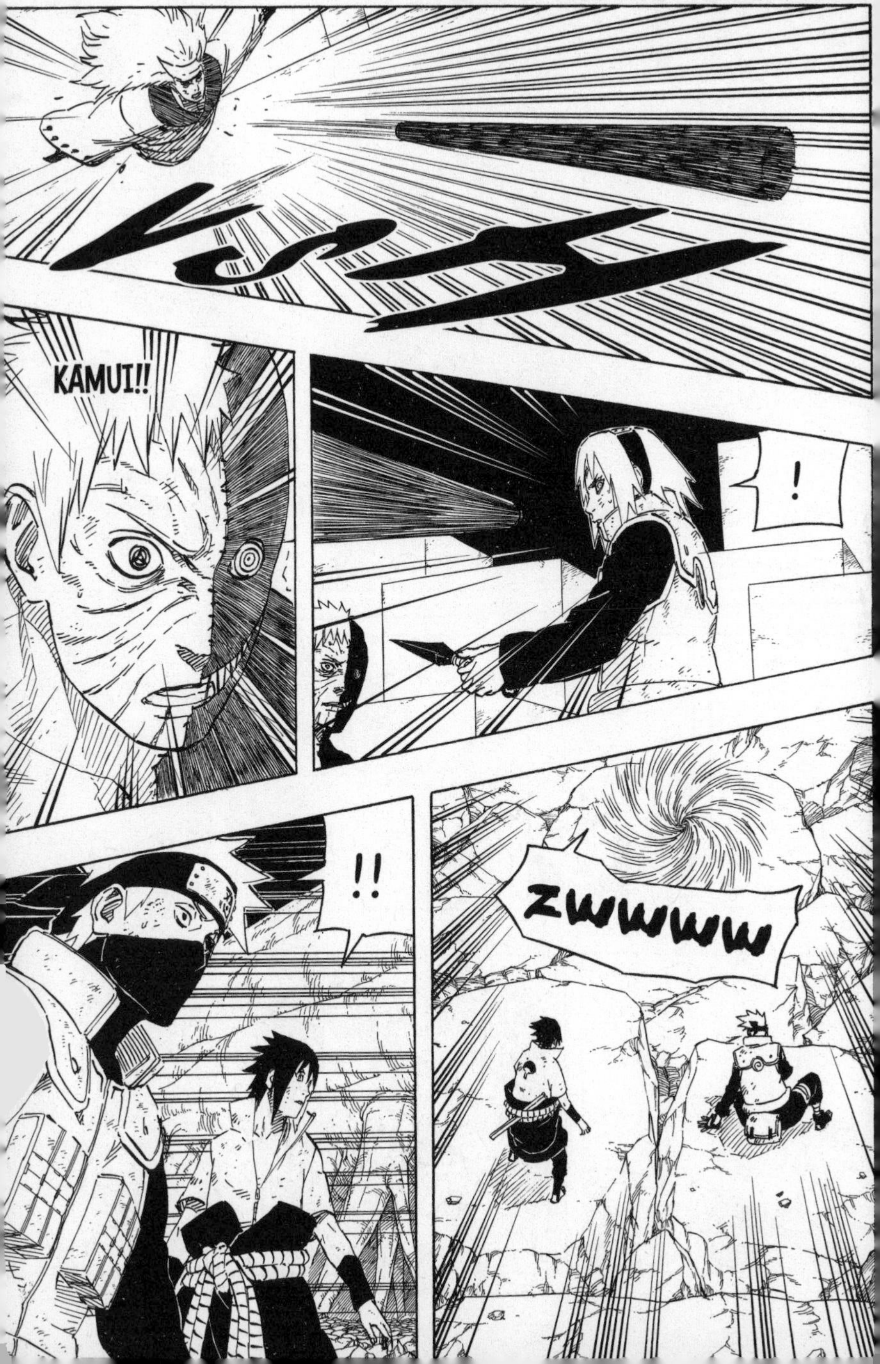
VSH
!
KAMUI!!
ZWWWWW
!!

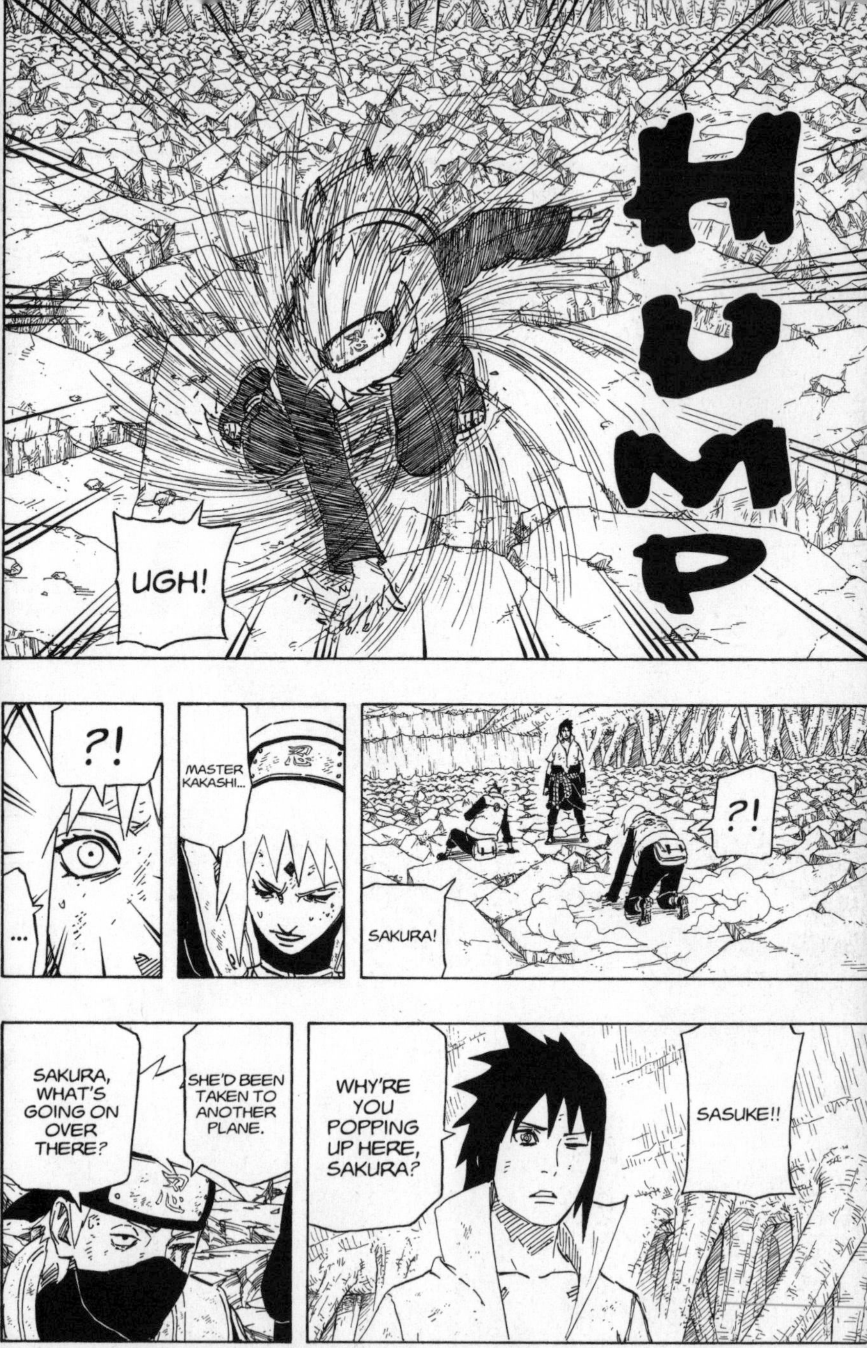
HUMP
UGH!
?!
SAKURA!
MASTER KAKASHI...
?!
...
SASUKE!!
WHY'RE YOU POPPING UP HERE, SAKURA?
SHE'D BEEN TAKEN TO ANOTHER PLANE.
SAKURA, WHAT'S GOING ON OVER THERE?

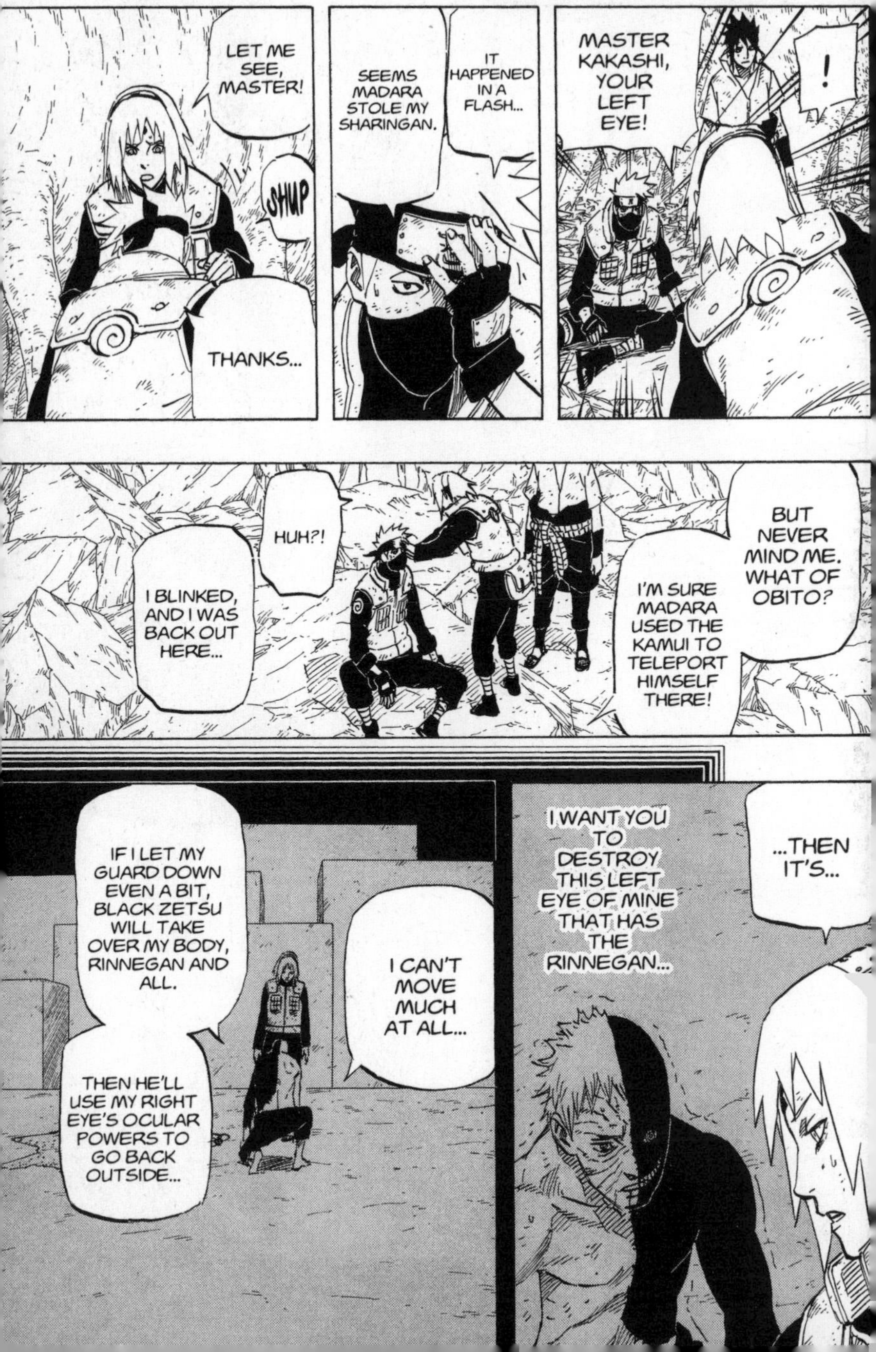
!
MASTER KAKASHI, YOUR LEFT EYE!
IT HAPPENED IN A FLASH...
SEEMS MADARA STOLE MY SHARINGAN.
LET ME SEE, MASTER!
SHUP
THANKS...
BUT NEVER MIND ME. WHAT OF OBITO?
I'M SURE MADARA USED THE KAMUI TO TELEPORT HIMSELF THERE!
HUH?!
I BLINKED, AND I WAS BACK OUT HERE...
...THEN IT'S...
I WANT YOU TO DESTROY THIS LEFT EYE OF MINE THAT HAS THE RINNEGAN...
I CAN'T MOVE MUCH AT ALL...
IF I LET MY GUARD DOWN EVEN A BIT, BLACK ZETSU WILL TAKE OVER MY BODY, RINNEGAN AND ALL.
THEN HE'LL USE MY RIGHT EYE'S OCULAR POWERS TO GO BACK OUTSIDE...

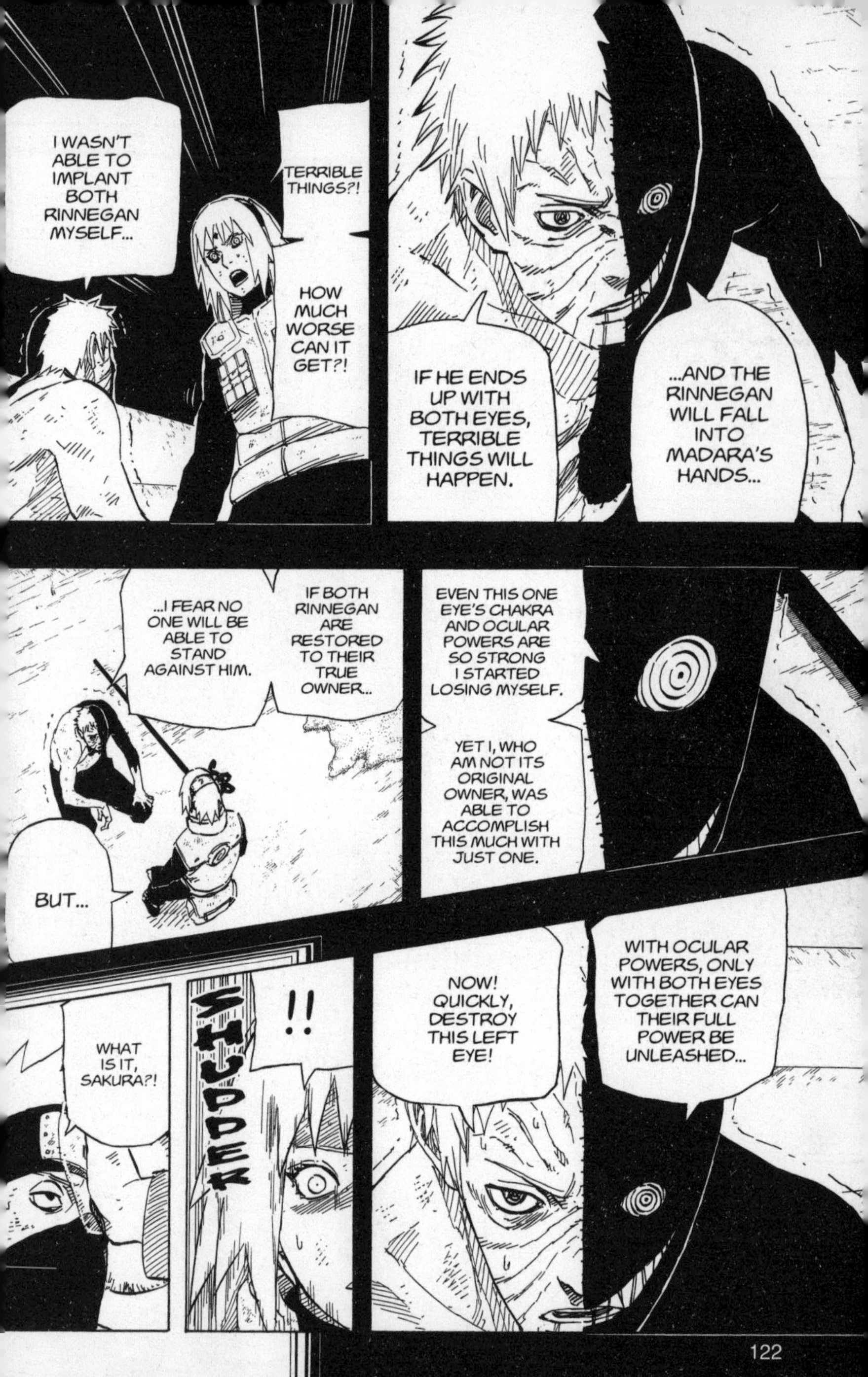
...AND THE RINNEGAN WILL FALL INTO MADARA'S HANDS...
IF HE ENDS UP WITH BOTH EYES, TERRIBLE THINGS WILL HAPPEN.
TERRIBLE THINGS?!
HOW MUCH WORSE CAN IT GET?!
I WASN'T ABLE TO IMPLANT BOTH RINNEGAN MYSELF...
EVEN THIS ONE EYE'S CHAKRA AND OCULAR POWERS ARE SO STRONG I STARTED LOSING MYSELF.
YET I, WHO AM NOT ITS ORIGINAL OWNER, WAS ABLE TO ACCOMPLISH THIS MUCH WITH JUST ONE.
IF BOTH RINNEGAN ARE RESTORED TO THEIR TRUE OWNER...
...I FEAR NO ONE WILL BE ABLE TO STAND AGAINST HIM.
BUT...
WITH OCULAR POWERS, ONLY WITH BOTH EYES TOGETHER CAN THEIR FULL POWER BE UNLEASHED...
NOW! QUICKLY, DESTROY THIS LEFT EYE!
!!
SHUDDER
WHAT IS IT, SAKURA?!

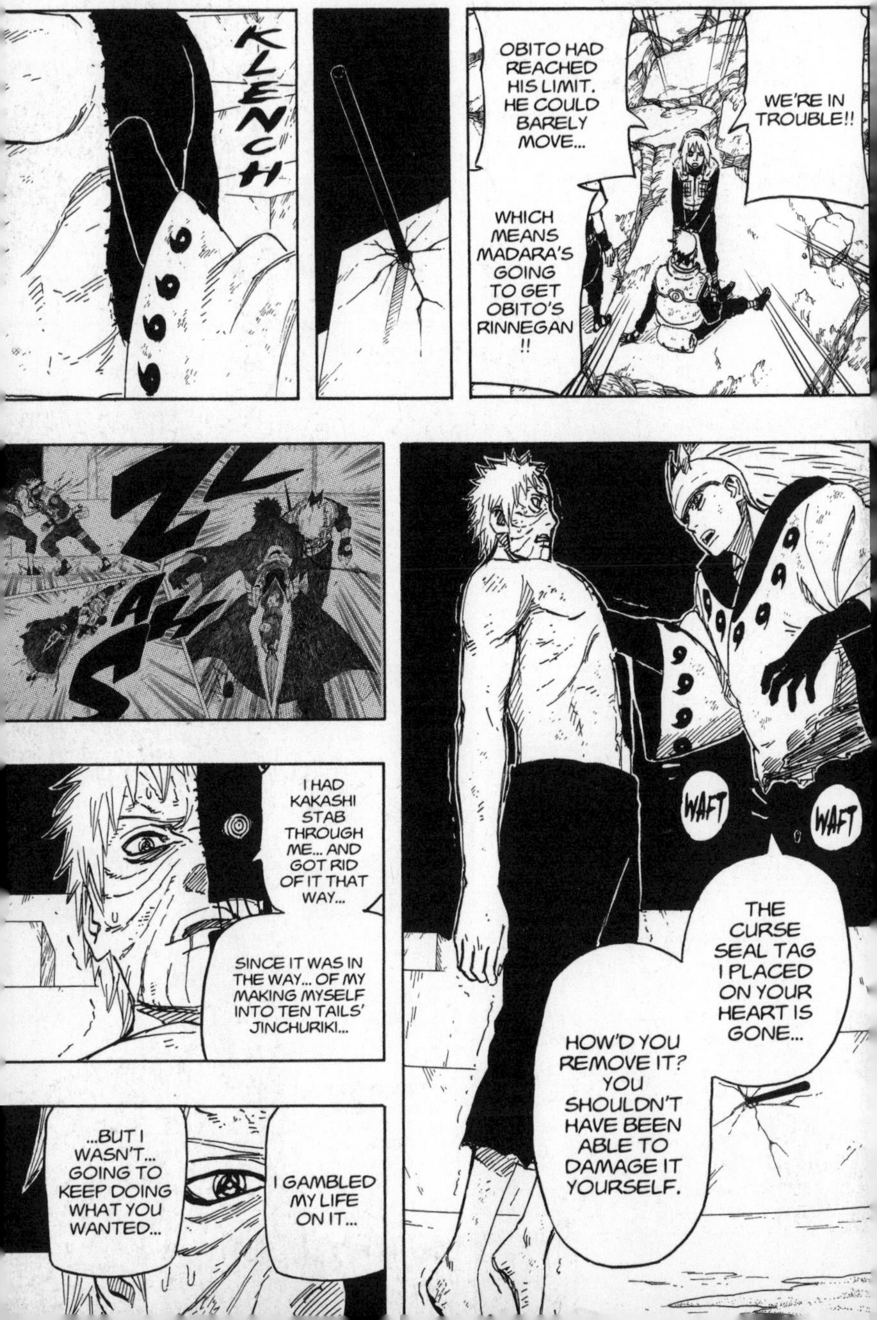
WE'RE IN TROUBLE!!
OBITO HAD REACHED HIS LIMIT. HE COULD BARELY MOVE...
WHICH MEANS MADARA'S GOING TO GET OBITO'S RINNEGAN!!
KLENCH
THE CURSE SEAL TAG I PLACED ON YOUR HEART IS GONE...
HOW'D YOU REMOVE IT? YOU SHOULDN'T HAVE BEEN ABLE TO DAMAGE IT YOURSELF.
WAFT
WAFT
I HAD KAKASHI STAB THROUGH ME... AND GOT RID OF IT THAT WAY...
SINCE IT WAS IN THE WAY... OF MY MAKING MYSELF INTO TEN TAILS' JINCHURIKI...
I GAMBLED MY LIFE ON IT...
...BUT I WASN'T... GOING TO KEEP DOING WHAT YOU WANTED...

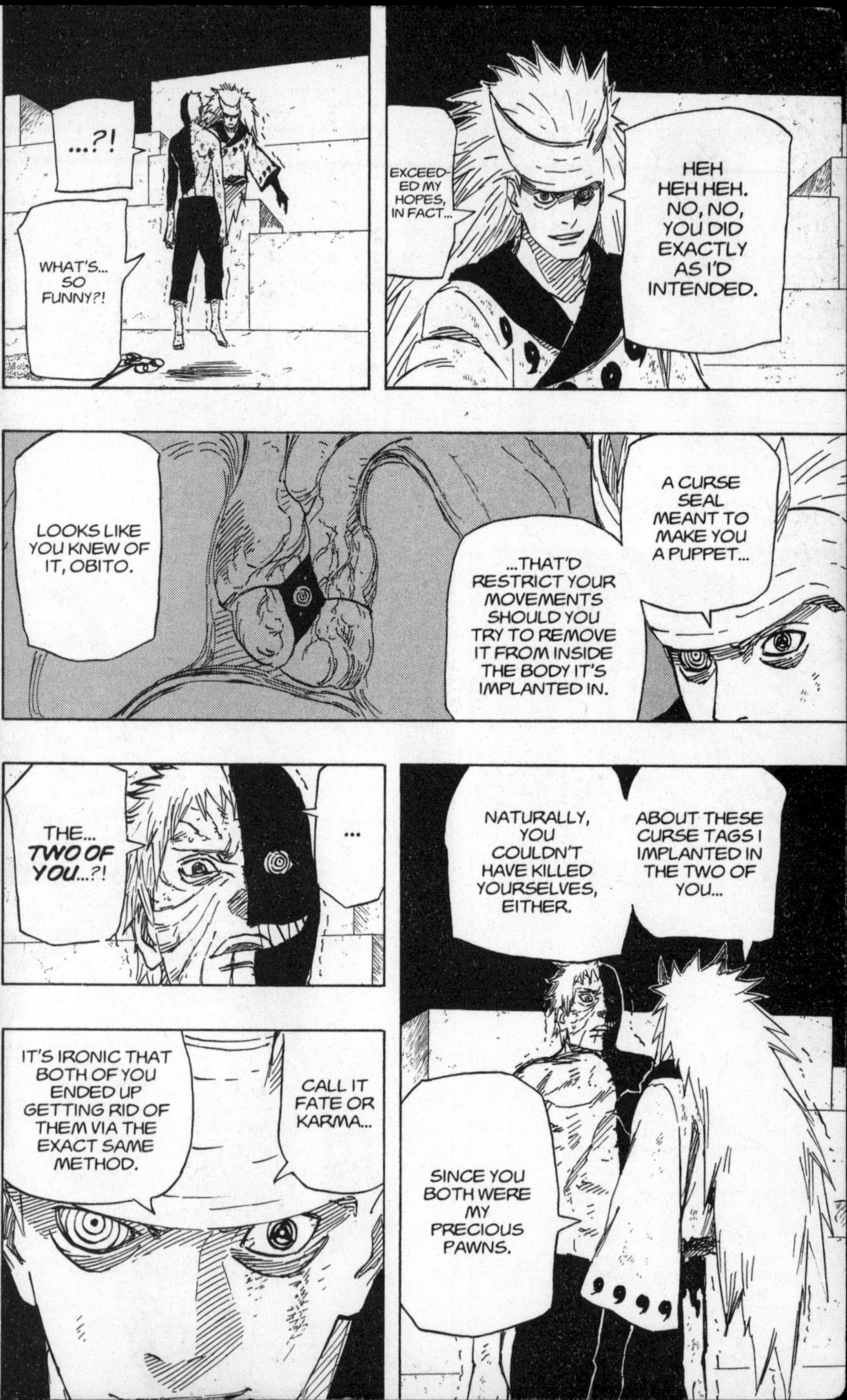
HEH HEH HEH. NO, NO, YOU DID EXACTLY AS I'D INTENDED.
EXCEEDED MY HOPES, IN FACT...
...?!
WHAT'S... SO FUNNY?!
A CURSE SEAL MEANT TO MAKE YOU A PUPPET...
...THAT'D RESTRICT YOUR MOVEMENTS SHOULD YOU TRY TO REMOVE IT FROM INSIDE THE BODY IT'S IMPLANTED IN.
LOOKS LIKE YOU KNEW OF IT, OBITO.
ABOUT THESE CURSE TAGS I IMPLANTED IN THE TWO OF YOU...
NATURALLY, YOU COULDN'T HAVE KILLED YOURSELVES, EITHER.
SINCE YOU BOTH WERE MY PRECIOUS PAWNS.
...
THE... *TWO OF YOU*...?!
CALL IT FATE OR KARMA...
IT'S IRONIC THAT BOTH OF YOU ENDED UP GETTING RID OF THEM VIA THE EXACT SAME METHOD.

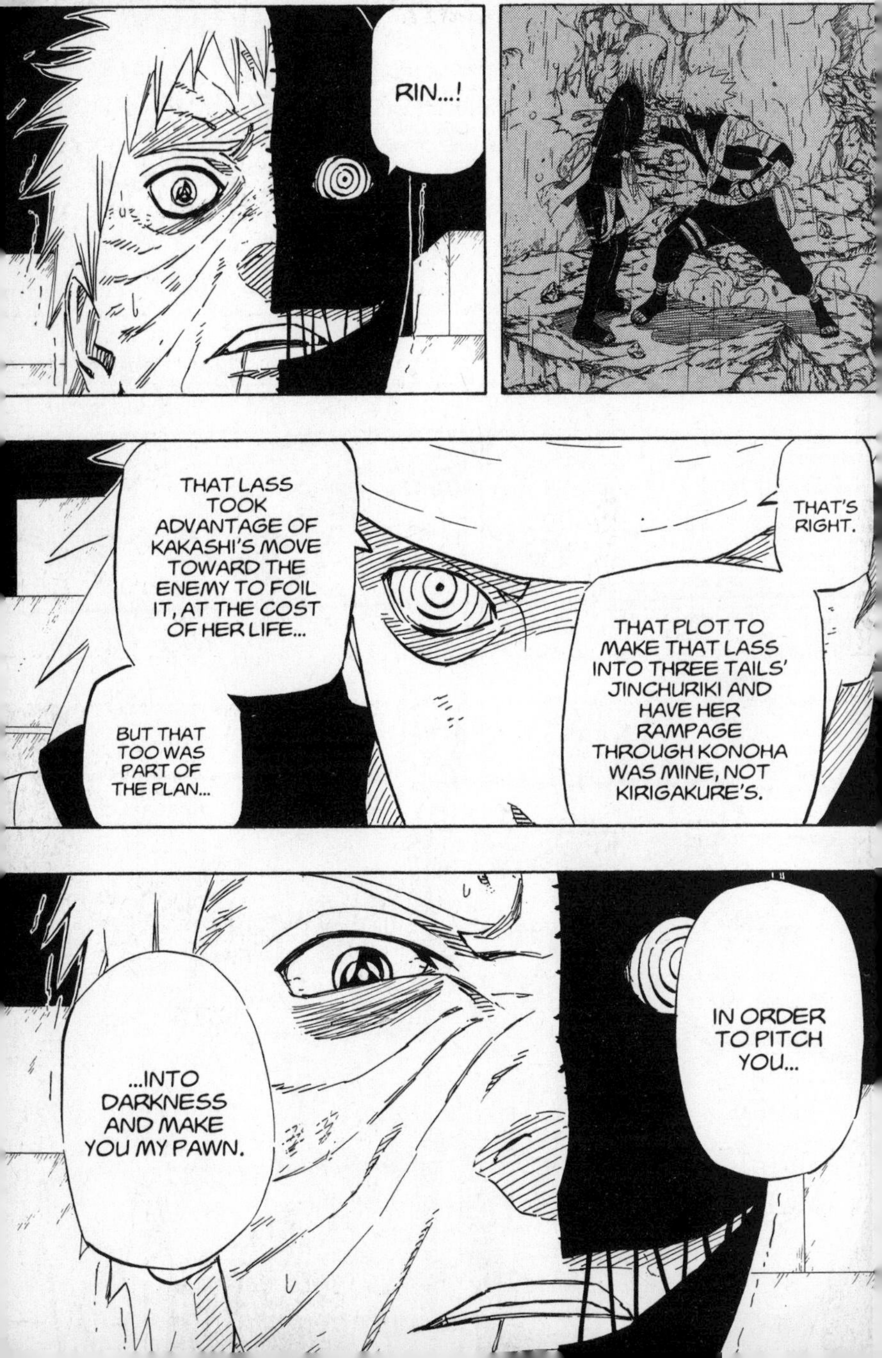
RIN...!
THAT'S RIGHT.
THAT PLOT TO MAKE THAT LASS INTO THREE TAILS' JINCHURIKI AND HAVE HER RAMPAGE THROUGH KONOHA WAS MINE, NOT KIRIGAKURE'S.
THAT LASS TOOK ADVANTAGE OF KAKASHI'S MOVE TOWARD THE ENEMY TO FOIL IT, AT THE COST OF HER LIFE...
BUT THAT TOO WAS PART OF THE PLAN...
IN ORDER TO PITCH YOU...
...INTO DARKNESS AND MAKE YOU MY PAWN.

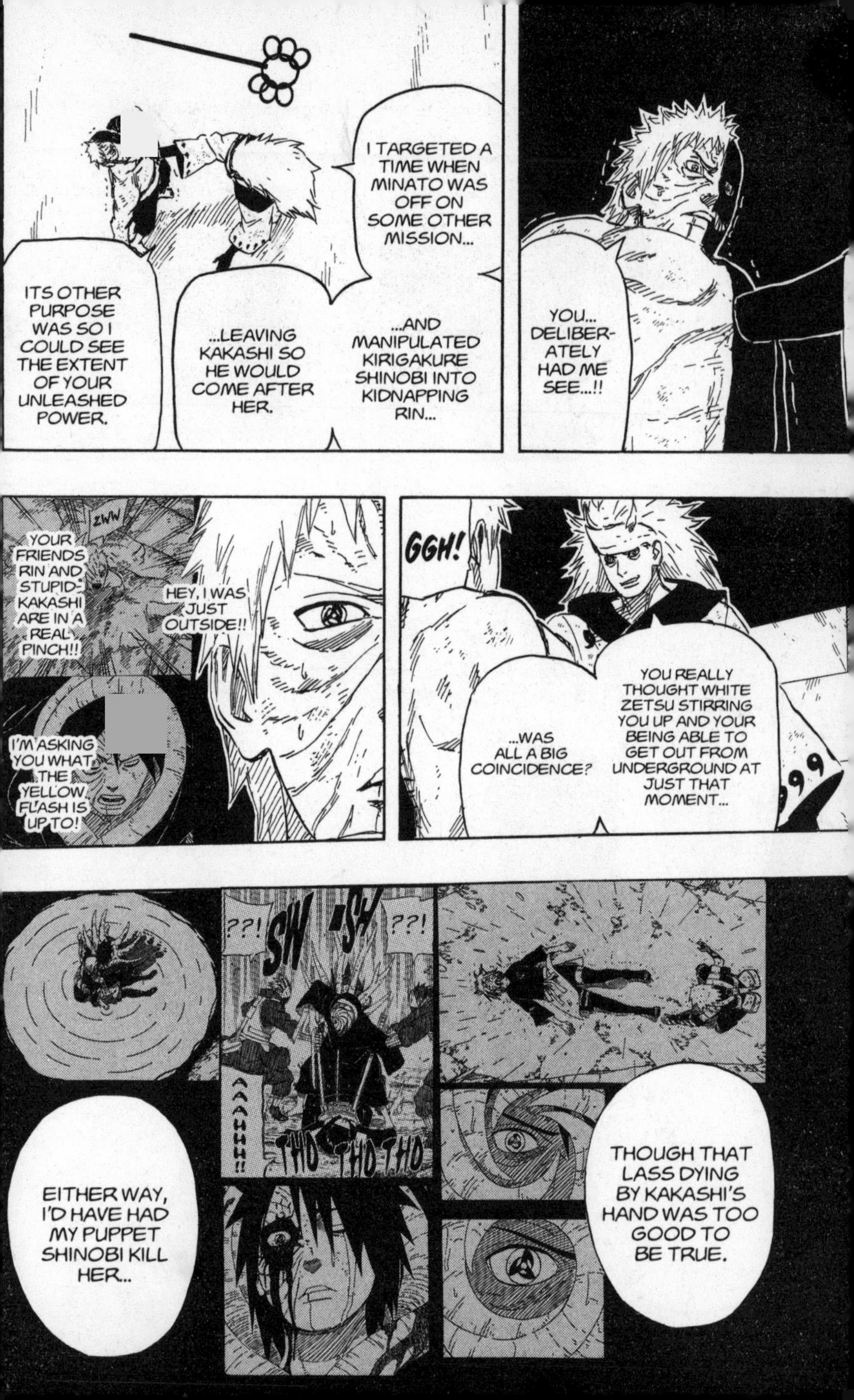
YOU... DELIBER-ATELY HAD ME SEE...!!
I TARGETED A TIME WHEN MINATO WAS OFF ON SOME OTHER MISSION...
...AND MANIPULATED KIRIGAKURE SHINOBI INTO KIDNAPPING RIN...
...LEAVING KAKASHI SO HE WOULD COME AFTER HER.
ITS OTHER PURPOSE WAS SO I COULD SEE THE EXTENT OF YOUR UNLEASHED POWER.
GGH!
YOU REALLY THOUGHT WHITE ZETSU STIRRING YOU UP AND YOUR BEING ABLE TO GET OUT FROM UNDERGROUND AT JUST THAT MOMENT...
...WAS ALL A BIG COINCIDENCE?
HEY, I WAS JUST OUTSIDE!!
ZWW
YOUR FRIENDS RIN AND STUPID-KAKASHI ARE IN A REAL PINCH!!
I'M ASKING YOU WHAT THE YELLOW FLASH IS UP TO!
THOUGH THAT LASS DYING BY KAKASHI'S HAND WAS TOO GOOD TO BE TRUE.
??!
SH
SH
??!
AAAHHH!!
THD THD THD
EITHER WAY, I'D HAVE HAD MY PUPPET SHINOBI KILL HER...

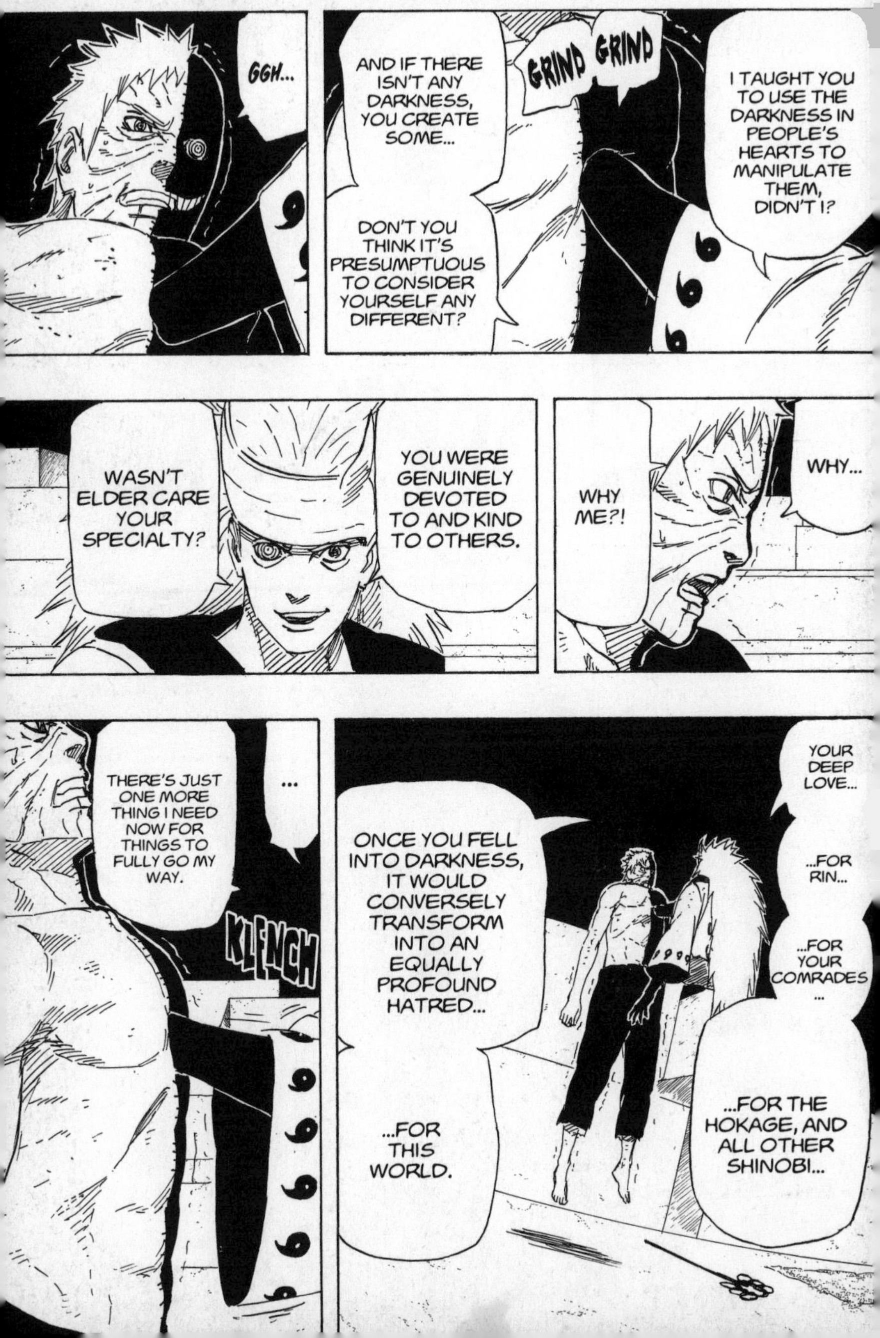
I TAUGHT YOU TO USE THE DARKNESS IN PEOPLE'S HEARTS TO MANIPULATE THEM, DIDN'T I?
GRIND GRIND
AND IF THERE ISN'T ANY DARKNESS, YOU CREATE SOME...
DON'T YOU THINK IT'S PRESUMPTUOUS TO CONSIDER YOURSELF ANY DIFFERENT?
GGH...
WHY...
WHY ME?!
YOU WERE GENUINELY DEVOTED TO AND KIND TO OTHERS.
WASN'T ELDER CARE YOUR SPECIALTY?
YOUR DEEP LOVE...
...FOR RIN...
...FOR YOUR COMRADES...
...FOR THE HOKAGE, AND ALL OTHER SHINOBI...
...FOR THIS WORLD.
ONCE YOU FELL INTO DARKNESS, IT WOULD CONVERSELY TRANSFORM INTO AN EQUALLY PROFOUND HATRED...
...
THERE'S JUST ONE MORE THING I NEED NOW FOR THINGS TO FULLY GO MY WAY.
KLENCH

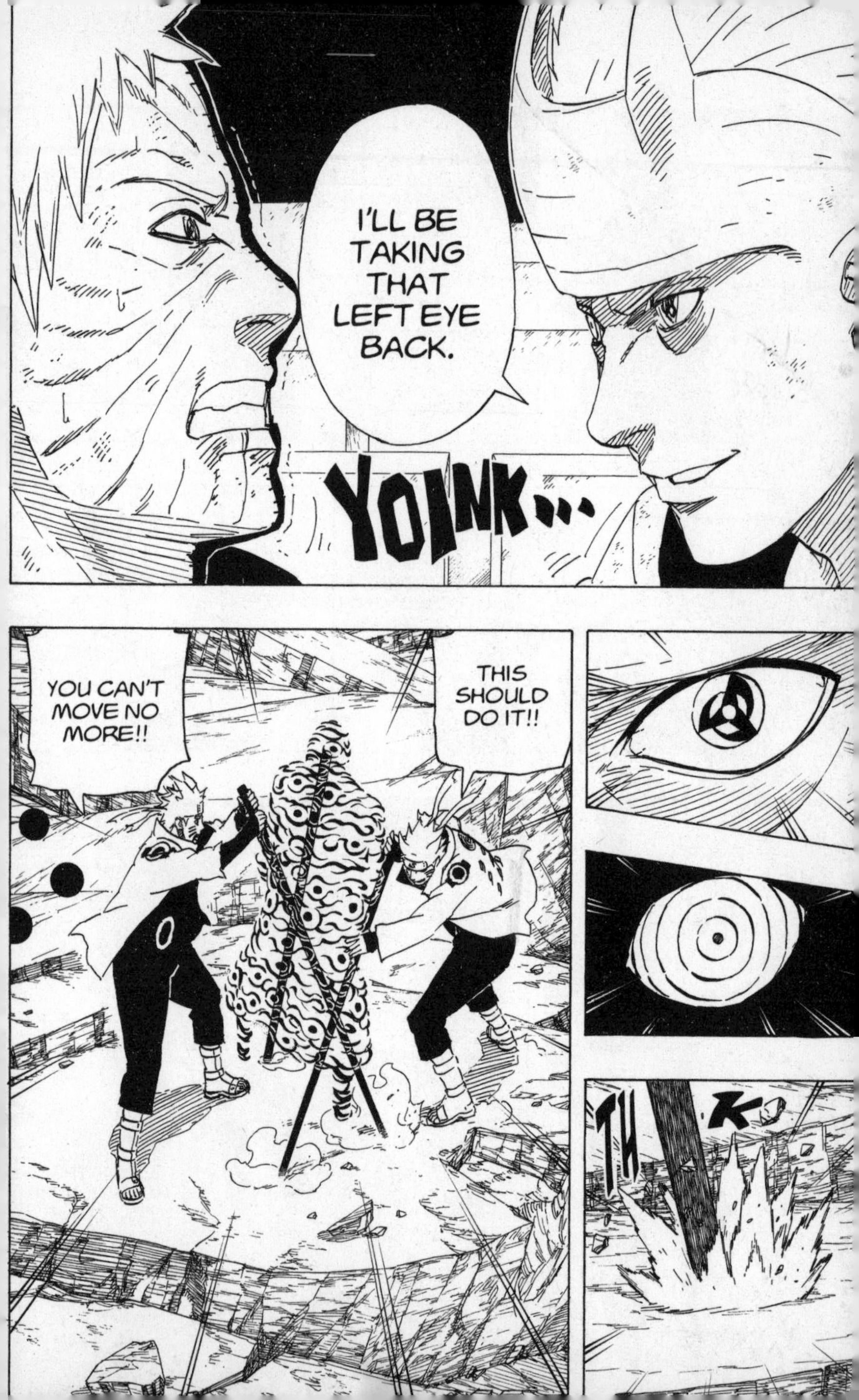
I'LL BE TAKING THAT LEFT EYE BACK.
YOINK...
TH K
THIS SHOULD DO IT!!
YOU CAN'T MOVE NO MORE!!

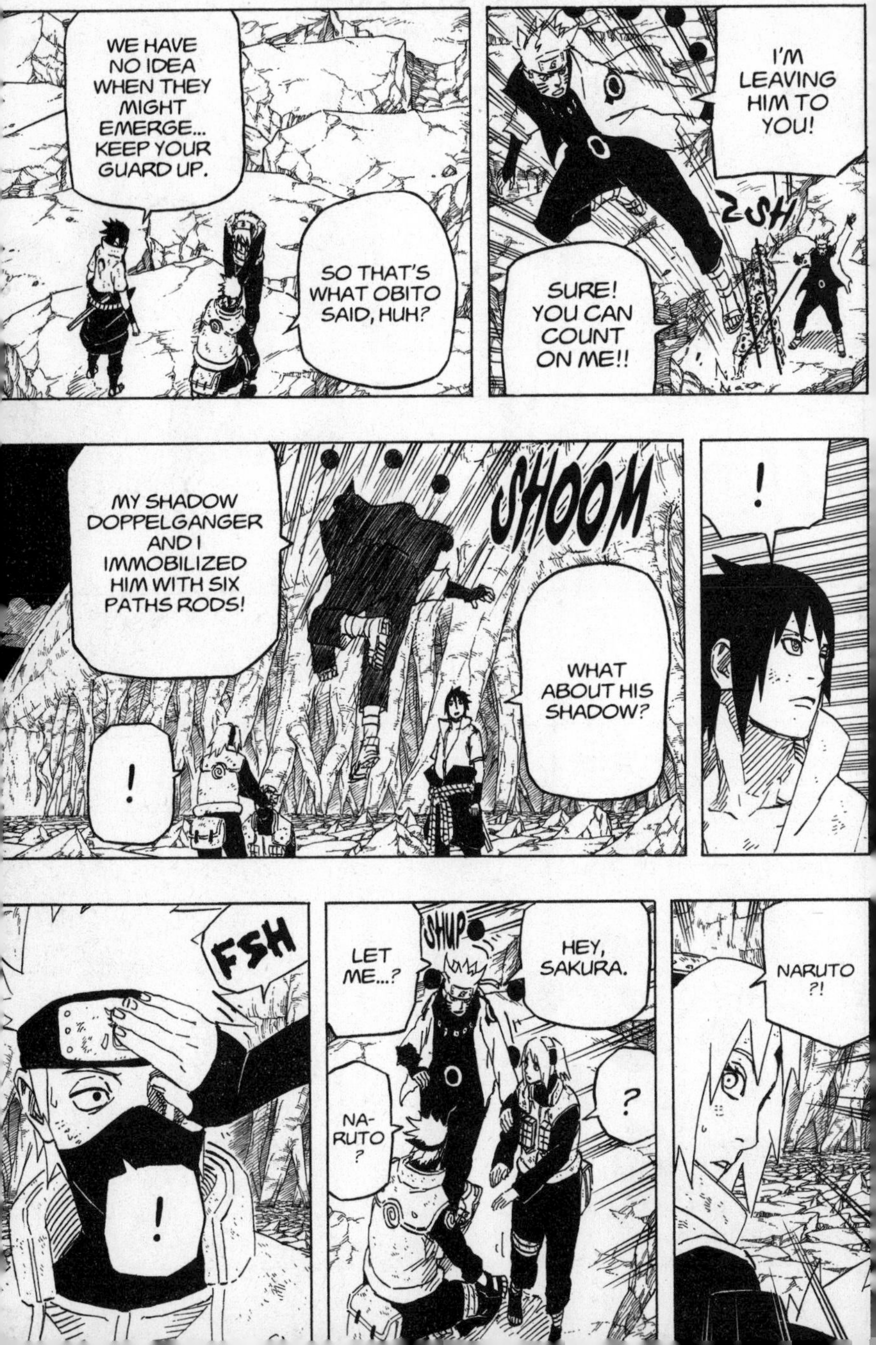
I'M LEAVING HIM TO YOU!
ZSH
SURE! YOU CAN COUNT ON ME!!
WE HAVE NO IDEA WHEN THEY MIGHT EMERGE... KEEP YOUR GUARD UP.
SO THAT'S WHAT OBITO SAID, HUH?
!
SHOOM
WHAT ABOUT HIS SHADOW?
MY SHADOW DOPPELGANGER AND I IMMOBILIZED HIM WITH SIX PATHS RODS!
!
NARUTO ?!
HEY, SAKURA.
SHUP
LET ME...?
?
NA-RUTO ?
FSH
!

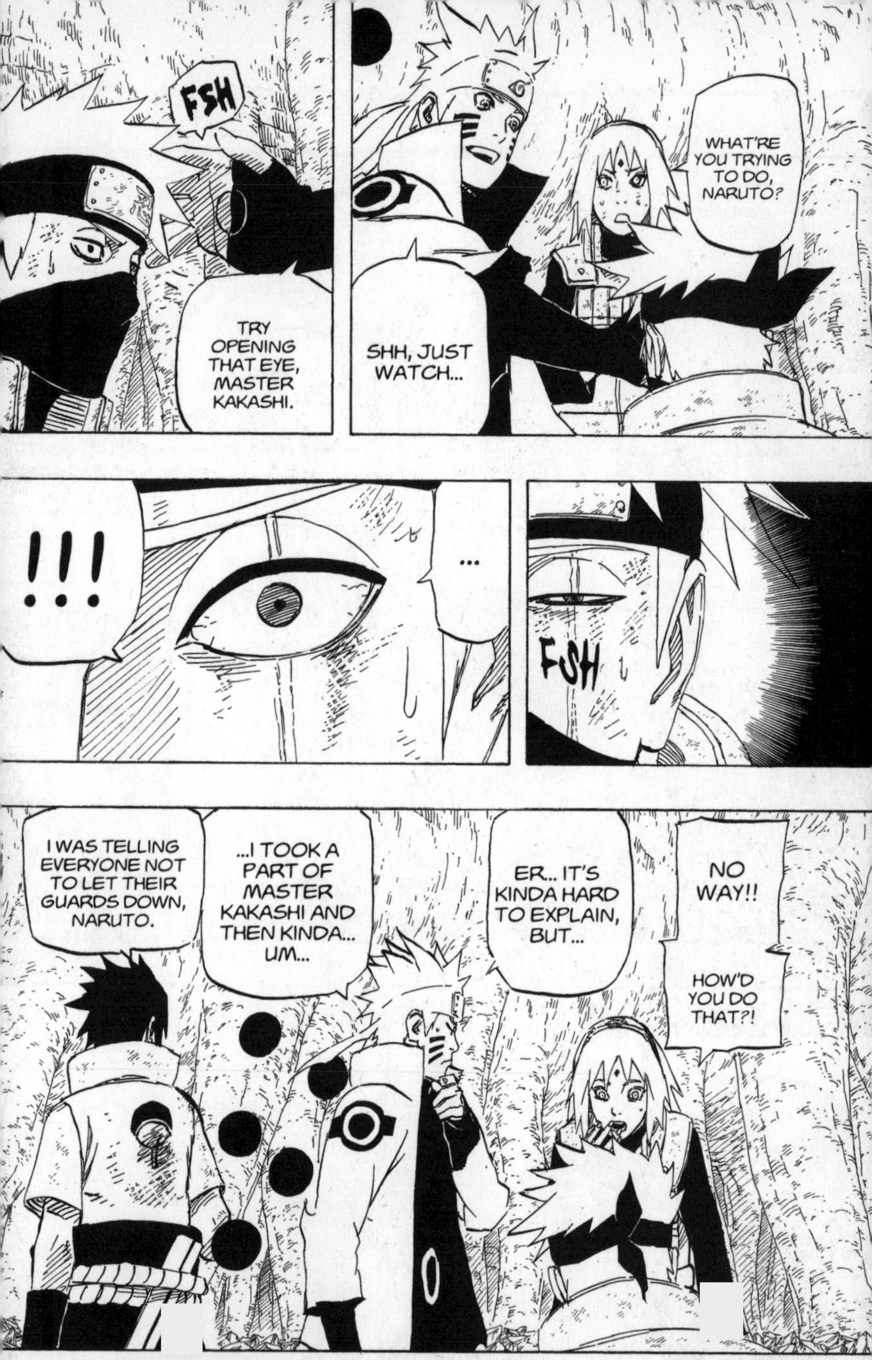
WHAT'RE YOU TRYING TO DO, NARUTO?
SHH, JUST WATCH...
FSH
TRY OPENING THAT EYE, MASTER KAKASHI.
FSH
...
!!!
NO WAY!!
HOW'D YOU DO THAT?!
ER... IT'S KINDA HARD TO EXPLAIN, BUT...
...I TOOK A PART OF MASTER KAKASHI AND THEN KINDA... UM...
I WAS TELLING EVERYONE NOT TO LET THEIR GUARDS DOWN, NARUTO.

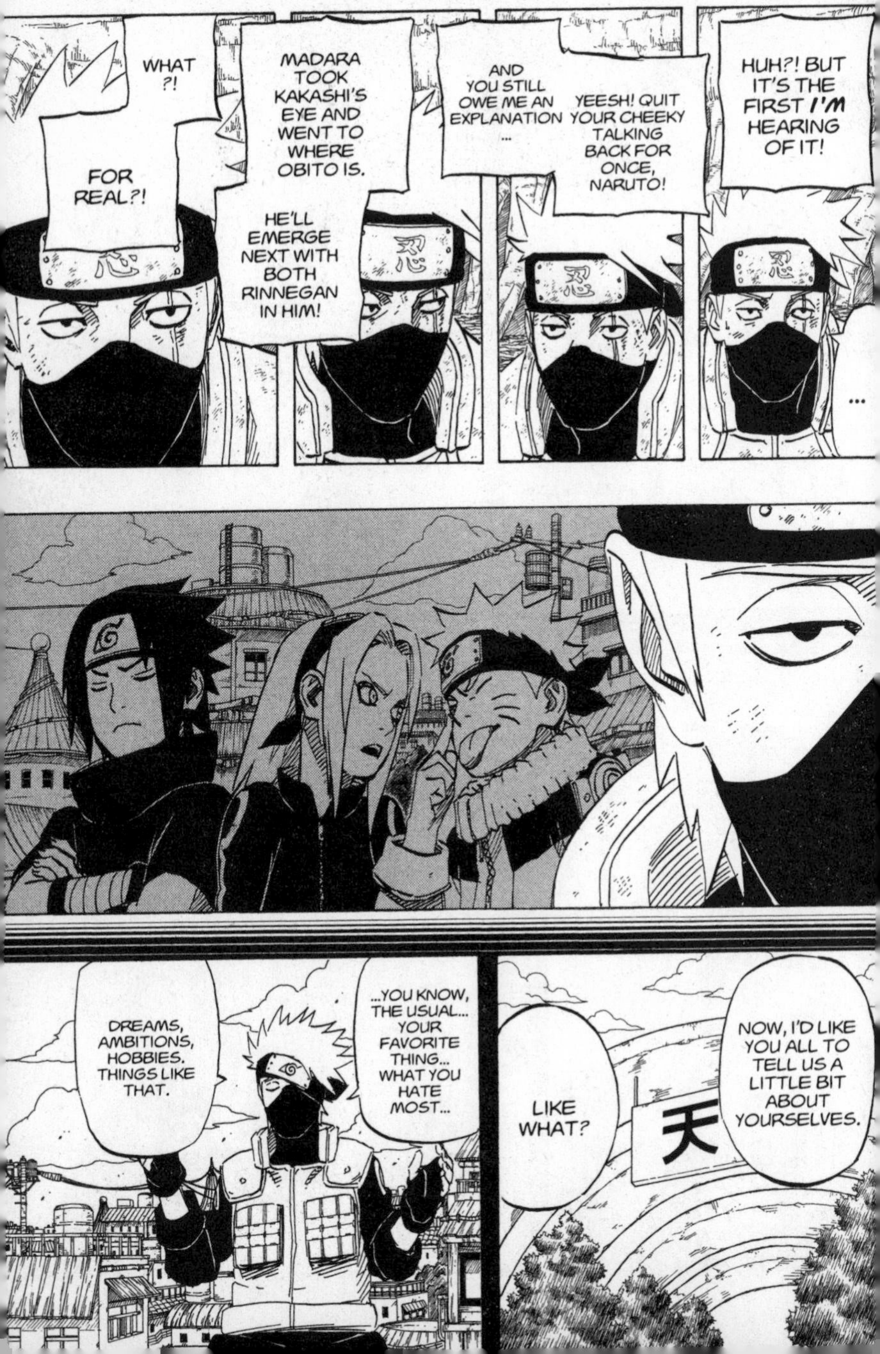
HUH?! BUT IT'S THE FIRST I'M HEARING OF IT!
...
YEESH! QUIT YOUR CHEEKY TALKING BACK FOR ONCE, NARUTO!
AND YOU STILL OWE ME AN EXPLANATION ...
MADARA TOOK KAKASHI'S EYE AND WENT TO WHERE OBITO IS.
HE'LL EMERGE NEXT WITH BOTH RINNEGAN IN HIM!
WHAT ?!
FOR REAL?!
NOW, I'D LIKE YOU ALL TO TELL US A LITTLE BIT ABOUT YOURSELVES.
天
LIKE WHAT?
...YOU KNOW, THE USUAL... YOUR FAVORITE THING... WHAT YOU HATE MOST...
DREAMS, AMBITIONS, HOBBIES. THINGS LIKE THAT.

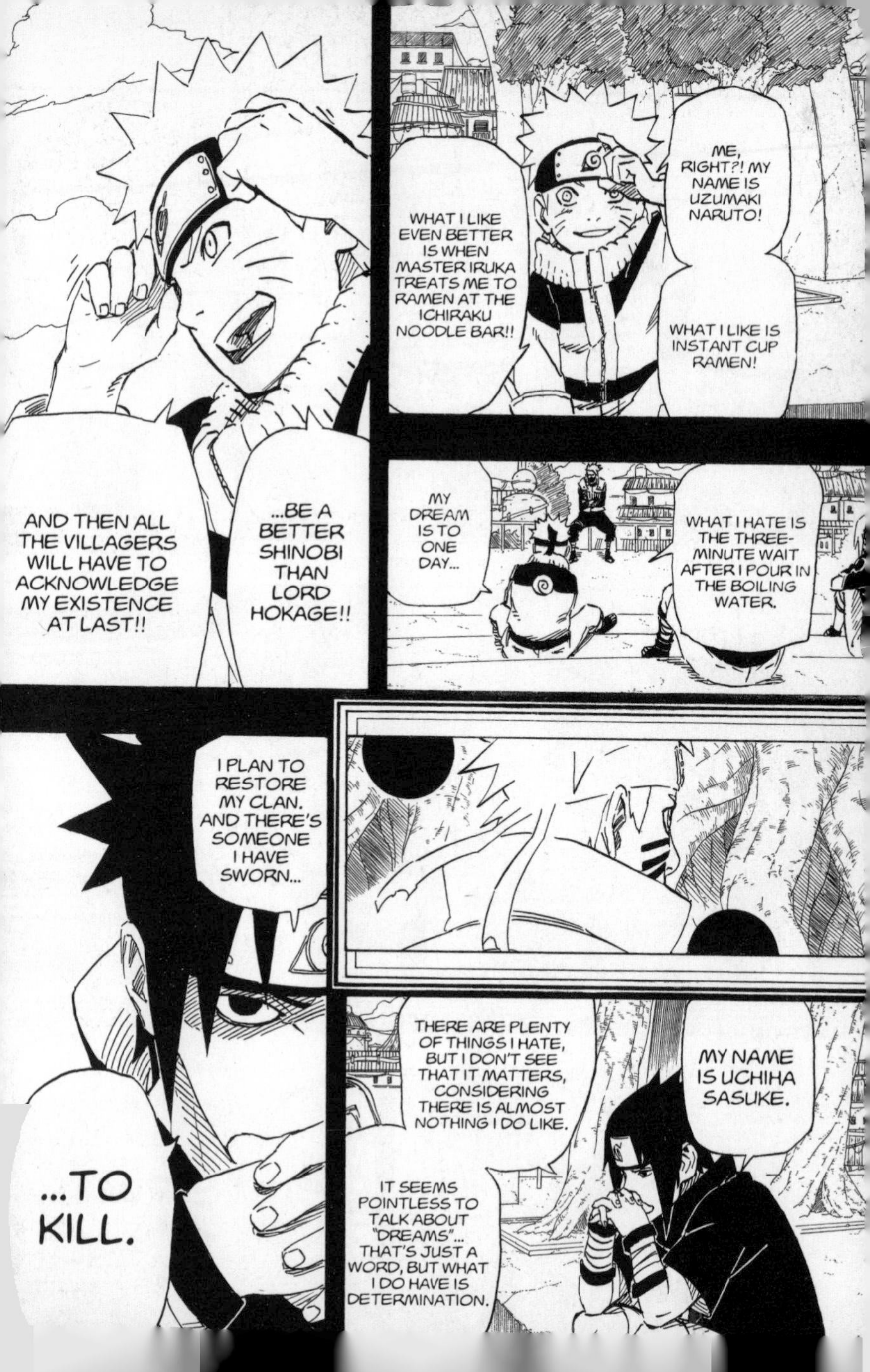
ME, RIGHT?! MY NAME IS UZUMAKI NARUTO!
WHAT I LIKE IS INSTANT CUP RAMEN!
WHAT I LIKE EVEN BETTER IS WHEN MASTER IRUKA TREATS ME TO RAMEN AT THE ICHIRAKU NOODLE BAR!!
WHAT I HATE IS THE THREE-MINUTE WAIT AFTER I POUR IN THE BOILING WATER.
MY DREAM IS TO ONE DAY...
...BE A BETTER SHINOBI THAN LORD HOKAGE!!
AND THEN ALL THE VILLAGERS WILL HAVE TO ACKNOWLEDGE MY EXISTENCE AT LAST!!
MY NAME IS UCHIHA SASUKE.
THERE ARE PLENTY OF THINGS I HATE, BUT I DON'T SEE THAT IT MATTERS, CONSIDERING THERE IS ALMOST NOTHING I DO LIKE.
IT SEEMS POINTLESS TO TALK ABOUT "DREAMS"... THAT'S JUST A WORD, BUT WHAT I DO HAVE IS DETERMINATION.
I PLAN TO RESTORE MY CLAN. AND THERE'S SOMEONE I HAVE SWORN...
...TO KILL.

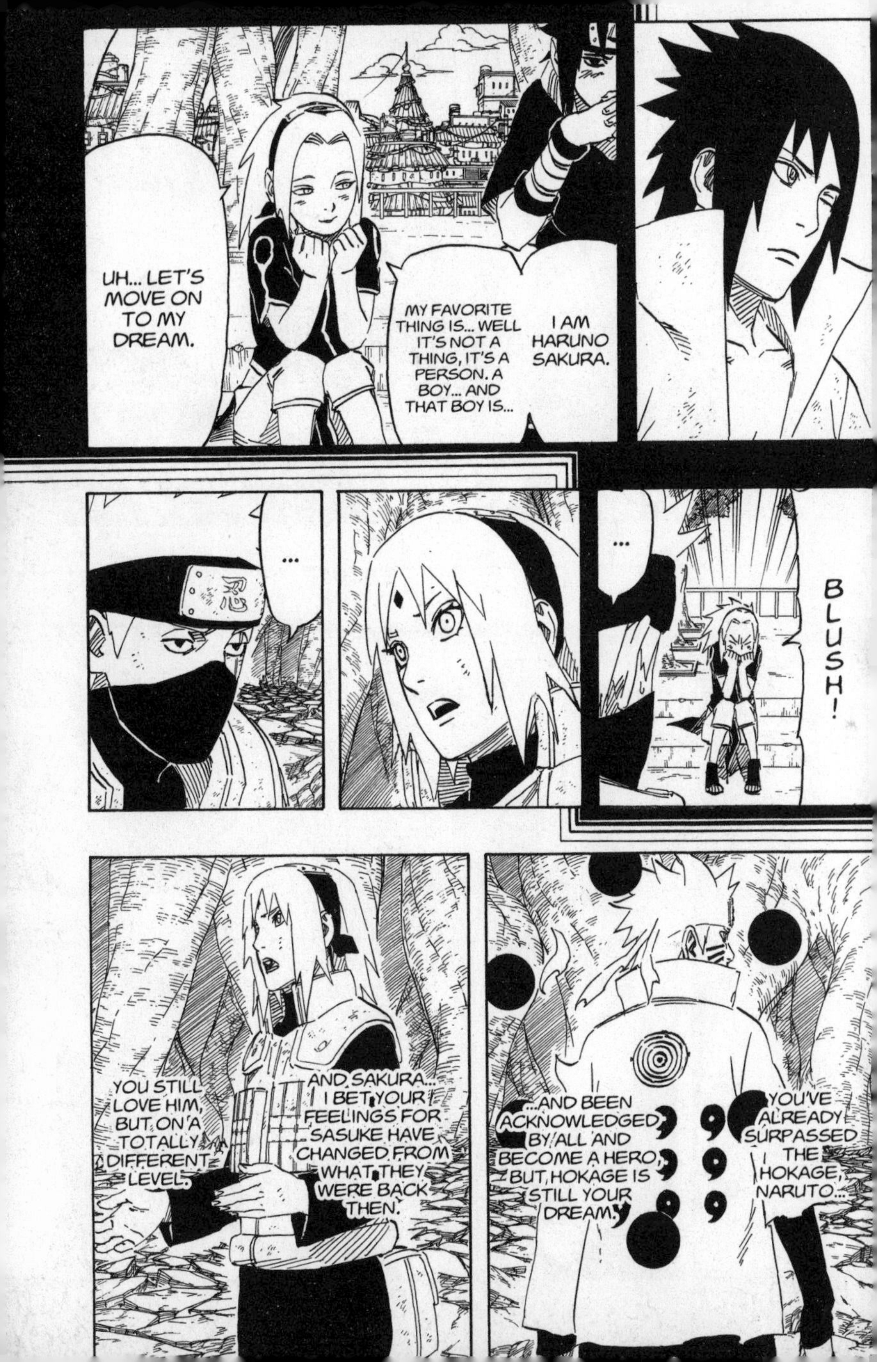
I AM HARUNO SAKURA.
MY FAVORITE THING IS... WELL IT'S NOT A THING, IT'S A PERSON. A BOY... AND THAT BOY IS...
UH... LET'S MOVE ON TO MY DREAM.
BLUSH!
...
...
YOU'VE ALREADY SURPASSED THE HOKAGE, NARUTO...
...AND BEEN ACKNOWLEDGED BY ALL AND BECOME A HERO, BUT, HOKAGE IS STILL YOUR DREAM.
AND SAKURA... I BET YOUR FEELINGS FOR SASUKE HAVE CHANGED FROM WHAT THEY WERE BACK THEN.
YOU STILL LOVE HIM, BUT ON A TOTALLY DIFFERENT LEVEL.

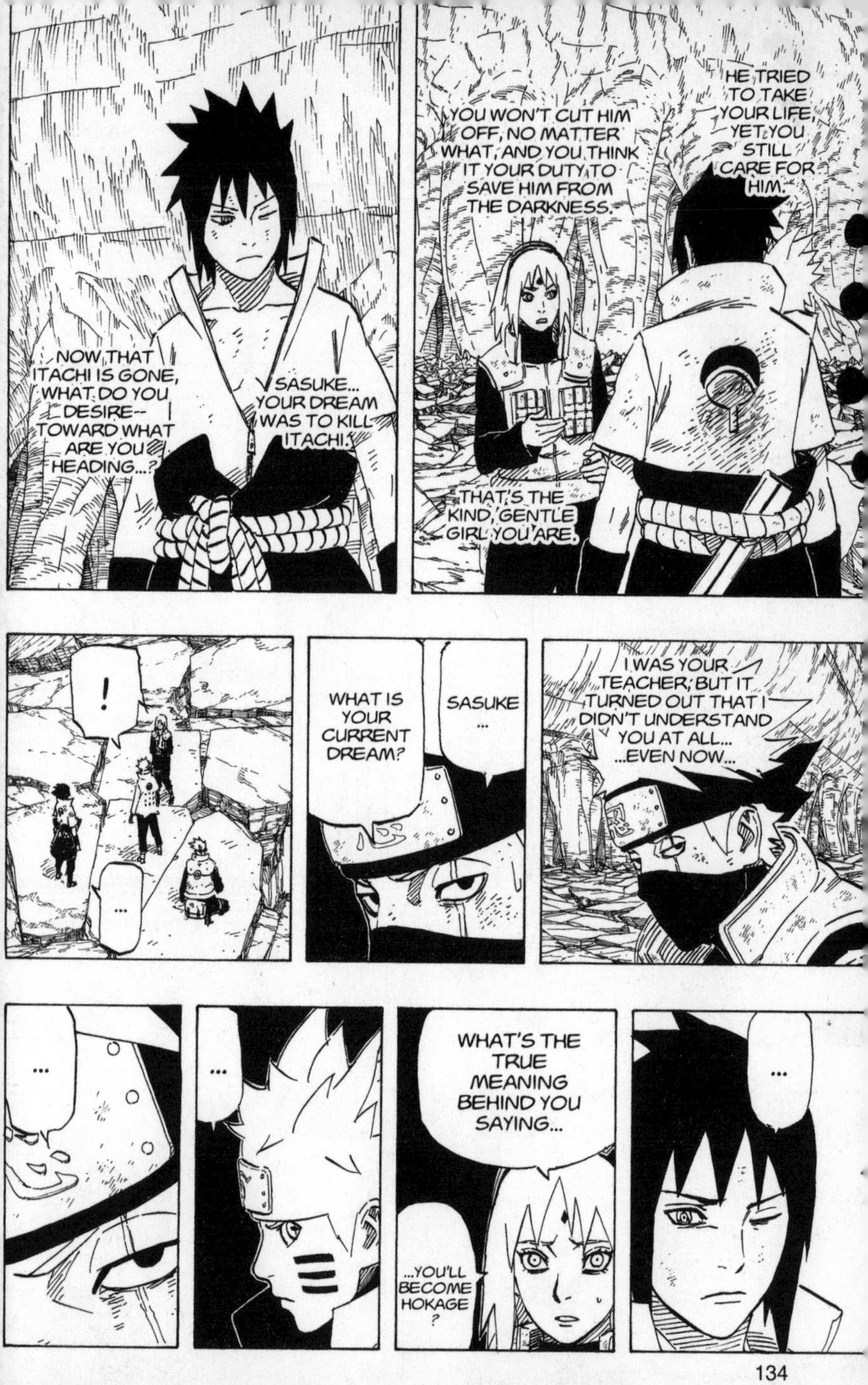
HE TRIED TO TAKE YOUR LIFE, YET YOU STILL CARE FOR HIM.
YOU WON'T CUT HIM OFF, NO MATTER WHAT, AND YOU THINK IT YOUR DUTY TO SAVE HIM FROM THE DARKNESS.
THAT'S THE KIND, GENTLE GIRL YOU ARE.
SASUKE... YOUR DREAM WAS TO KILL ITACHI.
NOW THAT ITACHI IS GONE, WHAT DO YOU DESIRE-- TOWARD WHAT ARE YOU HEADING...?
I WAS YOUR TEACHER; BUT IT TURNED OUT THAT I DIDN'T UNDERSTAND YOU AT ALL... ...EVEN NOW...
SASUKE ...
WHAT IS YOUR CURRENT DREAM?
!
...
...
WHAT'S THE TRUE MEANING BEHIND YOU SAYING...
...YOU'LL BECOME HOKAGE?
...
...

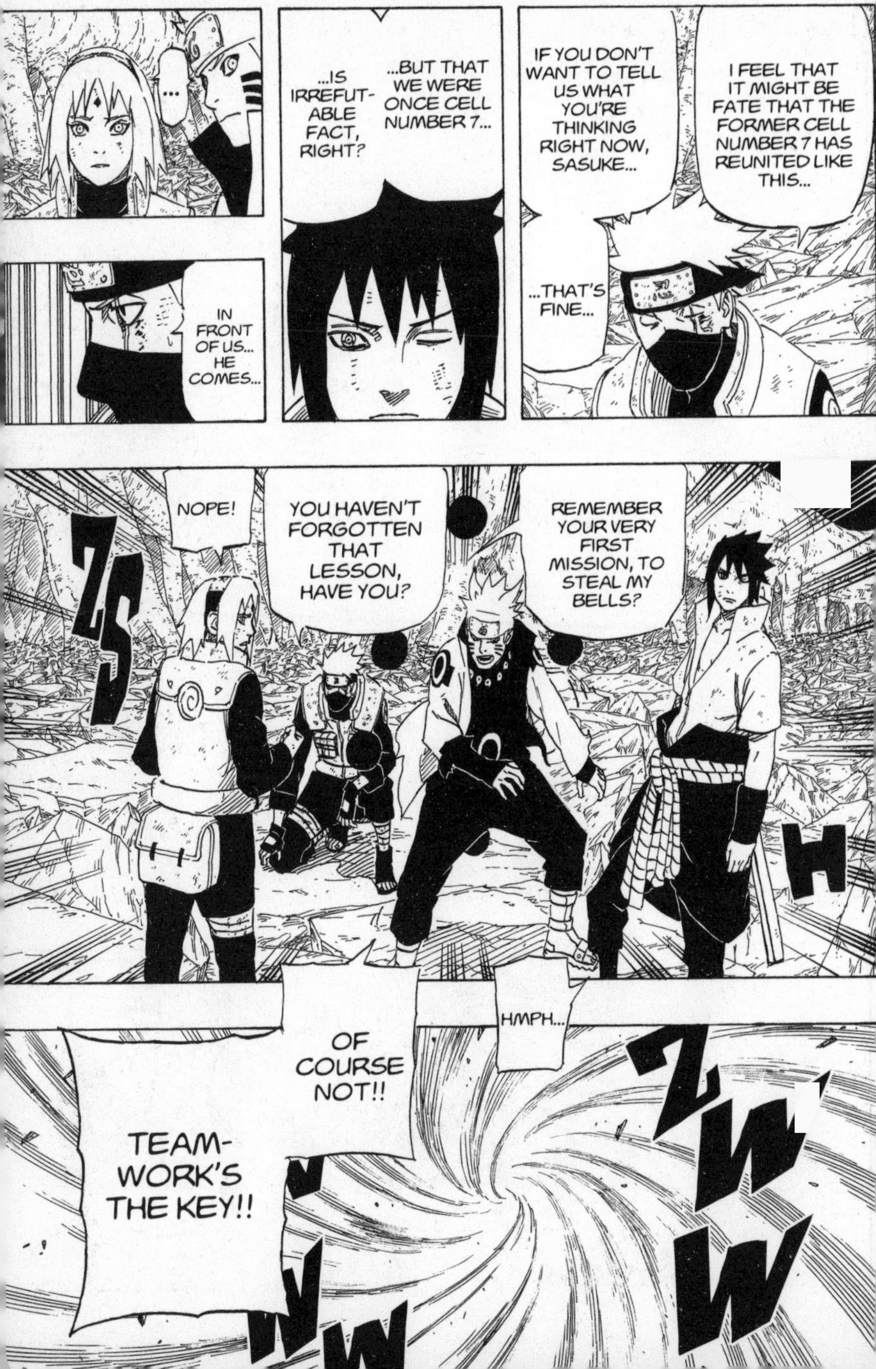
I FEEL THAT IT MIGHT BE FATE THAT THE FORMER CELL NUMBER 7 HAS REUNITED LIKE THIS...
IF YOU DON'T WANT TO TELL US WHAT YOU'RE THINKING RIGHT NOW, SASUKE...
...THAT'S FINE...
...BUT THAT WE WERE ONCE CELL NUMBER 7...
...IS IRREFUT-ABLE FACT, RIGHT?
...
IN FRONT OF US... HE COMES...
H
REMEMBER YOUR VERY FIRST MISSION, TO STEAL MY BELLS?
YOU HAVEN'T FORGOTTEN THAT LESSON, HAVE YOU?
NOPE!
ZS
HMPH...
OF COURSE NOT!!
ZWW
TEAM-WORK'S THE KEY!!
WWW

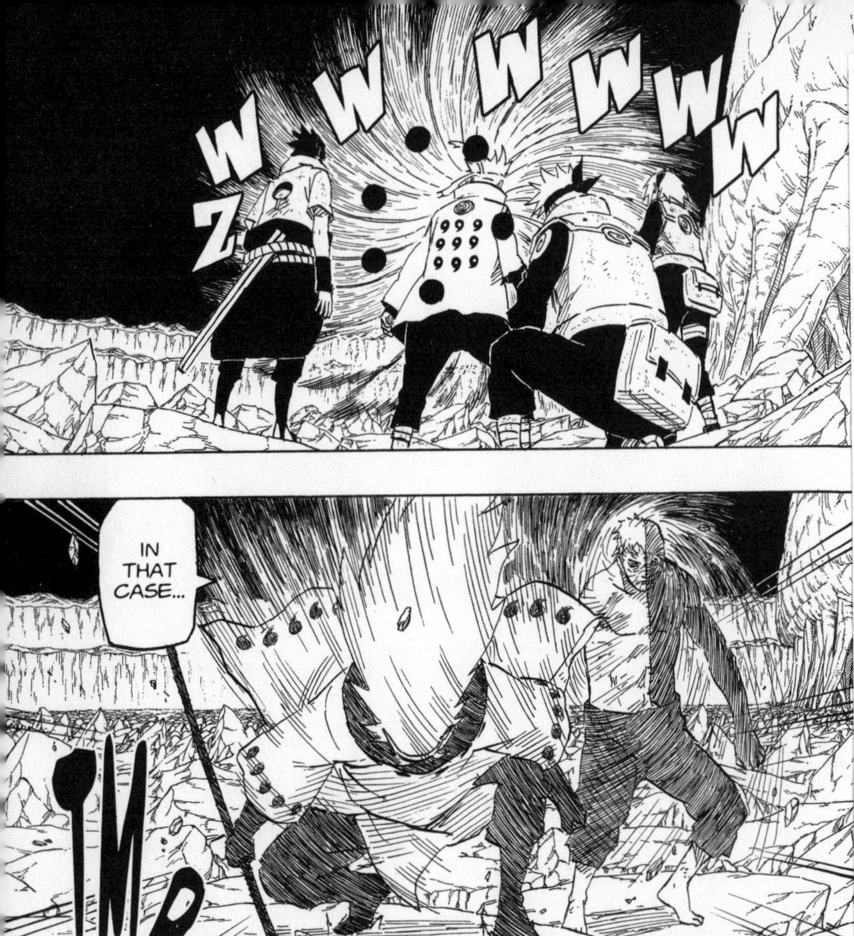
ZWWWWWW
IN THAT CASE...
TMP

## Number 676: The Infinite Dream

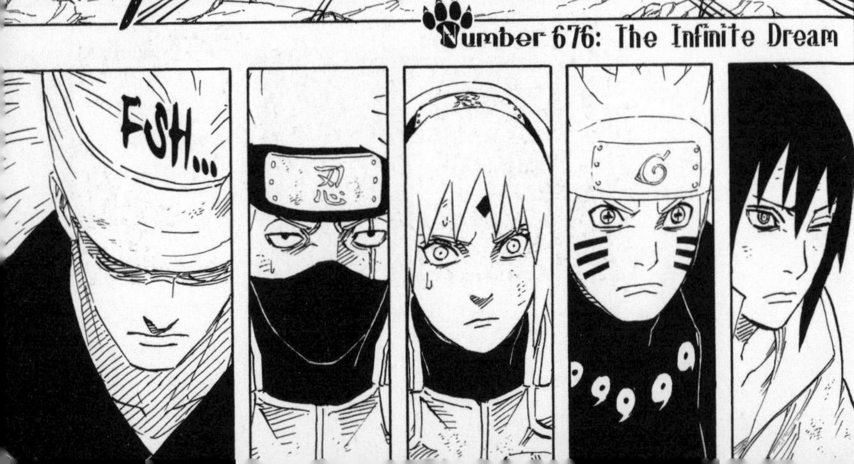
FSH...

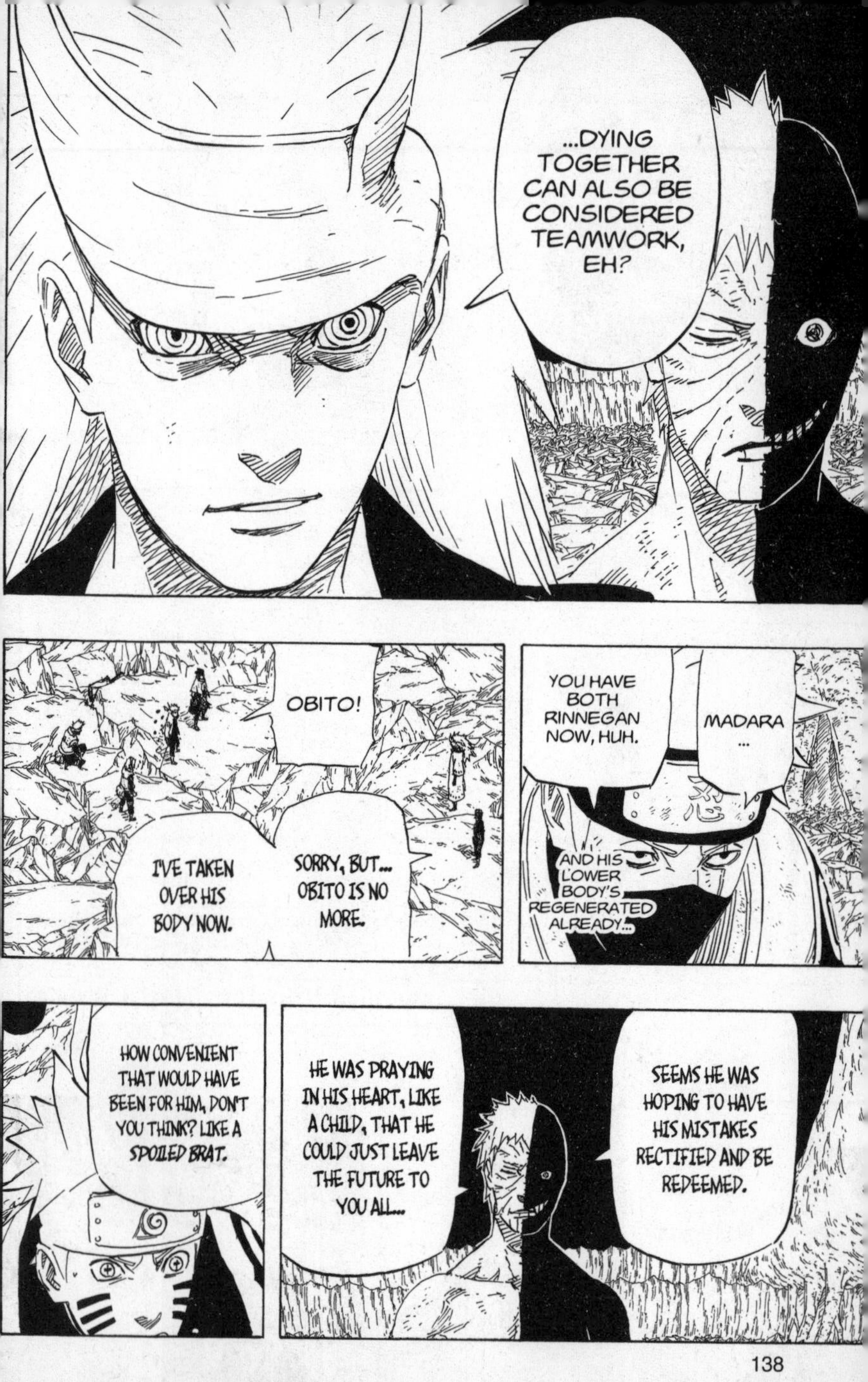
...DYING TOGETHER CAN ALSO BE CONSIDERED TEAMWORK, EH?
MADARA ...
YOU HAVE BOTH RINNEGAN NOW, HUH.
AND HIS LOWER BODY'S REGENERATED ALREADY...
OBITO!
SORRY, BUT... OBITO IS NO MORE.
I'VE TAKEN OVER HIS BODY NOW.
SEEMS HE WAS HOPING TO HAVE HIS MISTAKES RECTIFIED AND BE REDEEMED.
HE WAS PRAYING IN HIS HEART, LIKE A CHILD, THAT HE COULD JUST LEAVE THE FUTURE TO YOU ALL...
HOW CONVENIENT THAT WOULD HAVE BEEN FOR HIM, DON'T YOU THINK? LIKE A SPOILED BRAT.

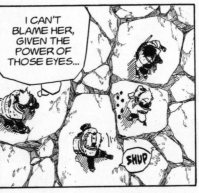

I CAN'T BLAME HER, GIVEN THE POWER OF THOSE EYES...

SHUP

SHUP!!

...

L'ADY TSUNADE, IT LOOKS LIKE I'VE FINALLY CAUGHT UP TO THEM!!

TMP

SHHF...

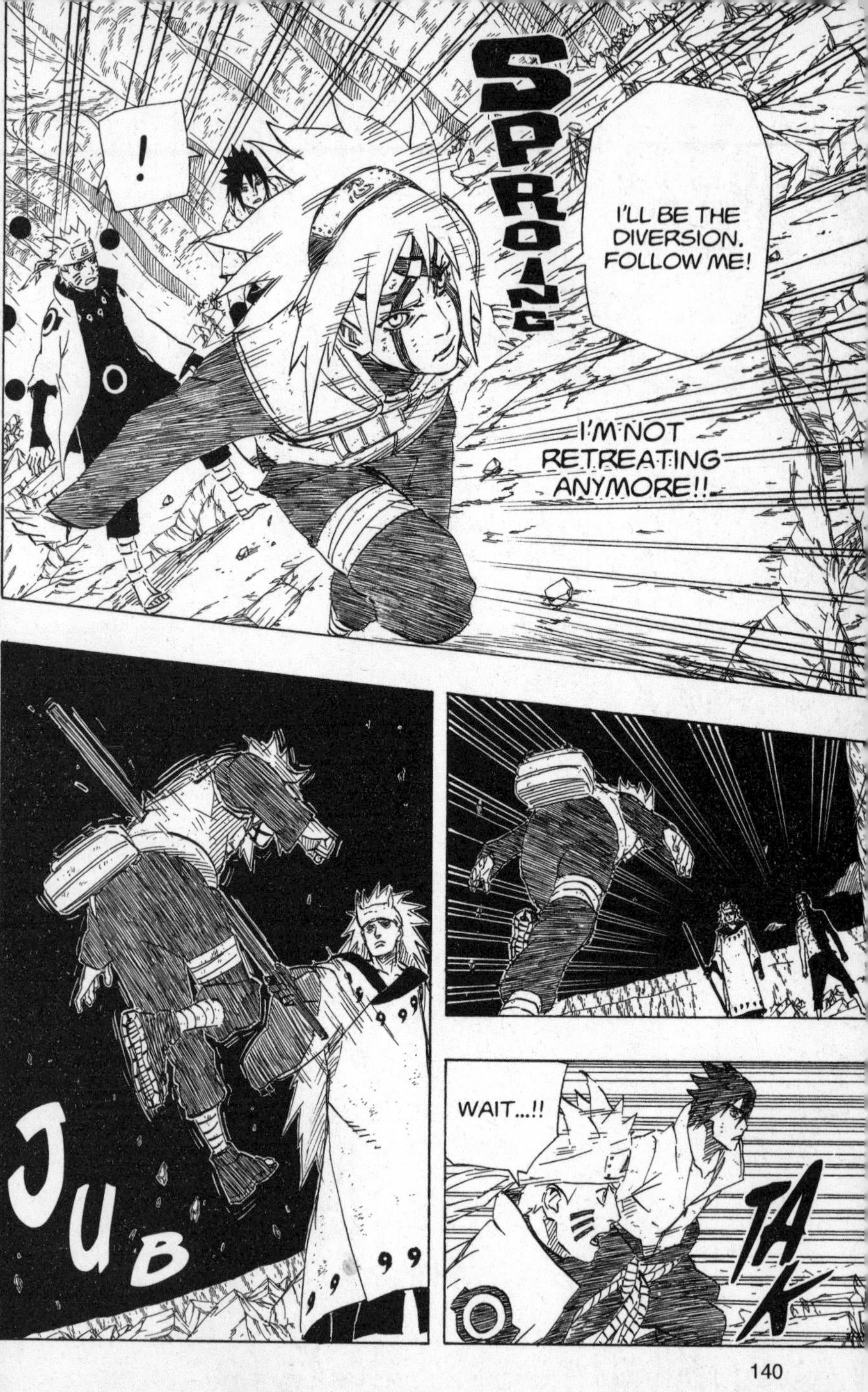
I'LL BE THE DIVERSION. FOLLOW ME!
SPROING
!
I'M NOT RETREATING ANYMORE!!
WAIT...!!
TAK
JUB

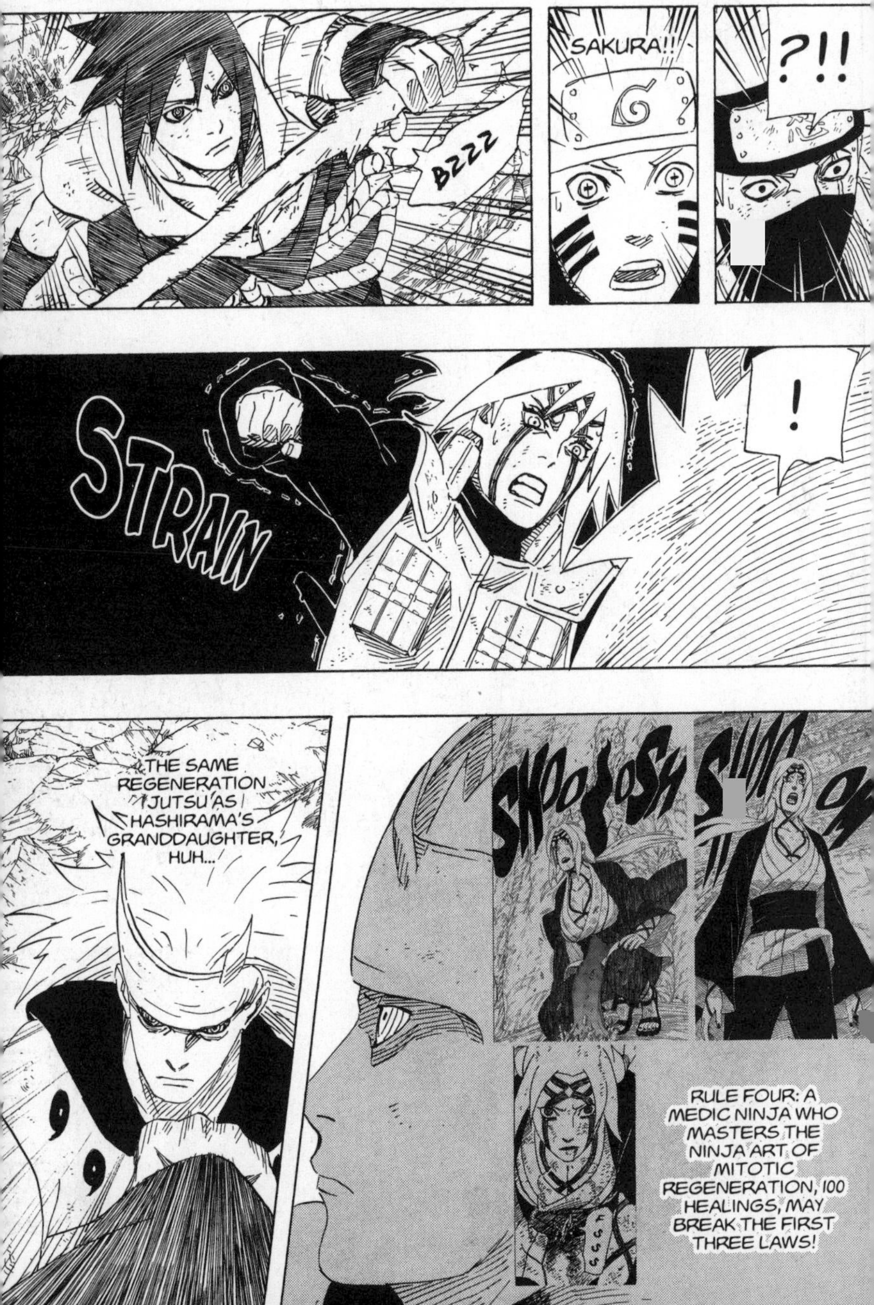
?!!
SAKURA!!
BZZZ
!
STRAIN
RULE FOUR: A MEDIC NINJA WHO MASTERS THE NINJA ART OF MITOTIC REGENERATION, 100 HEALINGS, MAY BREAK THE FIRST THREE LAWS!
THE SAME REGENERATION JUTSU AS HASHIRAMA'S GRANDDAUGHTER, HUH...

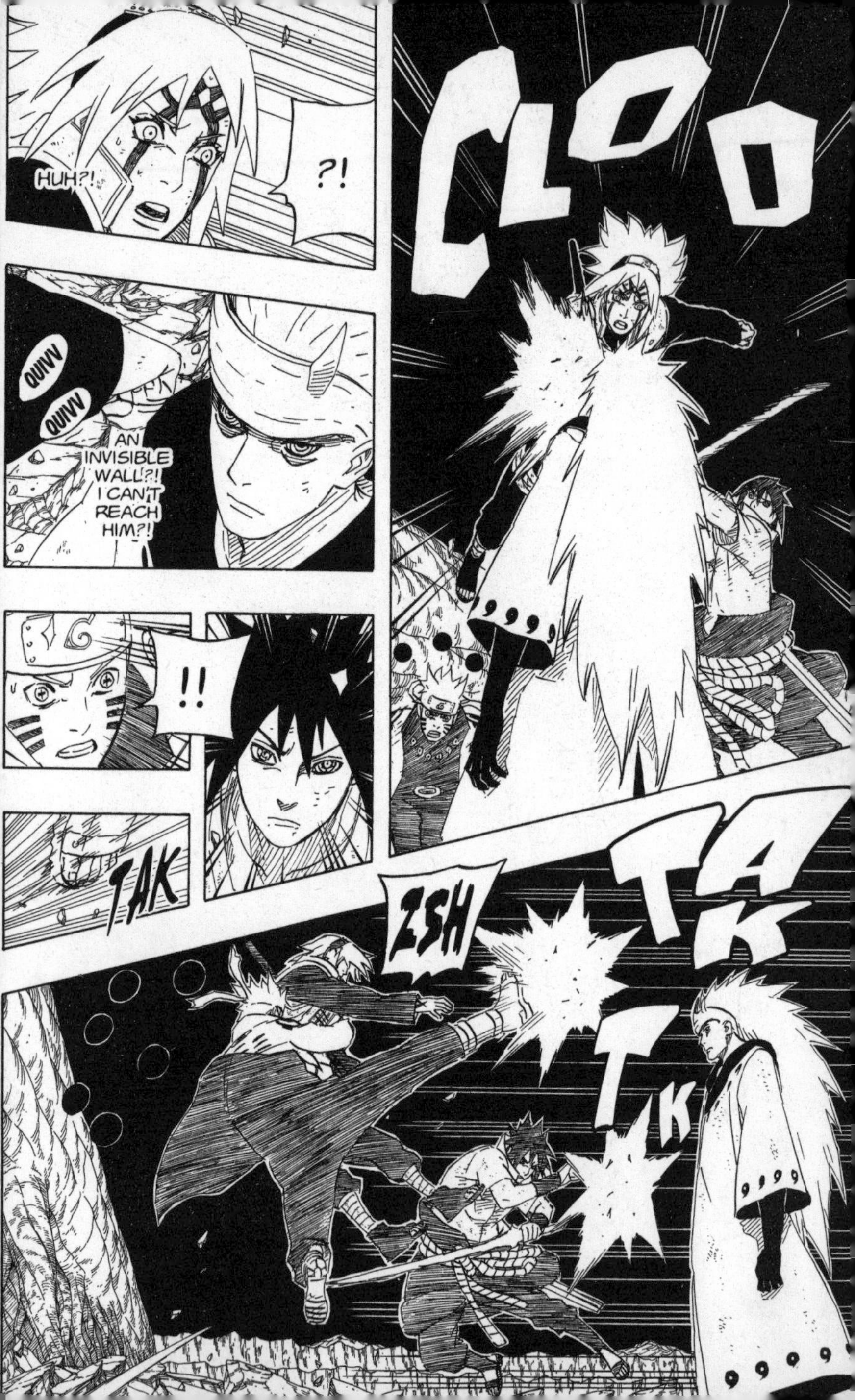
CLOOD
?!
HUH?!
QUIVV
QUIVV
AN INVISIBLE WALL?! I CAN'T REACH HIM?!
!!
TAK
TAK
ZSH
TK

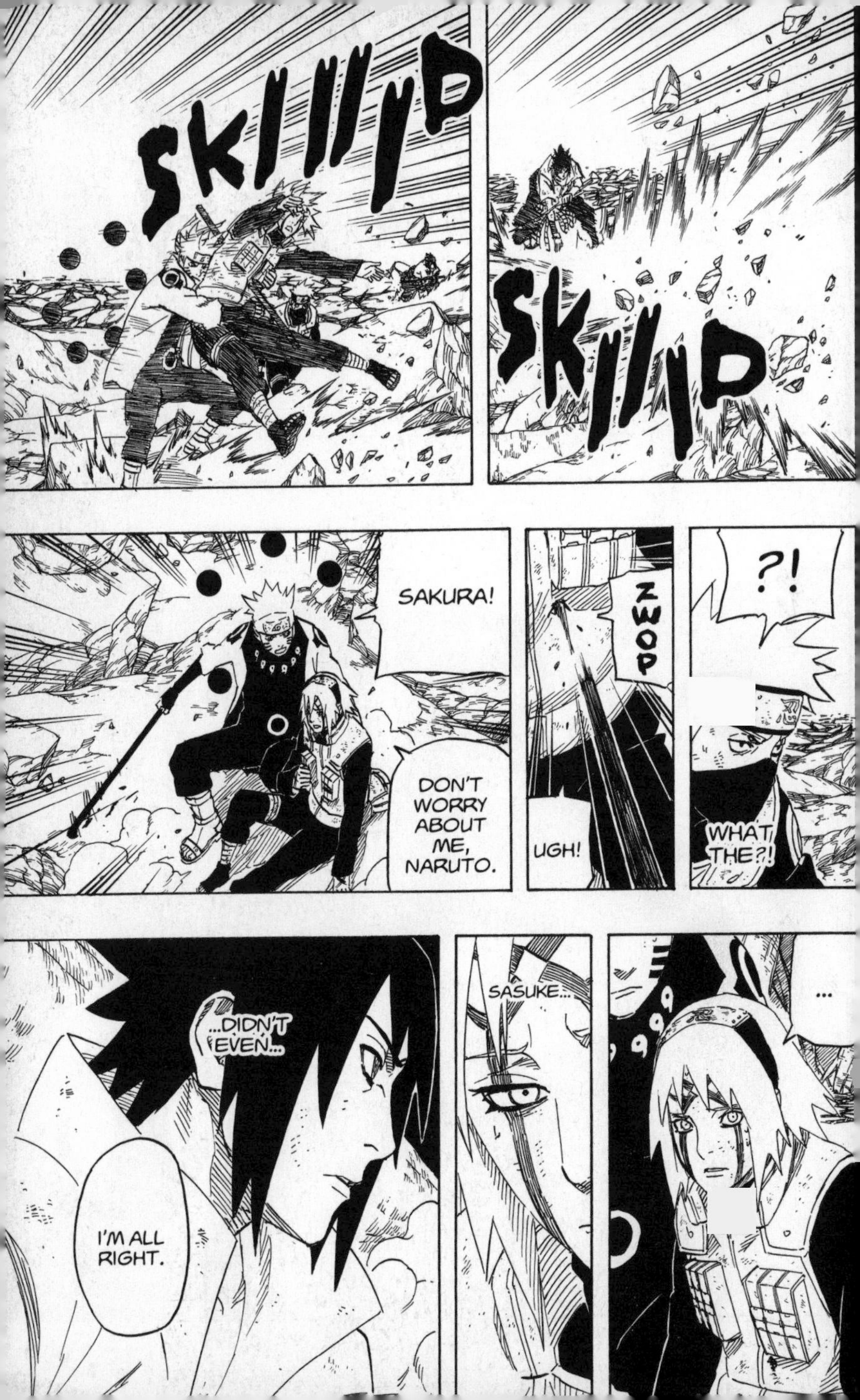
SKIIID
SKIIIID
?!
WHAT THE?!
ZWOP
UGH!
SAKURA!
DON'T WORRY ABOUT ME, NARUTO.
...
SASUKE...
...DIDN'T EVEN...
I'M ALL RIGHT.

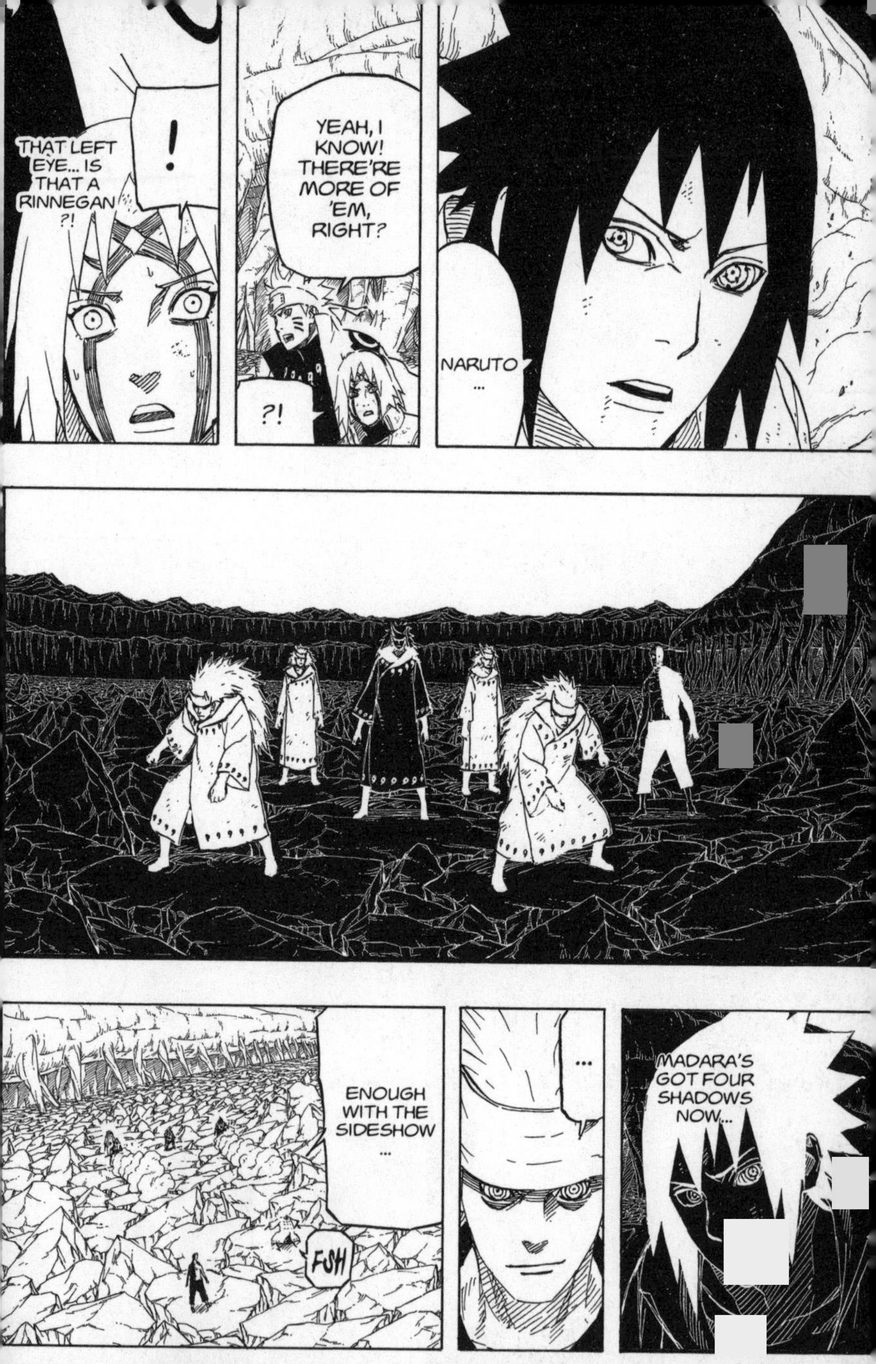
NARUTO ...
YEAH, I KNOW! THERE'RE MORE OF 'EM, RIGHT?
?!
!
THAT LEFT EYE... IS THAT A RINNEGAN ?!
MADARA'S GOT FOUR SHADOWS NOW...
...
ENOUGH WITH THE SIDESHOW ...
FSH

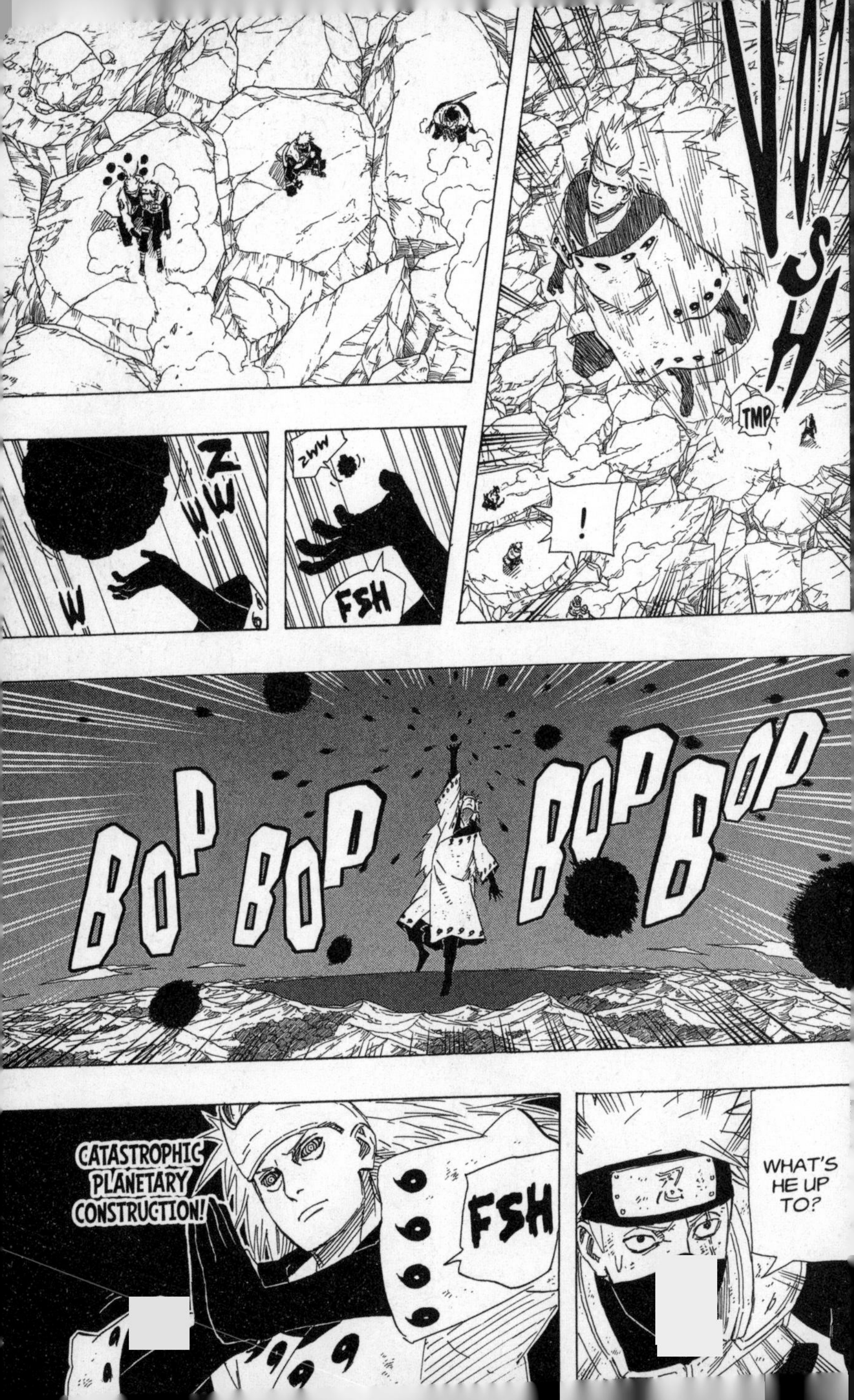
VOOSH
TMP
!
FSH
ZWWW
BOP BOP BOP BOOP
WHAT'S HE UP TO?
CATASTROPHIC PLANETARY CONSTRUCTION!
FSH

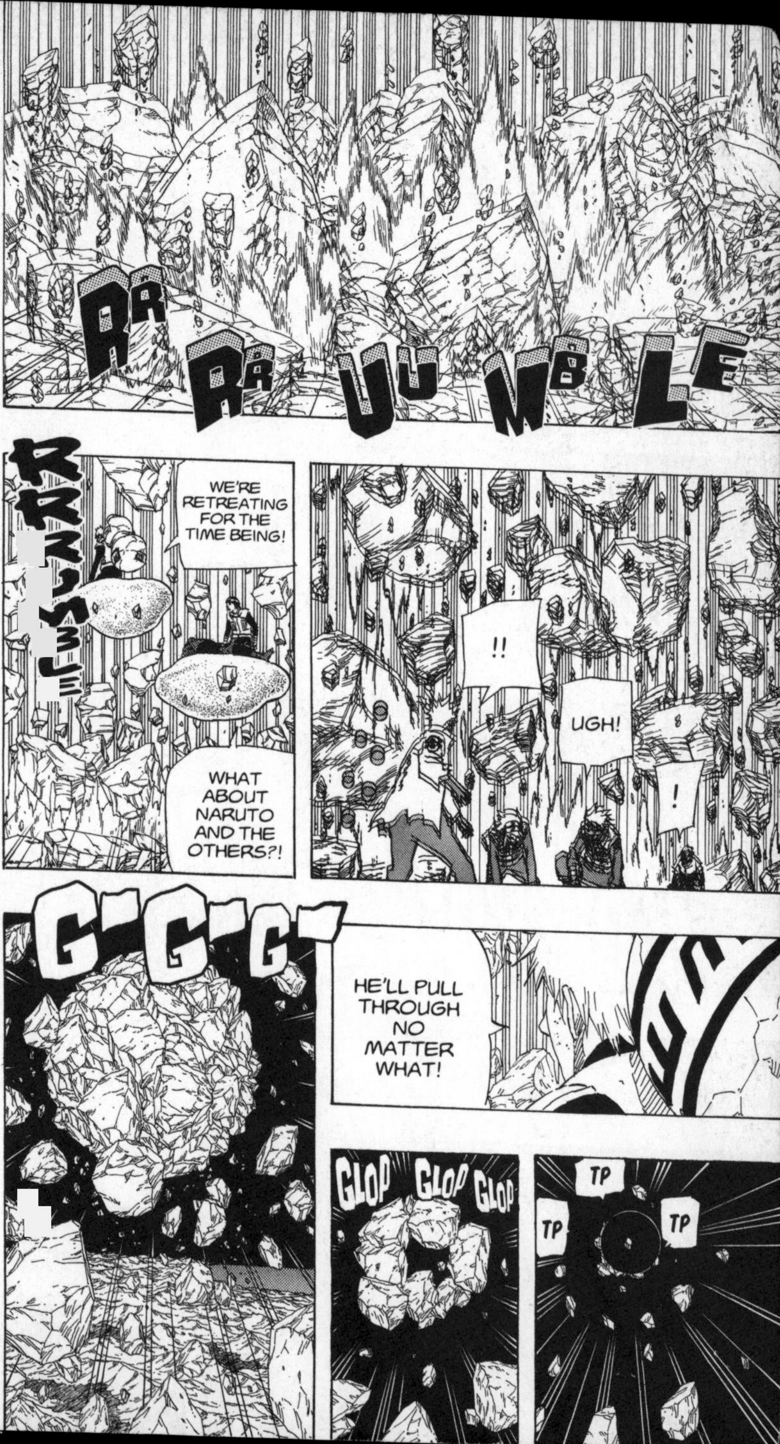
RARAUUMBLE
!!
UGH!
!
WE'RE RETREATING FOR THE TIME BEING!
WHAT ABOUT NARUTO AND THE OTHERS?!
RRRUMBLE
HE'LL PULL THROUGH NO MATTER WHAT!
G'G'G'
TP
TP
TP
GLOP GLOP GLOP

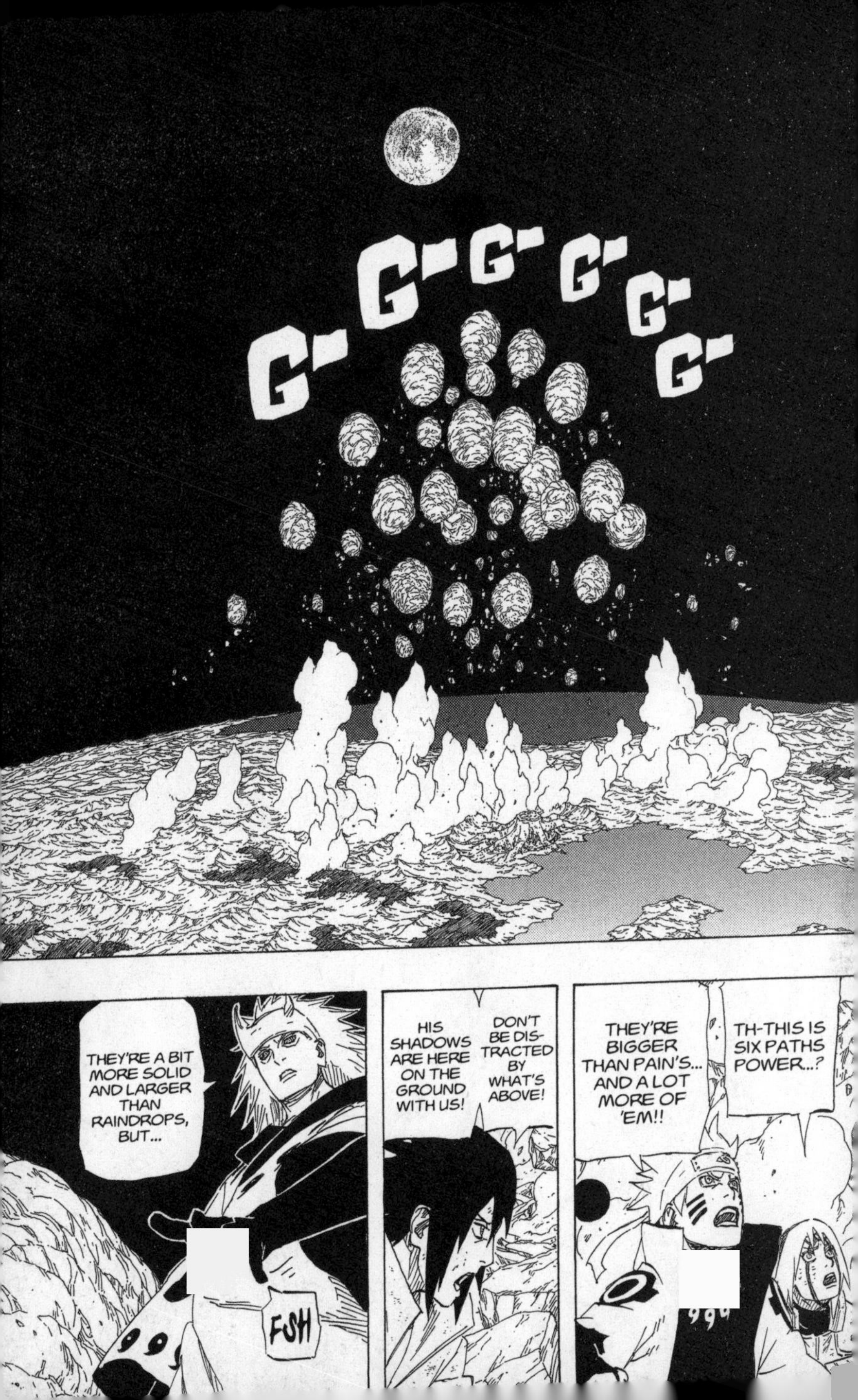
G- G- G- G- G- G-
TH-THIS IS SIX PATHS POWER...?
THEY'RE BIGGER THAN PAIN'S... AND A LOT MORE OF 'EM!!
DON'T BE DISTRACTED BY WHAT'S ABOVE!
HIS SHADOWS ARE HERE ON THE GROUND WITH US!
THEY'RE A BIT MORE SOLID AND LARGER THAN RAINDROPS, BUT...
FSH

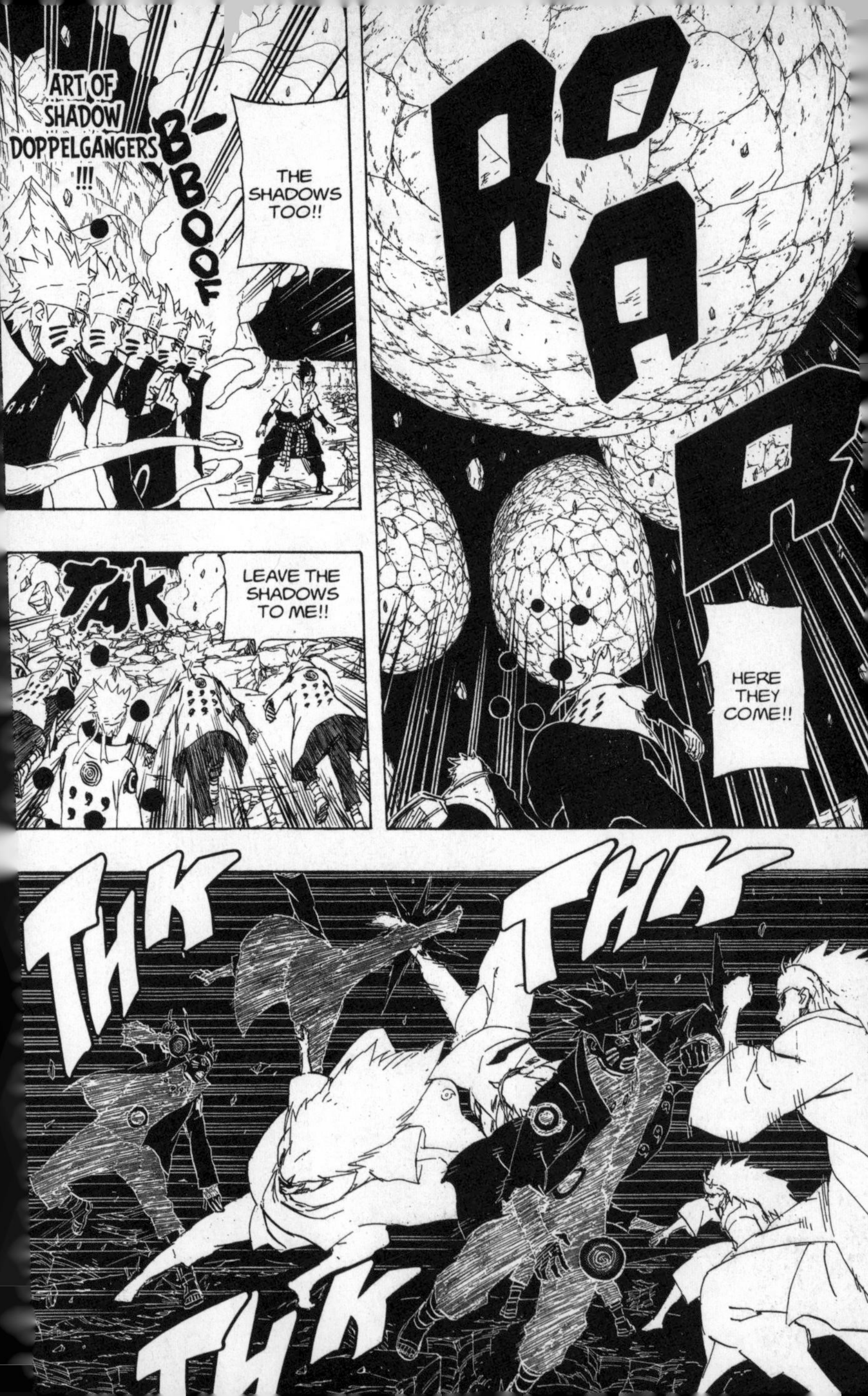
ROAAR
HERE THEY COME!!
THE SHADOWS TOO!!
B-BBOOF
ART OF SHADOW DOPPELGANGERS!!!
LEAVE THE SHADOWS TO ME!!
TAK
THK
THK
THK

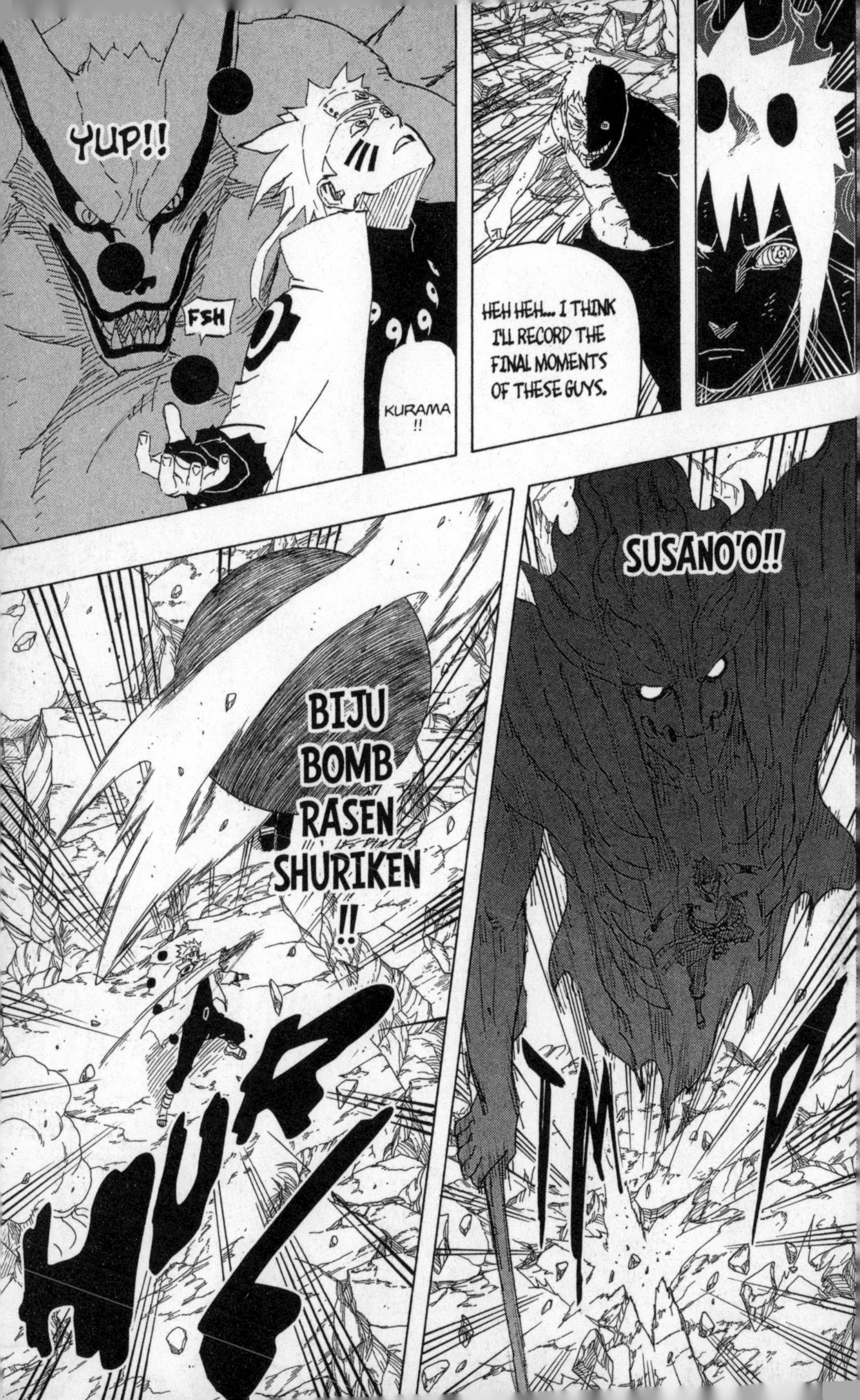
HEH HEH... I THINK I'LL RECORD THE FINAL MOMENTS OF THESE GUYS.
KURAMA!!
YUP!!
FSH
SUSANO'O!!
BIJU BOMB RASEN SHURIKEN!!

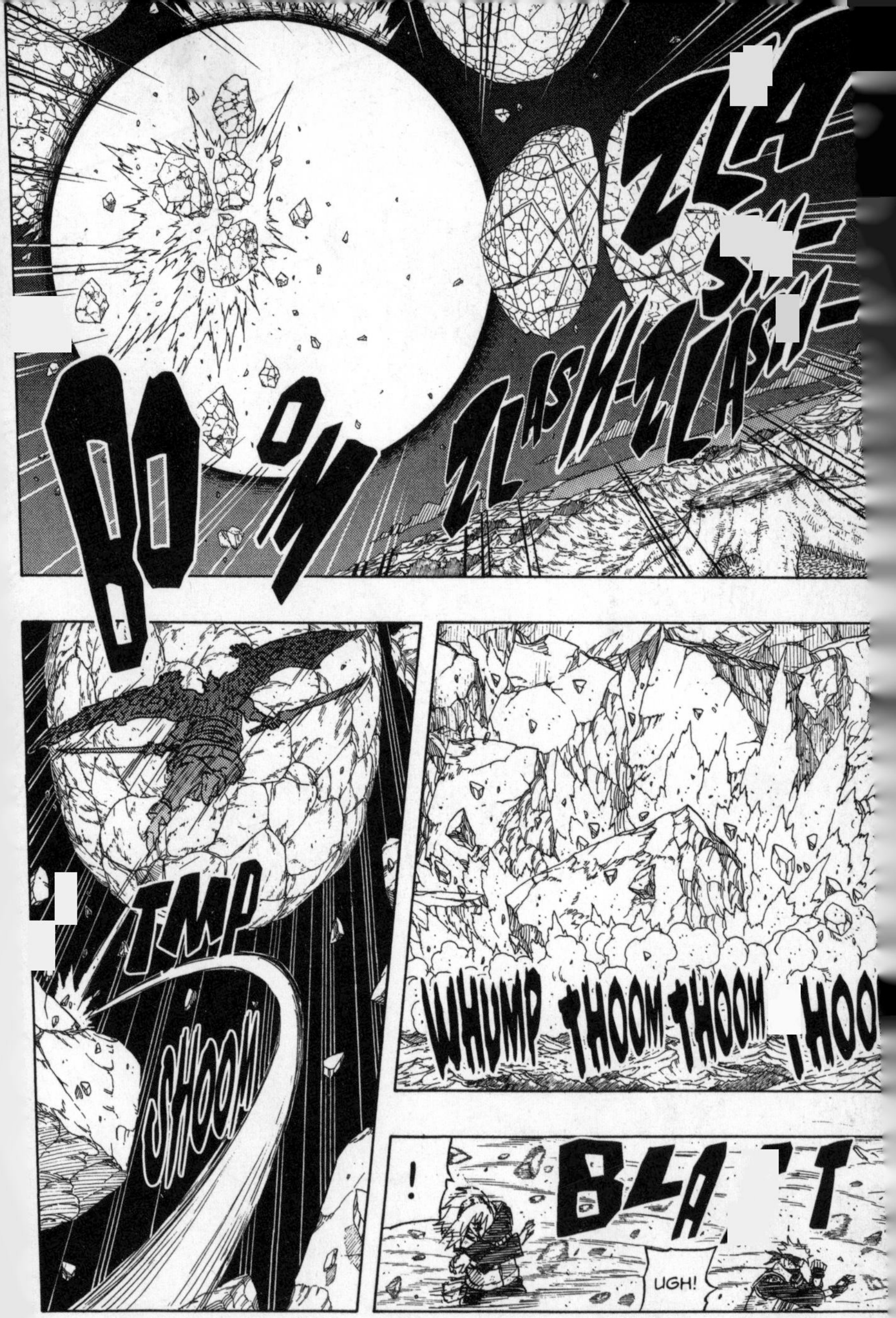
ZLA-
SH-
ZLASH-ZLASH-
BOOM
WHUMP THOOM THOOM THOO
!
BLA T
UGH!
TMP
SHOOM

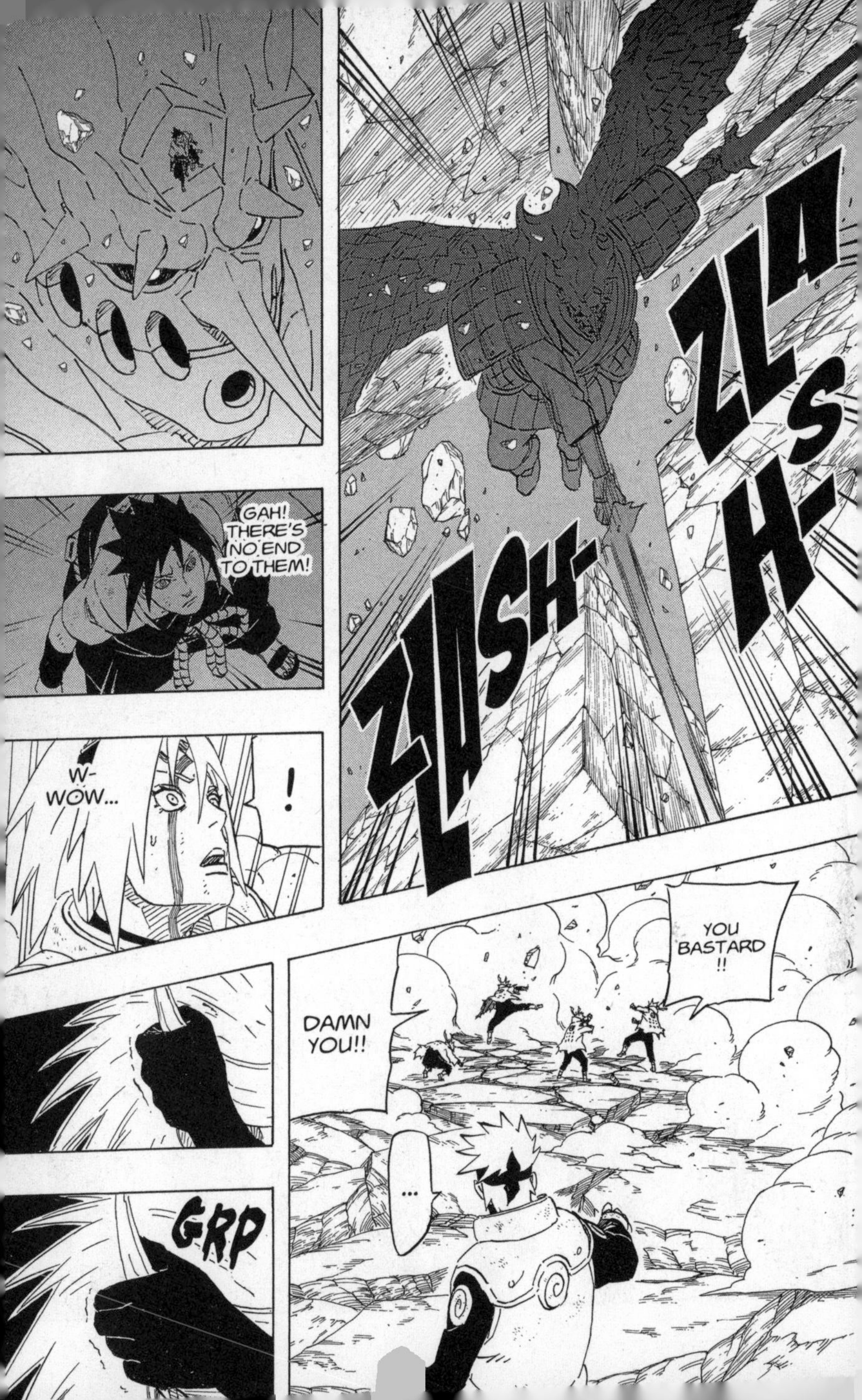
ZZASH-
ZZASH-
GAH! THERE'S NO END TO THEM!
!
W-WOW...
YOU BASTARD!!
DAMN YOU!!
...
GRP

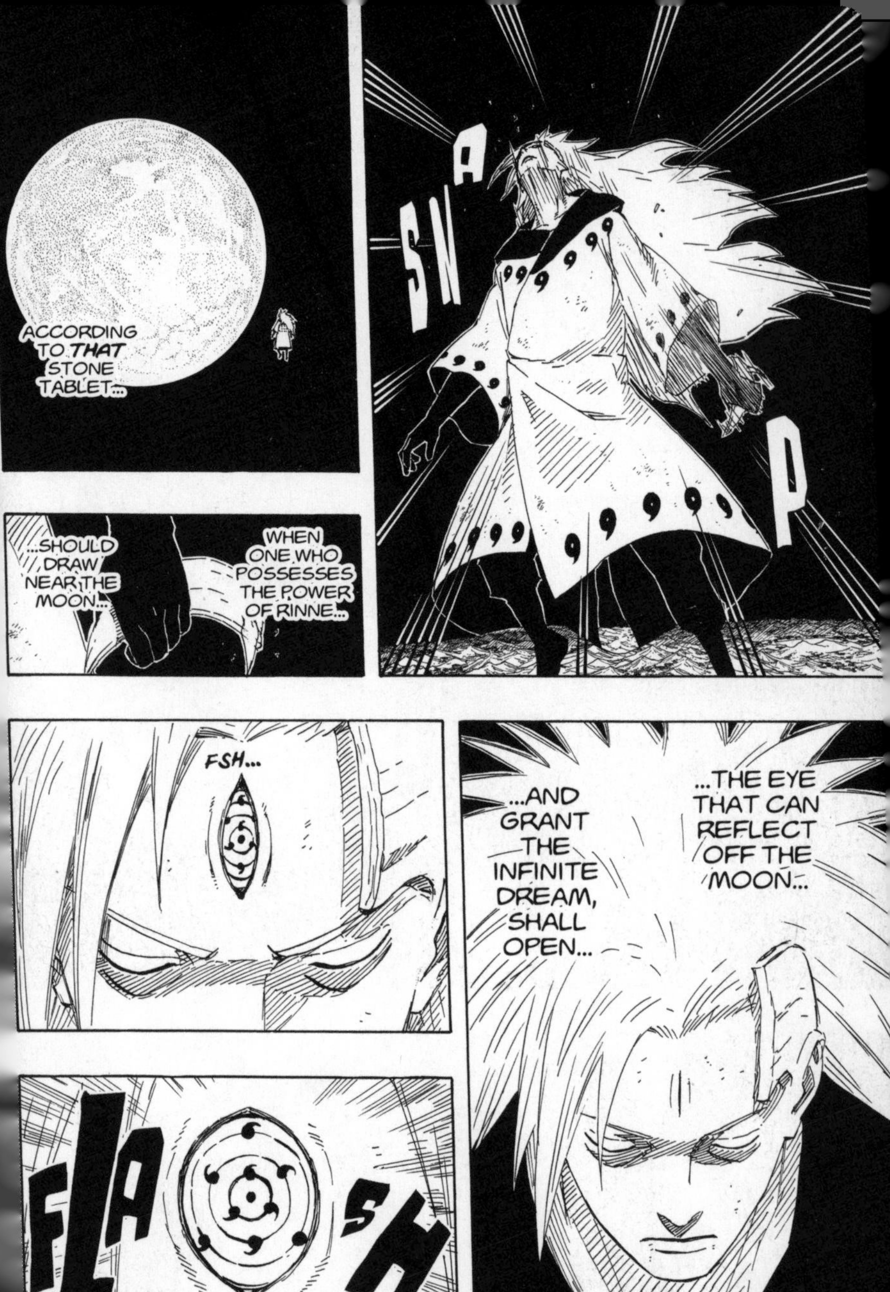
SNAP
ACCORDING TO *THAT* STONE TABLET...
WHEN ONE WHO POSSESSES THE POWER OF RINNE...
...SHOULD DRAW NEAR THE MOON...
...THE EYE THAT CAN REFLECT OFF THE MOON...
...AND GRANT THE INFINITE DREAM, SHALL OPEN...
FSH...
FLASH

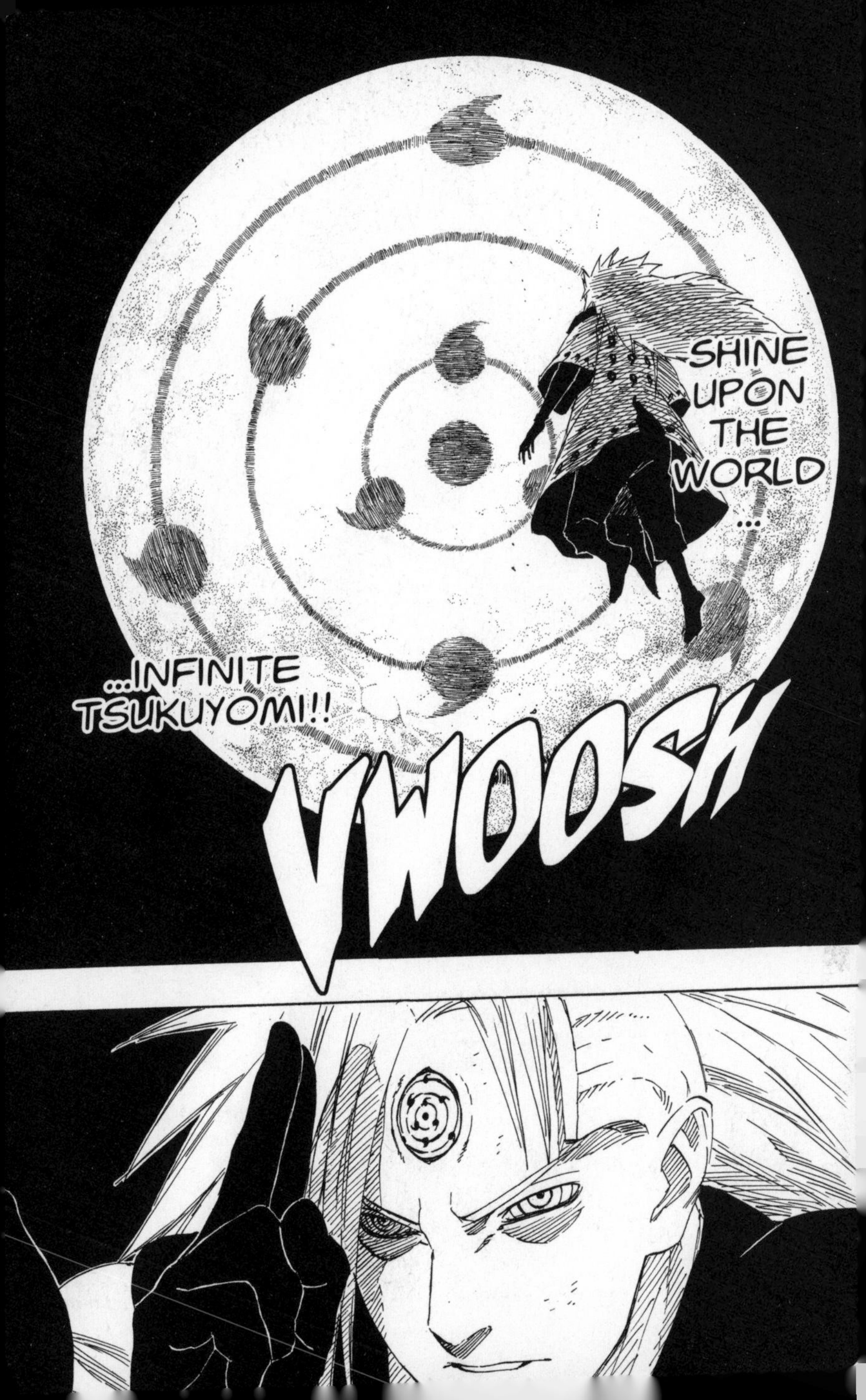
SHINE UPON THE WORLD...
...INFINITE TSUKUYOMI!!
VWOOSH

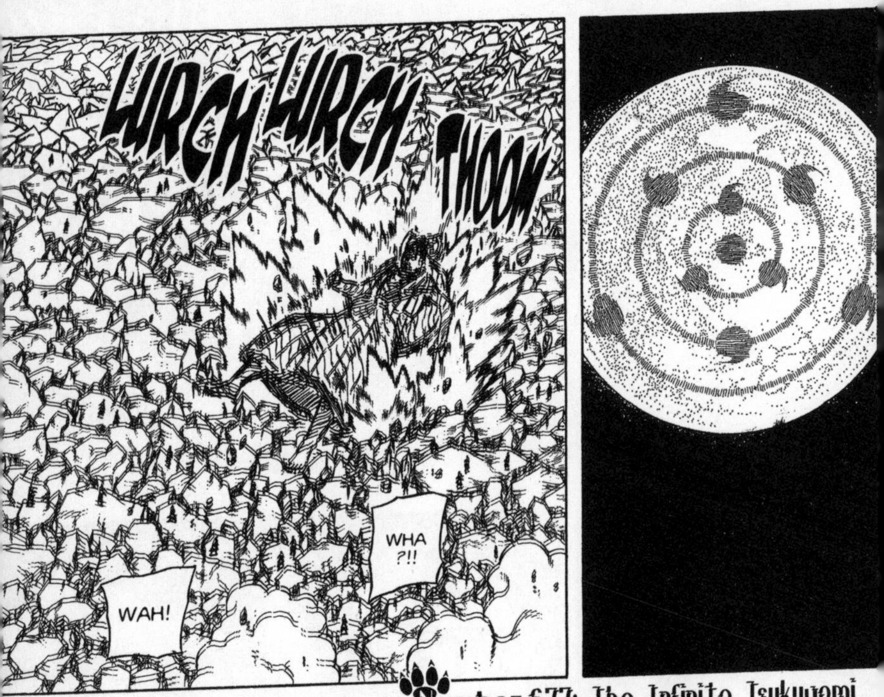
LURCH LURCH
THOOM
WHA ?!!
WAH!

## Number 677: The Infinite Tsukuyomi

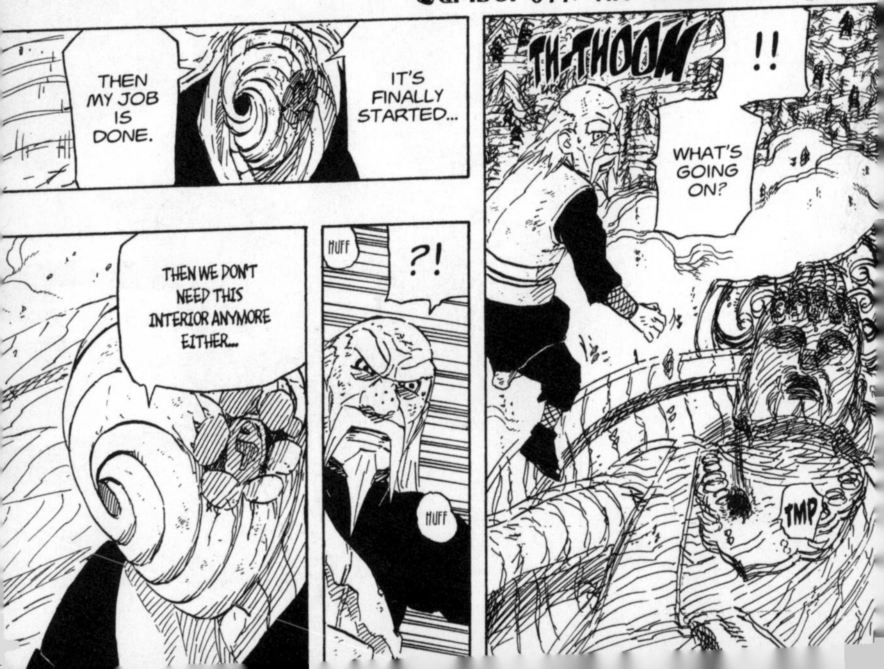
TH-THOOM
!!
WHAT'S GOING ON?
TMP
IT'S FINALLY STARTED...
THEN MY JOB IS DONE.
?!
HUFF
HUFF
THEN WE DON'T NEED THIS INTERIOR ANYMORE EITHER...

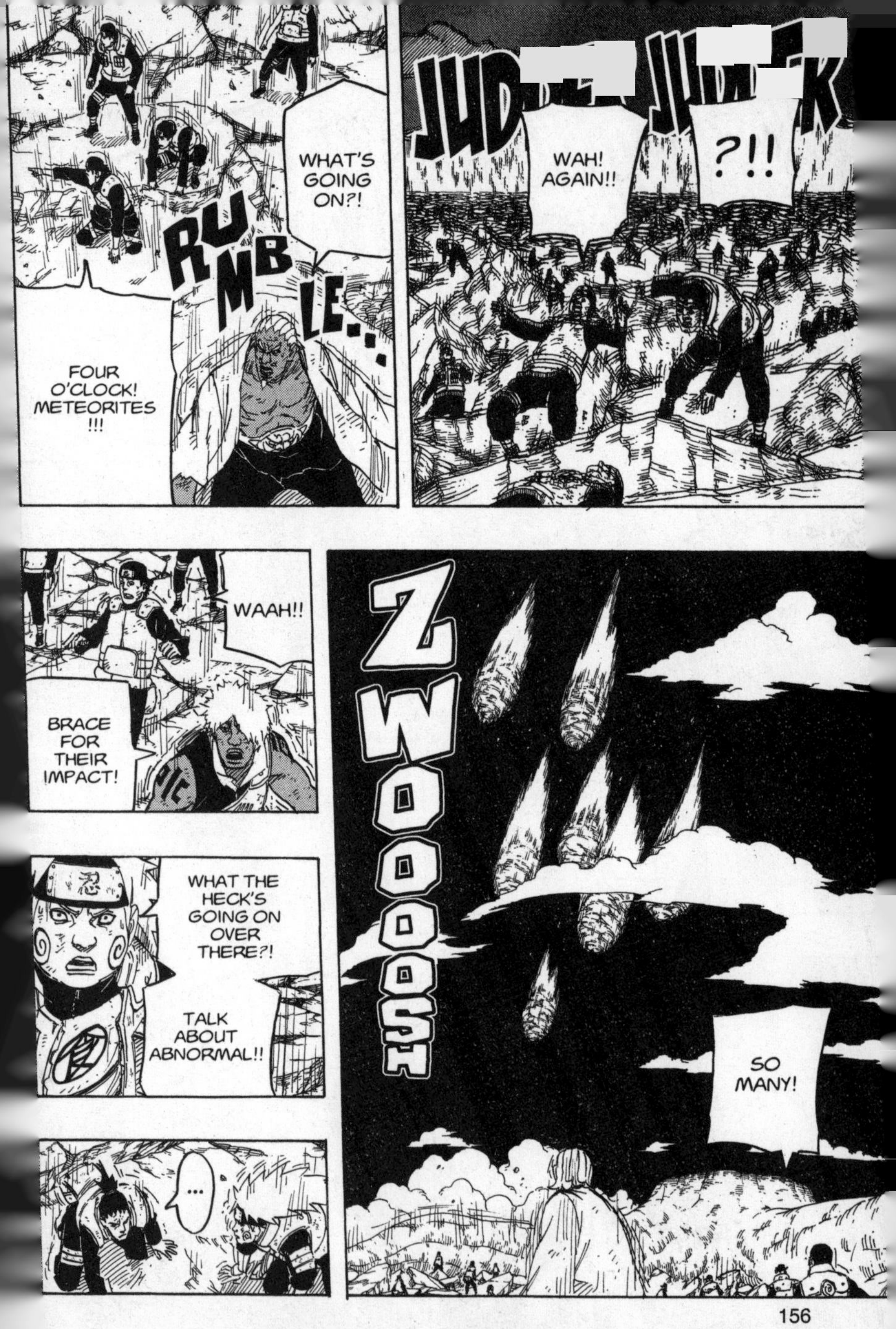
?!!
WAH! AGAIN!!
WHAT'S GOING ON?!
RUMBLE...
FOUR O'CLOCK! METEORITES!!!
ZWOOOOSH
SO MANY!
WAAH!!
BRACE FOR THEIR IMPACT!
WHAT THE HECK'S GOING ON OVER THERE?!
TALK ABOUT ABNORMAL!!
...

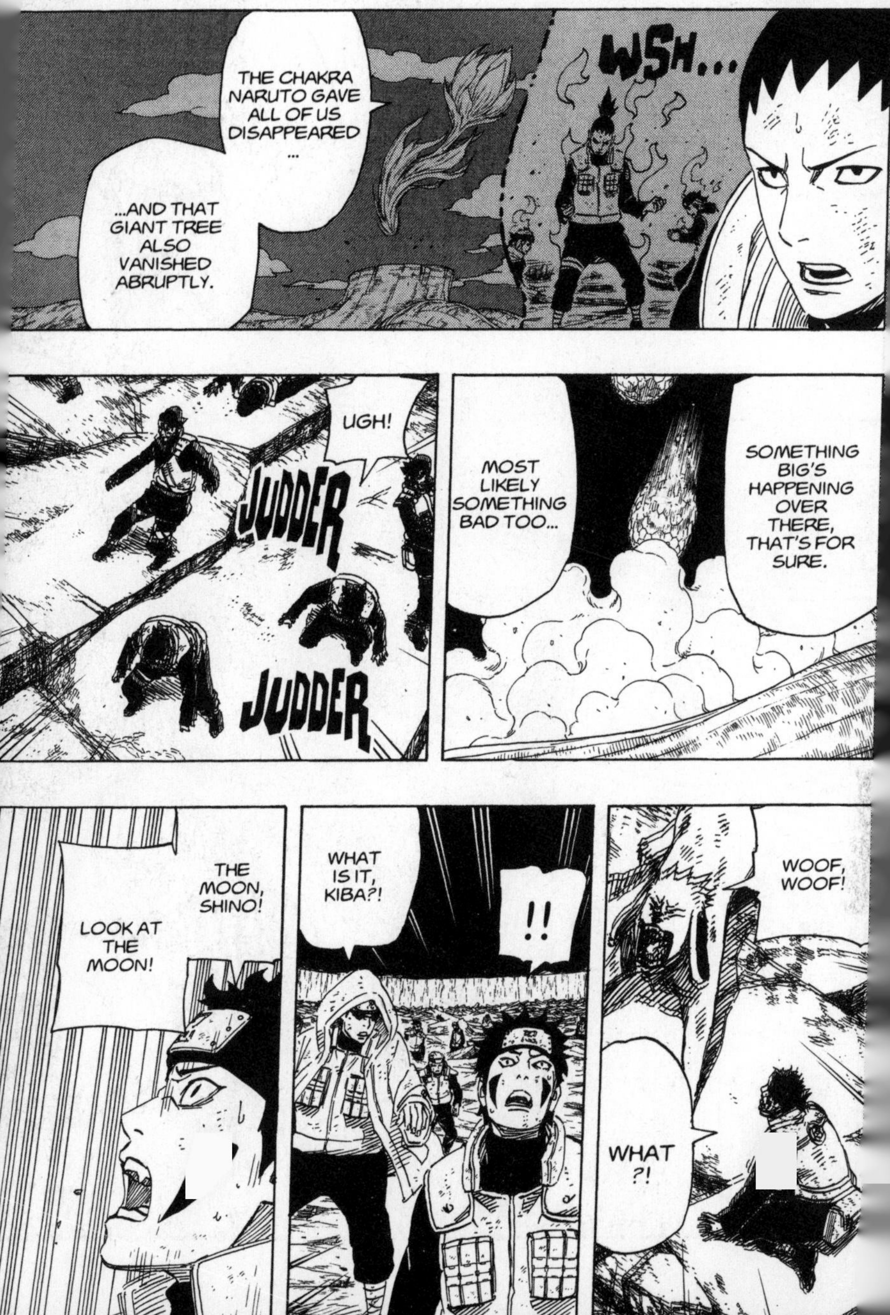
WSH...
THE CHAKRA NARUTO GAVE ALL OF US DISAPPEARED ...
...AND THAT GIANT TREE ALSO VANISHED ABRUPTLY.
SOMETHING BIG'S HAPPENING OVER THERE, THAT'S FOR SURE.
MOST LIKELY SOMETHING BAD TOO...
UGH!
JUDDER
JUDDER
WOOF, WOOF!
WHAT ?!
!!
WHAT IS IT, KIBA?!
THE MOON, SHINO!
LOOK AT THE MOON!

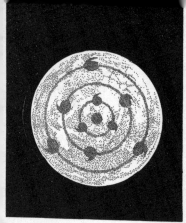

DON'T TELL ME THAT'S ...?!!

MY WORD!!

THIS IS REALLY BAD!

FWD

ZWISH

158

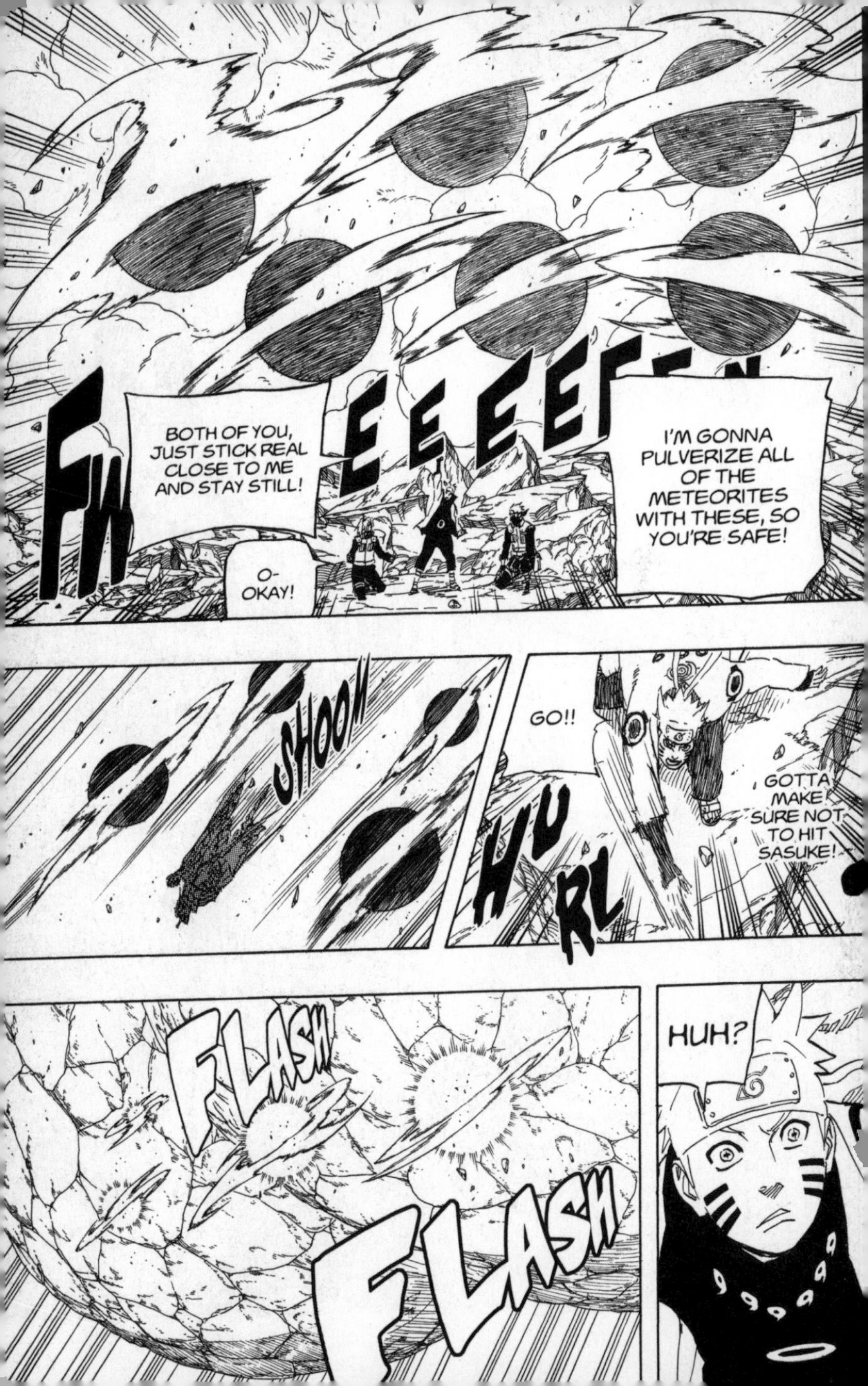
I'M GONNA PULVERIZE ALL OF THE METEORITES WITH THESE, SO YOU'RE SAFE!
FWEEEEEN
BOTH OF YOU, JUST STICK REAL CLOSE TO ME AND STAY STILL!
O-OKAY!
GO!!
GOTTA MAKE SURE NOT TO HIT SASUKE!
HWURL
SHOOM
HUH?
FLASH
FLASH

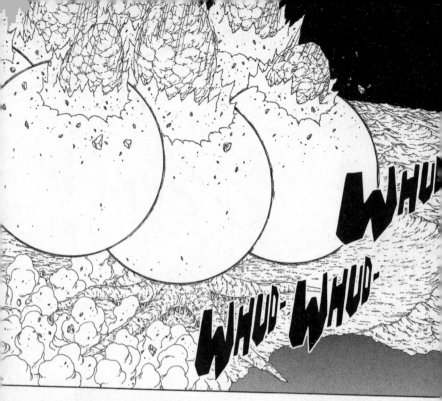

WHUD-WHUD-

WHUD-

WAH!!

EEP!

SASUKE, DON'T HEAD DOWN HERE SO SUDDENLY! I COULD'VE HIT YOU WITH A RASEN-SHURIKEN--

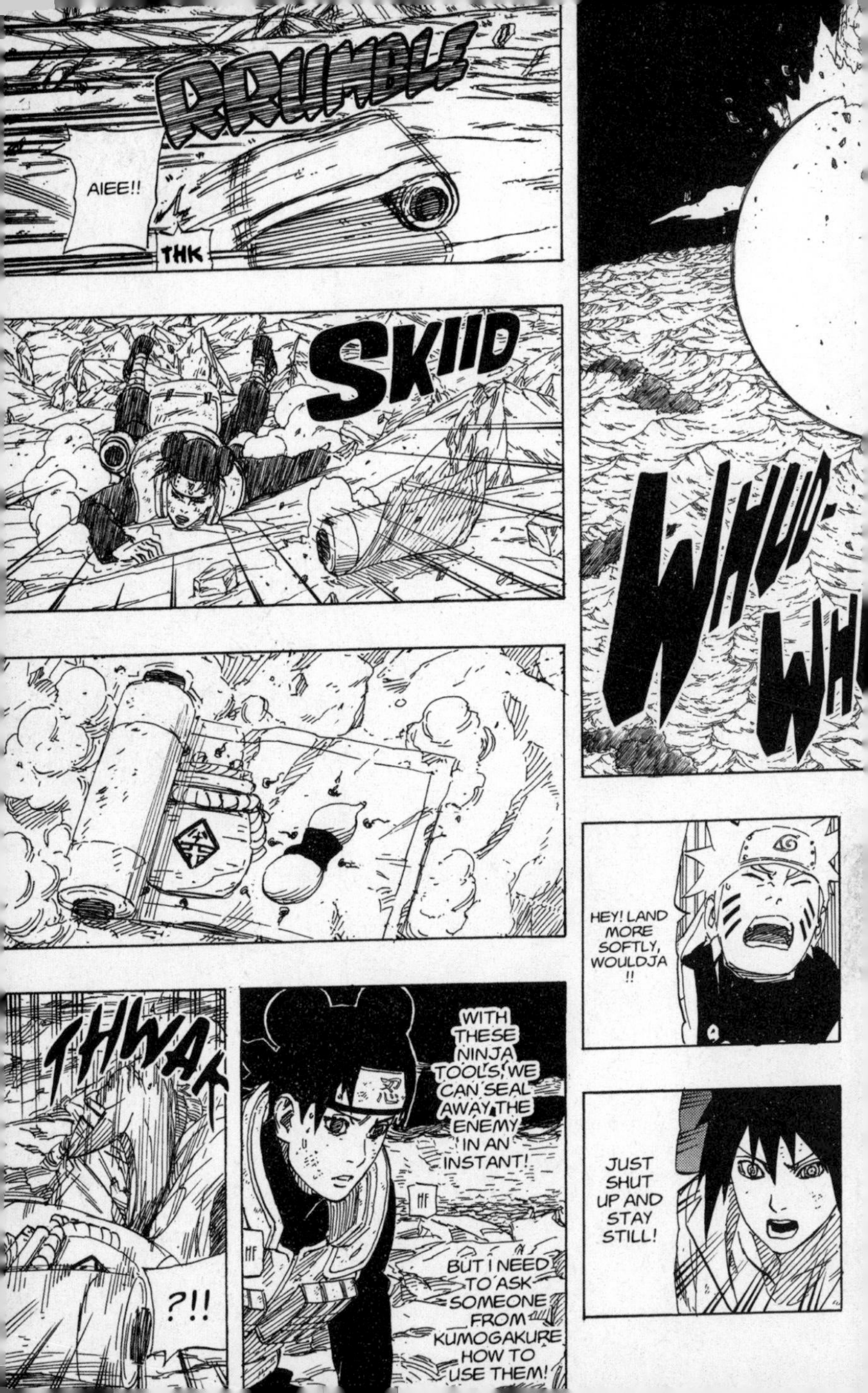

WHUD-
HEY! LAND MORE SOFTLY, WOULDJA !!
JUST SHUT UP AND STAY STILL!
RRUMBLE
AIEE!!
THK
SKIID
WITH THESE NINJA TOOLS, WE CAN SEAL AWAY THE ENEMY IN AN INSTANT!
HF
HF
BUT I NEED TO ASK SOMEONE FROM KUMOGAKURE HOW TO USE THEM!
THWAK
?!!

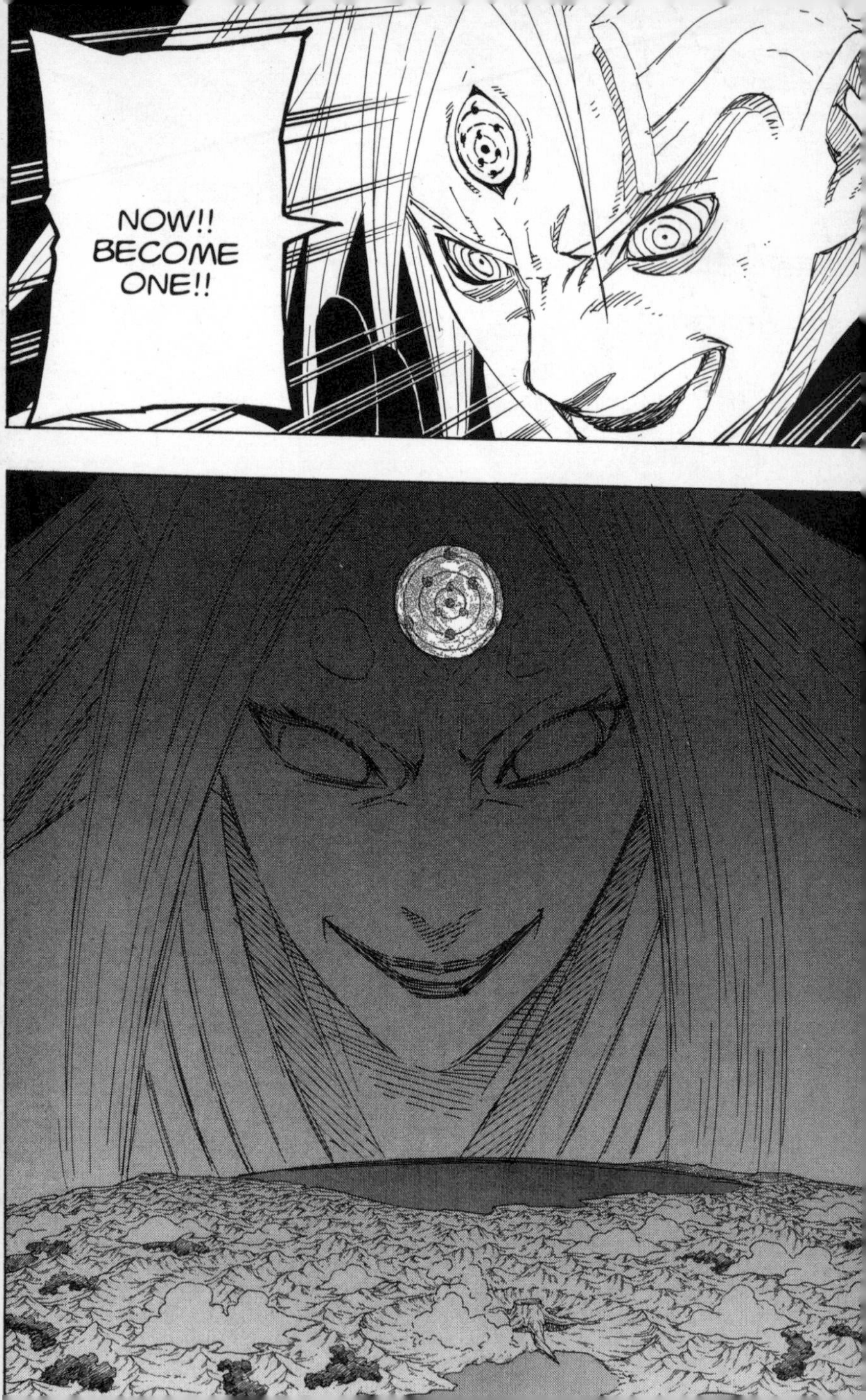
NOW!! BECOME ONE!!

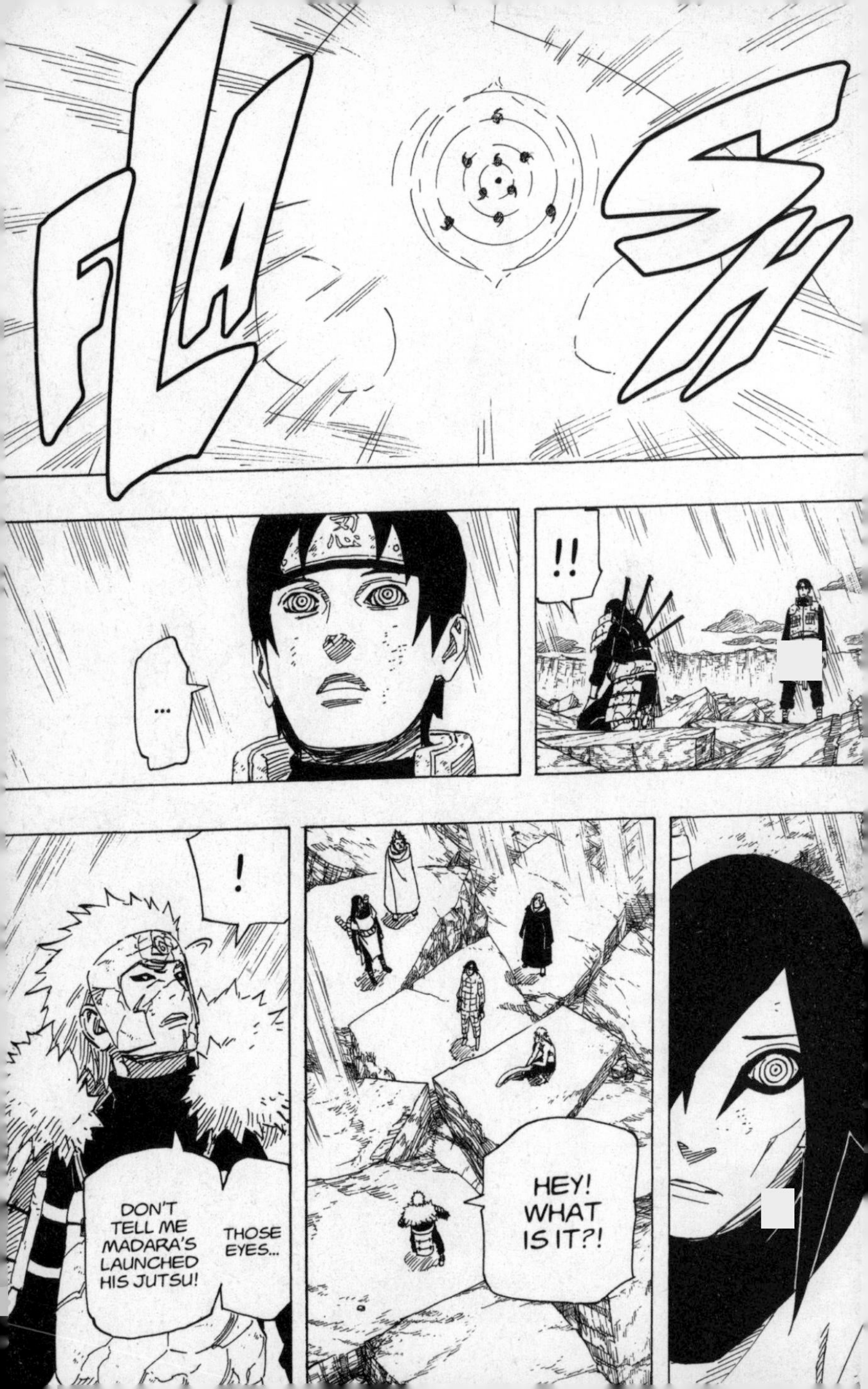
FLASH
!!
...
HEY! WHAT IS IT?!
!
THOSE EYES...
DON'T TELL ME MADARA'S LAUNCHED HIS JUTSU!

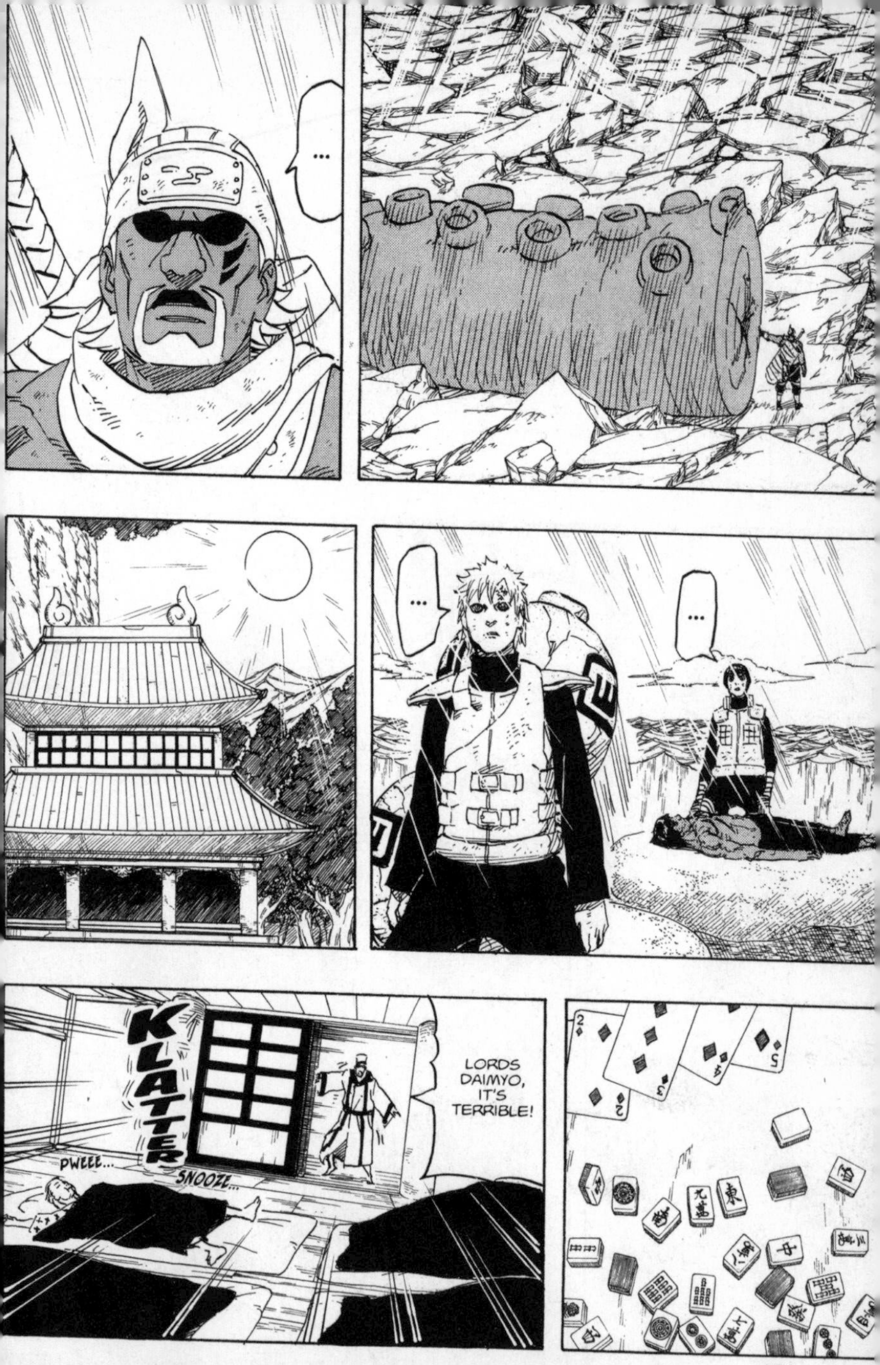
...
...
...
LORDS DAIMYO, IT'S TERRIBLE!
KLATTER
SNOOZE...
PWEEE...

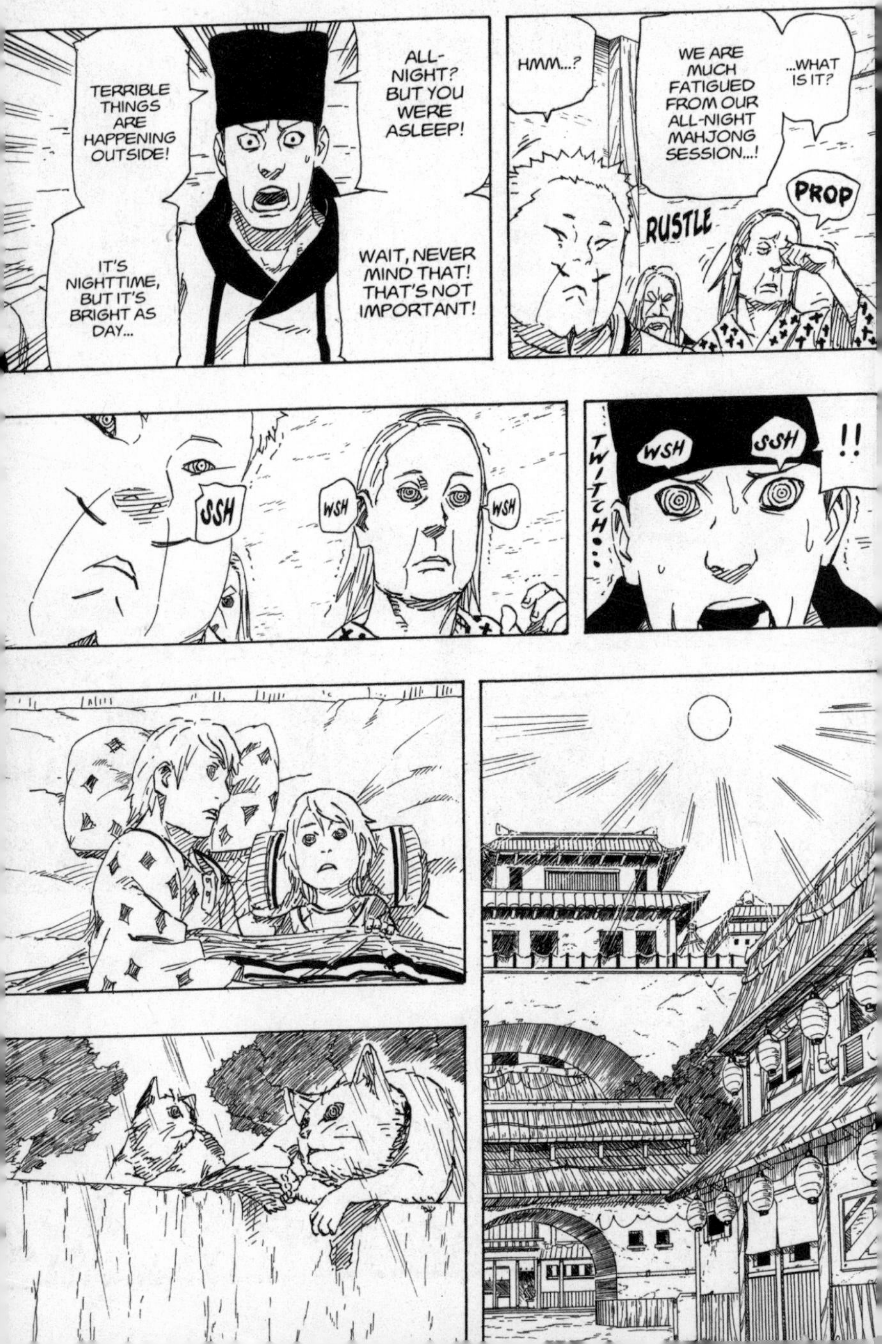
...WHAT IS IT?
WE ARE MUCH FATIGUED FROM OUR ALL-NIGHT MAHJONG SESSION...!
HMM...?
PROP
RUSTLE
ALL-NIGHT? BUT YOU WERE ASLEEP!
WAIT, NEVER MIND THAT! THAT'S NOT IMPORTANT!
TERRIBLE THINGS ARE HAPPENING OUTSIDE!
IT'S NIGHTTIME, BUT IT'S BRIGHT AS DAY...
!!
SSH
WSH
TWITCH...
WSH
WSH
SSH

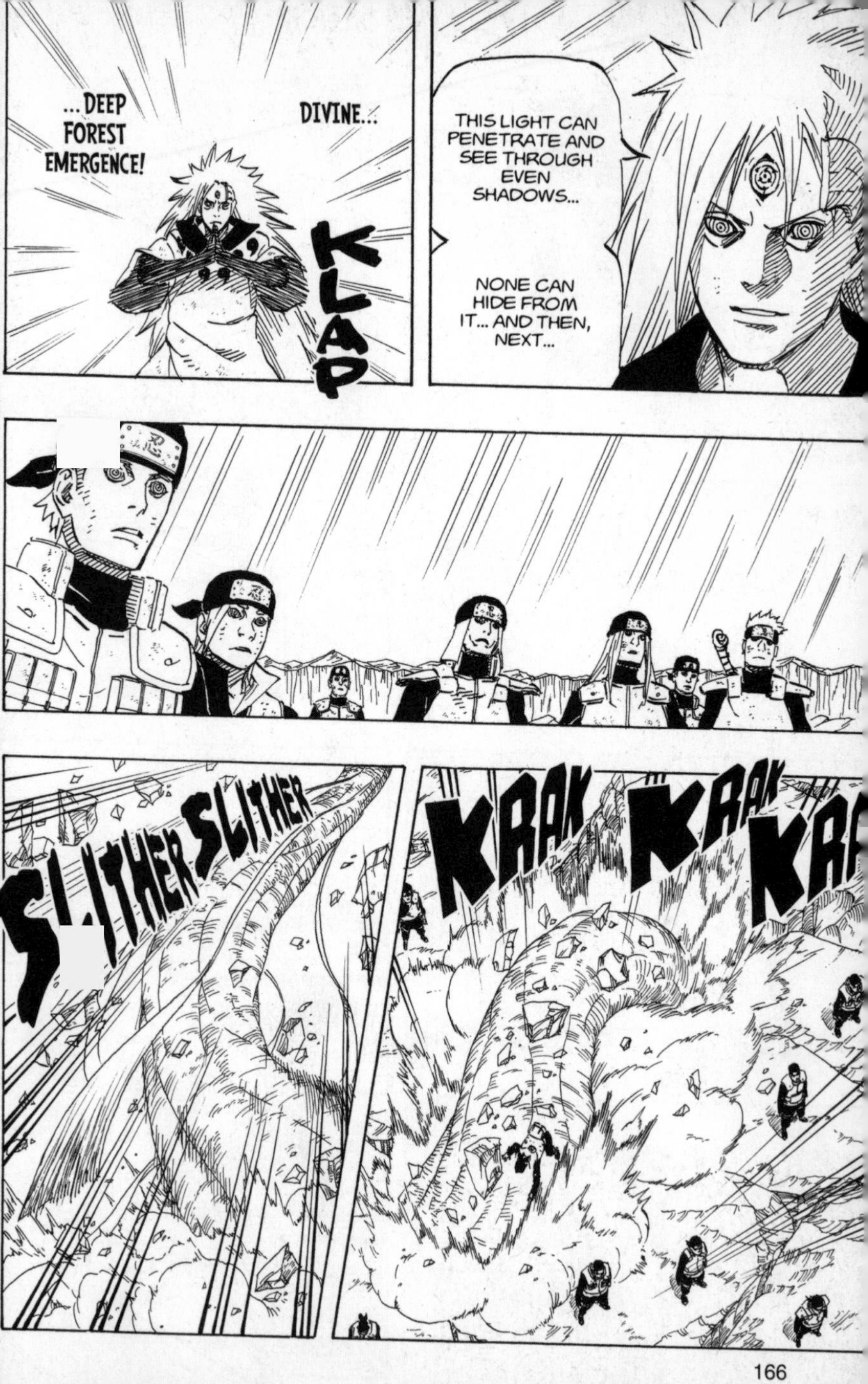
THIS LIGHT CAN PENETRATE AND SEE THROUGH EVEN SHADOWS...
NONE CAN HIDE FROM IT... AND THEN, NEXT...
DIVINE...
...DEEP FOREST EMERGENCE!
KLAP
KRAK
KRAK
SLITHER SLITHER

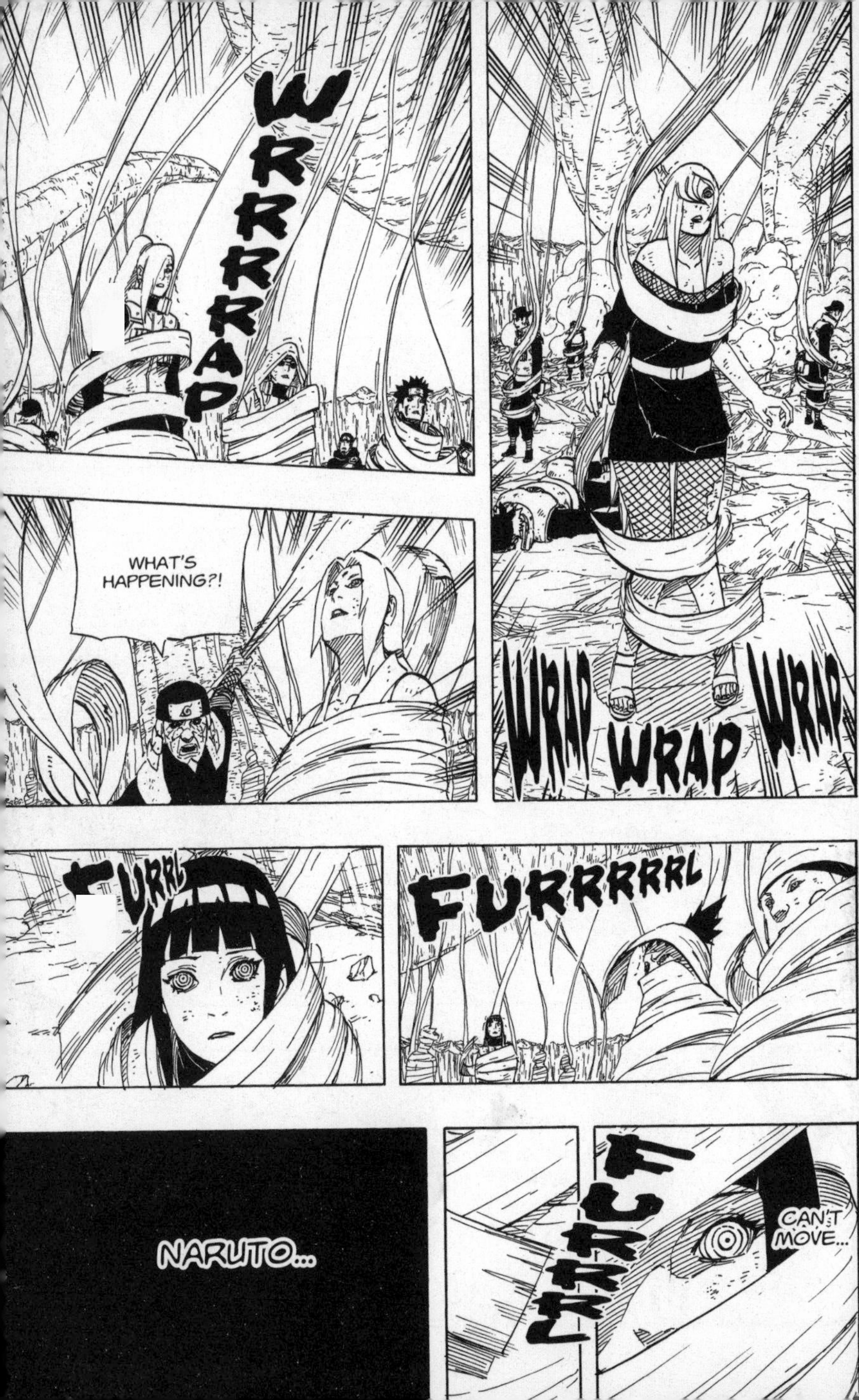
WRAP
WRAP
WRAP
WRRRRRAP
WHAT'S HAPPENING?!
FURRRRRL
FURRL
CAN'T MOVE...
FURRRL
NARUTO...

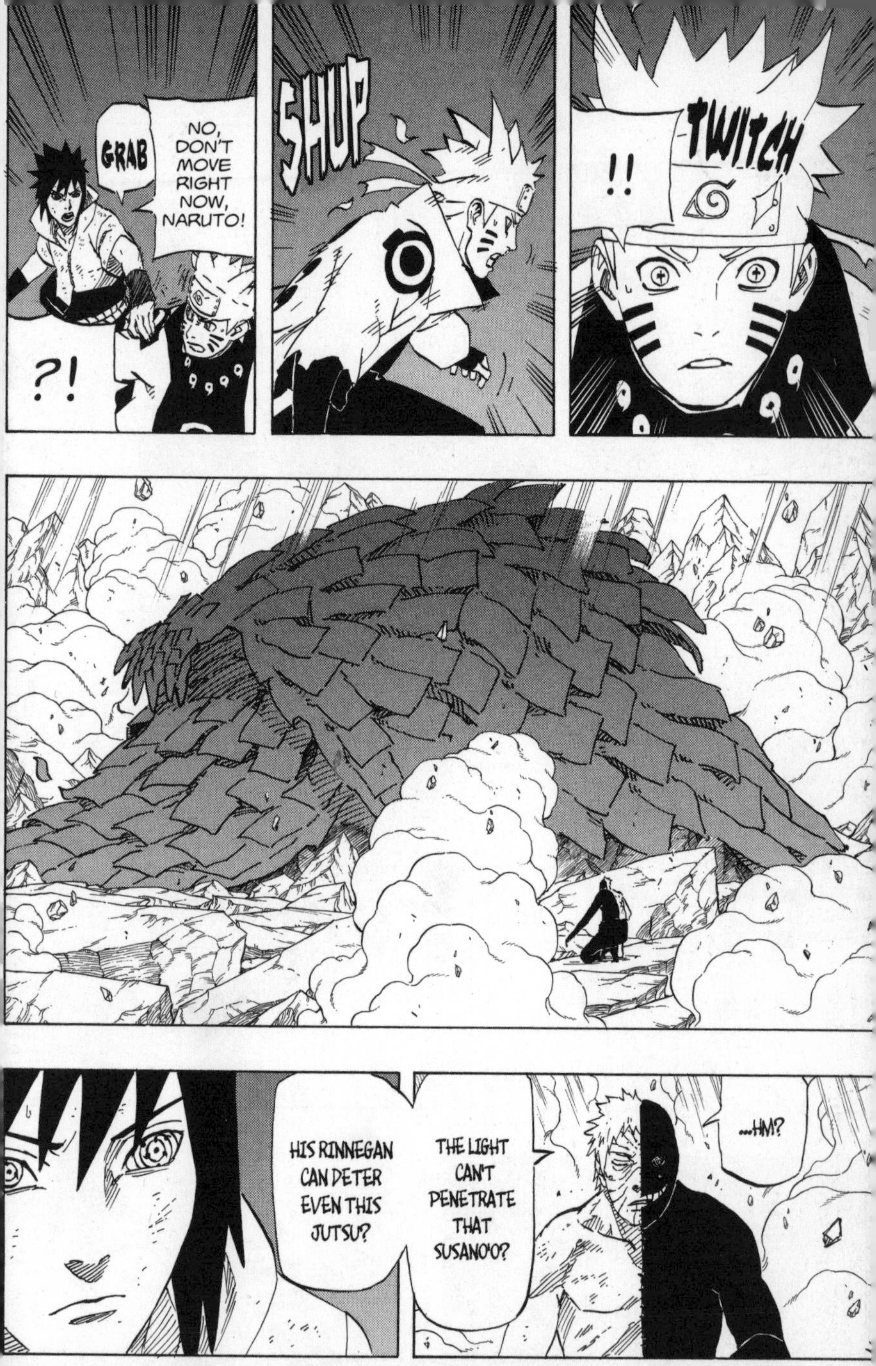
TWITCH
!!
SHUP
NO, DON'T MOVE RIGHT NOW, NARUTO!
GRAB
?!
...HM?
THE LIGHT CAN'T PENETRATE THAT SUSANO'O?
HIS RINNEGAN CAN DETER EVEN THIS JUTSU?

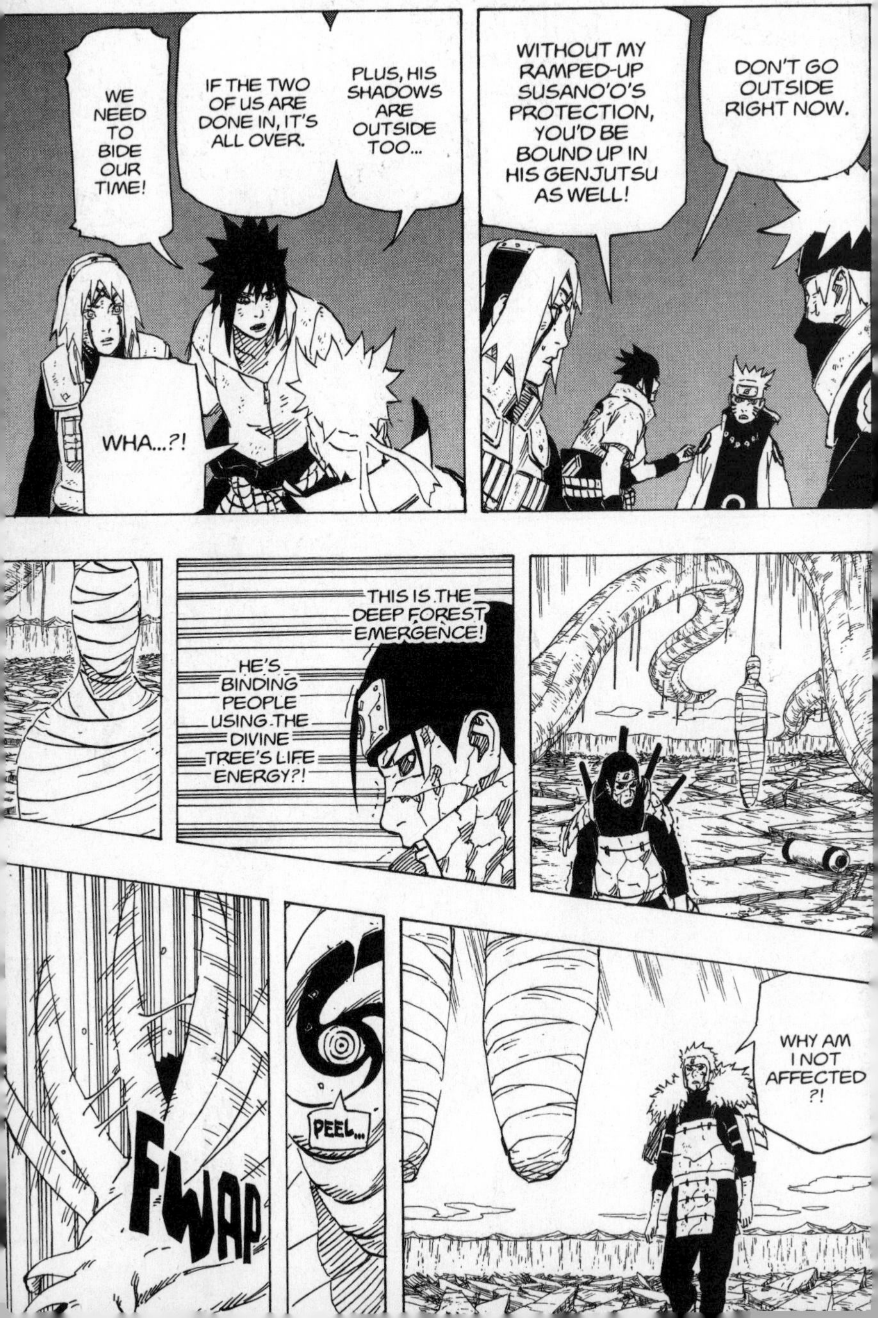
DON'T GO OUTSIDE RIGHT NOW.
WITHOUT MY RAMPED-UP SUSANO'O'S PROTECTION, YOU'D BE BOUND UP IN HIS GENJUTSU AS WELL!
PLUS, HIS SHADOWS ARE OUTSIDE TOO...
IF THE TWO OF US ARE DONE IN, IT'S ALL OVER.
WE NEED TO BIDE OUR TIME!
WHA...?!
THIS IS THE DEEP FOREST EMERGENCE!
HE'S BINDING PEOPLE USING THE DIVINE TREE'S LIFE ENERGY?!
WHY AM I NOT AFFECTED?!
PEEL...
FWAP

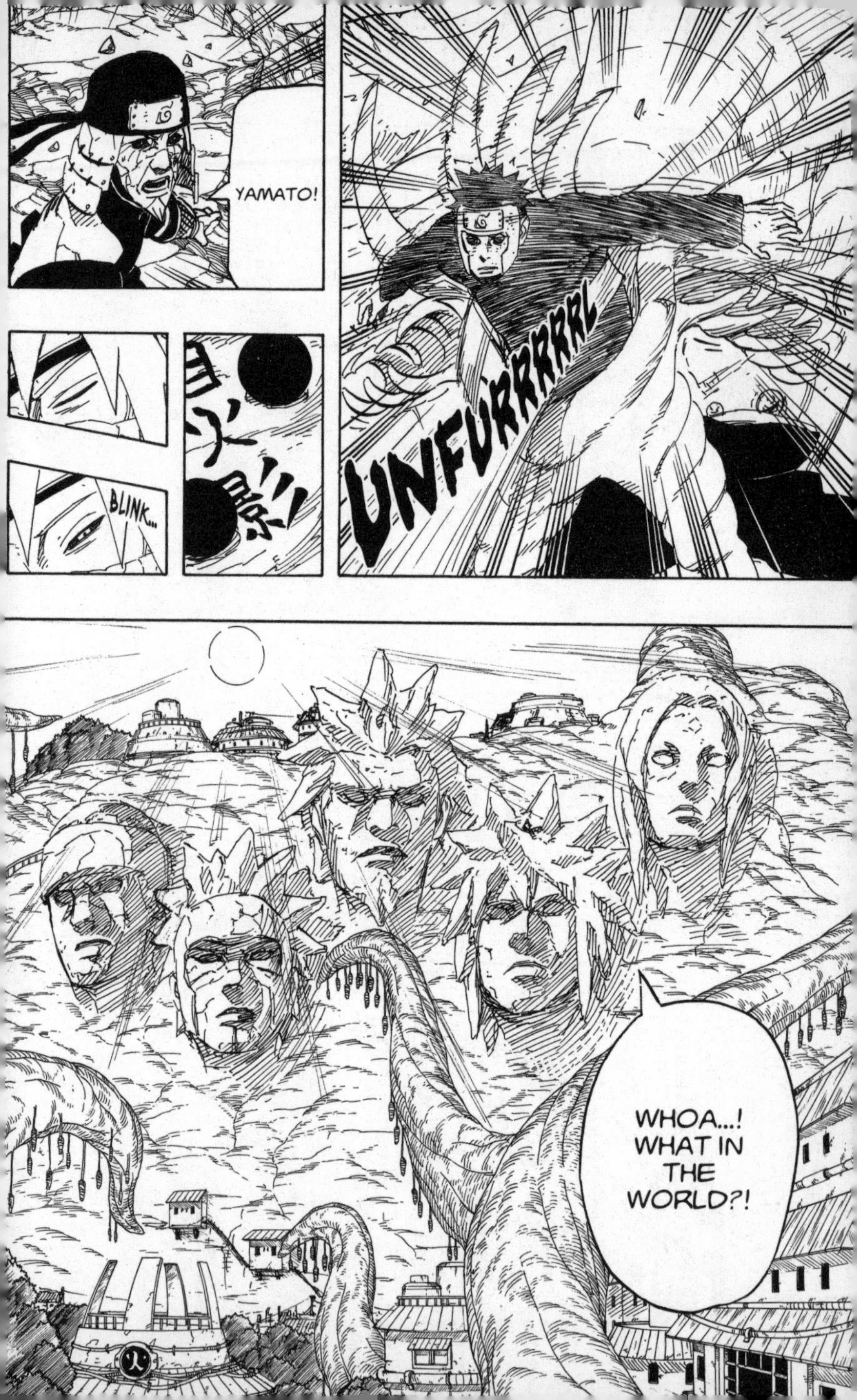
UNFURRRRRL
YAMATO!
BLINK...
WHOA...! WHAT IN THE WORLD?!

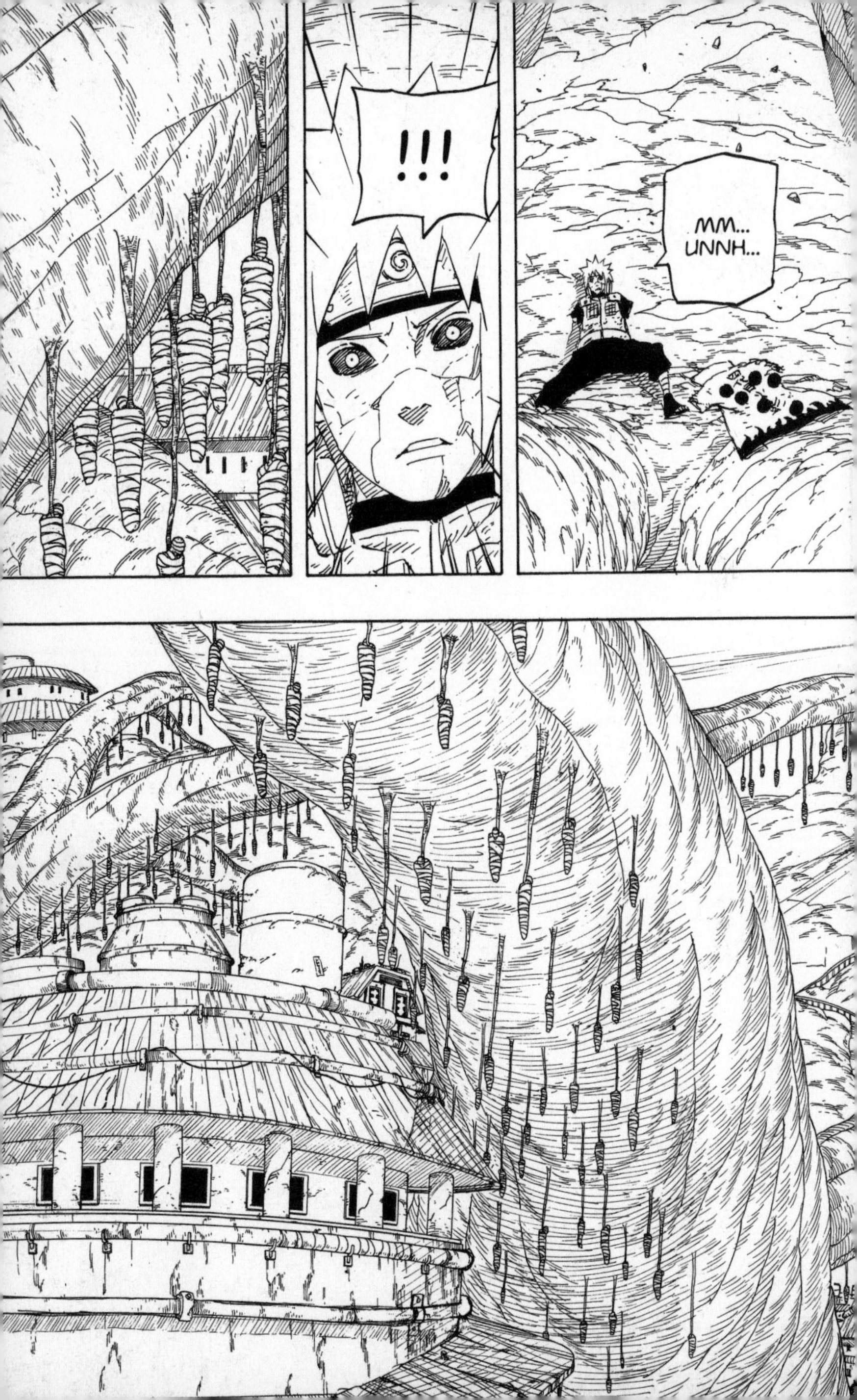
MM... UNNH...
!!!

# Number 678: My Will Is...

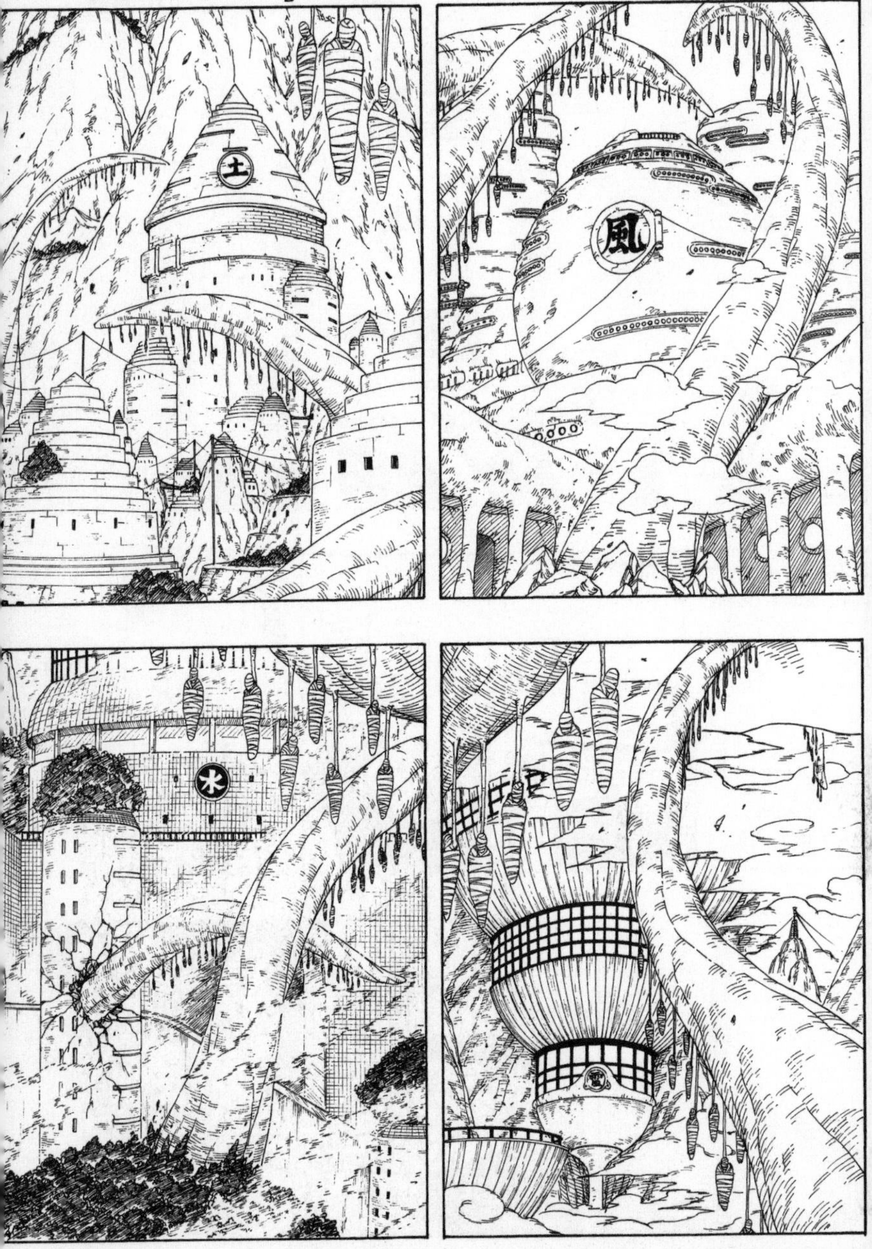

風
土
水

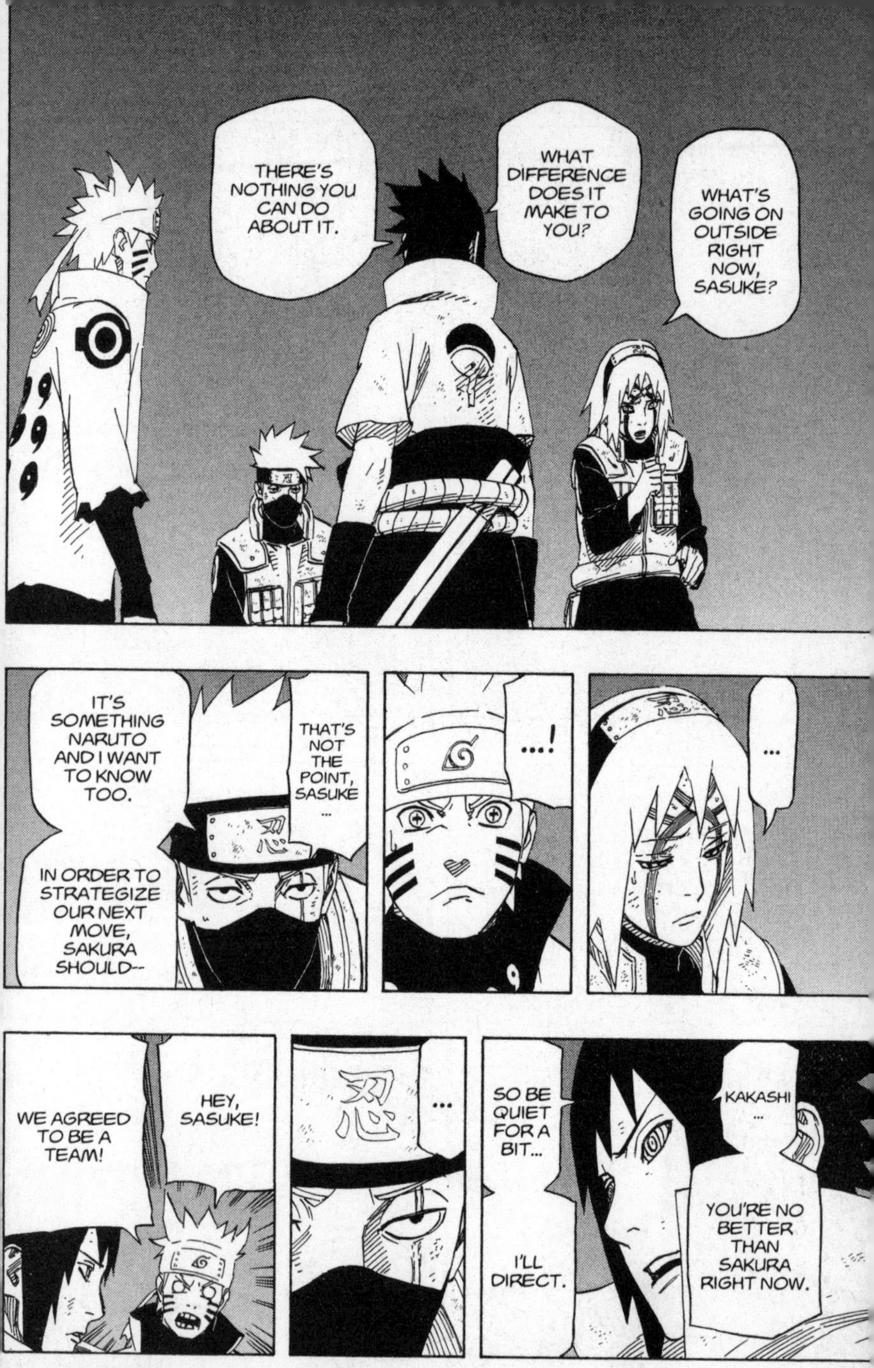
WHAT'S GOING ON OUTSIDE RIGHT NOW, SASUKE?
WHAT DIFFERENCE DOES IT MAKE TO YOU?
THERE'S NOTHING YOU CAN DO ABOUT IT.
...
...!
THAT'S NOT THE POINT, SASUKE ...
IT'S SOMETHING NARUTO AND I WANT TO KNOW TOO.
IN ORDER TO STRATEGIZE OUR NEXT MOVE, SAKURA SHOULD--
KAKASHI ...
YOU'RE NO BETTER THAN SAKURA RIGHT NOW.
SO BE QUIET FOR A BIT...
I'LL DIRECT.
...
HEY, SASUKE!
WE AGREED TO BE A TEAM!

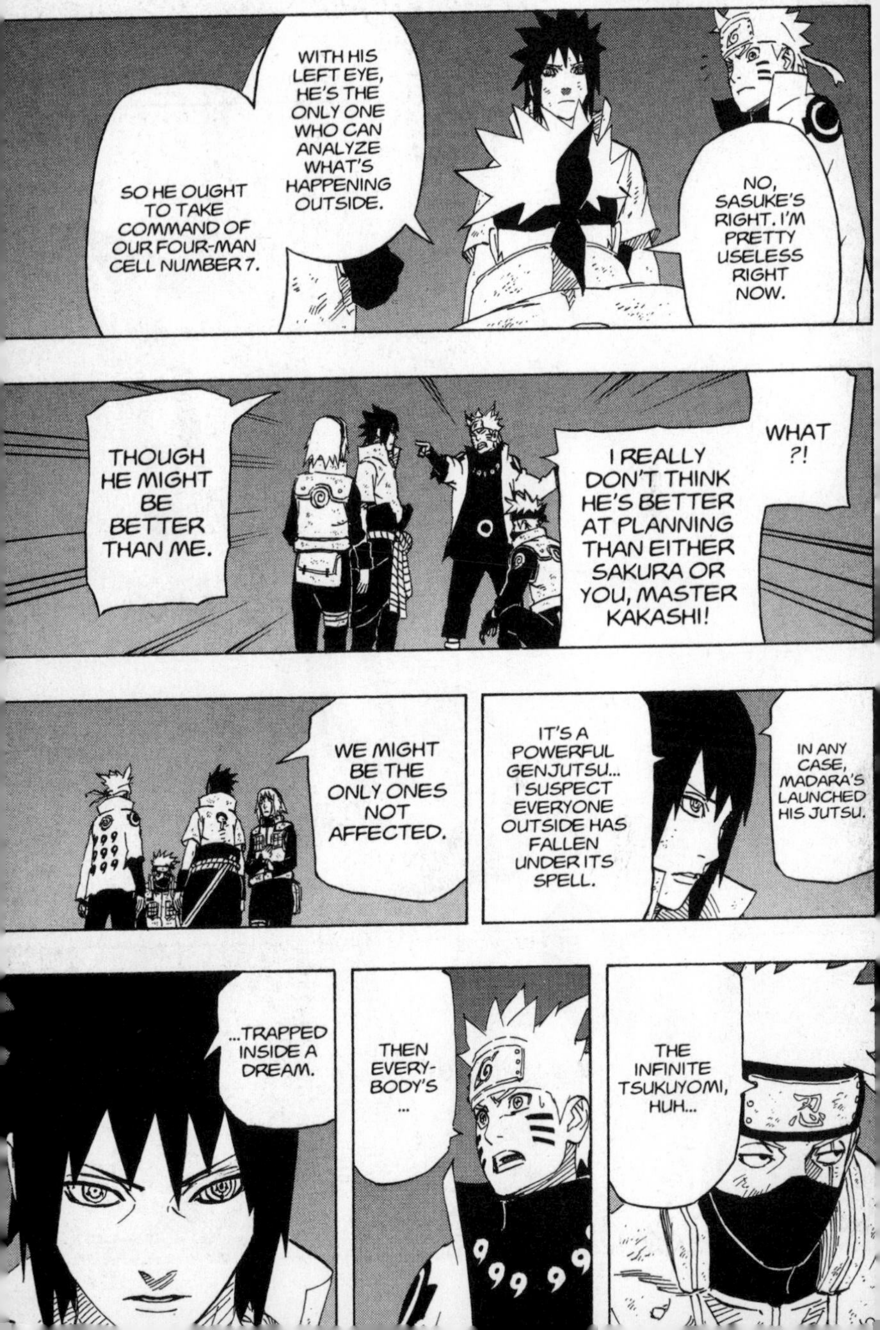
NO, SASUKE'S RIGHT. I'M PRETTY USELESS RIGHT NOW.
WITH HIS LEFT EYE, HE'S THE ONLY ONE WHO CAN ANALYZE WHAT'S HAPPENING OUTSIDE.
SO HE OUGHT TO TAKE COMMAND OF OUR FOUR-MAN CELL NUMBER 7.
WHAT ?!
I REALLY DON'T THINK HE'S BETTER AT PLANNING THAN EITHER SAKURA OR YOU, MASTER KAKASHI!
THOUGH HE MIGHT BE BETTER THAN ME.
IN ANY CASE, MADARA'S LAUNCHED HIS JUTSU.
IT'S A POWERFUL GENJUTSU... I SUSPECT EVERYONE OUTSIDE HAS FALLEN UNDER ITS SPELL.
WE MIGHT BE THE ONLY ONES NOT AFFECTED.
THE INFINITE TSUKUYOMI, HUH...
THEN EVERY-BODY'S ...
...TRAPPED INSIDE A DREAM.

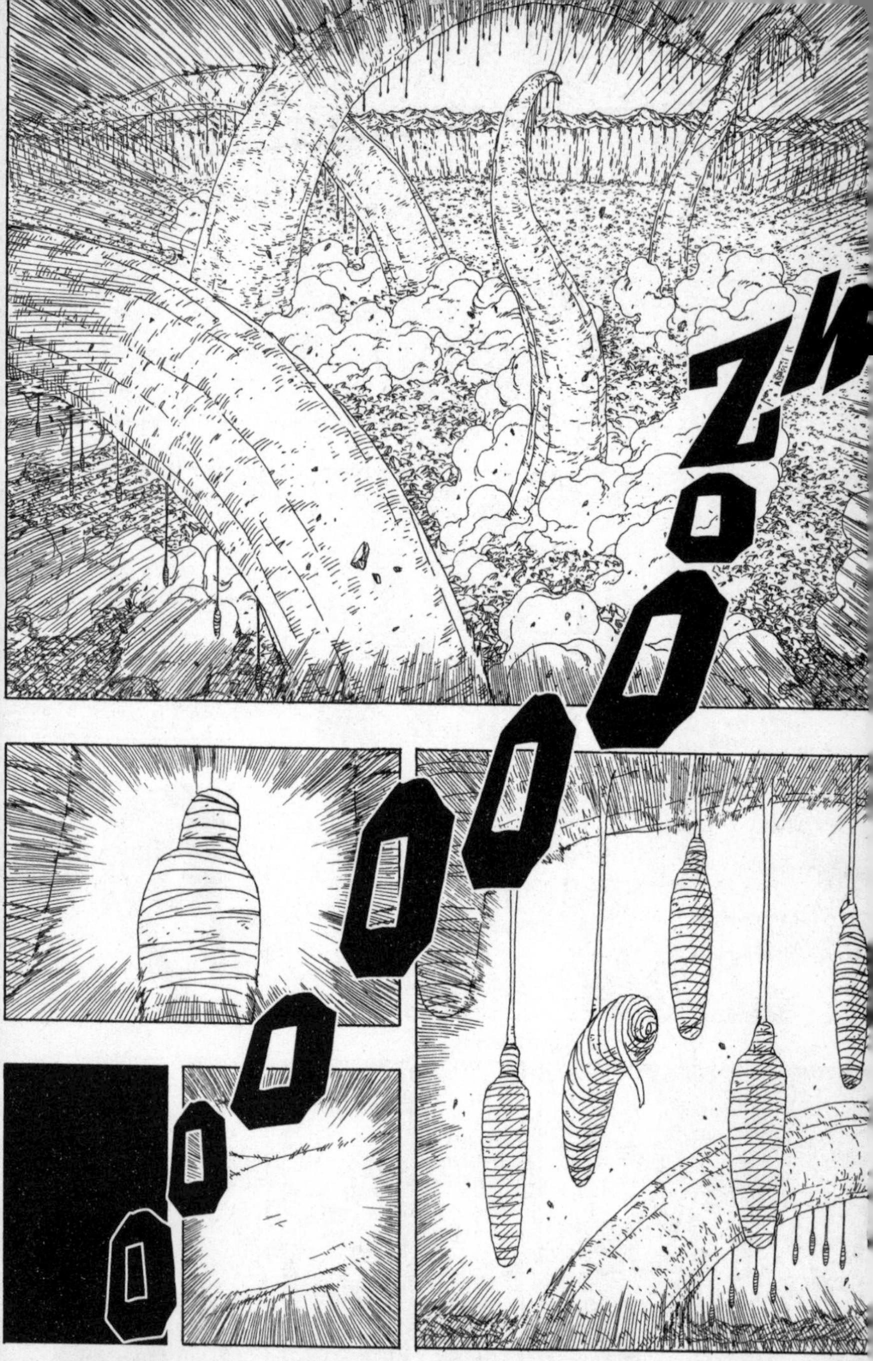
ZWOOOOOOO

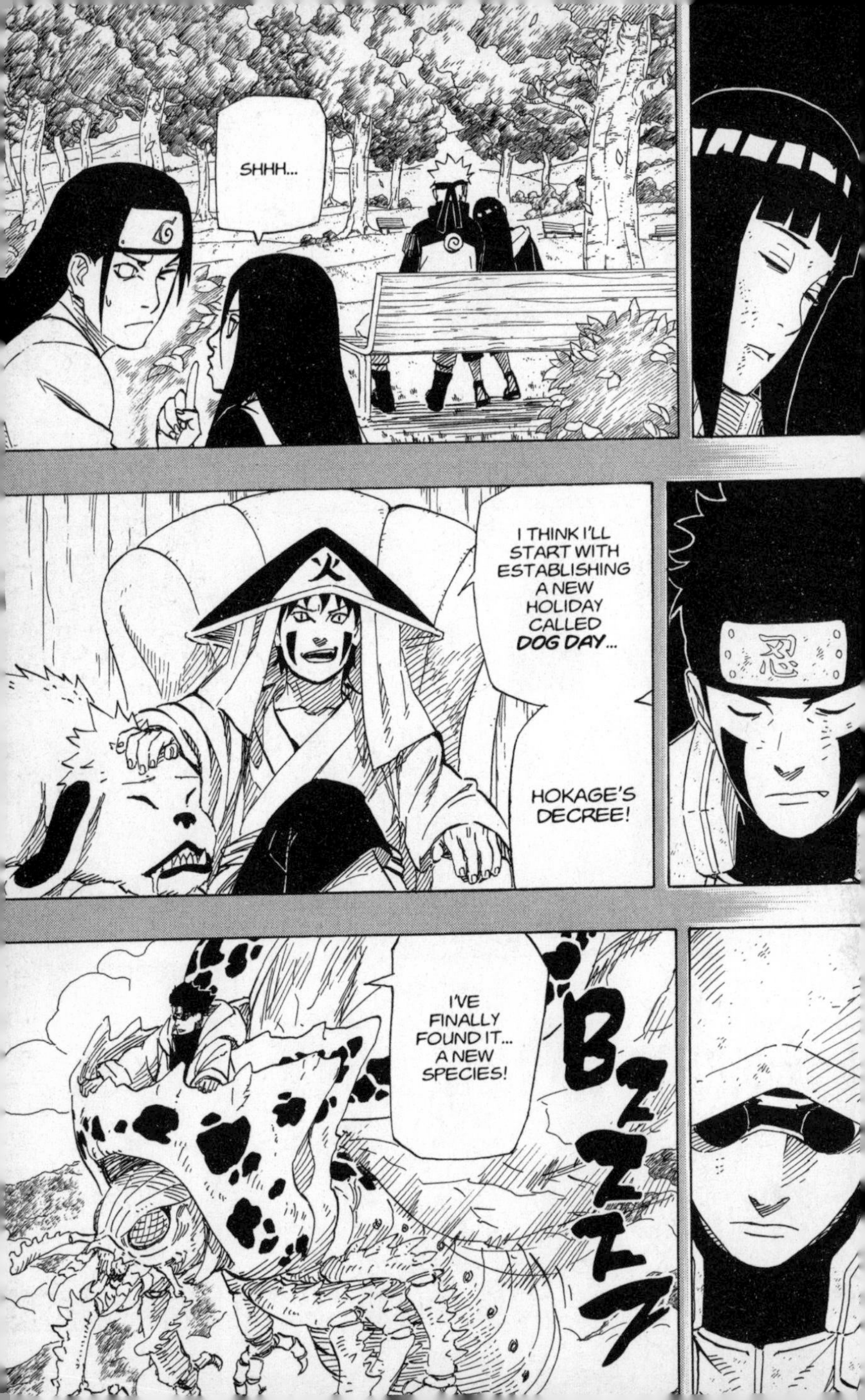
SHHH...
I THINK I'LL START WITH ESTABLISHING A NEW HOLIDAY CALLED **DOG DAY**...
HOKAGE'S DECREE!
BZZZZ
I'VE FINALLY FOUND IT... A NEW SPECIES!

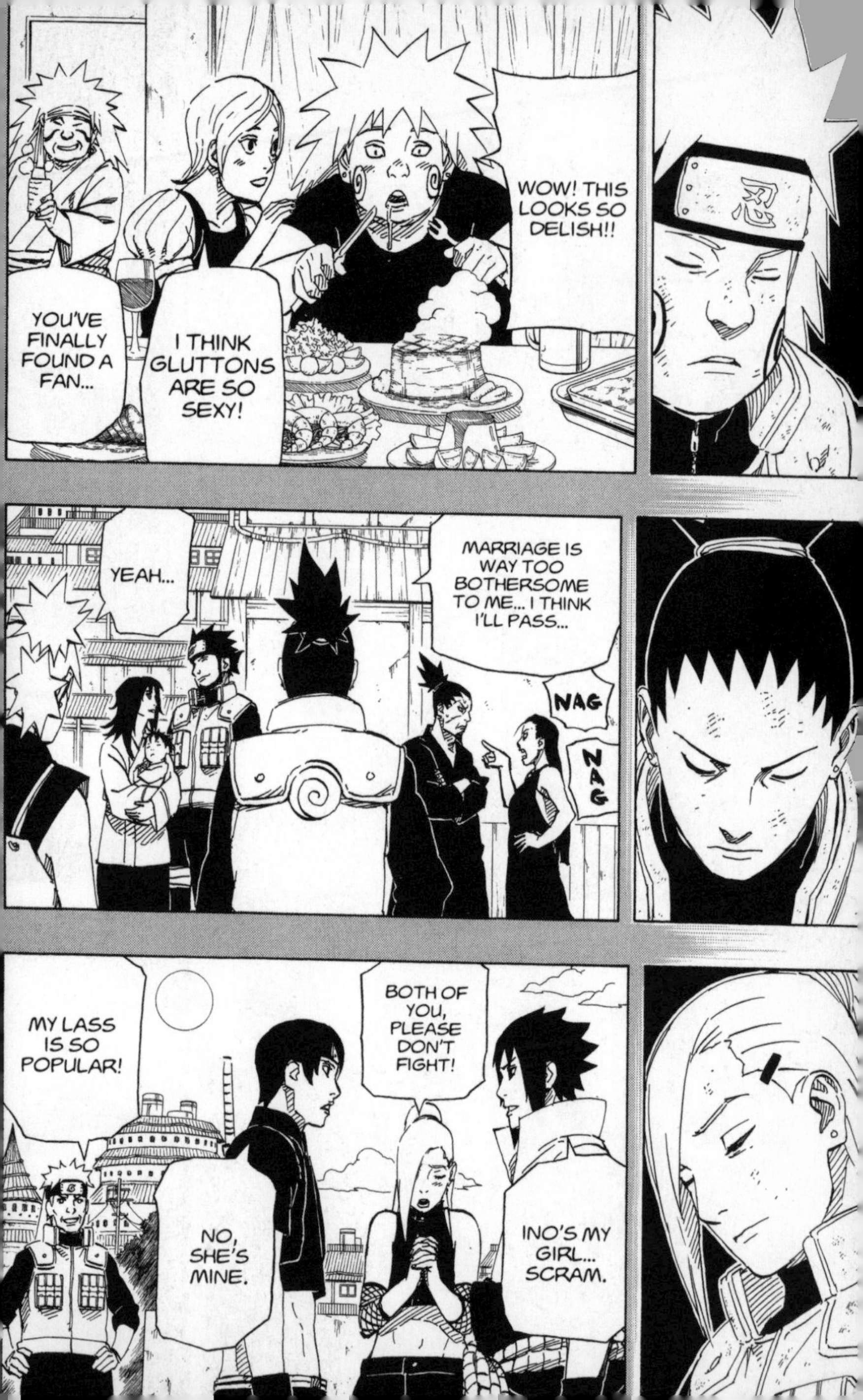
WOW! THIS LOOKS SO DELISH!!
I THINK GLUTTONS ARE SO SEXY!
YOU'VE FINALLY FOUND A FAN...
MARRIAGE IS WAY TOO BOTHERSOME TO ME... I THINK I'LL PASS...
NAG
NAG
YEAH...
BOTH OF YOU, PLEASE DON'T FIGHT!
INO'S MY GIRL... SCRAM.
NO, SHE'S MINE.
MY LASS IS SO POPULAR!

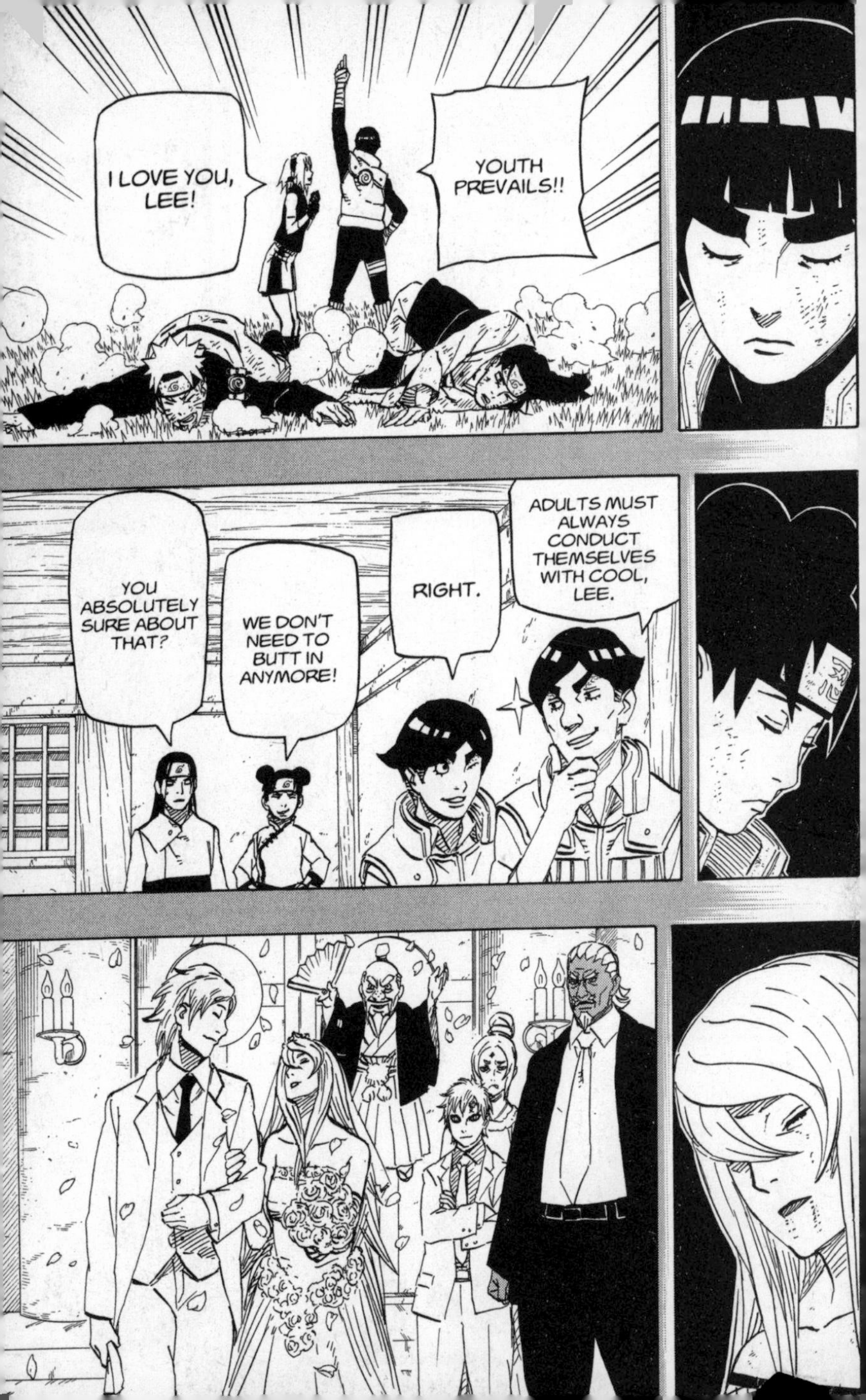
YOUTH PREVAILS!!
I LOVE YOU, LEE!
ADULTS MUST ALWAYS CONDUCT THEMSELVES WITH COOL, LEE.
RIGHT.
WE DON'T NEED TO BUTT IN ANYMORE!
YOU ABSOLUTELY SURE ABOUT THAT?

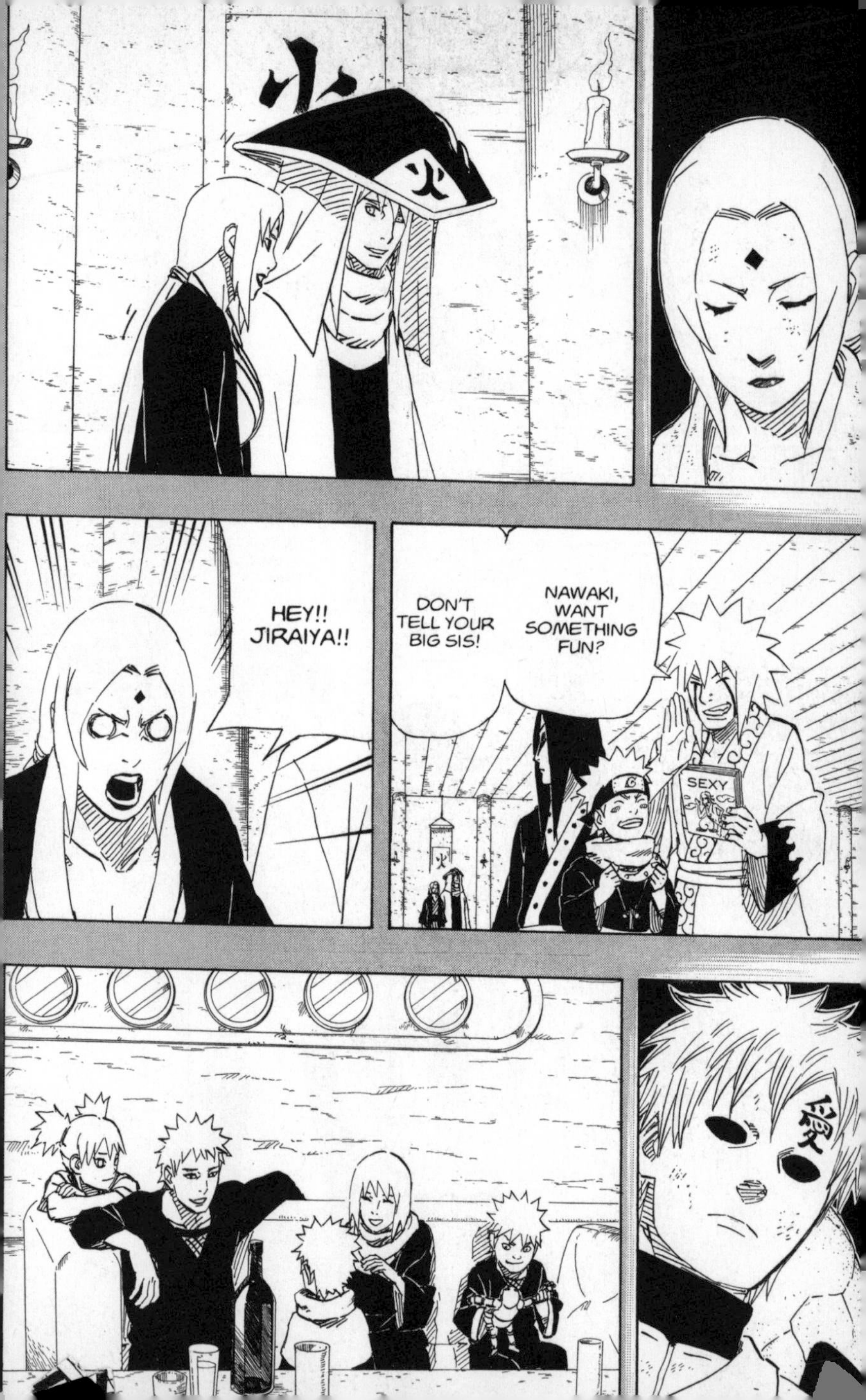
NAWAKI, WANT SOMETHING FUN?
DON'T TELL YOUR BIG SIS!
SEXY
HEY!! JIRAIYA!!

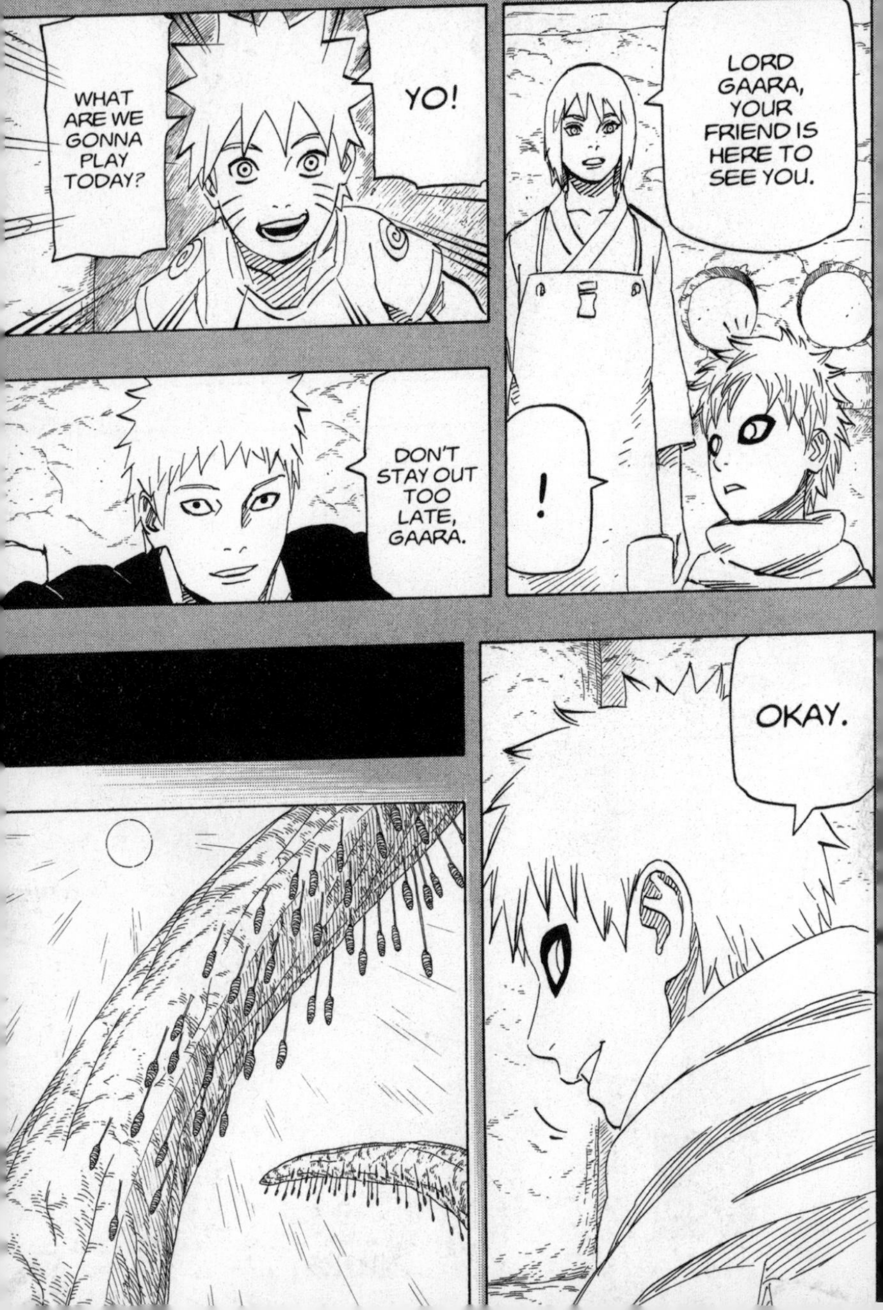
LORD GAARA, YOUR FRIEND IS HERE TO SEE YOU.
!
YO!
WHAT ARE WE GONNA PLAY TODAY?
DON'T STAY OUT TOO LATE, GAARA.
OKAY.

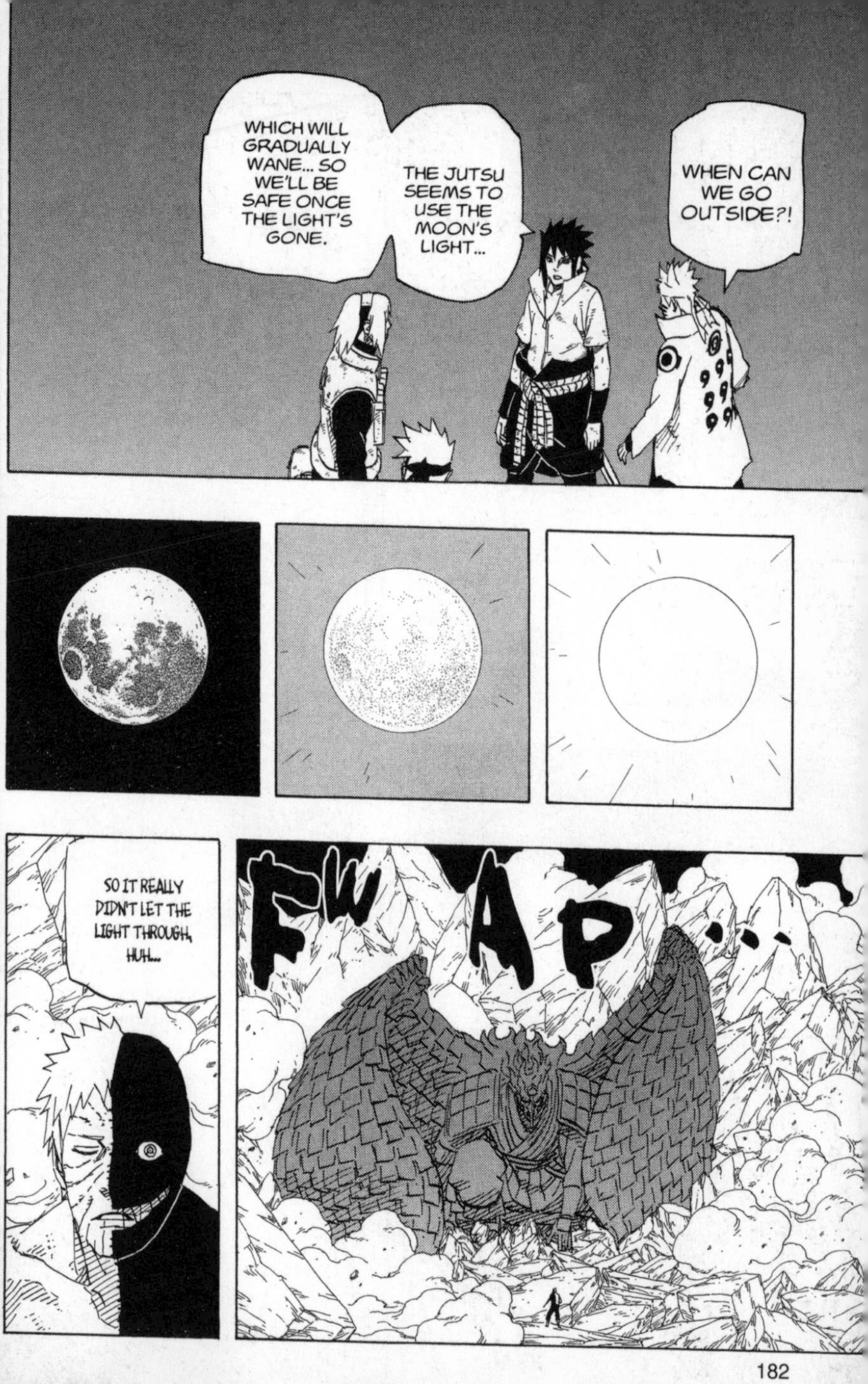
WHEN CAN WE GO OUTSIDE?!
THE JUTSU SEEMS TO USE THE MOON'S LIGHT...
WHICH WILL GRADUALLY WANE... SO WE'LL BE SAFE ONCE THE LIGHT'S GONE.
FWAP...
SO IT REALLY DIDN'T LET THE LIGHT THROUGH, HUH...

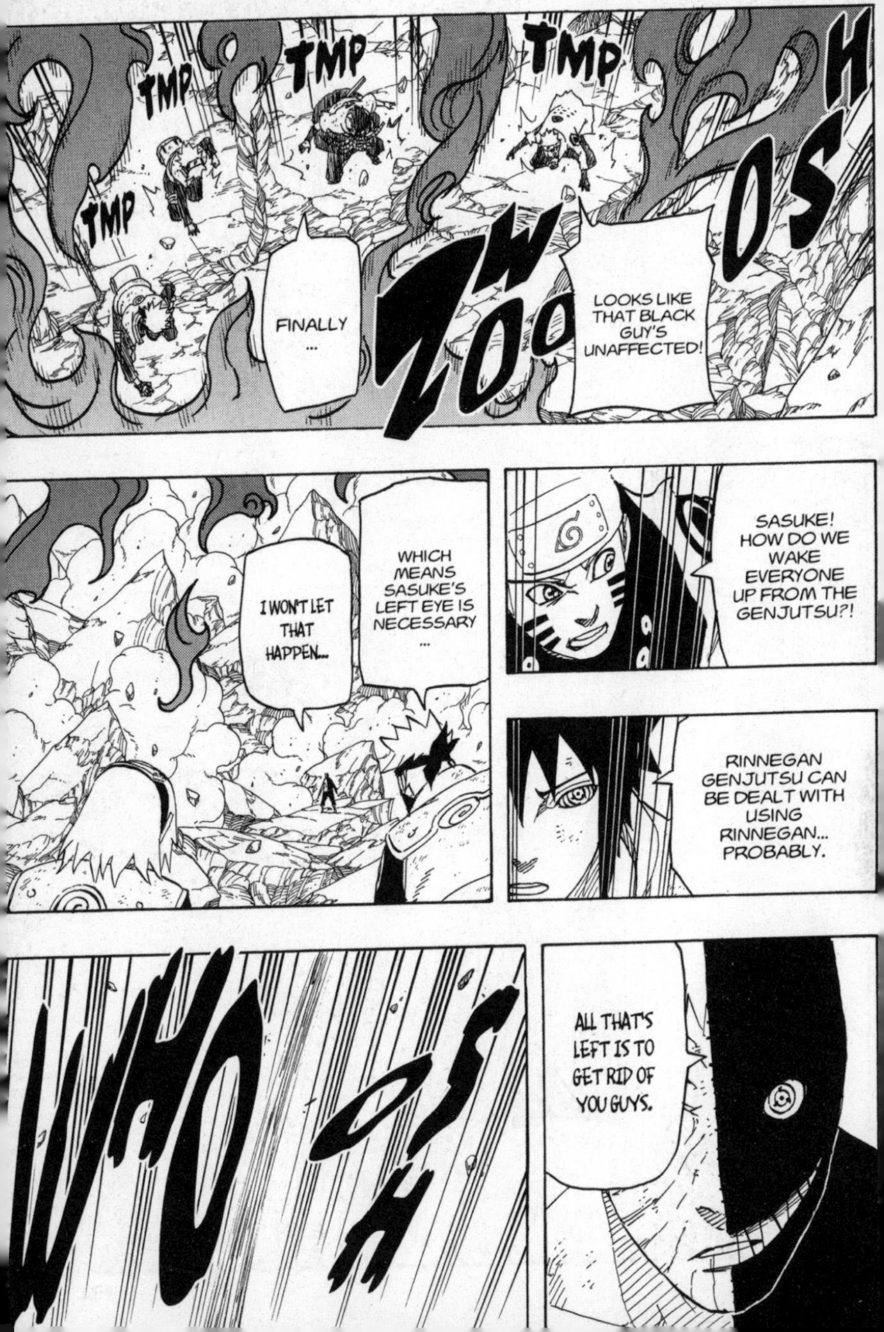

LOOKS LIKE THAT BLACK GUY'S UNAFFECTED!
ZWOOOSH
TMP
TMP
TMP
TMP
FINALLY ...
SASUKE! HOW DO WE WAKE EVERYONE UP FROM THE GENJUTSU?!
RINNEGAN GENJUTSU CAN BE DEALT WITH USING RINNEGAN... PROBABLY.
WHICH MEANS SASUKE'S LEFT EYE IS NECESSARY ...
I WON'T LET THAT HAPPEN...
ALL THAT'S LEFT IS TO GET RID OF YOU GUYS.
WHOOSH

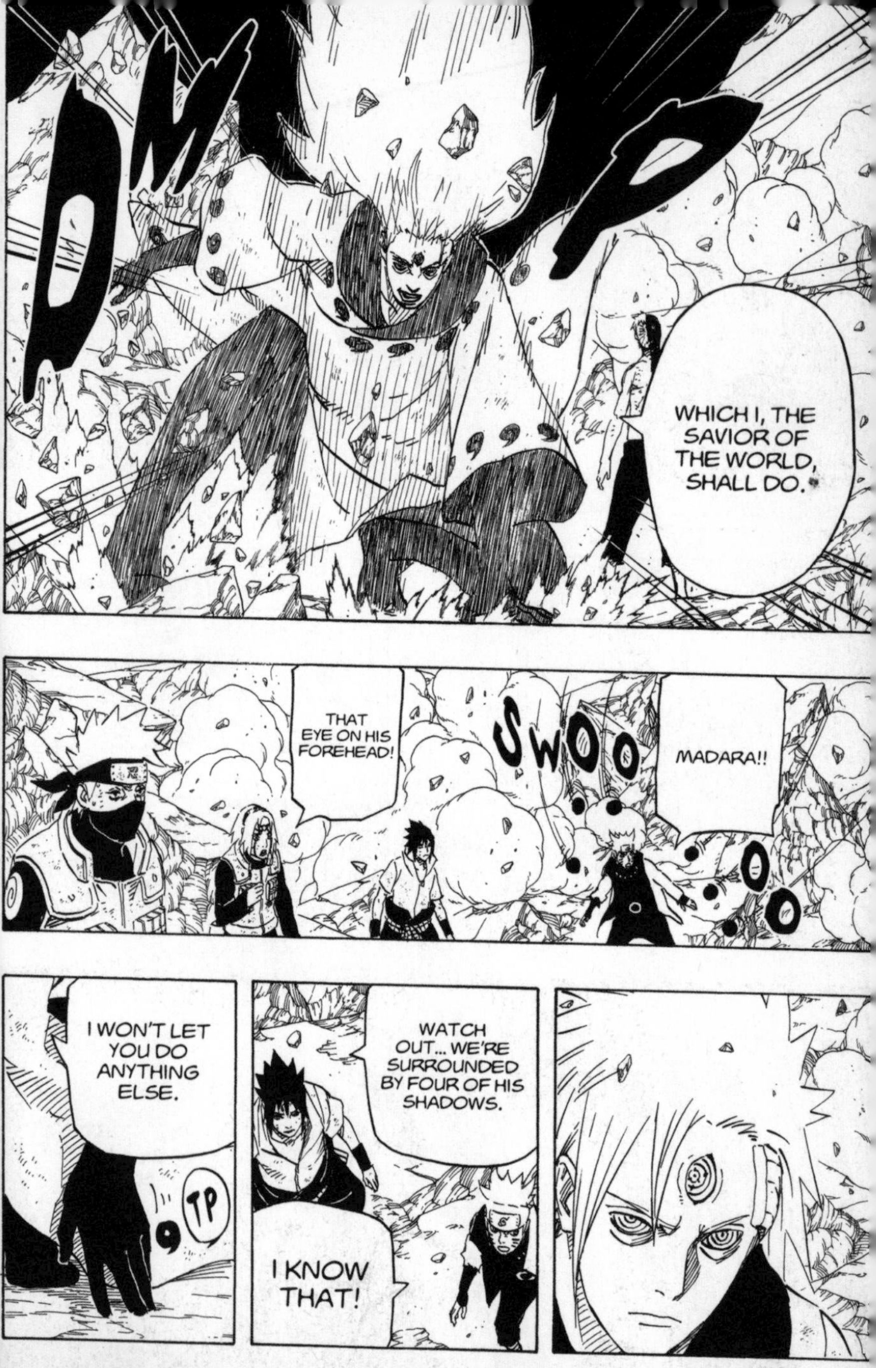
DMMP
WHICH I, THE SAVIOR OF THE WORLD, SHALL DO.
MADARA!!
SWOO
THAT EYE ON HIS FOREHEAD!
WATCH OUT... WE'RE SURROUNDED BY FOUR OF HIS SHADOWS.
I KNOW THAT!
I WON'T LET YOU DO ANYTHING ELSE.
TP

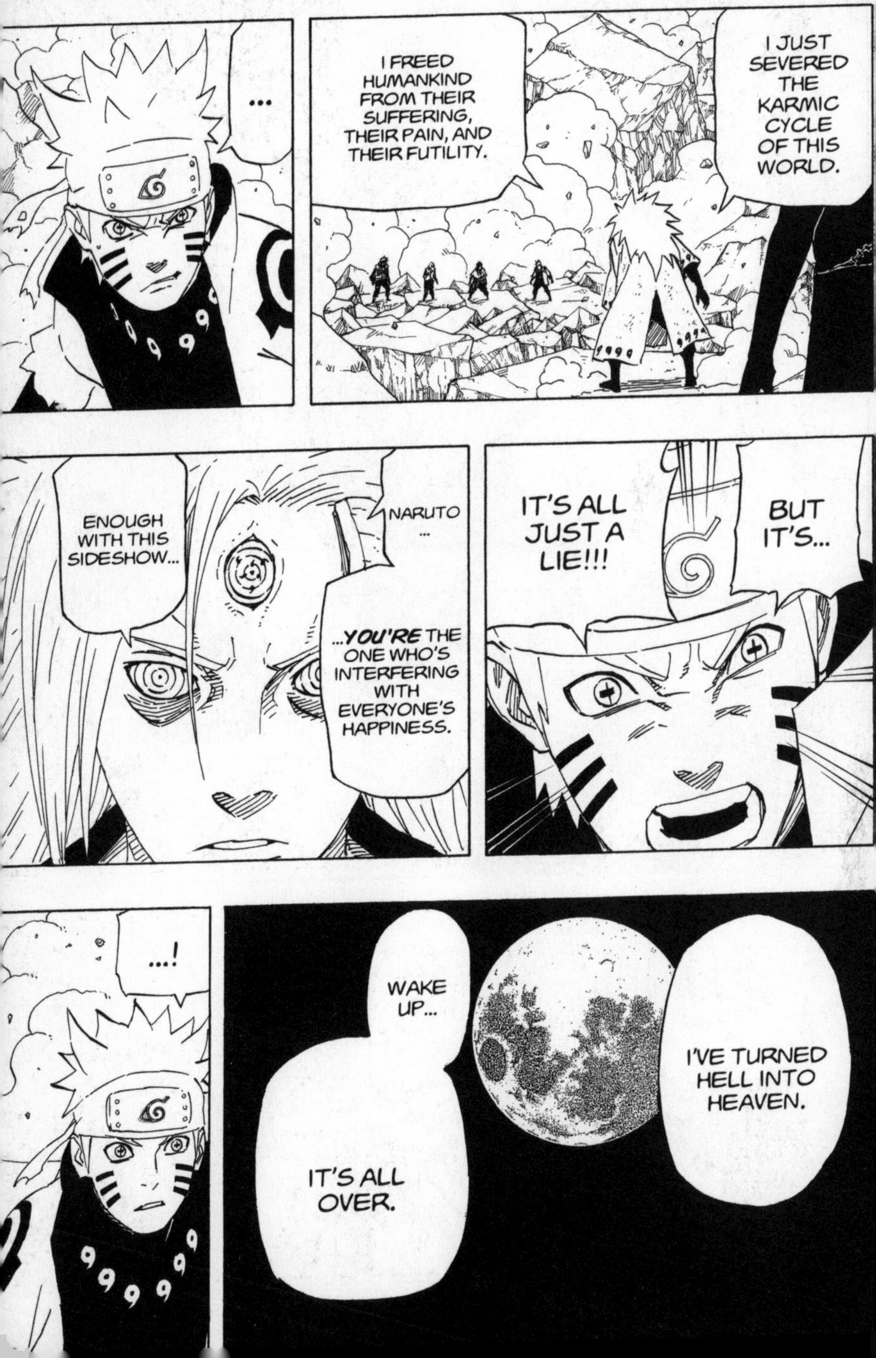
I JUST SEVERED THE KARMIC CYCLE OF THIS WORLD.
I FREED HUMANKIND FROM THEIR SUFFERING, THEIR PAIN, AND THEIR FUTILITY.
...
BUT IT'S...
IT'S ALL JUST A LIE!!!
NARUTO ...
ENOUGH WITH THIS SIDESHOW...
...*YOU'RE* THE ONE WHO'S INTERFERING WITH EVERYONE'S HAPPINESS.
I'VE TURNED HELL INTO HEAVEN.
WAKE UP...
IT'S ALL OVER.
...!

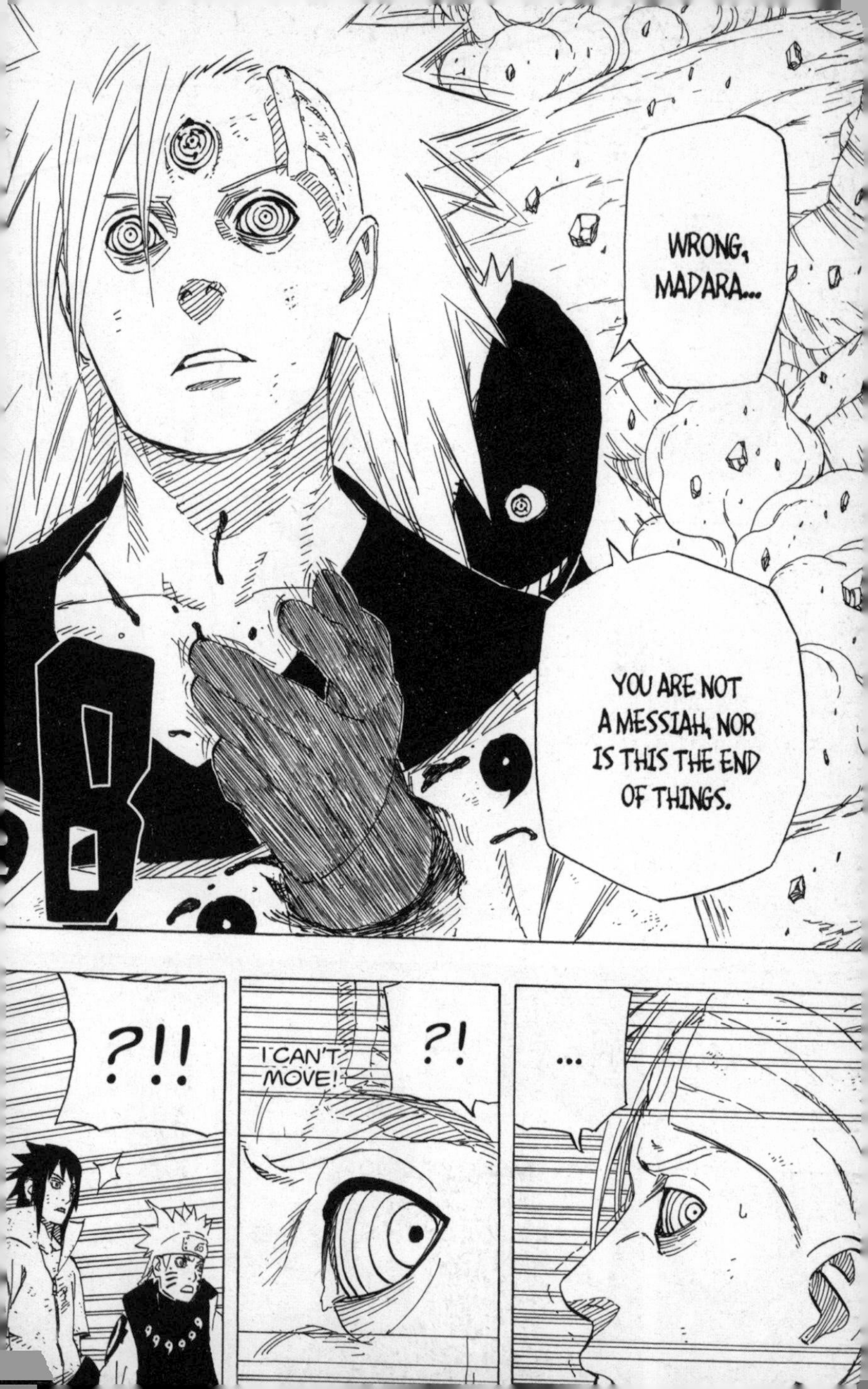
WRONG, MADARA...
YOU ARE NOT A MESSIAH, NOR IS THIS THE END OF THINGS.
...
?!
I CAN'T MOVE!
?!!

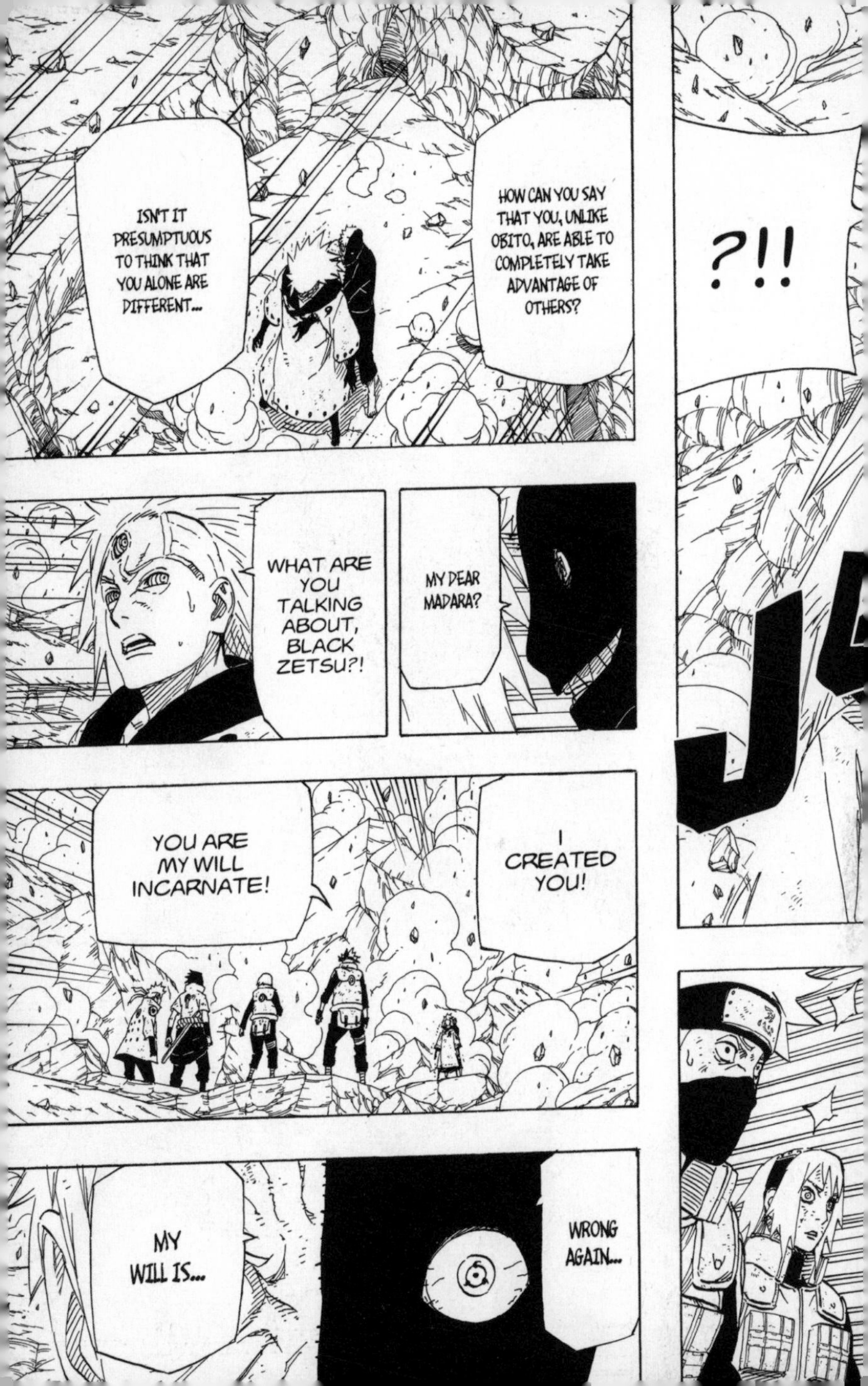

?!!
HOW CAN YOU SAY THAT YOU, UNLIKE OBITO, ARE ABLE TO COMPLETELY TAKE ADVANTAGE OF OTHERS?
ISN'T IT PRESUMPTUOUS TO THINK THAT YOU ALONE ARE DIFFERENT...
MY DEAR MADARA?
WHAT ARE YOU TALKING ABOUT, BLACK ZETSU?!
I CREATED YOU!
YOU ARE MY WILL INCARNATE!
WRONG AGAIN...
MY WILL IS...

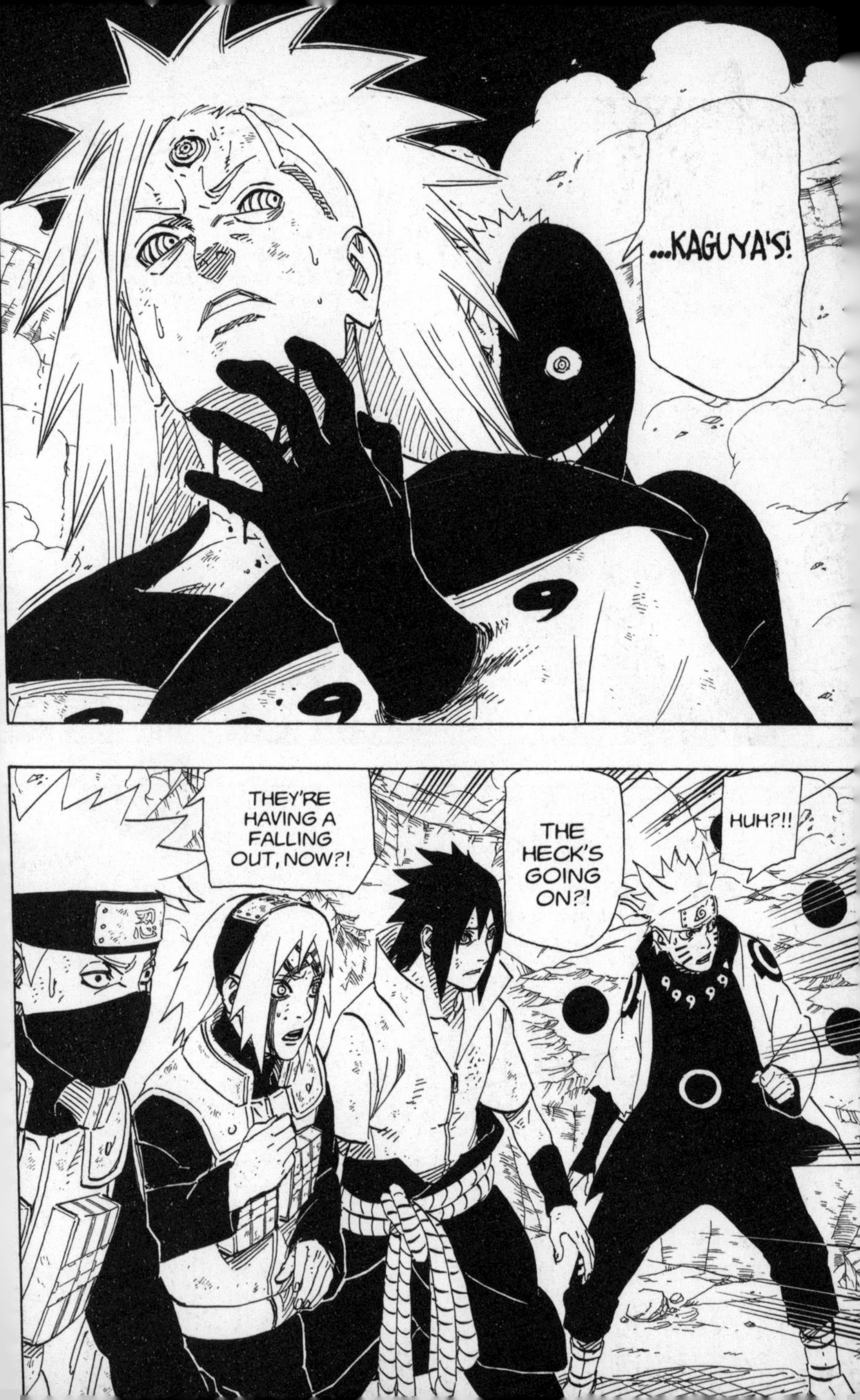
...KAGUYA'S!
HUH?!!
THE HECK'S GOING ON?!
THEY'RE HAVING A FALLING OUT, NOW?!

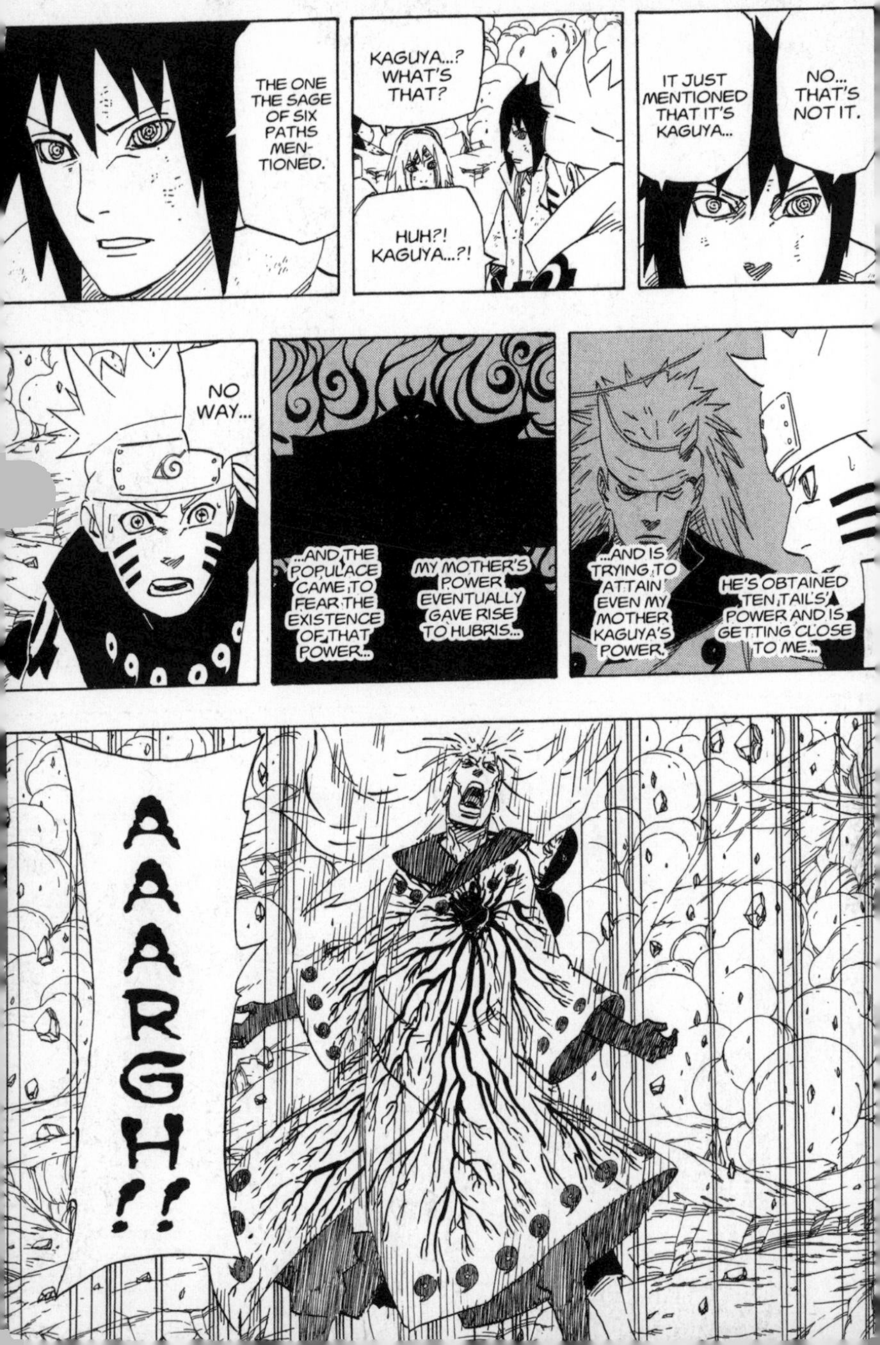
NO... THAT'S NOT IT.
IT JUST MENTIONED THAT IT'S KAGUYA...
KAGUYA...? WHAT'S THAT?
HUH?! KAGUYA...?!
THE ONE THE SAGE OF SIX PATHS MENTIONED.
HE'S OBTAINED TEN TAILS' POWER AND IS GETTING CLOSE TO ME...
...AND IS TRYING TO ATTAIN EVEN MY MOTHER KAGUYA'S POWER.
MY MOTHER'S POWER EVENTUALLY GAVE RISE TO HUBRIS...
...AND THE POPULACE CAME TO FEAR THE EXISTENCE OF THAT POWER...
NO WAY...
AAARGH!!

FWAP...

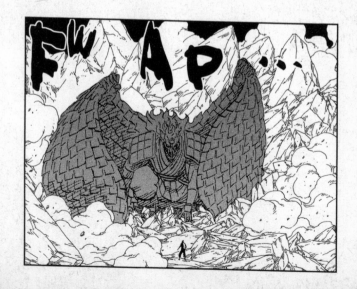

# Number 679: She of the Beginning

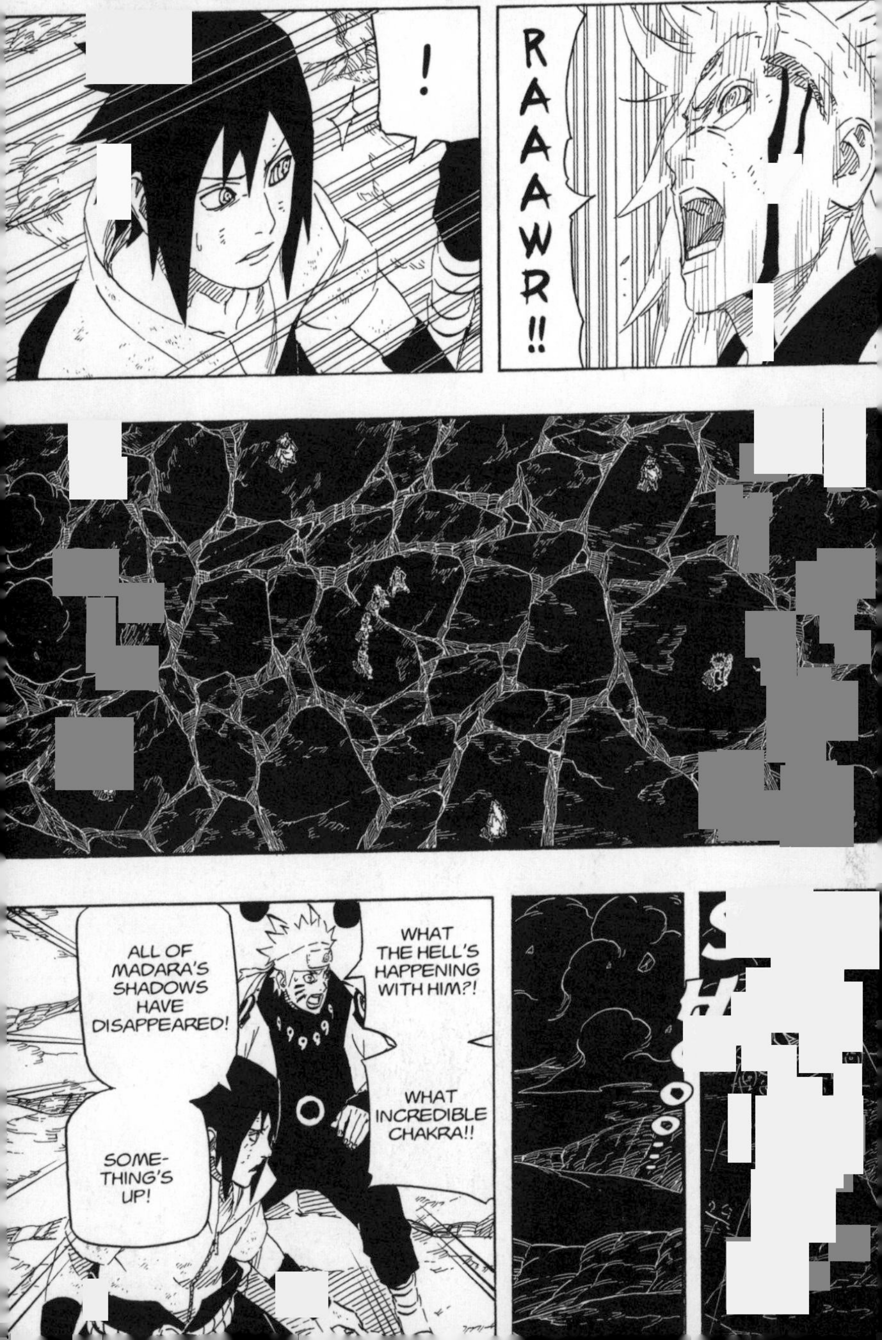
RAAAWR!!
!
WHAT THE HELL'S HAPPENING WITH HIM?!
ALL OF MADARA'S SHADOWS HAVE DISAPPEARED!
WHAT INCREDIBLE CHAKRA!!
SOME-THING'S UP!

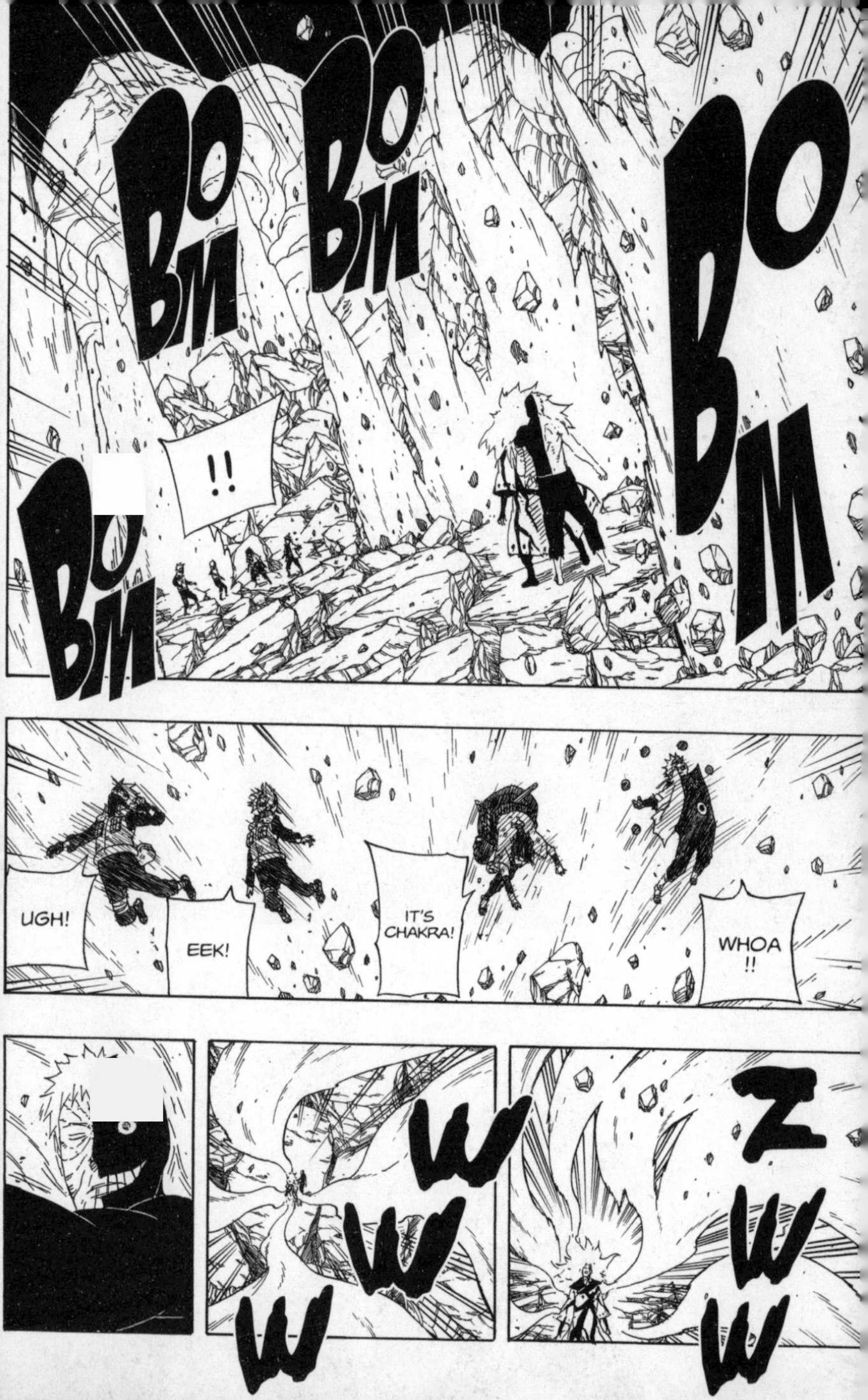
!!
WHOA !!
IT'S CHAKRA!
EEK!
UGH!

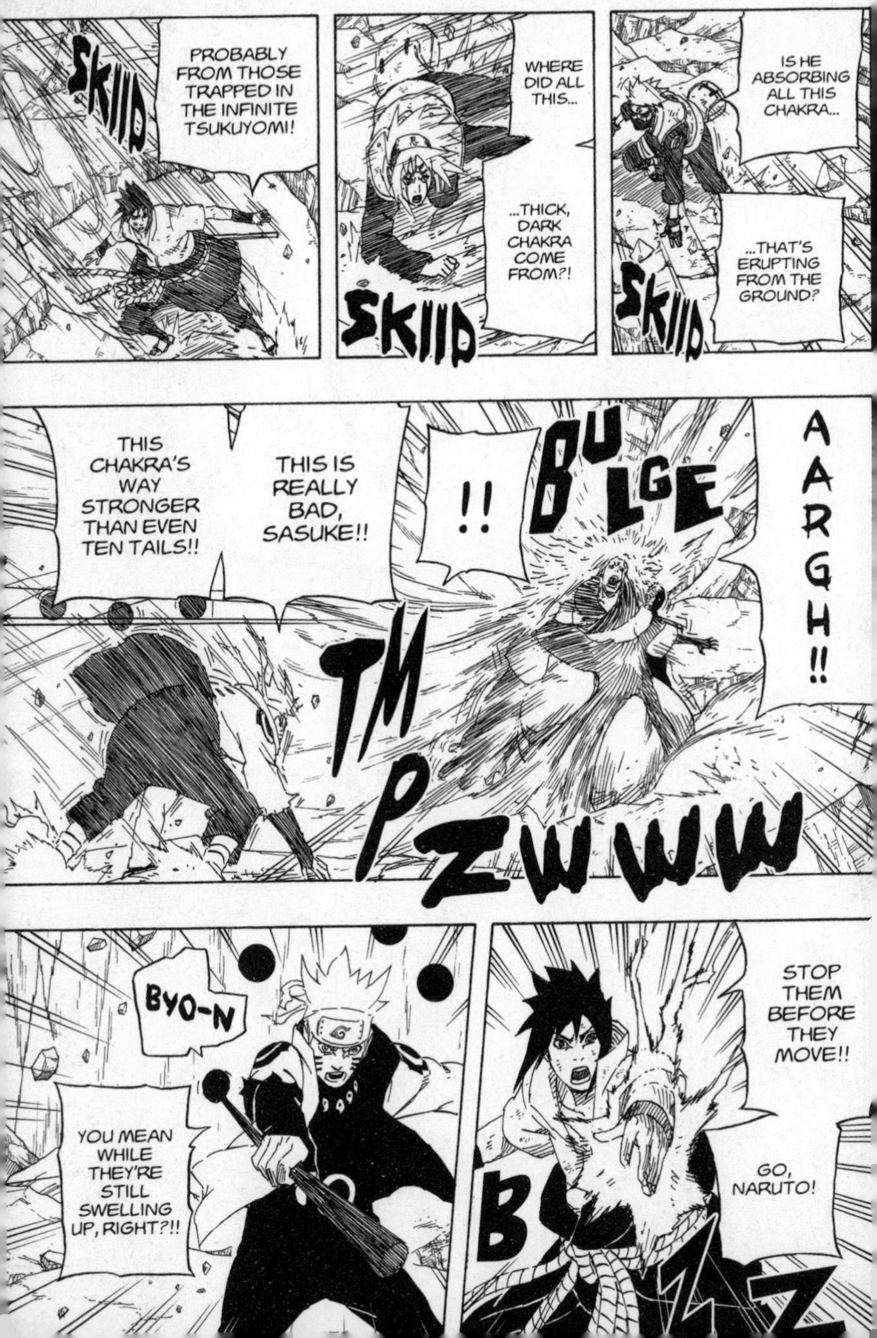
IS HE ABSORBING ALL THIS CHAKRA...
...THAT'S ERUPTING FROM THE GROUND?
SKIIID
WHERE DID ALL THIS...
...THICK, DARK CHAKRA COME FROM?!
SKIIID
SKIIID
PROBABLY FROM THOSE TRAPPED IN THE INFINITE TSUKUYOMI!
AARGH!!
BULGE
!!
THIS IS REALLY BAD, SASUKE!!
THIS CHAKRA'S WAY STRONGER THAN EVEN TEN TAILS!!
THMP
ZWWW
STOP THEM BEFORE THEY MOVE!!
GO, NARUTO!
B ZZ
BYO-N
YOU MEAN WHILE THEY'RE STILL SWELLING UP, RIGHT?!!

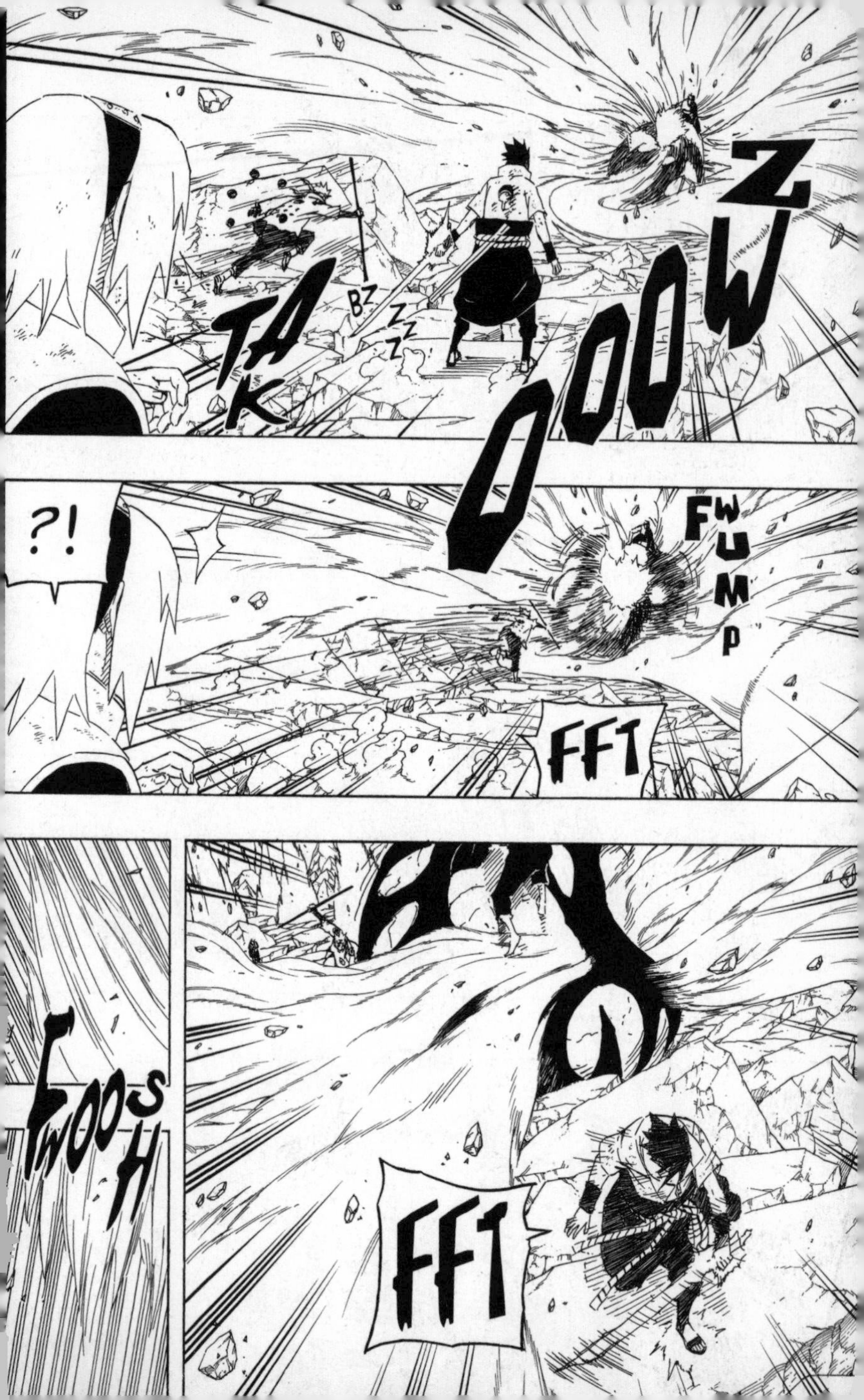

ZWOOOO
BZZZZ
TAK
FWUMP
?!
FFT
FFT
FWOOSH

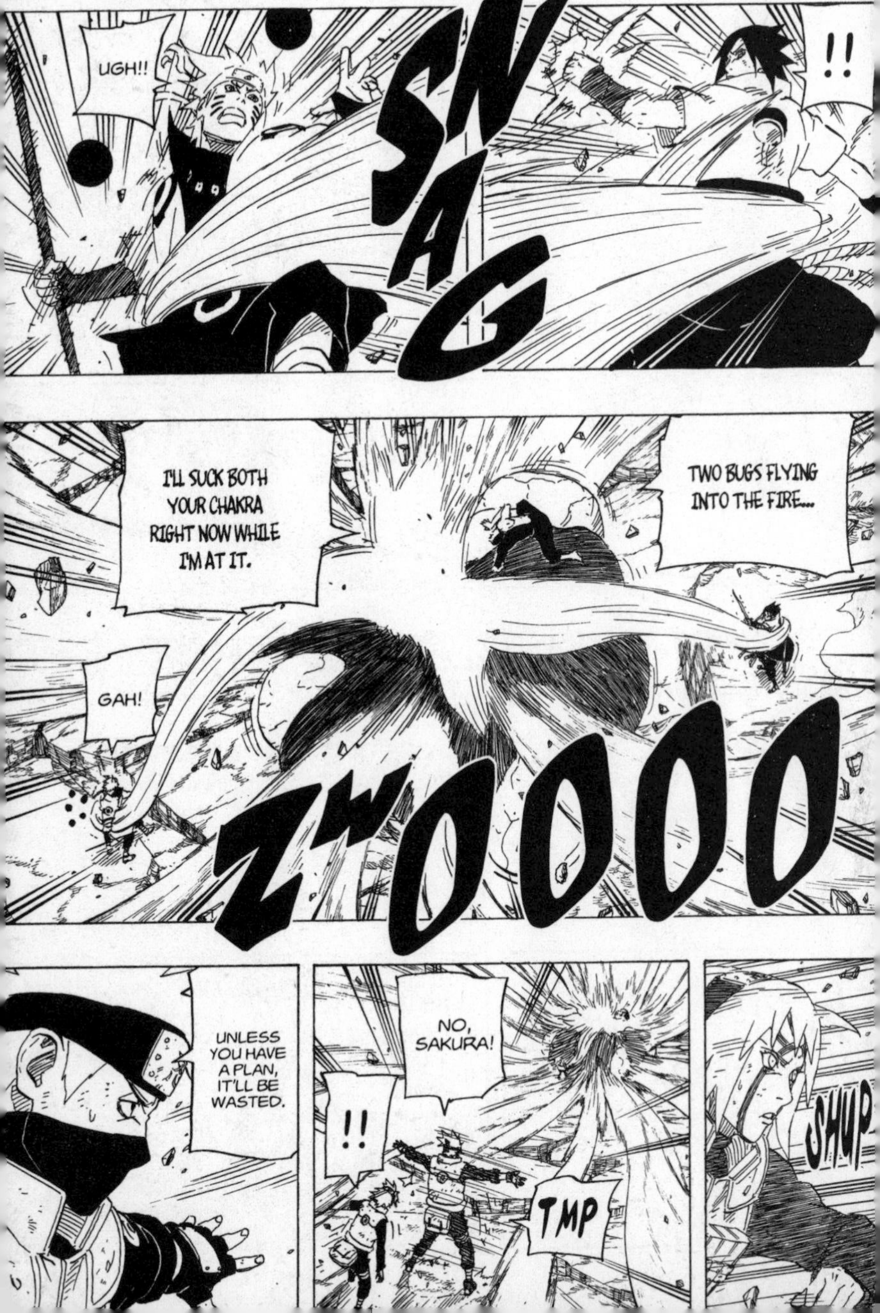
!!
SNAG
UGH!!
TWO BUGS FLYING INTO THE FIRE...
I'LL SUCK BOTH YOUR CHAKRA RIGHT NOW WHILE I'M AT IT.
GAH!
ZWOOOOO
SHUP
NO, SAKURA!
!!
TMP
UNLESS YOU HAVE A PLAN, IT'LL BE WASTED.

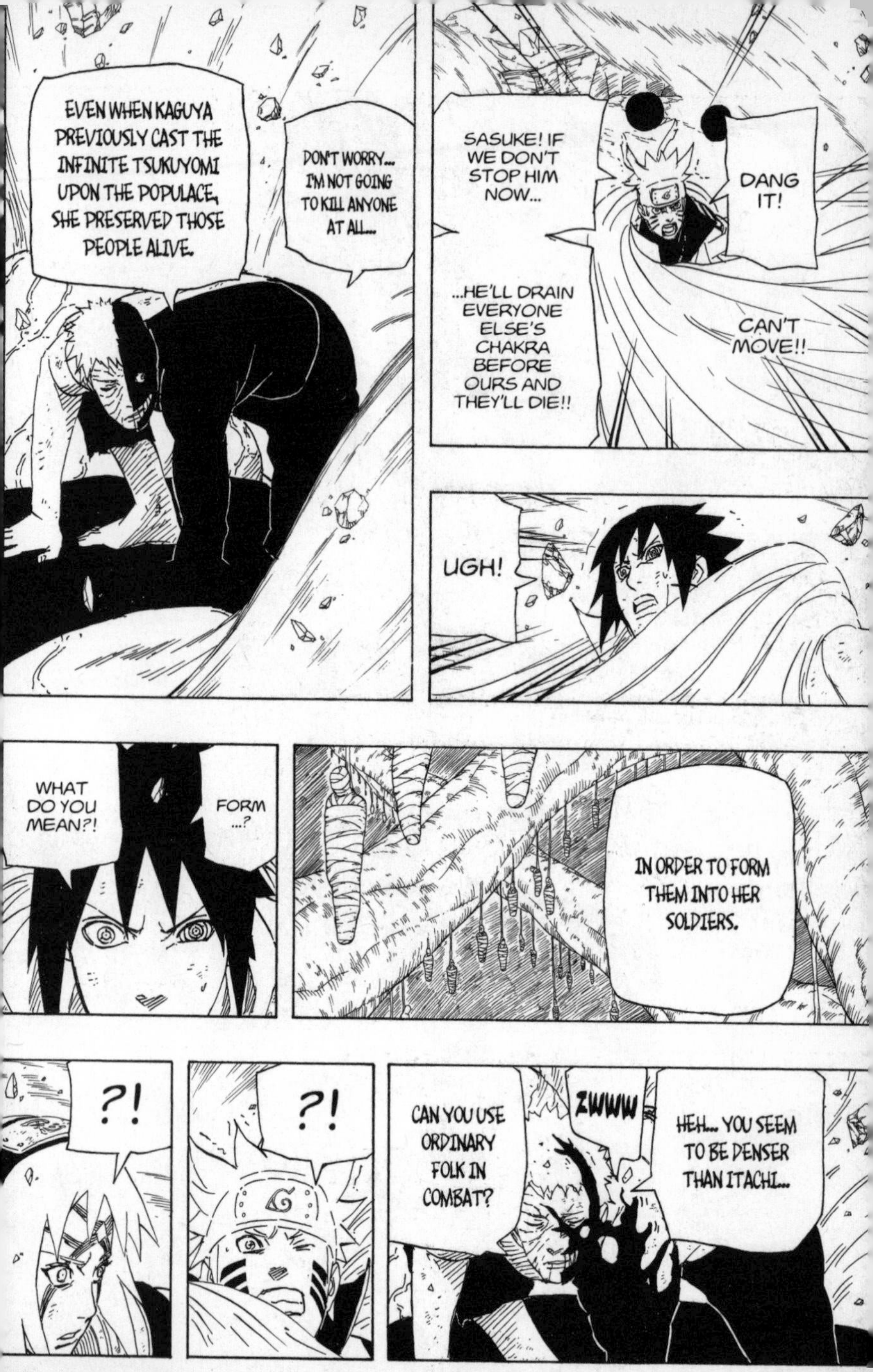
DANG IT!
CAN'T MOVE!!
SASUKE! IF WE DON'T STOP HIM NOW...
...HE'LL DRAIN EVERYONE ELSE'S CHAKRA BEFORE OURS AND THEY'LL DIE!!
UGH!
DON'T WORRY... I'M NOT GOING TO KILL ANYONE AT ALL...
EVEN WHEN KAGUYA PREVIOUSLY CAST THE INFINITE TSUKUYOMI UPON THE POPULACE, SHE PRESERVED THOSE PEOPLE ALIVE.
IN ORDER TO FORM THEM INTO HER SOLDIERS.
FORM ...?
WHAT DO YOU MEAN?!
HEH... YOU SEEM TO BE DENSER THAN ITACHI...
ZWWW
CAN YOU USE ORDINARY FOLK IN COMBAT?
?!
?!

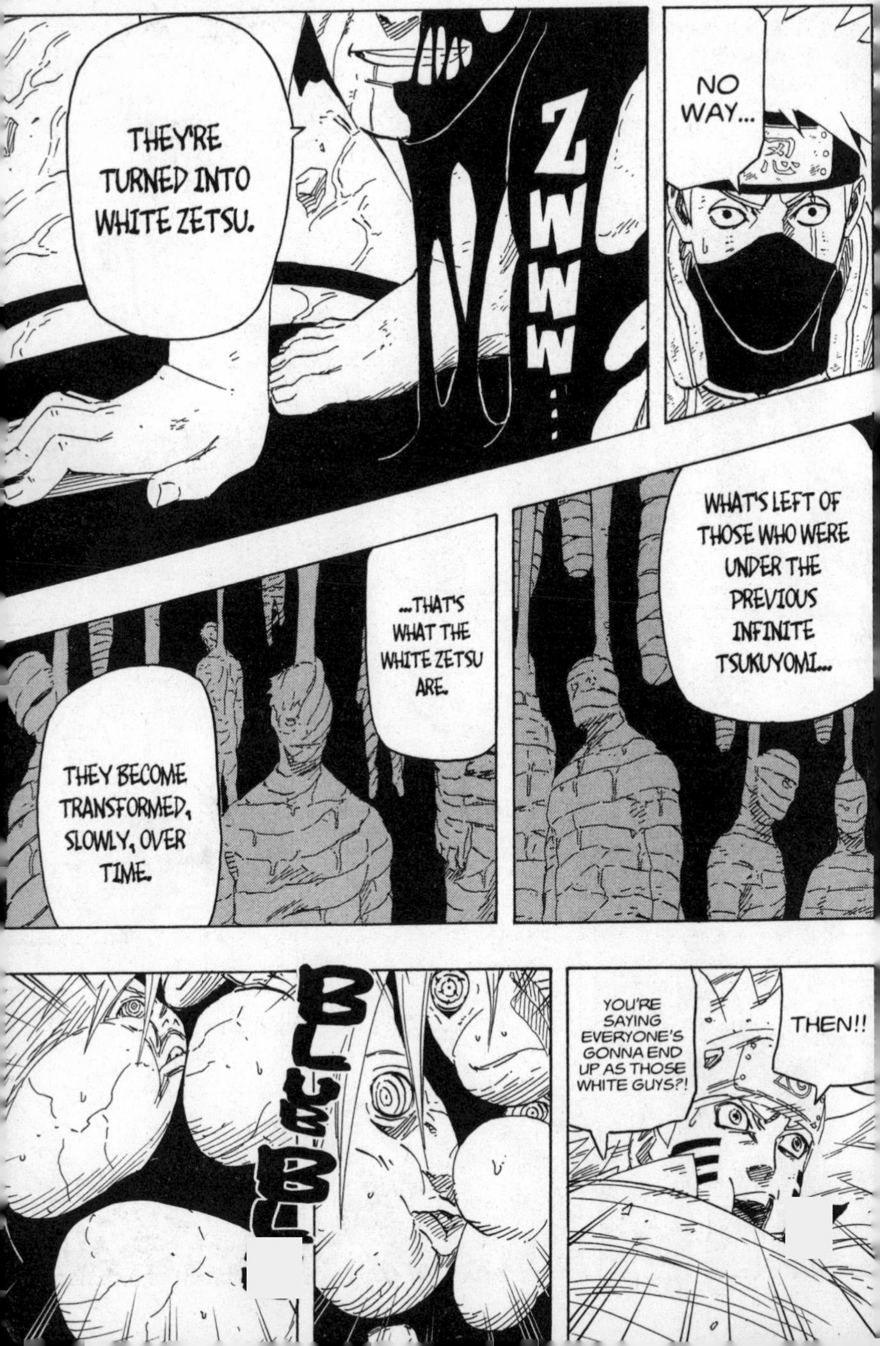
NO WAY...
ZWWW...
THEY'RE TURNED INTO WHITE ZETSU.
WHAT'S LEFT OF THOSE WHO WERE UNDER THE PREVIOUS INFINITE TSUKUYOMI...
...THAT'S WHAT THE WHITE ZETSU ARE.
THEY BECOME TRANSFORMED, SLOWLY, OVER TIME.
THEN!!
YOU'RE SAYING EVERYONE'S GONNA END UP AS THOSE WHITE GUYS?!
BLUBBL

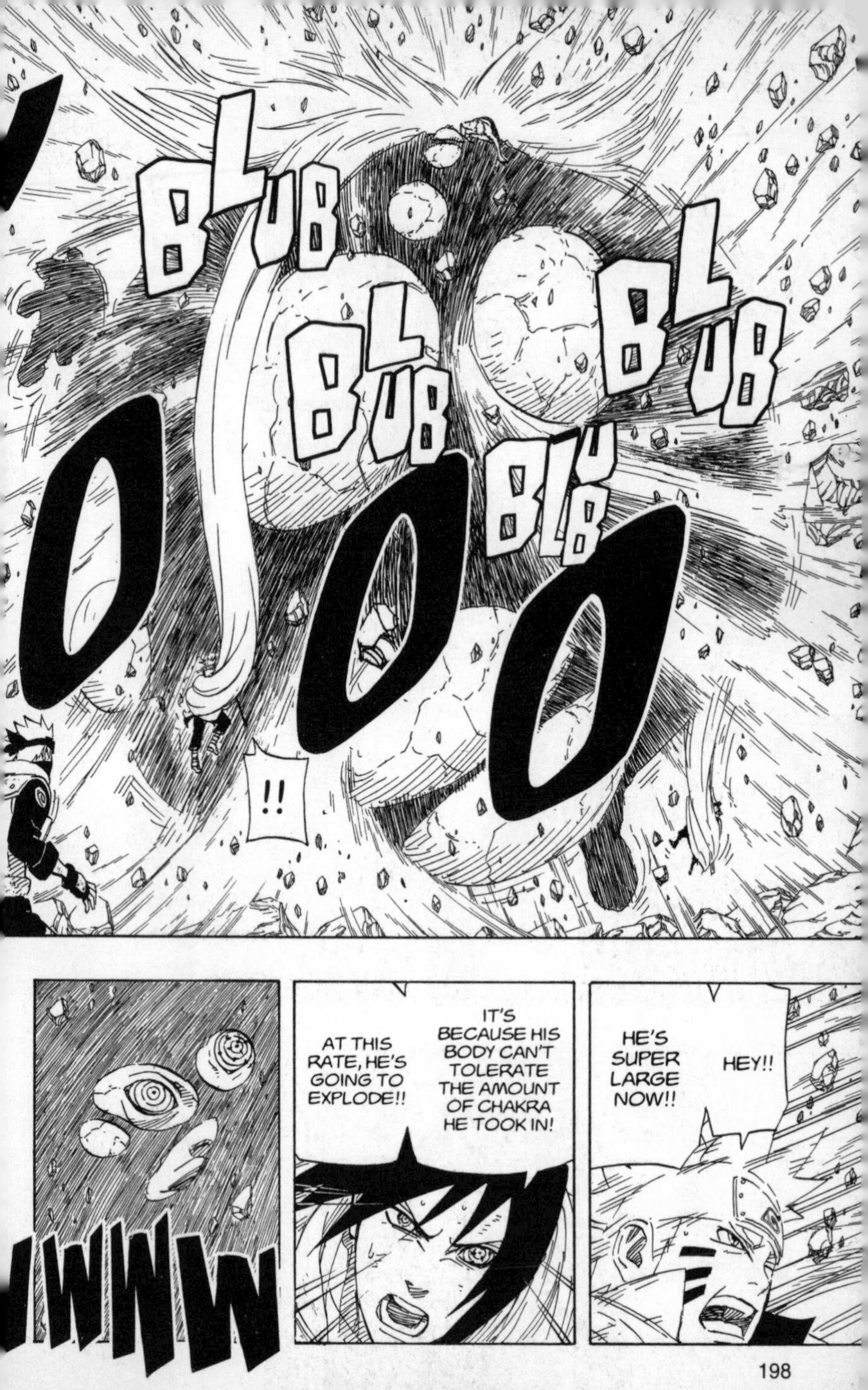
BLUB
BLUB
BLUB
BLUB
!!
HEY!!
HE'S SUPER LARGE NOW!!
IT'S BECAUSE HIS BODY CAN'T TOLERATE THE AMOUNT OF CHAKRA HE TOOK IN!
AT THIS RATE, HE'S GOING TO EXPLODE!!

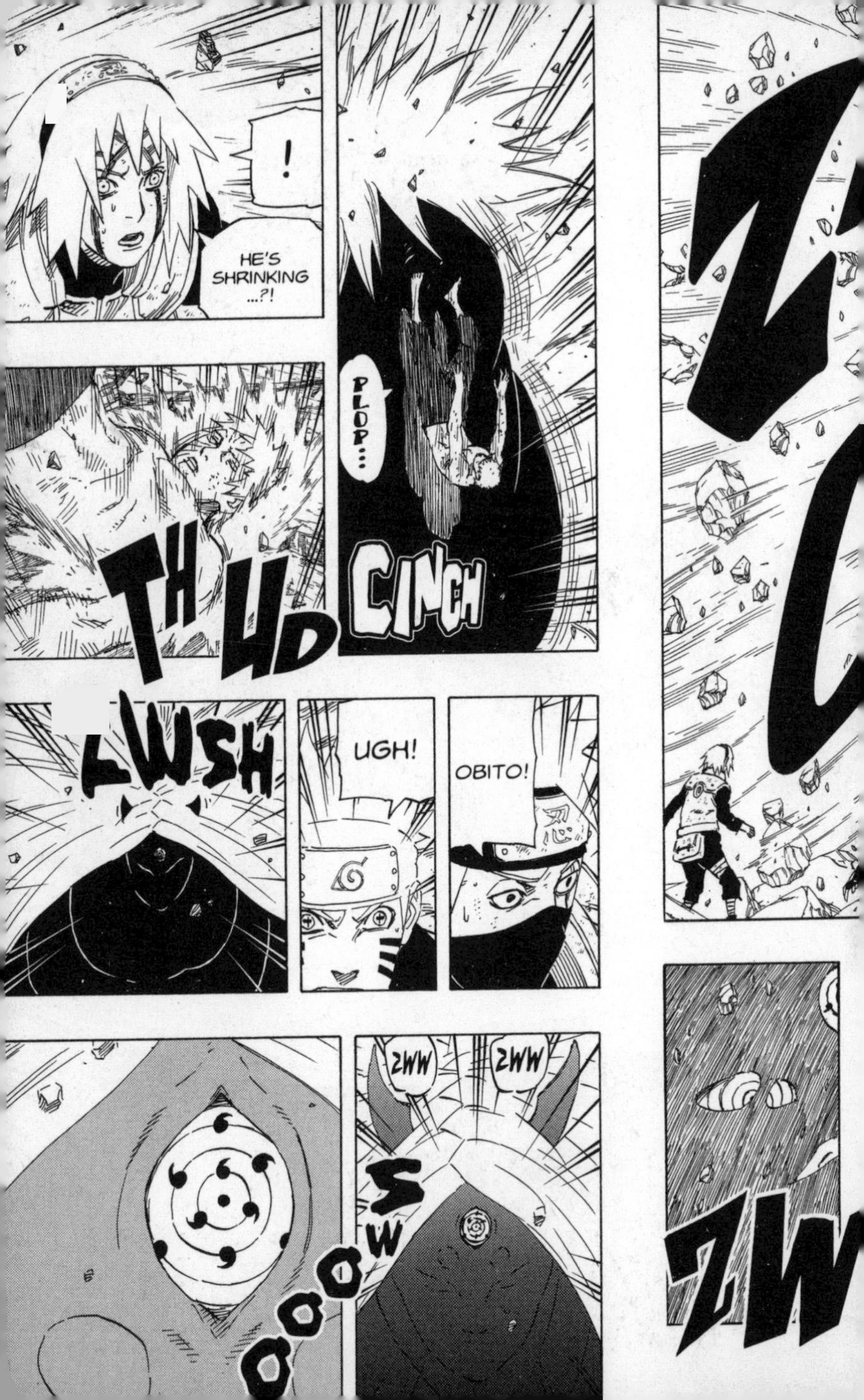

ZW
PLOP...
CINCH
!
HE'S SHRINKING ...?!
THUD
OBITO!
UGH!
WUSH
ZWW
ZWW
SWOOOOO

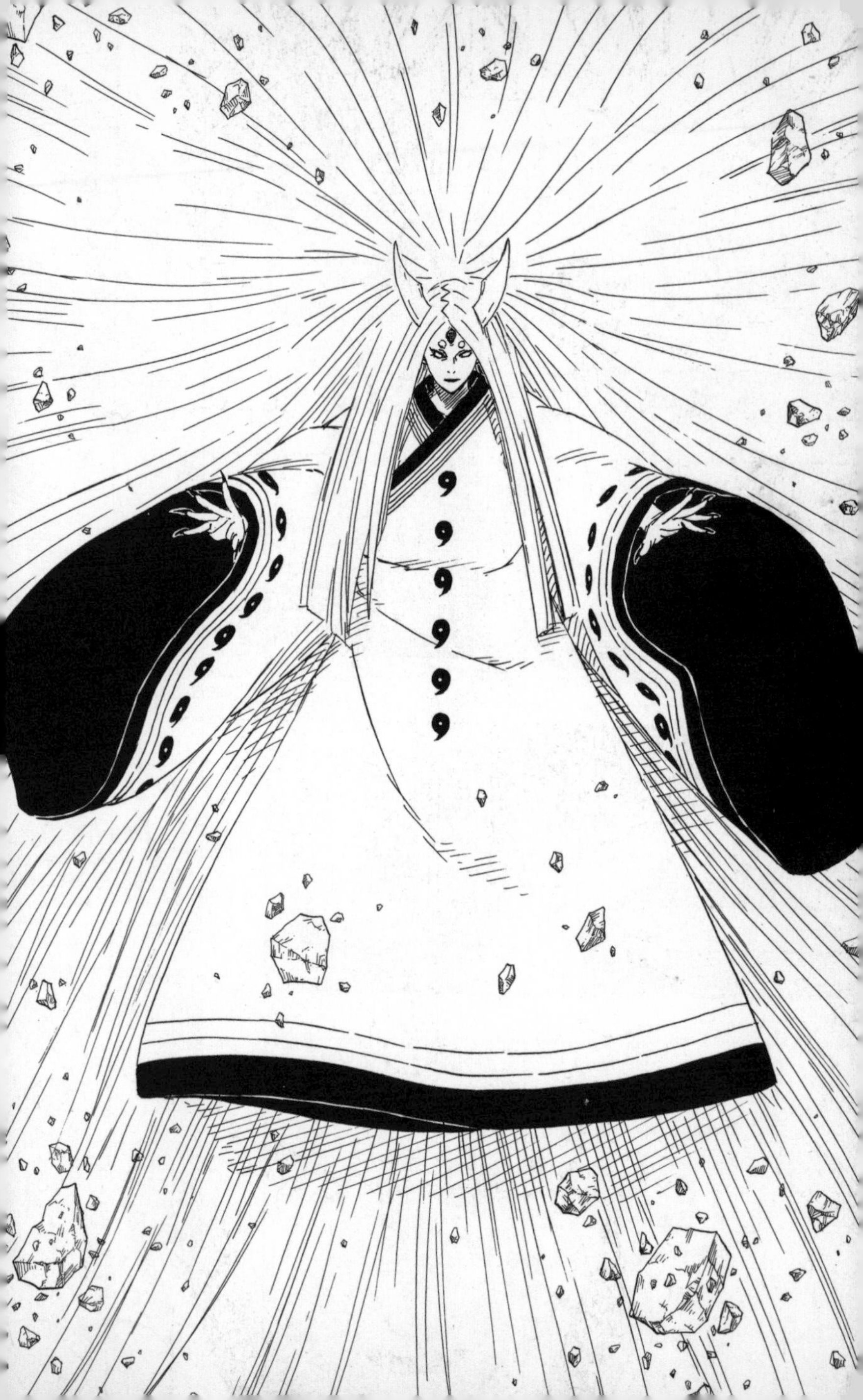

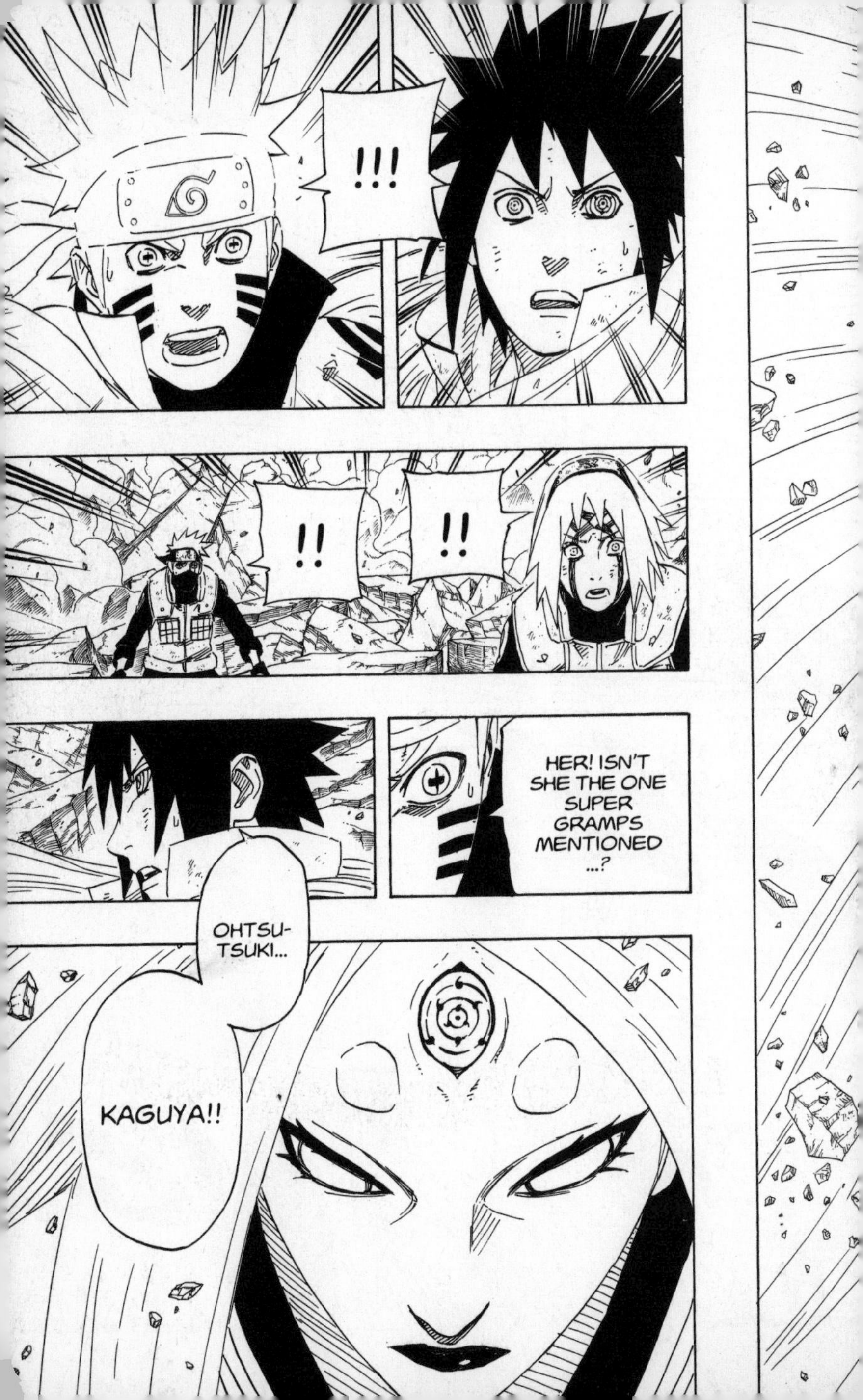

!!!
!!
!!
HER! ISN'T SHE THE ONE SUPER GRAMPS MENTIONED ...?
OHTSU-TSUKI...
KAGUYA!!

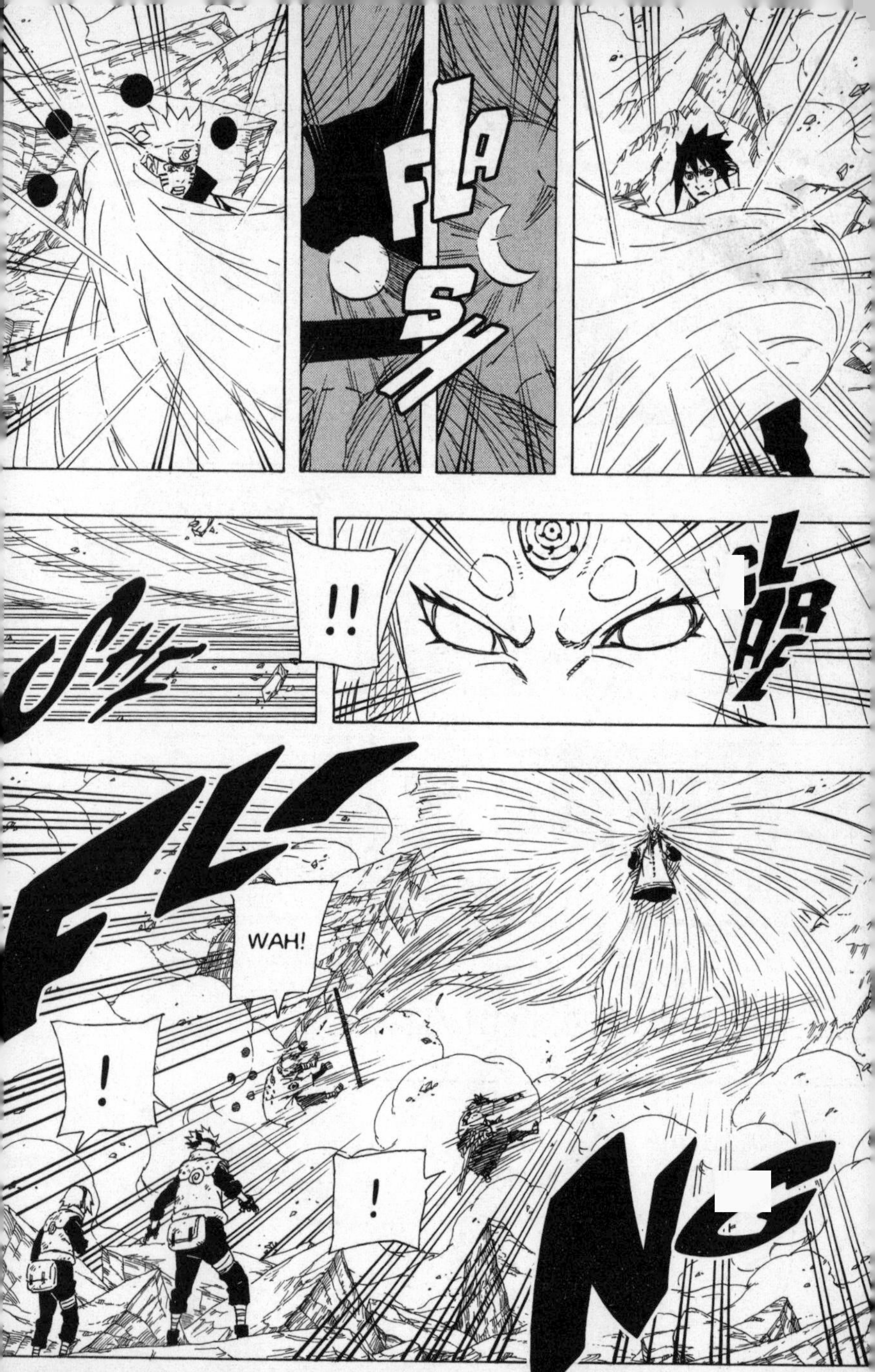
FLASH
!!
WAH!
!
!

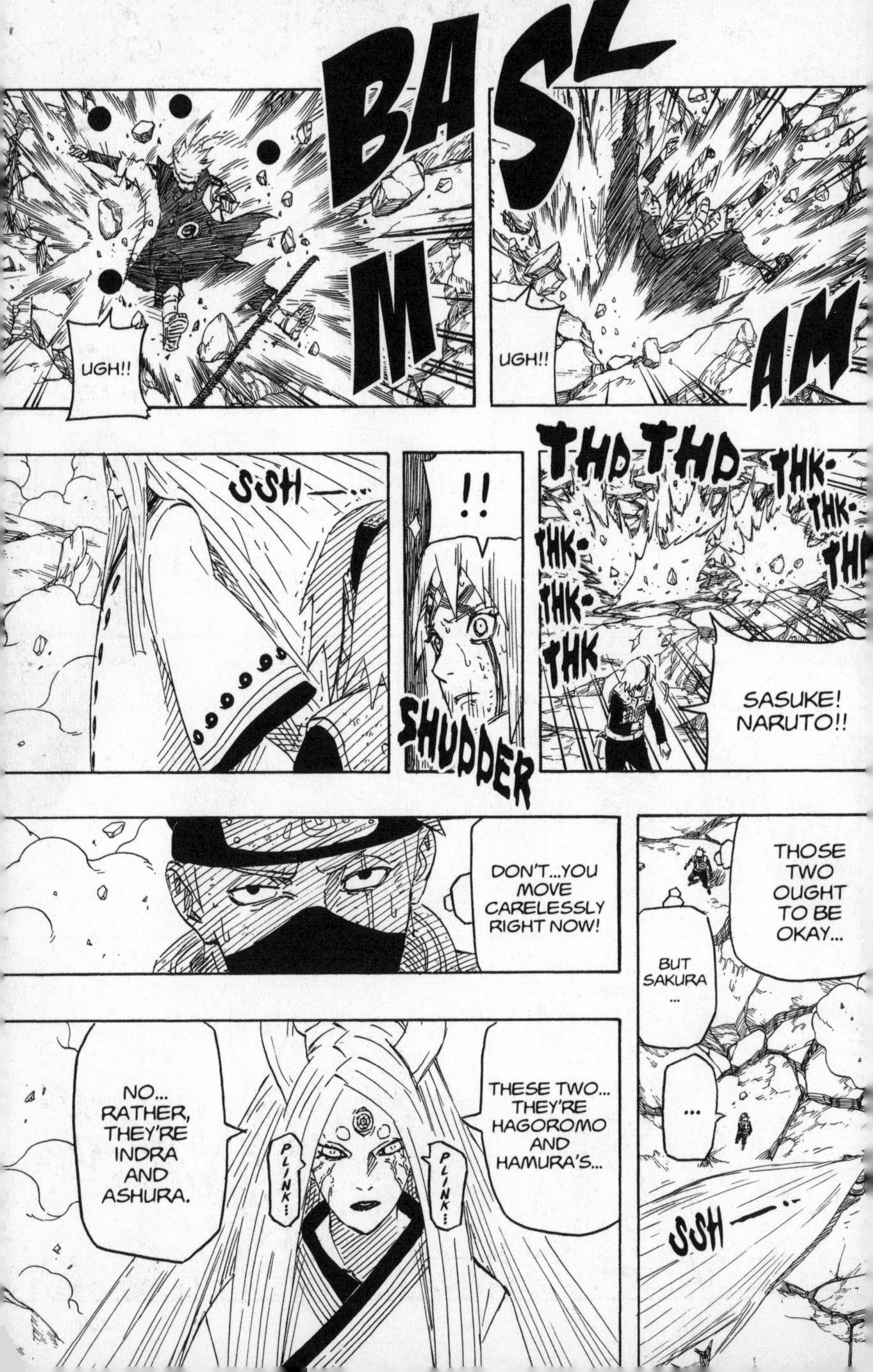

UGH!!
UGH!!
BAS
M
AM
THD THD
THK-
THK-
TH
THK-
THK-
THK
SASUKE! NARUTO!!
!!
SHUDDER
SSH—...
THOSE TWO OUGHT TO BE OKAY...
BUT SAKURA...
...
SSH—...
DON'T...YOU MOVE CARELESSLY RIGHT NOW!
THESE TWO... THEY'RE HAGOROMO AND HAMURA'S...
PLINK...
PLINK...
NO... RATHER, THEY'RE INDRA AND ASHURA.

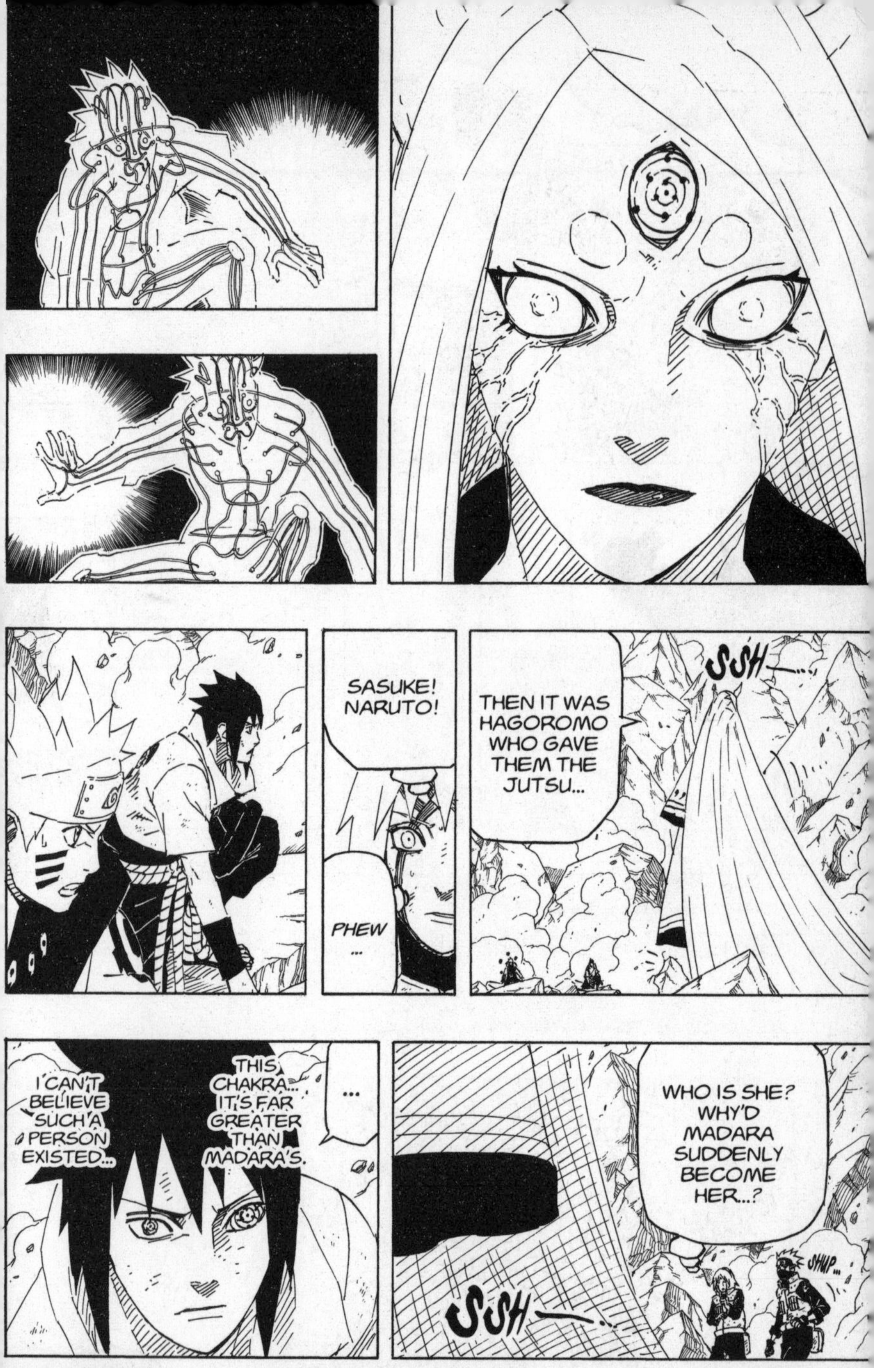
SSH...
THEN IT WAS HAGOROMO WHO GAVE THEM THE JUTSU...
SASUKE! NARUTO!
PHEW...
WHO IS SHE? WHY'D MADARA SUDDENLY BECOME HER...?
SHUP...
SSH...
...
THIS CHAKRA... IT'S FAR GREATER THAN MADARA'S.
I CAN'T BELIEVE SUCH A PERSON EXISTED...

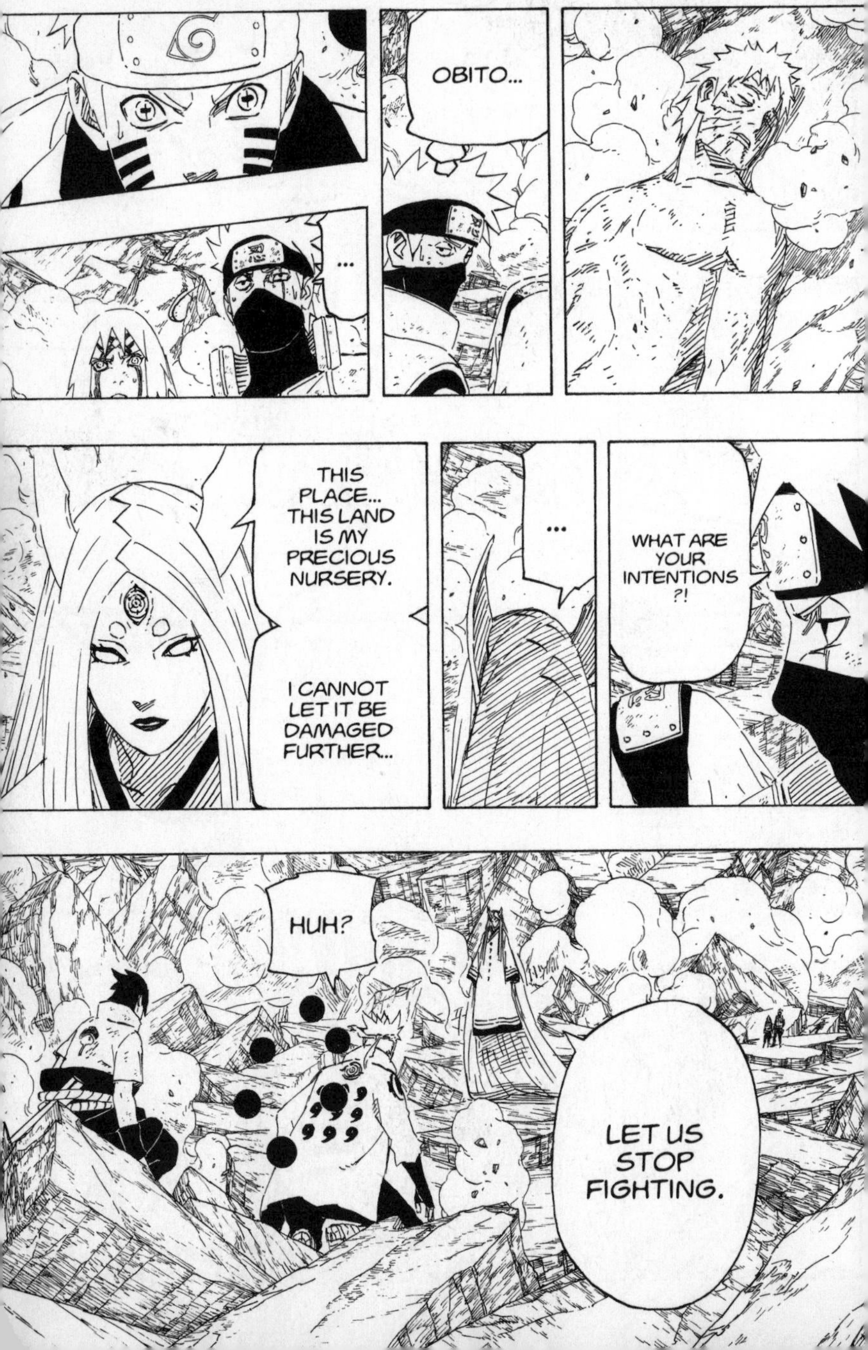
OBITO...
...
WHAT ARE YOUR INTENTIONS ?!
...
THIS PLACE... THIS LAND IS MY PRECIOUS NURSERY.
I CANNOT LET IT BE DAMAGED FURTHER...
LET US STOP FIGHTING.
HUH?

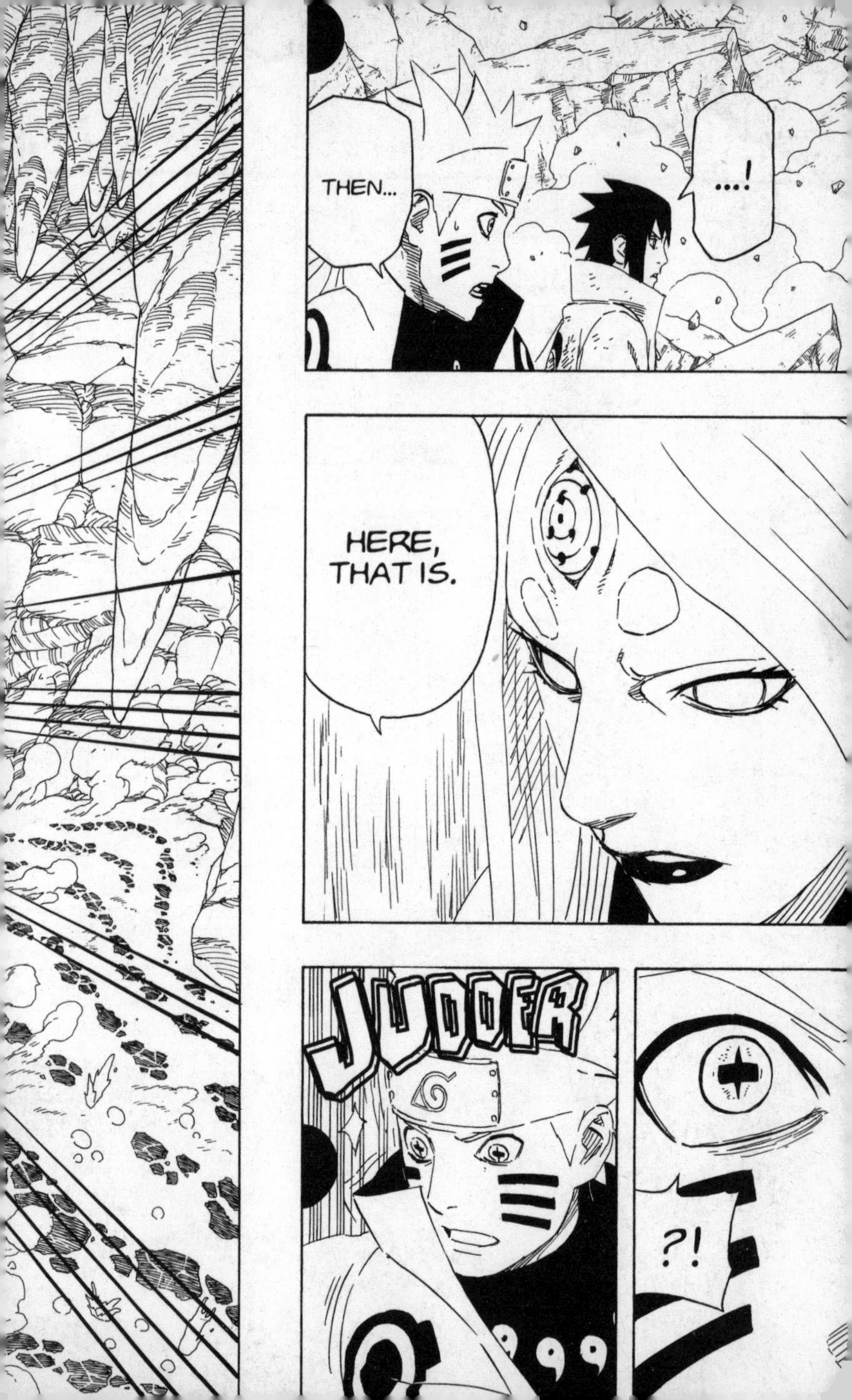
...!
THEN...
HERE, THAT IS.
?!
JUDDER

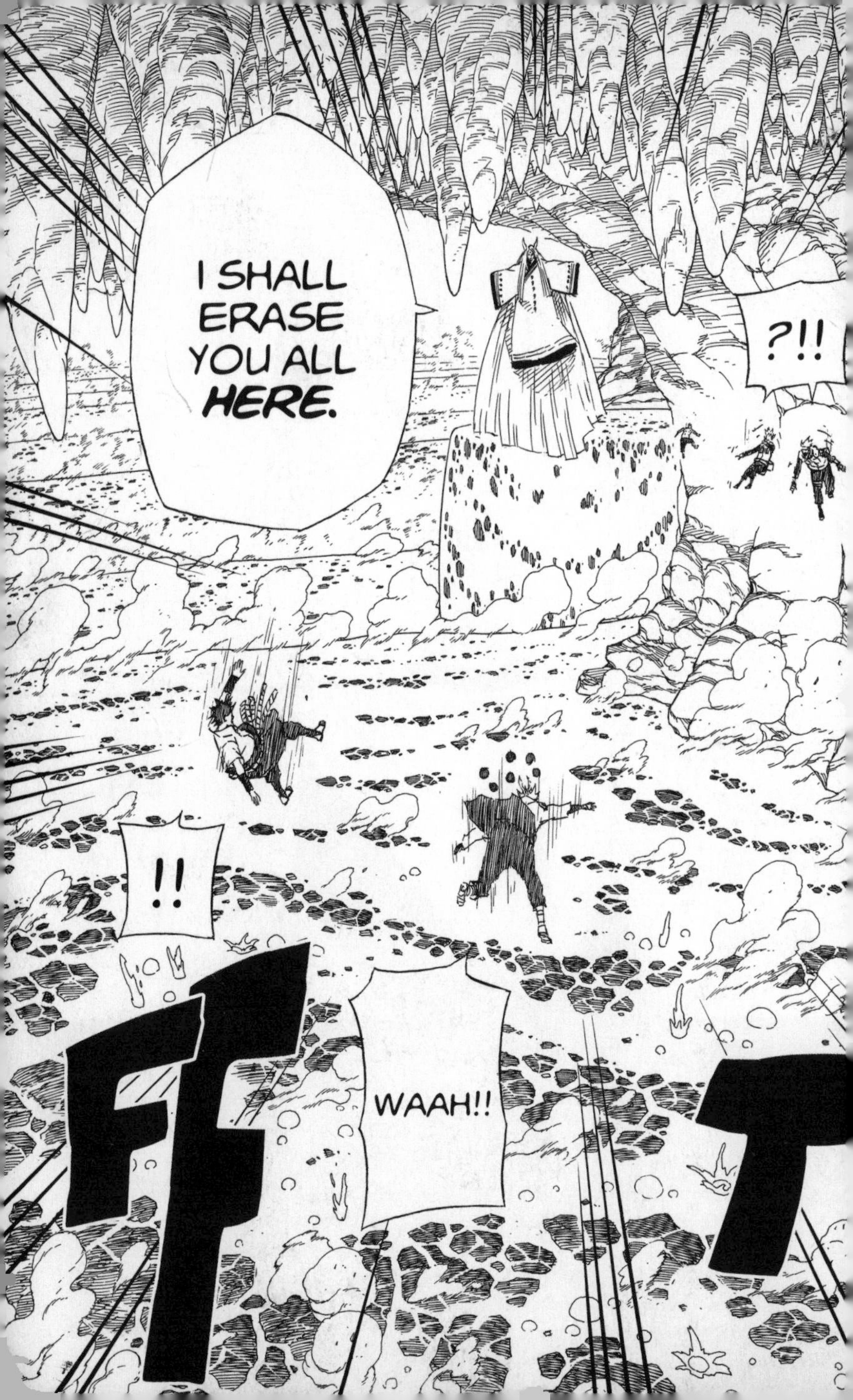
I SHALL ERASE YOU ALL HERE.
?!!
!!
WAAH!!
FFT

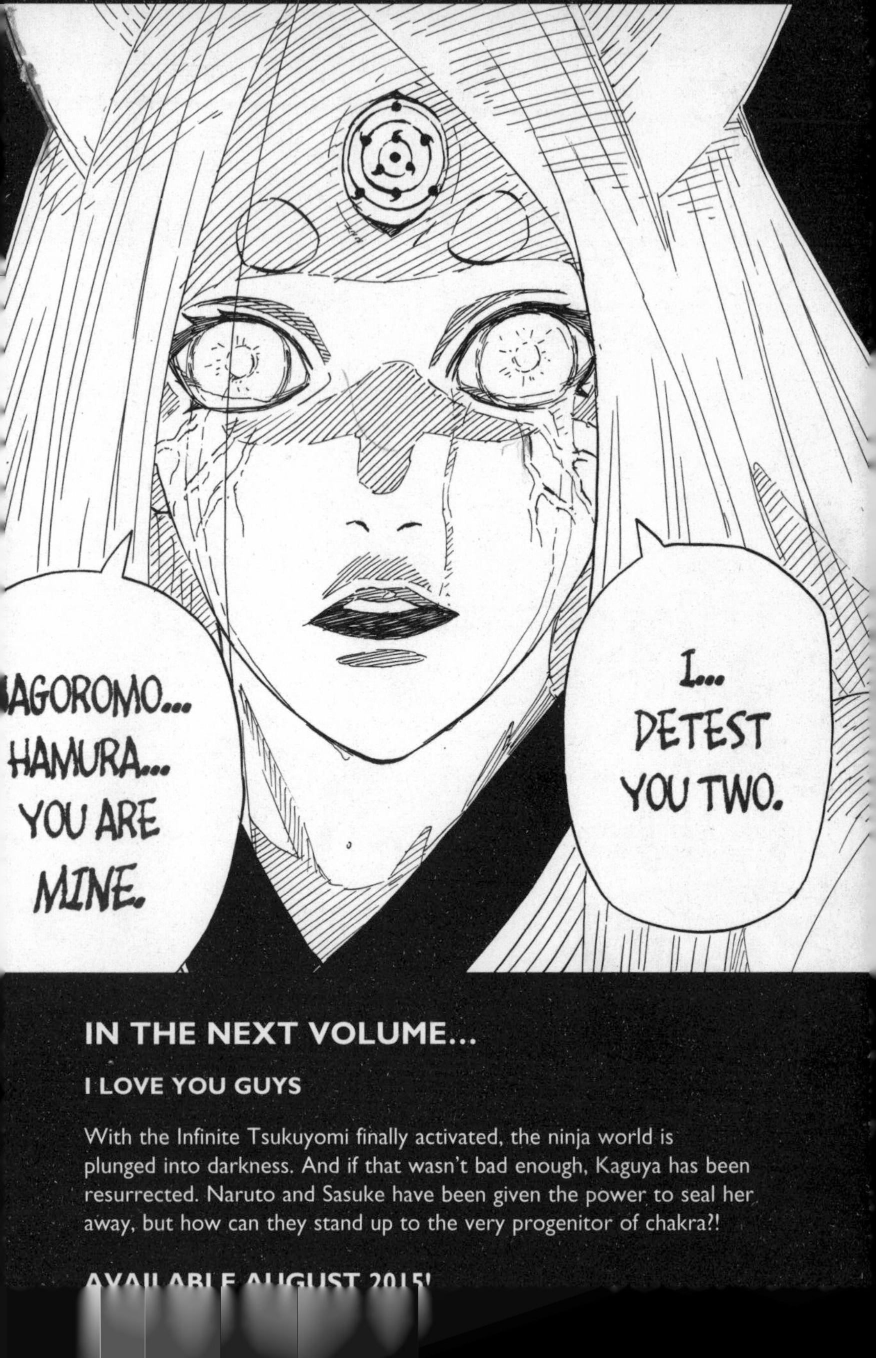
I... DETEST YOU TWO.
AGOROMO... HAMURA... YOU ARE MINE.

## IN THE NEXT VOLUME...

### I LOVE YOU GUYS

With the Infinite Tsukuyomi finally activated, the ninja world is plunged into darkness. And if that wasn't bad enough, Kaguya has been resurrected. Naruto and Sasuke have been given the power to seal her away, but how can they stand up to the very progenitor of chakra?!

**AVAILABLE AUGUST 2015!**